Many contemporary Christians feel a compelling need to believe that faith is consistent with the modern scientific view of the world. Standing in the liberal theological tradition dating from Schleiermacher, *Events of grace* addresses this need by contending that modern Christianity can be made compatible with a scientific, naturalistic world view. To do so "religion" and "God" must be understood valuationally, not ontologically. This approach to "religion" permits an existentialist account of faith entirely in terms of "modes of existing." *Events of grace* thereby weds Rudolph Bultmann's demythologizing program to Henry Nelson Wieman's naturalistic concept of God as creative transformation. Defending a strong doctrine of "justification by faith," Hardwick shows how both God and the knowledge of God can be conceived in terms of "events of grace" that transform possibilities of existence toward "openness to the future." On this basis, *Events of grace* gives a complete existential and naturalistic account of sin, faith, God, the knowledge of God, Christology, and the eschatological symbols that articulate Christian hope in the encounter with suffering and death.

EVENTS OF GRACE

EVENTS OF GRACE

Naturalism, existentialism, and theology

CHARLEY D. HARDWICK

The American University, Washington D.C.

CAMBRIDGE
UNIVERSITY PRESS

Published by the Press Syndicate of the University of Cambridge
The Pitt Building, Trumpington Street, Cambridge CB2 1RP
40 West 20th Street, New York, NY 1001–4211, USA
10 Stamford Road, Oakleigh, Melbourne 3166, Australia

First published 1996

Printed in Great Britain at the University Press, Cambridge

A catalogue record for this book is available from the British Library

Library of Congress cataloguing in publication data

Hardwick, Charley D.
Events of grace: naturalism, existentialism, and theology / by Charley D. Hardwick.
p. cm.
Includes bibliographical references and index.
ISBN 0 521 55220 6 (hardback)
1. Theology, Doctrinal.   2. Naturalism.   3. Christianity and existentialism.
4. Liberalism (Religion)   I. Title.
BT78.H275   1996
230'.046–dc20   95–20367 CIP

ISBN 0 521 55220 6 hardback

For my wife
Christina

Lo, I tell you a mystery . . . We shall all be changed, in a
moment, in the twinkling of an eye . . .

(1 Cor. 15:51f.)

What have you that you did not receive? If then you received
it, why do you boast, as if it were not a gift?

(1 Cor. 4:7)

I began to understand that the righteousness of God is that by
which the righteous lives by a gift of God, namely by faith. And
this is the meaning: the righteousness of God is revealed by the
gospel, namely the passive righteousness with which merciful
God justifies us by faith. . .

(Martin Luther)

It is not we who handle these matters, but we who are handled
by God.

(Martin Luther)

Contents

ix

Preface

This work is conceived entirely as an essay in constructive theology. Its distinctive viewpoint is an austere physicalist naturalism, dependent largely on John F. Post's nonreductive physicalism defended in *The Faces of Existence*. The choice of this theological strategy rests on my conviction that theologians must take far more seriously the possibility that naturalism provides the true account of our world, and indeed in its materialist or physicalist version. Theologians too readily – and too facilely – dismiss philosophical naturalism. They assume not merely that it is philosophically deficient but that its truth would render the Christian witness of faith impossible. The contemporary philosophical discussion presents ample reason to believe the first of these assumptions mistaken. This work aims to render the second mistaken as well. Even if I have failed, I remain convinced that the goal remains the deepest challenge facing theology in our time.

The evidence for the entirely theological motives underlying this work is that the single audience I am most in mind to reach are those responsible for training candidates for the Christian ministry in the care of souls. Generally speaking, the discipline of "practical theology" is doing a decent job in two of the three areas under its jurisdiction, the preaching of the Word and the administration of the sacraments. But the care of souls is a shambles today. At one end it ministers to one or another version of the latest self-actualization psychological gruel. At the other end, it has little if anything to offer to the troubled circumstances of tragedy, loss, suffering, and, most especially, death, except tired old eschatological symbols. These it continues to serve up largely unreflectively in mythological forms that scarcely any educated person believes today. Far more plain candor is required of the Christian ministry today, but there are few theological resources around to provide the basis of such honesty. This work offers one effort to provide them.

   This motive also accounts for my admiration for the work of
Stanley Hauerwas in Christian ethics, to which reference is made
from time to time in what follows. Hauerwas's genius is to identify
with unusual insight precisely those hard issues of "practical living"
under the Christian "form of life" for which the care of souls is
responsible and to make clear the commitment to honesty, candor,
and truth demanded by faith itself. Where I depart from Hauerwas is
on his persistent refusal to clarify the theological foundations that
permit his insights; instead he falls back unreflectively on theological
formulations that amount simply to mystification. I try to show that
what is most valuable in his work can be grounded on much more
austere, but also much more transparent, philosophical and theological
foundations than he is willing to entertain – though it will also be clear
that I depart from him entirely on his unwillingness to engage these
ethical issues on the basis of common reason. This work attempts to
show that there need be no conflict between the normative character
of the Christian "form of life" and human reason. Ethically this
means that the witness of faith requires Christians, especially Christians,
to have reasons which all in the human community can share for the
requiring that our ethical reasons require us to require of others.
   I must acknowledge my indebtedness to a number of persons and
agencies whose support – and criticism – have been invaluable. Most
especially I wish to recognize Schubert Ogden whose example as
teacher, theologian, and friend has inspired much that follows.
Though this work disagrees profoundly with Ogden's antinaturalism,
the reader will see that in certain respects, especially in the last half, it
is an extended engagement with his position. The reason is that in my
opinion, and despite our ultimate disagreement over ontology, no one
more consistently identifies the nub of theological issues with greater
precision than Ogden. He is especially good at holding theology tight
to the existential point of theological issues, and this has the effect
oftentimes (and with the most important theological doctrines) of
transforming our conception of what the proper theological questions
themselves are. Consequently, I have been compelled time and again
to develop my own arguments as a counterpoint to his. Thus, despite
the great differences in the two positions, I am grateful to acknowledge
my indebtedness to him. This extends so far as my having borrowed
two of his titles for the last two chapters.
   Some types of intellectual growth can occur only through
conversations that are ongoing over extended periods of time, but it is

rare after graduate school to find colleagues with whom one can be in constant and deep conversation over many years. I am gratified therefore to have the opportunity here to acknowledge four of my colleagues from The American University who have played this role in my life: Jeffrey Reiman, Phillip Scribner, Jon Wisman, and Barry Chabot (now of Miami University of Ohio). Our discussion group has provided me with an unparalleled opportunity for a vibrant intellectual life. None of them is a theologian and all have difficulty imagining how my efforts to do theology can succeed, or why I should care, yet their criticism, encouragement, and constant engagement with the widest theoretical issues of our day have provided the context for my intellectual growth for over twenty years. It was through this ongoing conversation that I gradually came to realize how my commitment to an existentialist method in theology also required a commitment to philosophical naturalism.

My thanks go to a number of others who have also provided criticism, support, and encouragement: the late Larry Axel, Fritz and Elsa Buri, James Duke, Nancy Frankenberry, the late Hans Frei, Langdon Gilkey, Ray Hart, Van Harvey, Robert Neville, Creighton and Frissy Peden, Wes Robbins, Marvin Shaw, Sarah Truelove and Jim Woelfel. I am grateful to the Highlands Institute for American Religious Thought which, under the leadership of Creighton Peden, Larry Axel, Nancy Frankenberry, and Marvin Shaw, devoted an entire week in 1991 to a seminar discussion of an earlier version of this work. I also want to thank Harley Chapman, Don Kleinfelter, Charles Milligan, and Jerry Stone, who were presenters at this seminar. Their criticisms and responses were extremely helpful in the final revisions. I am also happy to say a special word of thanks to Robert Neville and his wife Beth. They intervened with a crucial and delightful brainstorming session over lunch at a 1990 meeting in Highlands, North Carolina when I was having difficulty coming up with an acceptable title for this work. The present title grew out of that conversation. I probably would never have arrived at it without their help.

I also wish to acknowledge several agencies without whose support this endeavor surely would have been impossible: The Danforth Foundation, for support and encouragement during my years of study, and the Guggenheim Foundation and the American Council of Learned Societies for fellowships that made leisure and freedom from financial worries possible during the early stages of this project. I

wish to thank Richard Berendzen, the outstanding former President
of my university, and Milton Greenberg, Frederick Jacobs, Ann
Ferren, all administrative officers in his administration, and Betty
Bennett, Dean of our College of Arts and Sciences, for providing the
overall context of faculty development that has made The American
University a satisfying place to teach and work over the last decade. I
am also indebted to the Faculty Research Committee at The
American University for several summer research awards, stretching
as far back as 1976, that have enormously facilitated the development
of this project, and then, at last, for a sabbatical support grant during
1988–1989, that made its final writing possible.

Finally, I must thank two enchanting and beloved ladies: my wife,
Christina, and the city of Paris. The city of Paris was my constant
muse for a year while, day after day, I lost myself in the delights of
writing. Each time I surfaced it was to be surrounded anew with
loveliness and fresh inspiration. Little did I know that the same
loveliness and inspiration would surround me again when I returned
to Washington, DC to bring the draft to completion. For this I thank
Christina, who has made my life richer in every way and who already
knows. The dedication is for her.

Abbreviations

CM   Schubert M. Ogden, *Christ without Myth: A Study Based on the Theology of Rudolf Bultmann* (New York: Harper & Row, 1961).

CPA   John B. Cobb, Jr. *Christ in a Pluralistic Age* (Philadelphia: The Westminster Press, 1975).

FE   John Post, *The Faces of Existence: An Essay in Nonreductive Metaphysics* (Ithaca: Cornell University Press, 1987).

HB   Van A. Harvey, *The Historian and the Believer: The Morality of Historical Knowledge and Christian Belief* (New York: Macmillan & Co., 1966).

HMF   Rudolf Bultmann, "The Historicity of Man and Faith," in *Existence and Faith: Shorter Writings of Rudolf Bultmann*, trans. Schubert M. Ogden (New York: Meridian Books, Inc., 1960).

KBT   James Hall, *Knowledge, Belief, and Transcendence* (Boston: Houghton Miffline Co., 1975).

MUC   Henry Nelson Wieman, *Man's Ultimate Commitment* (Carbondale: Southern Illinois University Press, 1958).

NTM   Rudolf Bultmann, "Neues Testament und Mythologie: Das Problem der Entmythologisierung der neutestamentlichen Verkündigung," in H. W. Bartsch, ed., *Kerygma und Mythos*, vol. 1 (Hamburg: Herbert Reich-Evangelischer Verlag, 2nd ed., 1951). English translation = "On the Problem of Demythologizing," in Bultmann, *New Testament and Mythology and Other Basic Writings*, trans. Schubert M. Ogden (Phildalephia: Fortress Press, 1984), 1–43. Hereafter, citations to the English translation will be indicated by "ET." If the translation is my own, the reference to the German original is given first; otherwise Ogden's translation is cited first.

PC   Schubert M. Ogden, *The Point of Christology* (San Francisco: Harper & Row, 1982).

RESM   Henry Nelson Wieman, *Religious Experience and Scientific Method*
        (Carbondale: Southern Illinois University Press, 1954 [reissue
        of Macmillan, 1926].

RG   Schubert M. Ogden, *The Reality of God* (New York: Harper &
        Row, Publishers, 1963).

RR   Rem Edwards, *Reason and Religion: An Introduction to the
        Philosophy of Religion* (New York: Harcourt, Brace, Jovanovich,
        1972).

SHG   Henry Nelson Wieman, *The Source of Human Good* (Chicago:
        University of Chicago Press, 1946).

SMG   Paul van Buren, *The Secular Meaning of the Gospel Based on an
        Analysis of Its Language* (New York: The Macmillan Co., 1963).

SZ   Martin Heidegger, *Sein und Zeit* (Tübingen: Max Niemeyer
        Verlag, 9th unveränderte Auflage, 1960). Parentheses following
        are to the English translation, *Being and Time*, trans. John
        Macquarrie and Edward Robinson (London: SCM Press,
        Ltd., 1962).

ZPE   Rudolf Bultmann, "Zum Problem der Entmythologisierung,"
        in H. W. Bartsch, ed., *Kerygma und Mythos*, Vol. II (Hamburg:
        Herbert Reich-Evangelischer Verlag, 1952). English Trans-
        lation = "On the Problem of Demythologizing," in Bultmann,
        New Testament and Mythology and Other Basic Writings, trans.
        Schubert M. Ogden (Philadelphia: Fortress Press, 1984),
        95–130. Hereafter citations to the English translation will be
        indicated by "ET." If the translation is my own, the reference
        to the German original is given first; otherwise Ogden's
        translation is cited first.

PART I

Foundations for a naturalist Christian theology

CHAPTER I

Prospects for a naturalist theology

In one of the most provocative statements in contemporary theology, Rudolf Bultmann supports his demythologizing proposal by maintaining that "there is nothing specifically Christian about the mythical view of the world (*Weltbild*)" (NTM, 16 [ET, 3]). This seems to deny that faith contains common *beliefs* shared *across* world views (but not themselves mythical) that it would be the task of theology to explicate.[1] If there is nothing specifically Christian about

---

[1] The ultimate test of this claim will turn on how Bultmann renders the notion of "God" *theologically*, but his conception of God is a nest of difficulties. He probably simply assumed some version of classical theism (cf., for example, his assertions about an "objectively" existing God in ZPE, 196, 198–199 [ET, 110, 113–114]). Nevertheless, this commitment is by no means certain. The uncertainty arises from his proscriptions against objectification. But Bultmann is hard to sort out on this issue also. Sometimes, though not always, he seems to assimilate the issue of objectification to the issue of "proof." One can hold the objectively articulated content of an essentially existential meaning independently from one's own existential involvement, thus, at a crucial moment, betraying its very meaning. This reflexive structure makes objectification formally analogous to a "proof" since one can also entertain a proof independently from any existential involvement. When one proves something which by its nature includes existential involvement, then no matter what its formal validity, it becomes reflexively incoherent. Something like this seems to be Bultmann's meaning, and this makes it difficult to understand how he stands on the classical formulations of theism. (See ZPE, 196–206 [ET, 110–121] for examples of these mixed meanings.)

Though Bultmann may never have thought of himself other than as a personalistic theist, significantly, he almost always speaks of the "Word of God," not of "God" as such. For example, he says: "faith is the answer to the proclaimed word of God's grace," or "that encounter with God's word qualifies us whether we open ourselves to it or not is also known only by the faith . . .," or faith is "the hearing of Scripture as the Word of God" (ZPE, ET, 114 [199–200]). Such locutions open the door for the existentialist position to be defended in this work.

On the objectification issue, Schubert Ogden is probably correct that because Bultmann accepted objectification of the structures of existence (which as actual are essentially non-objective), he cannot avoid accepting the possibility of objectification about God provided that God is non-objective in an analogous fashion (see, CM, 90–94). But this point is merely formal. It may show how we can objectify a personal God if there is one, but it does not of itself determine that the correlate of faith is such a personal God. We shall see that faith can equally well be rendered on naturalist terms. It may turn out, in other words, that a proper understanding of the witness of faith also requires demythologizing the notion of a personal God as well!

3

the mythical world view, then it ought to follow that there is nothing specifically Christian about *any* world view. Bultmann suggests as much by distinguishing the content of faith from all *Weltanschauungen* because they tie faith to "anterior convictions" (ZPE, 197 [ET, 111–12]). Not a world view at all, faith, according to him, is an "existential self-understanding," and his method of "existentialist interpretation" is a strategy designed to free faith from any such "creedal" preconditions. This view receives added weight from Bultmann's statement that demythologizing is the "consistent application" of the doctrine of justification by faith "to the field of knowledge" (ZPE, ET, 122 [207]).

A straightforward reading of Bultmann's statement implies that faith cannot be identified with *any* particular world view or metaphysics. Such an implication is radical, for it loosens the connection between faith and any specific metaphysical entailments. But it also means that the truth of faith may be compatible with metaphysical views it is commonly thought to preclude, if, *on independent grounds*, one has reason to adopt such views. This latter implication provides the opening wedge for this book.

The present essay is an effort in Christian theological reflection. Its boundaries are set entirely by the task of comprehending the Christian witness of faith theologically. It is distinctive, however, because it is undertaken from the point of view of philosophical naturalism. For reasons to be detailed in a moment, I believe a strong case can be made that theology should consider such a naturalist option more seriously than it has. This book argues that this option is more attractive than is usually thought.

If the content of faith is an existential self-understanding, then we are not constrained at the outset by *any* metaphysical preconditions. Undertaking such an effort from a naturalist point of view will not import them. I shall show in a moment that naturalism will not so much dictate what faith must say as constrain what it *cannot* say. It frames the theological task but does not define it in detail. Though theological propositions must be consistent with naturalism, naturalism alone will not prescribe their positive content. If, following Bultmann, faith requires no anterior "creedal" convictions, if it is not tied to any particular world view, and if *on entirely independent grounds* we are convinced that philosophical naturalism gives a true account of the world, then we may ask what the Christian confession looks like from this perspective. Having become convinced of the naturalistic view of the world, we need not conclude that the Christian witness of faith is mere illusion, either on naturalist or on Christian grounds. The task remains strictly theological, but the endeavor will be focused against the background of philosophical naturalism. This procedure is made possible by Bultmann's (and Fritz Buri's[2]) claims (a) that the content of the gospel is the offer of a new self-understanding (not a set of doctrines or beliefs) and (b) that the theological task is to explicate this self-understanding existentially (not to offer up doctrines suitable for belief). Following Bultmann and Buri, I shall argue that an existentialist account of faith can be rendered on naturalist grounds.

Because of this unusual juxtaposition of normally incompatible positions, the reader is invited to view this effort as an experiment in thought. I invite the reader to examine what can be accomplished if certain assumptions are made. The effort is to show the attractiveness of a theological option by exhibiting its fruitfulness. It seeks to demonstrate that viable and indeed powerful conceptions of both religion and Christianity are possible on naturalistic grounds.

In this first chapter, I shall sketch an argument supporting the appeal of a naturalist approach to theology and develop a preliminary case for its possibility by introducing Henry Nelson Wieman's naturalist conception of God. Wieman's thought will be important for the argument but only as modified in the direction of a more austere physicalist version of naturalism as recently defended by John Post in *The Faces of Existence: An Essay in Nonreductive Metaphysics*. These philosophical foundations will be discussed in the next chapter.

THE APPEAL OF A NATURALIST THEOLOGY

Philosophical naturalism may conveniently be introduced by contrasting it to classical supernaturalism. Broadly construed, supernaturalism has been the basis of most Western religious views. It asserts that the world of nature fails to exhaust the "real" because reality consists of nature and a superordinate reality that grounds the natural world and provides its end. Contrasting it to supernaturalism, Rem Edwards describes naturalism by six "family resemblances" each of which diverges from a parallel element in supernaturalism.[3] These are: (1) that only the world of nature is real; (2) that nature is

---

[2] See, Buri, 1956, 1962, 1978. [3] See, *RR*, 133–141.

necessary in the sense of requiring no sufficient reason beyond itself to account either for its origin or ontological ground; (3) that nature as a whole may be understood without appeal to any kind of intelligence or purposive agency; and (4) that all causes are natural causes so that every natural event is itself a product of other natural events.

Beyond these basic features two additional ones have characterized most naturalisms. These are: (5) that natural science is the only sound method for establishing knowledge, and (6) that value is based solely in the interests and projects of human beings, a position that historically associates naturalism with "humanism." These features are more problematic than the first four and are, in any case, unnecessary for the basic metaphysical definition of naturalism.[4]

[4] Though any naturalism will affirm the world view of natural science as the final adjudicator of truth in some sense, the discrediting of the "verificationalist" conception of knowledge and meaning has left it unclear precisely how to construe this feature. Any claim to knowledge must be consistent with a conception of what is real derived from the natural sciences, especially physics, and with the horizons of truth that are set by that world view. But given our present limitations – both of the reality conditions established by the world view of natural science and of the methodological constraints imposed at the interfaces between those conditions and other realms of discourse – this affirmation is very "soft," and it is difficult to specify how it could be operationalized so as to transform it from a vague "feature" into a criterion. Far from setting the rules for conceptual claims in other realms, it has mainly negative force, establishing what *cannot* be claimed or, more powerfully, *meant* (as e.g., in alchemy). In some realms, especially religion, this kind of cognitive constraint can be powerful indeed. But these constraints are already implicit enough in the first four features, derived as they are from the implications associated with the historical development of the natural sciences, to make the fifth feature largely redundant. All that need be recognized – though it is all too often ignored in religious studies and generally in the humanities – is that what can count as knowledge (and interpretation) today are decisively constrained by natural science.

(One of the more deleterious effects of Thomas Kuhn's influential "perspectivalist" notion of "paradigm shifts" in the history of science is to have created the belief among humanists that the world view of natural science can be ignored by their disciplines. That at least is the way Kuhn is too often used by humanists. After a hasty reference, it is surmised that Kuhn legitimates the notion that natural science imposes no cognitive constraints on disciplines outside the sciences (as one of any number of examples, see Winquist [1978], 1). Kuhn's own careful qualifications of his position leave it unclear that he would license any of these uses to which his work is put, see Kuhn [1970].)

As for the association with humanism, naturalism at the outset simply leaves the question of the grounds of value open. Since it is almost impossible to separate humanism from axiological subjectivism, naturalists will take heart from recent philosophical discussions of value which give reason to believe that the Hume/Moore vise on these issues is about to be broken. (See, for instance, the almost causal way Thomas Nagel assumes the possibility of a naturalistic defense of value objectivity in Nagel (1986), 138–149. An even stronger physicalist defense is *FE*, esp. pp. 251–283. For a powerful theoretical ethics that grounds ethics in an objective conception of rationality and that must therefore challenge standard accounts of the naturalistic fallacy, see Reiman [1989].) There are also good *religious* reasons to challenge a humanist conception of value, and we shall see that a religious naturalism can ground value in God or objective nature as effectively as traditional theism. (From the standpoint of a naturalistic theism, Henry Nelson Wieman presented a number of powerful critiques of humanism [see, for instance, *SHG*, 9–16]).

Supernaturalism must reject each of the first four defining features of naturalism, and historically, the debate between naturalism and supernaturalism has centered on these issues. Alone, however, this debate might be thought outdated and no longer terribly interesting. In contemporary theology it is widely agreed that classical supernaturalist theism is untenable both philosophically and religiously.[5] It is commonly assumed, therefore, that the sole barrier to a truly contemporary theology lies in developing a revisionary metaphysical conception of God. The resources for such a project are drawn mainly either from Hegel or from the process thought of Whitehead and Hartshorne.[6]

It would be a mistake, however, to think that naturalism poses any less a challenge to revisionary theisms than to classical theism. Concerning the defining features of naturalism, classical and revisionary theisms share much more than they differ. If we assume, as I do in this book, that the world view of modernity is naturalist, then a revisionary theism must fail as effectively as classical supernaturalism to be adequate to the modern world, for no matter how successfully a revisionary theology reconceives God, it still shares far more important commonalities with classical theism.[7] For purposes of discussion we can identify three broad commonalities shared by both forms of

[5] This is even true of Langdon Gilkey. In Gilkey (1969), he sharply criticizes metaphysical theology, including process theology. But in Gilkey (1976), he accepts the process criticisms of classical theism and adopts a revisionary position very close to Whiteheadian views. See Gilkey (1969), 179–228, and Gilkey (1976), 226–299.

[6] An example of the Hegelian influence is Küng (1985b) (see also Küng [1980]). The still implicit conception of God in the work of Paul Ricoeur would also seem to lie in this direction (see Ricoeur [1970], 459–483). Much transcendental theology still assumes classical theism (as Schubert Ogden [1971] shows with Lonergan), thus failing to touch the underlying metaphysical issues. When transcendental philosophy does acknowledge those issues, it has tended to pursue either the Hegelian or Whiteheadian lines already mentioned (see, e.g., Gilkey [1970], 35–64 and [1976] and Winquist [1972]). The Whiteheadian line is widely represented in contemporary theology (see, e.g., Cobb [1965], Ogden [1963], and Ford [1978]). With the argument that because classical theism cannot truly affirm "this world," it has no resources for dealing with "secularism," Schubert Ogden has gone so far as to claim that the *only* fundamental issue confronting modern theology from the so-called "secular world" lies with the conception of God in classical theism (see *RG*, 1–20, 120–143). Ogden, of course, does not believe that all modern theological problems are solely metaphysical problems connected with a proper conception of God. In particular, he clearly sees the problem of mythology that any contemporary theology must address. But even here he closely associates its resolution with the revisionary theism upon which he insists. Cf. his "Myth and Truth" (*RG*, 99–119) and his well known discussions of analogy in relation to Bultmann's demythologizing program (*CM*, 90–93, 146–164 and *RG*, 144–163 and 164–187). (From a somewhat different angle, cf. Ogden [1977].)

[7] Because of these commonalities, "supernaturalism" is probably an inadequate term to draw out the deepest issues between naturalism and "non-naturalistic theisms," and I shall cease hereafter to use it.

theism: (1) that God is personal, (2) that some form of cosmic teleology is metaphysically true, and (3) that there is a cosmically comprehensible conservation of value.[8] These affirmations are revealing because each requires the falsity of one or more of the basic features of naturalism, and their truth requires the truth of very deep alternative metaphysical positions. Stating these shared affirmations thus starkly permits the ambitiousness of their underlying metaphysical assumptions to stand forth, and, I hold, thereby betrays their fundamental implausibility. It is the implausibility of these affirmations that marks the untenability of both versions of theism, no matter how ambitious (and even "successful") the revisionary efforts are. Let us take these affirmations in order.

The meaning of God's personal nature has always been fraught with metaphysical difficulties, not least having to do with the related issues of analogical predication and symbolic uses of language. For our purposes, there is sufficient agreement on *what* is intended (if not on *how* to make it metaphysically comprehensible). Classically, the primary intent was to ascribe *intelligence* and *intentional agency* (will) to the supreme being. These seem to be the minimal *ontological* conditions for the remaining traits the tradition has wanted to ascribe to God. These latter are perhaps best captured by the notion of a "living God," which is the content of the traditional idea of "Spirit." To the extent that the content of "life" or "Spirit" goes beyond intelligence and will, it is captured traditionally by "metaphorical" predicates such as "wisdom," "wrath," and, most especially, "love" and by the divine activities and attributes entertained under "governance" and "providence."[9] Christianity's deepest motive for affirming a personal God has been the idea that love belongs to God's very essence, thus the desire to ascribe to God the same caring, concernful love for his creation and for the least of its creatures that characterize a loving parent.

The idea of God as "Spirit" and thus as living and personal receives a new accent in modern thought. With the rise of modern philosophy, and especially with German idealism, the notion of "Spirit" is associated with the intense exploration of "consciousness" in modern thought and particularly with the exploration of "reflective" and "reflexive

---

[8] I arrive at this list by applying the following test. Ask of a classical or revisionary theology what beliefs are so fundamental that conviction of their falsity would require substantial alteration or abandonment of the entire position. These are the minimal, broad affirmations that pass this test in contemporary theology. Interestingly, this was not so much the case in the nineteenth century. See Gerrish (1978) for powerful analyses of positions taken on these and related issues by important nineteenth century thinkers.   [9] See Owen (1971), 17–44.

consciousness" in idealism.[10] But "life" is as important as "consciousness." That is, for a theism (or pantheism) along these lines, the basic model for both reality and a supreme being is organic.[11] Reality at the point of its utmost concreteness is not "dead matter" but organic life, infinitely rich and pulsating with depths of vitality entirely missed by the mere "surfaces" touched by the notion of "matter." The richness and complexity of "consciousness" serve as the model for describing this organic vitality.[12] This connection between the modern notion of "Spirit" (as consciousness and self-consciousness) and ontological organicism makes evident an underlying continuity between process thought and German idealism. Even though the explicit development of the categories of "Spirit" is less prominent in the former, they share an ontological and cosmic organicism.

At the same time, process thought, especially Hartshorne and his followers, has developed the metaphysical resources necessary to cash out the notion of a loving supreme being. Process thinkers see that crucial to the notion of a loving God is not merely loving *intent* but loving *response* (and indeed, the capacity for *responsiveness* as such). This idea has been richly developed with the notion of God's "consequent nature."[13] What is important is that where modern

[10] See Taylor (1975), 51–196.

[11] For this reason, Goethe and the romantic poets are as important for this turn taken by a strand of modern thought as is the internal history of philosophy from Descartes through the idealists to Nietzsche (and perhaps Heidegger). See Abrams (1971).

[12] The preeminent instance is, of course, Hegel's *Phenomenology of Spirit*, but the same metaphysical stance is at work in many others such as Fichte and both the early and late Schelling. Despite the weight given to the ontological concept of "existence" (in contrast to "consciousness") in existentialist philosophy, the tie between "life" (an ontological "organicism") and the depths of consciousness is still very close. This can be seen in the prominence given to "subjectivity" and, especially, "freedom." This connection between "Spirit" and an ontological organicism also probably accounts for both the power and the anomalies in Tillich's thought, which is otherwise so close to naturalism.

[13] Process thinkers correctly emphasize God's responsiveness, and they have made good arguments for its religious relevance. It is not so clear, however, that process thought is terribly cogent on the notion of divine intentional agency. Success here is certainly not achieved by Ogden's "What Does It Mean to Say 'God Acts in History'?" however successful this essay may be in elucidating God's historical action. (On this latter score, a careful reading will show that it certainly does not achieve the notion of God's *particular* action [see *RG*, 164–187].) Lewis Ford is one of the few process thinkers to devote explicit attention to this matter. He tries to conceptualize God's loving intentional action with the idea that God provides eternal objects for the subjective aim of each emerging concrescence (see Ford [1978], 15–69). Though this seems to be the direction a process theology would have to take, it requires far more extensive development than Ford devotes to it. As it stands, it suffers from two shortcomings. Either it is metaphysically vacuous (at the point of loving intent) since God provides eternal objects for all concrescences. Or, when this provision is particularized (as Ford does [see, esp., Ford (1978), 55ff. for Jesus]) it quite woodenly *reads back* into cosmology an overly literal and somewhat religiously naive conception of Christianity's constitutive "saving events."

thought has most powerfully contributed to the traditional concept of "Spirit," it has had to rely on a very strong metaphysical notion of cosmic, certainly ontological, organicism. A very great deal is made to hinge on the plausibility of this notion.

The second affirmation is of a cosmic or final teleology informing the ongoing passage of the world. This idea is closely related to that of a personal God. Just as the idea of an intelligent being who can act intentionally (carry out purposes) lies behind the attributes of a personal God, so also must such actions not merely be possible within the world but the world must be conceived so that its actuality is truly the outcome of such action. This is even the case when, as in most modern efforts, a major role is reserved for human freedom, for the issue is much wider, is indeed cosmic in scope, than merely to fit human freedom into the world.[14] Reality must be conceived so that divine activity within it is both possible and everywhere present. So, there is a close relationship between a personal God and a metaphysics which makes teleology possible and actual.

Connected with this issue is Christianity's stake in eschatological conceptions. Indeed, theologically, eschatology focuses cosmic teleology. This is even true of providence, for within Christianity, the doctrine of providence is given shape by an eschatological frame, as can be seen in figures as diverse as Augustine and Moltmann. And of course, it is the eschatological frame of Christianity that has decisively shaped Western notions of history. What is crucial again, as with a personal God, is that both forms of theism rely theologically on a very strong metaphysical claim, namely, that a metaphysical account of what is real can and must include teleology at its very center, indeed a teleology grounded in the acts of a personal divinity.[15] The metaphysical character of the theological claim is evident because the idea of

[14] It is revealing, though also entirely predictable, that Ford, in order to ground his account of divine intentional activity regarding humanity, must attribute the course of evolution itself to God's specific, quite particular provision (see Ford [1978], 56–63). On this basis, it is easy for him to formulate this same particularized activity culturally, historically, and religiously, especially in terms of a surprisingly orthodox (and parochial) conception of the election of Israel (see Ford [1978], 131ff.).

[15] The important but as yet unpublished work of my colleague Phillip Scribner demonstrates that an account of teleological causality can be given on entirely naturalistic terms. Indeed, Scribner pulls this rabbit out of the hat of a strongly reductionist physicalism. What is important in Scribner's path-breaking work, however, is that this causality is entirely mechanistic. In both classical and revisionary theism, in contrast, teleology must be seen as "intentional agency" in the widest sense. It must, if you will, be assimilated to "the point of view of the subject," and this point of view must be conceived as having the widest and deepest metaphysical efficacy.

"history" as a purposive or developmental process, decisively influenced by Christian eschatological sources, can be divorced from its cosmic background and given an entirely naturalistic account.[16] In other words, Christian conceptions of history require a cosmic, eschatological background even if the historical development for which they have otherwise been important can be rendered apart from it.

The third affirmation concerns the conservation of value and is most easily seen theologically in views concerning "survival of death," or in the way theologians discuss a final destiny for human beings and/or humanity beyond death. I have chosen a broad and lose term, the conservation of value, to characterize this affirmation because it is difficult to find another phrase that will fairly capture the issues at stake across the spectrum of theological views.[17] The difficulties in finding an appropriate term are themselves revealing. Theologians speak today with altogether too little candor about precisely what it is that non-theologians can be expected to believe about death and what is beyond death, on issues of "personal resurrection," "immortality," "God's eschatological promise," or a "destiny beyond death." At no other point in theological discussions today is it more common to find reference to tired, old formulas without theological elucidation. When theologians do discuss these issues, it is often difficult to figure out what is being affirmed – and denied.[18]

The hesitancy with which contemporary theologians affirm beliefs about "subjective immortality" is also revealing.[19] Until about the

[16] The "doctrine of progress" has, of course, been out of fashion for a long time. But apart from changes in fashion, important ethnographic, anthropological, archeological, and historical work since the 1930's, when the "doctrine" began to lose its allure, make it quite clear that, in a broad sense and taking sufficiently large spans of time and geography into account, something like a "progressive," or developmental, or structural view of human history is entirely plausible. Such a view can be developed without recourse to any notion of metaphysical teleology at all (see, e.g., Eisenstadt [1986].

[17] The only place I have found this phrase is in R. W. Hepburn's "Questions about the Meaning of Life" (Klemke [1981], 209–227, at 209, 221–225), though he does not use it to identify quite the same set of issues as here.

[18] See, for example, Gilkey (1976) 296 f. which is better than most. Gilkey speaks of "reunion" beyond death, and he insists that if death is final, then it is "ultimate" and therefore qualifies the ultimacy of our relation to the ultimate (not, to say the least, an entirely clear argument). But Gilkey makes it quite explicit that the final content of God's love is to "triumph over the conditions of our finitude" (Gilkey [1976], 318).

[19] It is often claimed that there is an essential difference between the Hebraic idea of resurrection and the Greek idea of immortality. This difference is located at two points: (1) unlike immortality, the resurrection faith envisages a renewal of the full psycho-physical identity of persons and thus includes their social existence. (2) Resurrection is not a natural, ontological condition (i.e., a *naturally* immortal soul) but is founded on the promise and gift of

19th century, subjective immortality filled the Christian confidence in a "destiny beyond death" promised by the "resurrection." But beginning in the 19th century, belief in subjective immortality became implausible, not merely in the general culture but among many theologians as well. Some simply gave it up, but more common was a retreat to vagueness. Today we generally find an unwillingness to say anything at all about subjective immortality, all the while continuing to use the formulas that traditionally suggested it, and either silence about the issue as such or a retreat to quite indeterminate language about a "destiny beyond death." A few theologians, such as Schubert Ogden, have addressed this whole nest of issues forthrightly. They recognize that subjective survival of death is not only metaphysically implausible (and perhaps incoherent) but also religiously unedifying (most especially in a religion as non-egocentric as Christianity). At the same time, they maintain that the resurrection faith essentially involves the promise of a defeat of death. This can be developed in process thought by a kind of "objective immortality" in which value attained in each actual entity is preserved and appreciated everlastingly, not in its own subjective mode (which would entail some version of "subjective immortality"), but in the ongoing consequent nature of God (which itself, of course, has a "subjective" dimension).[20]

For these reasons, it is difficult to find a single expression that captures all the views on what is nevertheless, I believe, a single affirmation broadly shared by classical and revisionary theists. I have chosen "the conservation of value" as sufficiently loose yet focused enough to state the issue. It has the virtue of covering Ogden's affirmation of a kind of objective immortality and also of capturing

God. Such distinctions are certainly intelligible, but it is difficult to understand what difference they make on the ultimate *religious* issue, the question of the finality of death. If I have an indefeasible faith in God's promise that the conditions of my finitude will be overcome at death, that my death will not be final, it is difficult to see how my additional belief that I will be a resurrected psycho-physical unity (and not "merely" a disembodied soul) is religiously different from my conviction that I am an immortal soul that will survive the death of my body (and perhaps *spiritually* commune with others). (For examples of this argument, see Niebuhr, [1937] 289–306 and Anderson [1951], 208–235.) The only point to these distinctions would seem to be the *symbolic* significance of the biblical conception of "resurrection" over "immortality." As Niebuhr points out, "resurrection" symbolically captures the biblical conception of human life as fully social which requires a strong notion of embodied existence (Niebuhr, [1937], 292–299). To take "resurrection" symbolically in this way, however, leaves unclarified the quite nonsymbolic issue of "destiny beyond death." Niebuhr and most theologians who follow this kind of analysis seem to want it both ways.

[20] This latter option is effectively stated by Ogden in "The Promise of Faith" (*RG*, 206–230, esp., pp. 220ff.), which will be dealt with at length in the last chapter.

the religious values at stake, namely, the issue whether the subjective consummations of our lives end in "perpetual perishing."[21] It also encompasses the wider spectrum, including subjective immortality, if the latter can be stated so as to avoid self-serving motives.

Across this diversity of views there is a general agreement that Christianity stands or falls with the promise of a destiny beyond death. This affirmation is perhaps best captured by Langdon Gilkey in the last sections of *Reaping the Whirlwind* with his repeated expression of a hope for a "final reunion, communion and completion" beyond history.[22] The "conservation of value" seeks to capture this consensus. As with the first two affirmations, the point again is that this consensus requires a background of very strong beliefs about the ultimate constitution of reality – irrespective of the specific theological formulations. Background *metaphysical* beliefs are required even if they are not formulated explicitly. In some sense, we must have a view of reality that includes and can make possible a conservation of value.

At no other point is the distinction between the stance of piety and the language of theology more important than with these three basic affirmations. This line has always been delicate, often fuzzy, and frequently obscured in actual theological practice, but today almost every theological decision requires a high degree of self-consciousness about it and about how one is negotiating between its two sides. The relationship between these stances is especially intimate with our three affirmations. Indeed, it seems that the *theological* warrant for these affirmations is often rooted directly in the stance of piety. The

---

[21] Concerning "annihilation" or "perpetual perishing," subjective immortality is too often defended with the religiously unedifying argument that a loving God would not permit to perish the values achieved precisely in and *as* subjective life on the part of the creatures he has lovingly created. Apart from its questionable mythological formulation, this is religiously unedifying because it is an essentially self-serving argument quite out of place for Christianity, at the very center of which is the claim that true life is defined by freedom from self *even unto death*. Surely one of the great distortions of Christianity has been the well-nigh universal acceptance that what is ultimately at stake is this kind of survival. It is difficult to avoid the impression that such beliefs amount to nothing more nor less than a massive denial of the *reality* of death, the childish affirmation that *we really do not die* (even though we pass through death). This impression is by no means alleviated by the equally common and facile argument that Christianity, unlike the classical belief in immortality, affirms the reality of death because life beyond death is grounded solely in the promise and the action of God. The consequence is exactly the same as far as the outcome of the belief goes. As Ogden sees, however, there may be a religious issue in the problem of perpetual perishing, when this issue is divorced from a self-serving subjective survival (see *RG*, 224–226). For a powerful statement of this issue on the part of one who as a naturalist had no illusions about the conservation of value, see Wieman (1946), 21–23. For Wieman's more extended discussion of the religious significance of death from a naturalist perspective, see Bretall (1963), 105–109.
[22] See, e.g., Gilkey (1976), 297–298, 318.

argument is that something is at stake *religiously* that requires or makes inevitable just these basic *theological* affirmations, the implication being that if the affirmations were surrendered, then piety itself, the very essence of religion, would somehow become impossible.

The religious stake in these affirmations is perhaps most apparent with the conservation of value. It is often assumed that if death is annihilation, if achieved values, including their subjective con-summations and the subjective life that is their condition, are lost at death, then life must be meaningless and despairing (because objectively achieved value and "influence" can persist only over brief cosmic epochs). This religious issue even seems to be at stake among those prepared to surrender subjective continuity in favor of some more objective immortality that defeats "perpetual perishing."[23]

Equally important are the religious issues involved in the other affirmations. Only a personal God, it would seem, can carry the religious centrality of love in Christianity. As has been proven again and again in modern theology, the role of love and of a God of love cannot be articulated in solely ethical terms, and even in modern theologies where the ethical component has predominated (as in Ritschl, Harnack, and Hermann), a personalistic theism has been so much taken for granted as not to require comment. A loving, personal God seems to be even more necessary for the drama of salvation in Christ, no matter how it is delineated theologically. How, for instance, can such central Christian notions as "forgiveness" and "justification" be rendered without a personal God?[24] Underlying these specifically Christian themes is the almost instinctive human need to relate religiously to the ultimate conditions of life in personal terms. Indeed, in the perspective of world religions, Christianity's uniqueness may lie in having given the deepest attention to this quintessential religious "need."

Here the notions of a personal God and final causality are most

[23] See, e.g., *RG*, 224.

[24] An important test case is Tillich. The background of Tillich's ontology is a kind of vitalistic organicism from Schelling and German idealism. Though this may ultimately support a personal or "trans-personal" (whatever that might mean) God, Tillich's concept of God as being-itself comes very close to being non-personal. In the closing pages of *The Courage to Be* he develops the idea of "the God beyond God" and forthrightly rejects theistic personalism, but there he is also closest to the religious roots of theological language. It is significant, therefore, that he cannot avoid highly personalized language about unconditional *acceptance*. At issue is whether he falls into complete incoherence here. One of the deep problems in this great work concerns how to elucidate "acceptance of acceptance" in the non-personal ontological terms he otherwise assumes (see Tillich [1952], 155–190).

intimately linked, for it is in connection with the idea of a "purposeful" ordering of the events of everyday life that the need to think of life's ultimate condition in personal terms most often comes to expression. This is seen in "popular" religion[25] in response to calamity, personal tragedy, or evil when the deepest consolation sought is the belief that such events "are for a purpose." At a less popular level, the same belief is often expressed in reaction to naturalism. Such a world, it is said, must be dead and without purpose, atoms in the void, a world "blind," indifferent, and utterly unresponsive to human values and purposes. It is assumed that in such a world life must be meaningless because nothing that one does can "make a difference" and therefore "cannot matter." There is a crucial (and indeed legitimate) link, in other words, between life being meaningful and life being purposeful. Though this link can be articulated without recourse to a personalistic theism, the centrality in these discussions of the language of "blindness" and "cosmic indifference," on the one hand, and "responsiveness," and a kind of encompassing "purposefulness," on the other, shows how closely personalistic conceptions of deity and final causality are connected.

There is, then, a kind of consensus that runs beneath contemporary theology. It runs, in particular, beneath its most significant division, between those who insist that the central Christian affirmations require classical theism[26] (even acknowledging the need for various other conceptual, methodological, and hermeneutical revisions[27]) and the advocates of a revisionary theism. I have tried to identify the basic ingredients in this consensus with the three affirmations analyzed above. Irrespective of their detailed articulation, they involve exceedingly strong metaphysical assumptions that must be made good in some fashion. In many cases, such as in Barth or Moltmann or Altizer, they are, of course, not made good metaphysically at all, but are simply assumed as a kind of frame within which a theological program is executed. In other cases, such as Ogden, Cobb, and Ford or differently in transcendental Thomism and Langdon Gilkey (whose essentially process stance is influenced by the transcendental method), an effort is made to render them straightfor-

---

[25] This term is not intended pejoratively but to refer to what I have called "the language of piety." It includes us all when we are *being* religious.

[26] See here the almost contemptuous rejection of process theism by Owen (1971), 82–89.

[27] I have in mind here the creative work of such Roman Catholic thinkers as Rahner, Lonergan, and Coreth who are sensitive to the conceptual situation created by modernity but who continue to affirm classical theism. Ricoeur also seems to belong here.

wardly. In all these cases the consensus is maintained, and it runs directly counter to the underlying affirmations of naturalism.

Taken together, the first four features of naturalism deny these three theological assumptions that form the contemporary theological consensus. Conversely, these theological affirmations require anti-naturalistic metaphysical positions. The most important of these center around the essential affirmations of personalistic theism: that the world is ultimately grounded and ordered by a metaphysical term properly conceived as intelligent, purposive agency. Such a metaphysical ground makes possible a purposive world, in terms of some account of teleology, which includes the conservation of value. Naturalism, in contrast, conceives the fundamental character of the world, the world under a "complete explanation," independently of any concepts that would introduce purpose or intelligence into an account of its most basic operation. All existence, all order, and all action can be accounted for without recourse to the operation of intelligent purpose. It follows, that teleological causes can only characterize some "micro-agents" within the world which, as "complex objects," are so constituted as to guide their behavior purposively. But teleology cannot account for order or action in the world as such, and those complex micro-agents that act purposively are themselves constituted by more fundamental objects that can be understood entirely non-teleologically. The features of naturalism also imply that there is no basis for a conservation of value (except across brief cosmic epochs). This is all the more true if, as in personalistic theisms, the conservation of value is essentially tied to metaphysical conceptions requiring personal agency and purposiveness on some cosmic scale (thus encompassing versions of both subjective and objective immortality). Value arises locally in a naturalistic world, but it is not conserved.[28]

My purpose in this opening chapter is to contrast naturalism and

---

[28] I have conducted this analysis without appeal to the second feature of naturalism which claims that the world of nature is ontologically necessary (see *RR*, 136, 138–139). The reason is that the denial of this feature is most closely related only to classical theism. Most forms of revisionary theism, certainly the Hegelian and process forms, would agree with naturalism that the "world as a whole" is ontologically grounded in itself, requiring no "supernatural" ground or no *causal* ground "beyond" its own internal, ordered givenness. On the other hand, these revisionary theisms, while agreeing very broadly with naturalism here, insist that the world as a whole nevertheless requires a "personal" and "teleological" ground or ordering to account for its sufficiency. This, for instance, is the role of Absolute Spirit in Hegelian thought and of the primordial nature of God in process thought. Another reason why I have ignored this issue is because Post shows the untenability of the principle of sufficient reason in debates over necessity and contingency (see *FE*, 80–84). If it is equally as coherent to think of nature as necessary as it is to think of God as ground, then theological decisions cannot be made on the basis of this issue.

the underlying non-naturalistic assumptions in the contemporary theological consensus as sharply as possible. I shall not attempt to demonstrate the truth of naturalism, nor shall I attempt to prove the impossibility of the metaphysical assumptions upon which the theological consensus is based. Starting *from* naturalism, I want to explore what can be done with it religiously and theologically. The attractiveness of this approach is suggested, however, by the present analysis. At bottom the theological consensus rests on exceedingly strong metaphysical affirmations that must be made good if its conception of theology is plausible. Since the 19th century, there have been any number of innovative theological efforts to address the modern theological situation. But their success must finally be assessed by judgments regarding their framing assumptions.[29] We now can see that these assumptions are relatively few and are metaphysically strong.

Taken together in this simplified way, these assumptions become, I hold, quite implausible. When we have precipitated these broad, simple, yet fundamental elements in the way we must think of the world as a whole in order even *to begin* theologically with the consensus today, then we cannot but be impressed with their implausibility. This is true despite the inventiveness of many contemporary theological efforts within those assumptions (often undertaken by almost ignoring them). We think, today, willy-nilly within naturalistic assumptions. Here, the kind of analysis Bultmann made when introducing his demythologizing proposal is still relevant (cf. NTM, ET, 2–5 [16–19]). When we cook on an electric stove, consult a doctor, or notice the latest discoveries in molecular biology or neuro-physiology, we think naturalistically.[30] When we notice how

[29] There are any number of revisionary theological efforts today that appear to prescind from the ultimately metaphysical issues I have attempted to elucidate. One thinks especially of efforts to develop a hermeneutical method that is entirely psychological, usually strongly influenced by Jung, as in the work of Charles Winquist and David Miller (see Winquist [1978] and Miller [1974]). Or there are other efforts, of which Raschke is a powerful example, which try to interpret theological content through an event theory of language. But the issue cannot be evaded. Either these efforts are already naturalistic, in which case this needs to be acknowledged because the proposals can only be fully developed and evaluated against this background. Or, as appears to be true in each of these examples, they are not naturalistic on the crucial issues I have outlined, in which case they are in the same position as the theological consensus, and the effect of these framing assumptions on their own positions needs to be more fully recognized and worked out.

[30] Perhaps the most obvious example here comes from chemistry, not physics. We now commonly think of the most basic operations of life (at the level of cells and of brain activity) in *molecular* terms. When one thinks of this and other examples, metaphysical attempts to make good on the affirmations of the theological consensus appear more and more like the old "God of the gaps" theology.

pervasive these naturalistic assumptions are throughout modern life, it is difficult to see how the views assumed by the theological consensus could even make an entrance into our conceptions of how the world goes. They receive whatever plausibility they have only by abstracting them from the naturalism that suffuses modern ways of approaching the world.[31]

Obviously, this amounts to no proof of naturalism, nor do I intend it as such. I want simply to elicit an impression of the magnitude of the conceptual leap the theological consensus requires. If we begin to feel the implausible weight of this leap, then a naturalistic view of the world becomes increasingly plausible. This is true even when we recognize, as we must, that naturalism comes in many versions and that none can be considered complete today. The issue is not metaphysical completeness at this point – certainly none of the alternatives to naturalism can be viewed as metaphysically complete – but starting point. Against the background of naturalism, which we everywhere wear almost as a second skin, the metaphysical load of beginning with the theological consensus is too great.

Of course, it is also widely assumed that we cannot begin, religiously or theologically, with naturalism. Viewing the world naturalistically, it is assumed, means viewing it non-religiously. Many versions of naturalism do have an anti-religious bias, and many naturalistic interpretations of religion are either pejorative or superficial. But, as we shall see, these accounts can be challenged and, perhaps, the deficiencies made good. There is no reason why a naturalist view of the world cannot provide a viable and attractive account of religion. Indeed, much, perhaps all, that is most deeply affirmed in the Christian witness of faith can be rendered on naturalist terms.

INITIAL PARAMETERS FOR A NATURALIST THEOLOGY

A viable naturalist theology would be very attractive in our contemporary theological situation. By a single stroke Christian affirmations would be aligned with the conceptual framework that otherwise underlies almost all contemporary culture. The issue here is not merely theoretical. Contemporary culture is not informed by naturalism in the first instance by theoretically formulated beliefs but behind or beneath them at the level of unstated assumptions and

---

[31] See Gellner (1974).

behavior. It would be attractive if the Christian faith could be aligned simply and directly with what we otherwise so readily take for granted in modern life. At the more theoretical level, it would make the "point" of the Christian faith (indeed of religion generally) once again available for broad reaches of the educated populace in modernized societies who are presently alienated from or indifferent to the issues of life that Christianity addresses. Finally, the Christian commitment to truth, at its high points, has always attempted a synthesis with the best philosophical thought of its time, and we should expect nothing less of ourselves.[32]

As it turns out, we are not without resources in this regard as there have been any number of modern attempts at naturalist appropriations of religion. The present book relies on one of these, the thought of Henry Nelson Wieman. In the remainder of this chapter I want to present certain aspects of Wieman's thought that will help us define the initial parameters of a Christian naturalist theology. This work is not simply about Wieman, however. Though his thought is more neglected today than it ought to be, Wieman never developed a complete philosophical position, and there is much in his work that is either dated or failed.[33] His naturalism tended to push him out of the mainstream after neo-orthodoxy came to prominence in American theology in the 1950's. For those seeking a more "liberal" alternative to the hard, supernaturalist side of neo-orthodoxy, Tillich, writing more in the "spirit" of the times, looked more attractive.[34] The theological situation today, however, is much different than it was when Wieman's influence waned. The strangle hold of neo-orthodoxy has been broken, but no clear way forward is evident. It is no longer certain what "orthodoxy" or the "tradition" require,[35] and it now appears that our theological situation is much more continuous with the 19th century than was clear when neo-orthodoxy dominated the theological scene. A bold willingness to experiment is called for in our

[32] See Post (1987), 332–336 for an excellent statement of why we should seek a synthesis between theistic religion and some version of physicalistic naturalism.
[33] This seems true, for instance, of Wieman's psychology of religion (Wieman and Wieman, [1935]) and of his *The Wrestle of Religion with Truth* (Wieman [1927]).
[34] Wieman's powerful criticisms of Tillich are still instructive, and indeed one of the best entrances to his thought (see, e.g., Wieman [1974a] and Wieman [1968]; see also *SHG*, 33, n. 1). On the other hand, he never really comprehended the power of Niebuhr's thought, and his discussions of him seem cranky (cf. Wieman [1961]).
[35] See Gerrish (1978), esp. 1–12, 181–188, for Gerrish's insightful comments, in reference to 19th century liberal thinkers in the Reformed tradition, about what continuity with the tradition means in the modern world.

time just as at the beginning of the 19th century. In this light Wieman's thought becomes interesting again. There are a number of powerful notions in his philosophy of religion that can serve to focus a naturalist account of the Christian faith. So, I shall appropriate Wieman selectively. The initial points for this selection are a number of brief but powerful theological essays sprinkled throughout his writings in which he interprets the basic Christian affirmations. These are like small systematic theologies, and they are very impressive. They are also in surprising conformity with almost all that a confessing Christian could affirm. Since he does this from the background of a naturalist philosophy of religion, it is worthwhile to "think backwards" from these essays and to examine how such basically "orthodox" statements of Christianity could have been rendered naturalistically. In a certain sense this entire book is simply an effort to provide this wider theological framework for Wieman's essays in Christian theology.

I shall first examine Wieman's naturalistic concept of God and show why it is significant for the existentialist approach to theology I shall defend. His concept of God will provide a basis for interpreting other broad themes in his work that link his notion of God with his naturalism. I shall conclude by alluding to certain parallels between Wieman's philosophy of religion and the biblical tradition.

Wieman's naturalism is especially worth renewed attention because of the powerful conception of God he succeeded in articulating on naturalist terms. Much of the argument of this book will develop from the possibilities opened up by this concept of God when it is brought to bear on Bultmann's method of existentialist interpretation. This correlation is opened because neither demythologizing nor existentialist interpretation mandate any particular view of the world in advance. Wieman's most incisive statement about God occurs at the beginning of his first book, *Religious Experience and Scientific Method* (1926). He wrote this before his naturalism was fully explicit, but it is consistent with naturalism, and there is nothing in his later work that either contradicts or improves upon it. I quote it at some length.

Whatever else the word God may mean, it is a term used to designate that Something upon which human life is most dependent for its security, welfare and increasing abundance. That there is such a Something cannot be doubted. The mere fact that human life happens, and continues to happen, proves that this Something, however, unknown, does certainly exist.

Of course one can say that there are innumerable conditions which converge to sustain human life, and that is doubtless a fact. But in that case either one of two things are true. Either the universe is a single individual organic unity, in which case it is the whole indivisible universe that has brought forth and now sustains human life; or else certain of these sustaining conditions are more critically, ultimately and constantly important for human welfare than are others. According to the first view God would be, or involve, the whole universe; according to the second he would be those most important conditions which, taken collectively, constitute the Something which must have supreme value for all human living. The word God, taken with its very minimum meaning, is the name for this Something of supreme value. God may be much more than this, but he is certainly this by definition. In this sense, with this minimum, God cannot be denied. His existence is absolutely certain. He is simply that which is supremely significant in all the universe for human living, however known or unknown he may be.

Of course this statement concerning God proves nothing about his character, except that he is the most beneficent object in the universe for human beings. He is certainly the object of supreme value. Nothing is implied by this definition concerning personality in God; but neither is personality denied. In fact, personality is by no means a clear and simple term. But two things are made certain: his existence and the supremacy of his value over all others, if we measure value in terms of human need. (*RESM*, 9–10)

I shall develop this conception more fully throughout the book. For the moment, several observations can be made. First, this conception is entirely formal. Though it is open-ended as to naturalism, as Wieman's reference to personality indicates, it is consistent with a naturalism. In his more mature work, Wieman made clear that personality could not intelligibly be attributed to deity (cf. *SHG*, 265–268). It is also important to notice how it skews the approach to God toward value rather than ontology. This becomes even more evident in Wieman's later thought. The framework, that is, from which theology should address the question of God makes it less appropriate to ask whether a being of such and such a sort exists than to ask about the character of a supreme devotion or loyalty.[36] This value orientation also gives it a functional cast. Instead of asking what qualities God must have to deserve an absolute devotion or worship – the normal way this issue is addressed theologically[37] – "God" is

---

[36] In this respect, it has similarities to Tillich's notion of "ultimate concern" (shorn of any ontological claims) and also to Royce's conception of loyalty.

[37] This type of argument is a crucial part of the critique process theologians make of classical theism, namely, that the God of classical theism cannot meet the criterion of religious adequacy, is undeserving of or cannot elicit an *absolute* devotion (see, e.g., *RR* 200–202).

defined functionally as that toward which we ought to direct a final devotion or loyalty. This functional strategy of defining God in terms of value has great advantages for the approach taken here because it leaves the theological ground neutral as between naturalism and non-naturalistic varieties of theism. In this sense, it opens the door for a naturalist theology (or what we might call, a "naturalistic theism"). In effect, Wieman is proposing to transform the very nature of the "God" question from ontology to value, thereby also transforming our understanding of the nature of religion. Much of the argument to be developed below will depend on the cogency of this double transformation.

Perhaps its most significant aspect is that God is comprehended as an actuality. If the passage is interpreted theistically, this would be no great surprise, of course, but it is truly significant that Wieman here achieves an actual God on terms compatible with naturalism. Within naturalistic circles this is quite unusual. Those naturalists who show an interest in the philosophy of religion – such as Santayana, Dewey, or Randall – have an easy enough time conceiving a *real* God, but one whose reality is *ideal*, not actual. Wieman's naturalist God is not merely ideal but is the actuality in which value is grounded. Because this God is an actuality, Wieman's thought is much more open for Christian theological use than would otherwise be the case. Finally, we need simply note that this conception of God is also neutral regarding the three basic affirmations analyzed above. Nothing is presumed about the personal character of God, about final causality, or about the conservation of value, and the definition would continue to be serviceable if, as in naturalism, these affirmations were all denied.[38]

---

[38] An exception, it might be argued, is the conservation of value. One might argue that the conservation of value is essential to the constitution of value for human beings given the reflective and historical manner in which value is achieved at the human level of nature. Wieman's orientation to supreme beneficence and human need might then be taken to require the conservation of value. Ogden, for instance, seems to take something like this position with his argument that the experience of meaning (and of the meaningfulness of life) as such presupposes an affirmation of God (see *RG*, 30–43, 120–143). A less sophisticated version occurs when theologians ground "immortality" in the love of God by arguing that the Christian God *would not* (*could not?*) permit to pass into annihilation those values achieved in the subjective temporality of the creatures he has created in his image. Irrespective of the merit of these arguments – and as I have noted, the latter appears suspiciously self-serving and religiously unedifying – they need not be read back into Wieman. For Wieman such arguments get the matter backwards. We cannot dictate the conditions of reality by starting with human need. Reality either does or does not support the conservation of value. If it does not, then it does not follow, as Ogden seems to presume, that value is made nugatory. Process theology itself recognizes that not all value is compossible – this is essential to typically process approaches to the problem of evil. The structure of value appreciation at the human level

In *Religious Experience and Scientific Method* and in his early thought generally, Wieman was inclined to speak of this "Something of supreme value" as the "total event" of the world. By this he meant the "total event" as it comes to focus in experience. In *The Wrestle of Religion with Truth* (1927), his least successful book, he toyed with a speculative version of Whitehead's consequent nature of God to describe this "total event." But throughout the remainder of his career, speculative efforts to describe the "Something of supreme value" receded into the background. Indeed, the avoidance of speculative interest became one aspect of his "empiricism." He argued that what should drive the philosophy of religion (and theology) is a religious, not a speculative interest, and he became unconcerned with all questions except those of how we can know, serve, and enhance our relationship to the source of value.

Wieman's nonspeculative naturalism is especially attractive for the approach I am proposing. His empirical, non-speculative approach accords nicely with Bultmann's existentialist interpretation, for the focus in both is the existential and thus religious force of basic Christian affirmation. Or rather, each shows that the force of basic Christian affirmation is always existential and thus religious. Naturalism operates here as a kind of boundary condition. It dictates by setting boundaries to what *cannot* be contained, mainly by implication, in the existential content of faith. Wieman's naturalist, yet non-speculative, concept of God serves to anchor the existential content of faith in a real and actual object of faith which can be conceived entirely existentially. It serves in this respect, exactly as Bultmann insisted, to protect the notion of existential self-understanding from subjectivistic misunderstanding.[39]

Wieman came increasingly to associate the notion of God with "creativity." Undoubtedly drawn from Whitehead's thought, the "empirical" bent of Wieman's interest turned this notion in a more existential or religious direction. His most mature development of the idea of God was presented in *The Source of Human Good* (1946). By this time, he had come to define God as "the creative event," a notion which turns on his distinction between "creative good" and "created

includes the recognition that some values are indeed not compossible, are doomed to disappointment. A naturalist account of value must, of course, address the almost instinctive human fear of annihilation and perpetual loss which seems to have been so fundamental to the history of human religiosity, and this will be a theme in the following. But nothing requires that we build into our account of the source of value from the beginning an ontological ground for overcoming this fear.   [39] See, ZPE, ET, 113–116 (198–201).

good." This distinction, in turn, required him to develop a more complete theory of value. The "creative event" and "creative good" are synonymous and interchangeable. God is "the creative event" because "God" refers to the source of value; thus, the creative event is also "creative good." "God" refers to those processes in nature, whatever they are, that are productive of value. The notion of value is developed here by the notion of "quality." Quality or value arises in nature when natural processes develop at a physical level which give rise to events within physical objects that are qualitative in character. "Qualities" occur as intrinsic events within complex physical objects that register responsiveness to an environment.[40] In this very basic and primitive sense, "qualities" are values, and probably arise at a minimal level in cells. The notion of quality gives Wieman a naturalistic account of value. At this basic level, value can increase in nature as more complex physical systems develop that are capable of greater richness of quality. Richness of quality can increase through greater intensity, through contrast, and through greater complexity which permits mutual reinforcement and hierarchical relating and ordering of qualities.

But value in nature is strictly limited as long as it is limited to quality since quality is immediate and ephemeral, with little or no temporal depth and restricted to the physical boundaries of the object undergoing it. To account for a growth of value beyond this level,

---

[40] Though very suggestive, Wieman's discussion of value as quality is condensed and not fully elaborated, especially in terms of its physical basis. My presentation attempts both to be faithful to it and to elaborate it in a more physicalist direction. In my opinion, Wieman's tentativeness about elaborating it fully had to do with his ambivalence toward process metaphysics. Clearly, much of the inspiration for his conception of creativity and of value came from the Whiteheadian view of experience. At the same time, he was not, I believe, comfortable with accepting a Whiteheadian ontology as an account of naturalism. Very much under the influence of Dewey, he simply prescinded from giving any ontological account of experience and settled for a minimal set of distinctions that would account for the structure of value in experience and could serve to move his own theory forward toward the religious issues that were his chief concern.

By "complex physical objects" I mean physical objects that are complex physical systems resulting from the combination of more primitive physical objects. Cells are the most basic of such complex objects, being themselves complex, interactive systems of molecules. Complex physical objects have the functional characteristic of interacting with their environments by maintaining a set of uniformly varying spatial relationships among their parts. (I am indebted to the work of Phillip H. Scribner for this latter way of construing complex physical objects.)

This discussion of Wieman's theory of value is drawn from *SHG*, 16–23 where he confines himself entirely to the notion of "qualitative meaning." A comparison of his discussion with mine will show that my interpretation of what he must mean by "quality" goes considerably beyond (or behind) what he himself says.

Wieman introduces the concept of "qualitative meaning." Qualitative meaning is still constituted by qualities, but by qualities that have become "sign events." At a certain point, sufficiently complex physical organisms develop with capabilities for qualities that can stand for other qualities. Events within the organism registered as qualities come to stand for, or "mean," other qualities. Immediacy is broken because qualities can now signify qualities that are not immediately present, residing either in the past, as the physical basis for memory, or in the future, as the physical basis for anticipation, planning, projection, imagination, foresight, and resolve. Qualities that are physical events producing qualitative meaning are also the physical basis of learning. When the capability of qualitative meaning is reached, the potential for growth and richness of quality becomes infinite. In sum, to quote just one of Wieman's formulations: "Qualitative meaning is any structure of interrelated events, together with their possibilities, when these events have appreciable qualities and when the structure as a whole can be represented by signs. Signs are those events belonging to the structure which serve to represent the structure as a whole. The possibilities pertaining to such a structure make up that part of the structure not now embodied in actual events" (*SHG*, 21).

Qualitative meanings are available to many nonhuman organisms though they are probably limited to organisms with a central nervous system. For our purposes we can confine ourselves largely to the human level. Even here, however, neither qualitative meaning nor quality are confined to consciousness. Wieman was a "radical empiricist," and this position (disregarding its questionable tendency to build a metaphysics into the notion of experience) insistently questions limiting experience to focused consciousness. In the same vein, Wieman also associated the richness of experience with the penumbral and the vague, not merely with focused attention. Thus, just as quality and qualitative meaning extend beyond human beings, even within human beings, some qualities and qualitative meanings are always present in the background and on the edges of any focused attention. This great swell of interlacing quality comprises Wieman's notion of the richness of experience. But throughout, it is qualitative meaning, both implicit and penumbral as well as focused, that raises the richness of value to a new level. The defining mark of such increase in value is that qualities break the mere passage of existence into discriminable events so that from the continuity of passage, mute, blind, and unmodulated, a world emerges. Greater capacity for fineness of quality, to be understood in terms of brain events, provides a more richly grained capacity for the discrimination of events, so that at the human level with an infinite capacity for qualitative meaning, especially through language,[41] a world of extraordinary discriminative richness arises.[42]

The creative event (or creative good) refers to those processes in nature that produce value, quality, and qualitative meaning. The creative event is always productive. It accounts for changes in physical conditions that in the sweep of evolutionary history underlie the rise of capacities for quality and qualitative meaning. With those capacities already established, it also accounts for new combinations of quality or qualitative meaning (or their intensities) by which new richness of quality occurs. In both senses, but especially in the latter, the creative event is always *transformative*, either of whatever physical conditions obtain (resulting in the transformative production of capacities for quality as such) or, more normally, in new interrelationships of qualities productive of new quality and thus of new qualitative meaning. This notion of the creative event (God) as transformative will be important for the theological development to follow. At the level of qualitative meaning, Wieman attempted to describe the formal structure of this creative event, and at the appropriate point below, we shall examine and extend his analysis. For the present, we can ignore his full theory in the interest of concentrating on the outlines of his naturalistic conception of God. For these purposes we need see only that "the creative event" is always a productive or transformative event in the sense just described.

To develop the concept of the "creative event" more fully, we must introduce its contrast which Wieman termed "the *created* event" or "*created* good." *Created goods* refer to the actualizations of value produced by the creative event. They are, if you will, the precipitates in experience of the creative event's transformative action. They are value as experienced – as long as we hold in view the broader conception of experience Wieman is presupposing. Value is always

---

[41] Language is on this account one but not the sole form of qualitative meaning. It is, in any case, itself based on events in the brain which are themselves qualities. Language is an expressive outcome of qualitative meaning, but it has a physical basis in qualitative events in the brain.

[42] This discussion of quality as discrimination of events is drawn from a section entitled, "Creative Event Biologically Interpreted" (*SHG*, 70–74). This concept of "world" of course shows Wieman's naturalism at its most Deweyian.

quality since even the infinitely greater richness of qualitative meaning is built up out of events that are themselves qualitative in nature (and ultimately of a physical kind, brain events, if you will). Created good, then, is value as quality. We can even say that value is always quality as experienced (even though, strictly speaking, the latter phrase is redundant).

This conception of value and experience already provides a bridge to theology. If we define the relationship between man and God by the relationship between the creative event (productive, transformative events) and created good (events as experienced), then theology becomes an axiological discipline. This also implies the hermeneutical rule that theological ideas must have their content in terminations of experience. This is why Bultmann's method of existentialist interpretation can be given a naturalist turn. We shall return to this point again and again in the following.

The distinction between the creative event and created good serves an intricate, but decisive, purpose in Wieman's philosophy of religion. Wieman begins *The Source of Human Good* with a description of various theories of value: value as object valued, as a state of mind, as a transcendent or transcendental quality, indefinable or concrete, temporal or nontemporal, as the case may be, or as some complex relationship, especially between desire and thing desired, and, from a specifically naturalist point of view, as goods, as satisfaction, as quality, and as power in the sense of human control (*SHG*, 3–16). In general Wieman approves identifying value with relationships, with "a total complex context." His reason, however, is not so much theoretical as pragmatic. He says: "Both in practical action and in intellectual inquiry, we can do more with value when we take it this way. The 'context' is circumscribed to include just those things with which we must operate whenever we choose and act and reflect in a way to determine a future that can be more or less continuously approved" (*SHG*, 6). Thus, when Wieman examines and rejects the four naturalistic conceptions of value, it is not because they are inadequate as theories of value; in fact, he approves each of them after a fashion. His reason is that each of them, on its own terms, fails in "providing principles for human conduct and choice" (*SHG*, 16–17). He then rather abruptly introduces the creative event, "a creative process working in our midst which transforms the human mind and the world relative to the human mind" (*SHG*, 17).

Wieman, in other words, is not interested in a theory of value for its own sake. His concern is with how value increases and with how its increase may be served.[43] When he introduces the creative event as "the creative process working in our midst" and analyzes it in terms of qualitative meaning, he refuses to say specifically why qualitative meaning is always good – it can in fact be shown to be good on any of the alternative theories. The right question, instead, concerns the proper "guide" to its achievement. "The guiding thread – the thread that guides infallibly because it does not break and fail in the midst of great disasters, frustrations, and destructive conflicts – is not qualitative meaning, but it is what produces qualitative meaning. Therefore, we can find it best by tracing qualitative meaning to its source" (*SHG*, 20). Wieman's argument, then, concerns how we can serve goodness, and to this question he gives an essentially religious answer. This accounts for the religious passion with which so much of his writing is filled. We serve goodness by serving God, the creative event, and in serving God we serve the supreme good, for God is supremely good because God is the source of goodness. This argument intimately involves the distinction between the creative event and created good. Wieman is saying that we cannot answer the decisive question – how to find value, how goodness may increase – by turning to created good. We must, instead, serve the process by which value comes into being. To do this is to serve God, for God, defined now axiologically (and functionally), just is this process. Stated in this way the distinction between the two is relatively innocuous, being merely a way for Wieman to identify the source of good. Once he makes this basic point, however, the distinction turns out to be far from innocent, since it provides him with the outlines of an entire theological anthropology.

It is not merely that we ought not to look to created good, the goods already precipitated in experience, for the growth of value. Rather, it is precisely there that we are always inclined to look, and looking there, we defeat the processes by which value does increase. In other

[43] Wieman discusses Dewey as an example of conceiving value relationally in terms of power or human control. His comment is revealing of his argument as a whole: "If Dewey means that the outcome of control may be fuller release and more potent working of a transformative process, which we must not try to control in the sense of determining what it shall produce but only serve by holding all our values subject to the transformation which it will work upon us, then Dewey's assertion is true. But most of the time he seems to be saying that we can foresee the consequences of value, can appraise them as the best possible prior to our attainment of them, and can then direct the course of events to their attainment" (*SHG*, 16). Much of Wieman's entire argument is devoted to defeating the claim made by this last sentence.

words, the notion of created good contains, embryonically, a conception of human sin. We are always inclined to think of value in terms of goods already achieved. But beyond this relatively innocent tendency more is at stake. In looking to created goods, we tend, practically, to absolutize them, thus placing them at the center and blinding ourselves to other possibilities and to the process, if Wieman is correct, by which value and the goods we so ardently desire are sustained and increase. There are three sources of this blindness. The first is simply "the limited range of human appreciation." Values appreciated in a moment of focus are only a small range of the values present at any instant, especially if one adopts Wieman's notion of the richness of experience. The second is the distortion, indeed perversion, introduced into any apprehension of value by self-concern, egoism, and involution upon self. Finally, there is the "resistance to change in the structure of appreciative consciousness" which any structure of achieved values carries with it. Such inertia is especially powerful when it is linked, as it always is, to self-concern (*SHG*, 27–29). Wieman makes no great effort to expand upon these "faults of the human value-sense" (*SHG*, 27). For the purposes of my later argument, it is important to recognize, however, how compatible this analysis is with the powerful descriptions of the human predicament in contemporary theology. In particular, Wieman's points about blindness, self-concern, and inertia can easily be deepened by the existential analyses of Niebuhr, Tillich, and Bultmann who argue that it is the human existential situation that inclines, "tempts," us to elevate ourselves to the center of the world and then to attempt to subjugate the world thus centered to ourselves.

The distinction between the creative event and created good, elaborated by this embryonic conception of sin, completes Wieman's conception of God. By refocusing theology axiologically, it makes possible an entirely naturalist concept of God. Such an axiological orientation is not theologically unprecedented since it has partial antecedents in Augustine, Luther, Calvin, and Ritschl. The distinction between creative event and created good provides an essentially religious analysis for why this axiological concept of God is important. Again not unprecedented, Wieman shows why the question of value, which is at the center of all human concern, is fundamentally and at bottom a religious concern. What is unprecedented, the very root of Wieman's genius, is his entirely naturalistic framework for achieving these traditional theological objectives.[44] Finally, the distinction between the creative event and created good provides the structure for a powerful conception of the human predicament, and this is especially significant given his fundamentally soteriological aims.

We can conclude this chapter by noting three powerful biblical parallels with Wieman's conception of God. First, his philosophy of religion places the problem of idolatry (and conversely, the first commandment) at the very center of theological orientation in direct continuity with the prophetic tradition. His notion of how created goods tend to replace the creative event as the orientation of value (and thus of religious concern) is a formal equivalent to the notion of idolatry. It is not simply that "created good" serves as a contrasting term to the true God ("the creative event"). "Created good," as with any powerful notion of idolatry, also functions to show how the distortion and perversion of idolatry come about. For this reason, Wieman himself adopts the language of idolatry and speaks of how created goods (or qualitative meaning) become demonic:

Qualitative meaning becomes unreliable the moment it usurps the greater good of which it is merely the product and for which it must function as a servant. It has a way of pretending to a completeness of meaning and value actually offered and given only by a reality with a goodness incomparable to its own. All qualitative meaning lies open to this perversion, and every good is in danger of becoming thus demonic. The greater the good, the greater the danger of this perversion. The gravest peril that men have to face resides in the way qualitative meaning, created good, can arouse an absoluteness and supremacy of loyalty which only its source, creative good, the generating event, really commands.

What renders a perilous situation even more perilous is the way, diversely and subtly manifested, in which good turned demonic conceals its treacherous claim and character by assuming and feigning the guise of its master. The terror and treachery of demonic good resides in the hidden deceptions that graven images always perpetrate on men – they claim and appear to be otherwise than what they actually are. (*SHG*, 24)

The parallel with the traditional "critique of idolatry" is more than merely formal. Any theology that takes idolatry as a central problem must show why idolatry deserves religious critique as "false worship" (rather than, for example, merely as moral wrong); it must specify both God and idol so as to show how the attributes of deity can be bestowed upon an idol. It must, that is, move some distance toward

[44] See Wieman's classic essay on the situation of modern theology, "The Need of Philosophy of Religion," Wieman (1975b), 114–128.

existentializing both "God" and "idol," and in this respect it must move beyond a merely abstract treatment of God. It must specify the relationship of God/idol by some set of markers drawn from the human situation that explain how and why idolatry is religiously important. This is the movement by which the notion of idolatry gains its weight, and Wieman makes it with his analysis of a false orientation toward value. This is where the theological substance of a critique of idolatry is "cashed out," and at this point Wieman's analysis has the power of any good critique of idolatry, despite the unconventionality of his notion of God. His notion achieves this power because his concept of "created good" is, as we have seen, more than just a contrasting term to "God" but contains the seeds of an argument about how created goods acquire their usurping power in human life. In both of these respects, both as formal contrast and as material elucidation, the contrast between creative event and created good shares many of the same characteristics with Tillich's "Protestant Principle" and Reinhold Niebuhr's critique of idolatry.[45]

Second, Wieman's thought also has a Pauline structure. The contrast of creative event to created good is structurally similar to Paul's analysis of "life after the flesh" and "the life of faith." This similarity is accented by Wieman's anti-speculative bent which grows out of his underlying religious interest and makes the general form of his thought soteriological through and through. The movement by which he accounts for the usurping power of created goods ("life after the flesh") is contained in his list of the faults in human value appreciation (blindness, self-concern, inertia, or reluctance to change). He may be faulted perhaps for failing to develop fully how and why orientation to created good receives its distorting power through these faults. For instance, though he certainly recognizes self-concern, he fails to give a theologically informed account of its sources and power, and the same could be said for the linkages between inertia and self-concern. Wieman's analysis of the idolatrous power of created goods must therefore be supplemented by a more complete existentialist analysis of the human situation before God. But the resources for completing this analysis are readily at hand and require no substantive alteration of his conception of God's working in human life.

As in Paul, for Wieman "sin" is fundamentally "life after the flesh."

[45] See Tillich (1948), 32–51, 162–176, 226–229, and Tillich (1967), III, 223–224, 244–245; Reinhold Niebuhr, (1941), I, 165–166, 178–186.

As we have been taught by twentieth century biblical scholarship, "flesh" is to be understood not as the body or sensuality, but as a total orientation of life in refusal of God, and "the life of faith" is a structure of life in orientation to God. In both cases, the value of "God" (and the contrasting values of sin) are found in the structure of life as lived, by existential co-efficients, not by speculative or cognitive concerns. As we shall see, Wieman's creative event/created good structure, as it works itself out in human life, bears striking relationship to Bultmann's existentialist interpretation of Pauline theology and to Niebuhr's equally Pauline analysis of the source and role of pride in human sinfulness. The same Pauline parallel may also be found in the role of justification by faith in Wieman's soteriology, but I shall not expand upon this point until later.

Third, and finally, we can also observe a Johannine parallel in Wieman. By this I mean the way in which John conceives salvation as eternal life. John's eternal life is sharing in the life of God understood as love. The force of such terms in John is soteriological, not speculative. John should be seen as redefining the very nature of life. God is eternal life, and one receives eternal life precisely in accepting the gift of one's own life in the life of God. "Eternal life" just is one's own life as a sharing in the life of God. The same is true with Wieman. The force of his attempt to orient the understanding of God to value, to the source of value, is basically a religious argument redefining the nature of life. Like John, Wieman is saying that true life is not "more life," but a new kind of life that arises out of orientation to God. And, as we shall see, like John, Wieman also is saying that such life, grounded in God's life as love, is entirely a gift.

CHAPTER 2

Physicalism and philosophical naturalism

We now have the outlines of a surprisingly powerful naturalist conception of God. Because my concern is theological, I shall not develop a full naturalistic philosophy. Such an enterprise is unnecessary because almost all contemporary philosophy is already naturalist in a broad sense. Still, we need a general description of the naturalist position which lies in the background of this project. There have been many forms of naturalism. The strongest, most austere form remains the one deriving from classical, Democritian materialism, today termed *physicalism*. Since I want to emphasize the *constraints* naturalism places upon theological formulation, I shall adopt a physicalist version of naturalism, one defended recently with elegance and power by John F. Post in *The Faces of Existence*.

Loosely, physicalism states that only the basic objects of mathematical physics exist and that everything at a higher or more complex level can occur only if there is a corresponding occurrence at the level of physics. Physicalism requires a realist conception of truth because some naturalisms such as positivism and pragmatism define truth non-realistically by appeal to practical success (for instance, experimentation or predictability), thereby remaining agnostic about the ontological status of theoretically defined non-observable entities and leaving the referential status of physical science indeterminate. Their understanding of natural science is consequently epistemic alone. Physicalism, in contrast, says that finally it is the world or existence (not scientific practice) that defines what is known in physics.

There is ample precedent within contemporary philosophy for physicalism and a realist conception of scientific truth. The central debate lies elsewhere, over reductionism. Physicalism seemingly demands that terms from other domains must ultimately be defined solely by terms from physics. This would be physical reduction. But there is widespread agreement that all forms of reduction either fail or are too weak to establish the required relationship. Post's contribution is to defend a nonreductionist physicalism and to relate it powerfully to broad issues in ontology and metaphysics, including some having religious and theological implications.[1] My argument will depend on this version of naturalism in the sense defined earlier, namely, that it places constraints on theology largely of a negative kind, in what theology *can not* affirm rather than in defining it positively in detail.

This chapter will give only an abbreviated outline of Post's position. Presenting his full position would require an extensive discussion of some of the most difficult and technical issues in contemporary philosophy. My purpose is simply to use Post's work to frame a theological position. Though bounded and limited by this physicalistic naturalism, the theological position itself has a certain autonomy, as I have already indicated. The reader should consult Post himself for a more elaborate engagement with his position, and some readers may want to skip the present chapter and go to the next one where the directly theological argument begins. I shall first present an outline of the basic physicalist position, illustrating it with two revealing examples of how it deals with emergent properties. I shall then describe Post's physicalist account of value. This account will provide the basis for a "valuational theism."

NONREDUCTIONIST PHYSICALISM

The minimal physicalist principles

A "minimal version of physicalism" requires, according to Post, just three principles: "(i) 'Everything is physical'"; "(ii) 'No difference without a physical difference'"; "(iii) 'All truth is determined by physical truth.'" Though probably already implicit in these principles, a fourth principle, a realism about truth, is required, Post notes, if "the kind of systematic unity that (i)–(iii) presuppose requires our

---

[1] Though I shall follow Post's nonreductionist physicalism, I want to prescind from the ongoing reductionism debate *per se*. It is not yet evident, in my opinion, that some version of reductionism may not succeed. Philip Scribner is developing a powerful version of physicalism which requires reduction in at least some form. But Scribner's work is not yet available, and it is uncertain how it will address the classical problems of reduction. It is also uncertain whether it will permit some of the same positions allowed by Post's nonreductive version. Given the comprehensive and elegant character of Post's argument, it is safe enough to use for my purposes. Some of the technical issues remain open, and Post's position will probably require modification as this discussion develops. On the basic issue of "ultimate ontological inventory status," Post's is a well conceived version of the position any physicalistic naturalism must adopt.

physical theories to be true, not merely empirically adequate, as seems likely" (*FE*, 161).

The first two of these principles need little comment. The first requires specification of what physical existents are, but they can be defined simply by some explicit list of predicates drawn from the best physics of any given time,[2] and set theory can resolve the ontological status of abstract mathematical entities. The following disjunctive formulation permits Post to remain neutral as between mathematical Platonists and nominalists: ". . . everything is *mathematical*-physical; everything is either an abstract entity of mathematics or a concrete entity of physics" (*FE*, 168, Post's emphasis). By making physical entities the first set (including the null set), set theory is compatible with either option.[3]

Any physicalism requires the second slogan, "no difference without a physical difference," but it poses difficulties since it seems to imply reductionism. After pointing out problems with Quine's "full coverage" principle, Post uses modal possible worlds theory to formulate the slogan nonreductively (a "Modal Nonreductive Discernibility Principle"): "For any *P[physical]*-world *W*, if *x* and *y* are *N[non-physically]*-discernible in *W*, then they are *P*-discernible in *W*, where *x* and *y* are *P-(N-)*discernible in *W* iff [i.e., "if and only if"] there is some *P-(N-)*property, relations included, that *x* but not *y* has in *W*" (*FE*, 176–177).[4] This principle operates as a regulative ideal given the success science has had, time and again, in meeting its equivalent. The principle is consistent with holistic thinking since the distinguishing *P*-property may apply to *x* only when *x* is considered in terms of functional or intentional roles it has in a wider environment (cf. *FE* 176–177).

The last slogan, "all truth is determined by physical truth," when combined with this "Modal Nonreductive Discernibility Principle," is crucial for distinguishing these minimal principles from reductionism. In order to see why this is important, let us review typical objections to metaphysical materialism. Every metaphysics since Thales has claimed that there are some few basic unifiers of which all else is a manifestation (see *FE*, 210–213). Critics of materialism object not because it posits unifiers but because of the consequences nothing but physical unifiers are thought to have. Among these are reductionism,

---

[2] See Post (1987), 118–128.   [3] See Post (1987), 168–173.
[4] The reductionist version is: "If there is a distinction between *x* and *y* expressible by terms from some domain, there are terms solely from physics which express that same distinction" (*FE*, 174).

all varieties of which assert that terms from all domains are ultimately individuated as concrete particulars and then defined solely by terms from physics. Materialisms are also thought to require an identity claim whereby "all properties and states of things are really physical properties and states" (*FE*, 162–163).[5] Physicalism is therefore taken to require elimination: other domains and their discourses (sentience, intentions, consciousness, persons, culture, etc.) must be illusory, there being really only one domain, physical entities, and only one kind of legitimate talk about it, physics. Furthermore, materialism is believed to seek an invidious form of universal explainability, implying not merely that physics can explain everything but also that other domains lack their own explanatory autonomy. These and other objections come to the same thing: materialism amounts to an elimination or reduction of features of life and thought that are regarded as so important and obvious as to be beyond question.

To avoid these objections a physicalist must, at the same time, (1) claim that underlying all domains there is a unity in which all truth is determined by truths at the level of physics, yet (2) not assert that these other domains are either identical to or nothing more than the domain of physical entities and the discourse in physics about them. This means in turn that we must accord autonomy, including explanatory autonomy, to various domains above physics, including emergent properties (such as sentience, consciousness, persons, intentions, culture, and irretrievably subjective points of view such as "what it is like to be a bat" or my knowing that I am going to die). How can physicalism achieve this? The issue turns on what Post terms the relation of *determination*: what we mean when we say that something is determined by something else.

Because determination is an alternative to reduction, it permits a formulation of physicalism that avoids the objections above. In ordinary usage, "*to say one thing determines another . . ., is to say the first delimits or fixes one and only one way the second can be.*" Further, "ordinarily, if we wonder why a certain thing is as it is, our question is answered when . . . we learn that it had to be that way, given the way some other thing is. In short, the matter is accounted for or explained, in an important sense, when we learn that it is determined by something else. . . " (*FE*, 181–182, my emphasis). This loose statement of determination is metaphysically neutral since every

---

[5] If this is not simply a restatement of reductionism.

metaphysics must claim determination in this sense for its ultimate unifiers. Its specifically physicalist form can be stated with Post's "Principle of the Determination of all Truth by Physical Truth": "Given any two *P*-worlds, if the same *P*-sentences are true in both, then the same *N*-sentences are true in both, where to say that the same *P-(N-)*sentences are true in both is to say that for every such sentence Φ, Φ is true in one iff Φ is true in the other." The principle "is a way of saying that given a distribution of truth-values over the *P*-sentences, there can be one and only one distribution over the *N*-sentences" (*FE*, 184–185). Post shows that it is the world that determines truth independently of questions about determinate reference;[6] thus, even though the principle is about sentences, it is the world that determines their truth (including the truth of the principle itself) (*FE*, 185).[7]

These minimal principles, especially the third principle's specification of determination, avoid the traditional objections to materialism by avoiding the reductionist identity conditions normally associated with it. Determination permits physical metaphysical unifiers, but it refrains from saying that all existents must be identified and articulated by the basic level of physics, and it denies explanatory monopoly in terms of that basic level. Post formulates the underlying point by an oft repeated and seemingly paradoxical statement upon which his entire position might be seen as a commentary: "nothing but mathematical-physical entities exist, yet not everything is nothing but a mathematical-physical thing"

[6] It is worth noting that the determination relation holds no matter what the outcome in the contemporary debate about reference. The debate concerns whether there is a fact of the matter about reference, taking reference in the nonintentional sense. If there is, then "all reference is determined ultimately by physical truth"; if there is not, "then there is no truth of the matter to be determined," and the principle still holds (*FE*, 190). In another context discussing the inscrutability of reference, Post shows that "a realist concept of truth does not presuppose an objective or determinate relation of reference between terms and pieces of the world. . . . [For] the truth-values of our whole sentences are nevertheless determined by the world" quite independently of determinateness of reference. "So even if there is no fact of the matter as regards reference, still our words do not stray so far from the world as to frustrate realism or a correspondence theory of truth" (*FE*, 190–191). (For an earlier context, see *FE*, 25–51.)

[7] See *FE*, 25–51 for an earlier argument. The principle is minimal because, among other reasons, it does not require that all *N*-phenomena are determined by *P*-phenomena within specific spatiotemporal regions. It leaves open whether "there are nonphysical truths about the world that are true only in virtue of the totality of the *P*-phenomena," in other words, whether in some instances the relevant *P*-phenomena may not be local but global (*FE*, 188). Thus, it may be that some nonphysical phenomena (perhaps minds) can only finally be determined by a unified field in which the gravitational force derives not from an exchange of particles in a field but from the curvature of space.

(*FE*, 195).[8] This means that in addition to being nonreductive, the position is also broadly pluralist about other domains, claiming no identity, elimination, or reduction, and conferring autonomy on them (including explanatory autonomy). Post even denies the legitimacy of saying "that physics describes 'the only real world,' or perhaps *the* world, *the* way things really are" (*FE*, 206), for the language of every domain is conditional on our interests, the particular questions we are asking.[9] Physicalism claims greater metaphysical and ontological comprehensiveness (assuming meta-physical comprehensiveness is our interest), but this does not amount to maintaining that there is only one way things are and only one way of saying it. It also means that there is a quite legitimate sense in which nonphysical things and emergent properties (both taken to be denied by traditional materialism) are real. Finally, the determination relation permits Post to address the objectivity of value on physicalist terms.

What it is like to be a bat: emergent properties and nonreductive states

To see how Post's paradox amounts to an answer to the typical objections to materialism, it will be helpful to examine more closely how he treats emergent properties and nonreductive states. This discussion is quite technical, but for our purposes we can limit ourselves mainly to two examples, one from culture and another from irretrievably subjective states.[10] Let us first briefly examine the issue of emergence.

If there are nonphysical domains of entities, properties, and states (e.g., organisms, persons, languages, cultural artifacts and their properties) and if, as physicalism asserts, nothing exists but math-ematical-physical entities, then those domains must be emergent in the following sense: "An entity or property is emergent or 'novel' with respect to a domain (such as physics), roughly, if our term for it cannot be defined by any terms from the domain (hence not 'predicated' by any truths from the domain)" (*FE*, 162; cf. 197–198).[11] The domain for defining, say, a "person" might be exhausted by

---

[8] For other contexts in which Post invokes this seeming paradox, see also *FE*, 196, 197, 205, 206, 212.   [9] See *FE*, 203–208, 286–287, 293–304.

[10] For the full discussion, see, esp., *FE*, 166–174, 194–203.

[11] Note that this definition already assumes something like a determination relation (that is, some alternative to reductionism), else emergence cannot be defined while still remaining within physicalism.

nonphysical and therefore emergent properties (e.g., consciousness and intention), but this would not exclude it from the physicalist inventory (it is still *identical* with the inventory of basic physical entities). It simply means that a "person" is not individuated solely by physical terms and its properties are not statable by (i.e., reducible to) physical properties. As we shall see, the crucial physical determination relation will still hold.

The problem with emergence and the nonphysical is especially well illustrated with "states." "States" have been critical for the problem of mind (intentional states) and for other areas that critics of physicalism have identified with the problem of reduction. Functional states (i.e., states that bear causal or other relations to other things and states) and intentional (as well as logical) states are thought not to be identifiable with any particular physical state because any state "can be realized or embodied in an indefinite variety of distinct physical systems, perhaps even in an indefinite variety of physically specifiable states of the same physical system" (*FE*, 161), say, different neuro-states of the same brain. In the philosophy of mind, it seems impossible to define the identity that would be required to reduce intentional states to physical equivalents (since any number of physical states can realize the nonphysical ones), but the problem is general, extending far beyond the philosophy of mind, even to physical states themselves. The reason is that "states typically are not defined by reference to the stuff of which the entities are made that can realize them. Entities composed of very different stuff could all realize one and the same state, whether the stuff is biological, electronic, bionic, or mental. . . [A] functional state, for example, typically is not defined by reference to any physically specifiable states of the entity . . . Thus one and the same functional state could be realized in the same entity (or system) x when x is in any one of a perhaps indefinite variety of distinct physical (or structural) states" (*FE*, 198).

Post's two principles we have already discussed, the "Modal Nonreductive Discernibility Principle" and the "Principle of the Determination of all Truth by Physical Truth," permit the determination relation to address these issues physicalistically.[12] The first "implies that for any difference in the emergent states x realizes, there is some physical difference between x in one of its emergent

---

[12] For the corresponding discussions in Post, see *FE*, 176–177 and 182–189, respectively.

states and x in another" (*FE*, 200). This is sufficient for determination, and it is nonreductive. The second "implies that truths at the level of physics determine which emergent states x realizes" (*FE*, 200). This also is nonreductive in that it does not affect the domain status (perhaps entirely nonphysical) of the language used to express the state. Furthermore, Post emphasizes, the determination relations required by both principles do not necessitate that the physical entities, truths, or states determine x in isolation from some wider environment. Thus, if x is partially nonphysical, say an organism or a person, some of the truths about it may range over nonphysical domains such as its cultural, or intentional, or linguistic role. But at some point all such truths will themselves be anchored (in the sense of determined) by truths at the level of physics and then back through the series to x – even if such truths are so complex that they could never be expressed. The determination relations are thus consistent with physicalism and are yet nonreductionist.[13]

Post illustrates these points with a discussion of the slabs of heavy rock in Chaco Canyon, New Mexico, constructed as a solar marker by the Anasazi Indians between 950 and 1150 A.D. From a purely objective standpoint, the configuration of the slabs and the angles of the sun explain physically the patterns of light cast by the slabs (not the configuration by the pattern) (cf. *FE*, 107). Yet we can recognize them as a solar marker only because their physical states and configuration are realized in a cultural role (*FE*, 200). From this perspective, the patterns explain the configuration after all, and the asymmetry, and thus objectivity, of explanation seem endangered. Furthermore, anthropologists can comprehend the positioning and role of the slabs only by reconstructing the intentions of the

---

[13] Note, for instance, the things that are *not* included in the relations between the physical and emergent states: "Expressible or not, what is the relation between this physical state P and the emergent state N that x also realizes? They cannot be identical, or the same state, since by hypothesis N is emergent. Nor can we say in general that necessarily if x realizes N, then x realizes P. For N might be defined in such a way that x can realize N when x is in the physical state P and also when x is in a different physical state. We cannot even say, in general, that whenever x realizes P, then x realizes N. For N might be defined in such a way that no structural-physical state of x is sufficient for x to realize N. Instead, it may be that x realizes N only when x realizes a certain (sort of) structural-physical state in some wider context. If so, the relations x bears to certain other things – via its cultural role, say, or its linguistic role, or (other) intentions about it – must be taken into account, in addition to x's structural-physical state. The relations between x's physical states and x's emergent states often obtain only or largely in virtue of x's place in a wider environment" (*FE*, 199). None of these cases precludes the determination relations defined by the principles of physical discernibility and physical truth.

Anasazi. In this sense, "the property of being a solar marker is emergent with respect to physics and indeed natural science." The slabs yield a "clear case in which the physical truths about x in isolation (the system of the slabs) hardly suffice to determine that x does (or does not) instantiate a certain emergent property," that is, a cultural role (*FE*, 200). Even if he had all the physical truths about both the slabs and the Anasazi, the physicist, with those truths alone, could not tell that they are a solar marker. He could not derive the intentions even from the totality of physical truths, so the autonomy of the anthropologist's domain is secure.

Yet it does not follow that the Anasazi's intentions are not determined by truths at the level of physics or that, in principle, the physicist could not express those truths (at the level of physics). A wider set of truths from physics (not just about the slabs and their configuration alone) could determine what it is about the Anasazi, their culture, and the slabs that make the latter a solar marker. It would then follow that the objectivity of explanation still holds. The patterns do not after all, in the deepest sense, explain the configuration.

Generalizing from this example, we can say that physicalism must allow irreducible nonphysical vocabularies to express the properties essential for entities "that realize certain properties in virtue of some functional-intentional role," such as hammers or inscriptions. "[N]o physical-structural truths about hammers and inscriptions even in their wider context could tell us that they are cultural entities," and with inscriptions, such truths could not tell us that they belong to a language or what meaning in a language they have (*FE*, 201). Also, with most emergent entities such as cultural artifacts and persons, the relations between the natural states that the natural sciences can explain physically and the nonphysical states that they cannot is "accidental, historical, particular, and novel. There is no general sort of connection – hence no lawlike connection or even constant conjunction" between the physical states and the emergent properties, "between the slabs' structural-physical state and their being a solar marker" (*FE*, 202). For this reason anthropologists, historians, artists, and others need not fear for the integrity of their domains. None of this, even their accidental, historical, particular, novel and nonphysical natures, undermines physical discernibility of all discernibles or the determination of all truth by physical truth.[14] Yet the latter need not be reductive.

A second example is Thomas Nagel's famous argument about what it is like to be a bat. This is a particularly powerful case because Nagel is taken to have shown that purely subjective phenomena fall irretrievably outside the physicalist's net. Such phenomena include what it is like to be a bat, or what it is like to have an idea of ourselves as the source of our own actions, or to have a personal identity, or to be persons experiencing our own temporality or moral dilemmas. The reason is that all such phenomena are *essentially* connected with having a single point of view. Given the objectivity that physicalism must claim, Nagel argues, the physicalist must eliminate or fail to account for such points of view.[15] Nagel, however, defines the central problem as reduction: "The reductionist program that dominates current work in the philosophy of mind is completely misguided, because it is based on the groundless assumption that a particular conception of objective reality is exhaustive of what there is" (Nagel [1986] 16). "The reduction can succeed only if the species-specific viewpoint is omitted from what is to be reduced."[16] Yet we have seen

---

[14] Though physicalism need not be an identity theory, Post points out that "like all versions of physicalism, the theory must require that any entity mentioned outside physics – a person, say – is identical with *something* in the physicalist's inventory of what there is." The theory is a token-identity (not type-identity) theory, and this means "that each particular entity or event of some general type N is identical – token-identical – with a particular mathematical-physical entity or event, even if the type N is not itself identical – type-identical – with any physical type." Post further notes that "an entity or state x could be token-identical with something in the physicalist's inventory *without* being token-identical with something in the inventory that satisfies a term (or a complex of terms) from physics or even the neurosciences . . . The vocabulary of physics and neuroscience, in this sort of case, would be incapable, by itself, of picking out or individuating x; for x would not be denoted by any term from (or definable by) such a vocabulary. . ." Any metaphysics must be a token-identity theory in this sense "insofar as it must claim that everything at bottom is somehow token-identical with or constituted from certain basic entities or processes, whether physical, mental, spiritual, or whatever" (*FE*, 163, Post's emphases). The minimal physicalist principles show how this kind of identity can be articulated in terms of determination relations without entailing identity in the sense of reduction.

[15] The classical statement of this argument is Nagel (1979). These arguments are elaborated in a somewhat different fashion in Nagel (1986), 7–8, 15–19, 32–43, 49–51.

[16] Nagel (1979), 175. In the later work, Nagel expands as follows: "Physicalism, though unacceptable, has behind it a broader impulse to which it gives distorted and ultimately self-defeating expression. That is the impulse to find a way of thinking about the world as it is, so that everything in it, not just atoms and planets, can be regarded as real in the same way: not just an aspect of the world as it appears to us, but something that is *really there*. I think part of the explanation of the modern weakness for physicalist reduction is that a less impoverished and reductive idea of objectivity has not been available to fill out the project of constructing an overall picture of the world. . . The central problem is not whether points of view must be admitted to the account of the *physical* world. Whatever may be the answer to

that physicalism can be defined nonreductively. As Post responds, "the nonreductive varieties can cheerfully admit that indeed there is (or may well be) something it is like to be a bat; that what it is like is inexpressible and unknowable; and that even if what it is like could be expressed, still it could not be expressed by, or otherwise reduced to, scientific or any other objective discourse" (*FE*, 245).

The question is whether essentially subjective phenomena are beyond even determination by purely objective phenomena. They are not if there is a fact of the matter about what it is like to be a subject. Nagel concedes that there are facts of the matter about such instances. Having an irretrievably subjective point of view, what it is like to *be* it, is a fact "about what mental states are like for the creature having them."[17] Such facts may be inexpressible, "beyond the reach of human concepts."[18] But, as Post says: ". . . expressibility is beside the point. Contrary to Nagel, physicalists need not 'insist that everything real must be brought under an objective description'."[19] Given Nagel's admission that such phenomena are facts, then physical determination can be accommodated in three steps.

First, subjective facts must be in the physicalist inventory of what there is. For Nagel, a fact is "the truth of a proposition, humanly expressible or not" (*FE*, 246). Parallel with properties, propositions can be "functions from possible worlds to truth-values. As such, they are mathematical entities, hence mathematical-physical as regards their inventory-status" (*FE*, 246). As with properties, so with propositions, expressibility, agreeing with Nagel, is irrelevant for inclusion in the inventory. Second, the determination relation between the two realms, the objective and subjective, can now be defined by extending the "Principle of the Determination of all Truth by Physical Truth": ". . . in *P*-worlds the Φ-facts determine the Θ-facts iff given any two such worlds, if the same Φ-facts obtain in both, then the same Θ-facts obtain in both" (*FE*, 246). Again, expressibility need not be an issue.

Finally, there is the question of "how we could ever tell in practice whether some given subjective phenomenon (humanly expressible or not) is determined by certain objective phenomena." For those subjective phenomena that are expressible, connective theories, to be

---

that question, we shall still be faced with an independent problem about the mind. It is the phenomena of consciousness themselves that pose the clearest challenge to the idea that physical objectivity gives the general form of reality" (Nagel [1986], 16–17).

[17] Nagel (1979), 201.   [18] Nagel (1979), 168.   [19] *FE*, 245; Nagel (1979), 210.

discussed in a moment, are required which relate relevant intervening disciplines. As Post notes, "since determination is transitive, no direct relation between physics and the subjective need be claimed," the work being done by the intervening disciplines and families of connective theories. There is no problem in observing such phenomena, for Nagel either, "for to observe it is not to have it or even to be able to understand what it is like to have it. . . And we can observe certain correlations between the occurrence of the experience and various organic states, including the determination correlation." Such determination does not require identity in the sense that the subjective phenomena could be read off the physical operators. "No term that expresses what the experience is like for the experiencing organism (even if there is such a term) need be even accidentally coextensive with any term . . . from the sciences or indeed from any objective discourse. Hence the subjective experiential state need not be type-identical with any structural-physical state of the organism. . . The same subjective state might even be realized at different times in the same organism via different structural-physical states." The humanly inexpressible subjective phenomena, such as what it is like to be a bat, can be handled on grounds of continuity and simplicity, which is common with theoretical extension in many disciplines. If the physicalist can claim that the expressible experiences are physically determined, "there appears to be no relevant difference, between the expressible and the partly or wholly inexpressible experiences, in virtue of which the former but not the latter could be granted determination. If reducibility or translatibility were being claimed, then degree of expressibility would matter. But determination is a relation among the phenomena, expressible or not" (*FE*, 246–248).

The experience of time, the subjective experience of a now and of passage, seem especially to support Nagel's resistance to physicalist objectivity, for physics "deals with spatiotemporal invariants, deliberately abstracting from point of view, frame of reference, or what things are like for us now," and contemporary physics seems to warrant such abstraction by the very ontology of space-time. Nagel's resistance would hold if reduction, not determination, were the issue. ". . . [T]he irreducibility or ineliminability of our subjective temporal experience and our use of tenses is irrelevant as regards whether the corresponding subjective phenomena are determined by the objective phenomena with which physics deals" (*FE*, 248). Such physical determination has a fourfold sense; it is physically determined: "(a) that there are such phenomena, (b) which ones there are, (c) what it would be like to experience them, and (d) what their (other) properties are" (*FE*, 245). Such determination need not demote subjective temporal experience. There is no claim that the physicist's tenseless discourse reduces tensed discourse, and there is no monopoly claim that the physicist's discourse is somehow more fundamental. Priority here is relative to some purpose, and that is true of the physicist's discourse as well. In the manner broadened by physicalism's wider claims, physics enjoys the metaphysical priority of inclusiveness and comprehensiveness, *when that is our aim*. But there are many other kinds of aim and priority. Physicalist objectivity, contra Nagel, does not amount to the claim that it provides "the *right* way for the individual to look at the world and his place in it."[20] There simply is no such *one* right way – though as we shall see, there may be a right way to exist for physical objects that are mortal human beings. Again, Nagel's argument fails with determination, irrespective of its success with reduction.[21]

We see then that determination permits a physicalist metaphysics without the reduction or eliminativism so feared by its opponents.[22]

[20] *FE*, 249; Nagel (1979), 197.

[21] Post goes on to comment: "Only when we are pursuing the relevant purpose or purposes need we employ an objective idiom. We remain free to be interested in other things, and sometimes we are obligated to be... Furthermore, there are many ways of unifying the phenomena, and subjective ways are surely among them. A map of everything in polar coordinates centered on us is no less a map, and no less inclusive, than a map that is coordinate-free. The important thing is to know which map to use on what occasion for what purpose. Such knowledge is less a matter of metaphysics, traditionally conceived, than of wisdom... How things look or feel from here now is itself determined by purely objective phenomena, according to the physicalist. Thus the objective phenomena also determine why the subjective point of view often is nearly true, or true with certain qualifications, or true relative to some time and place. In this extended sense, determination of all truth by physical truth applies not only to strict truths from a given domain, but also to 'truths' couched in a subjective idiom, such as 'You promised me a rematch here today'. Even if this sentence could not be turned into an eternal one by supplying names, locations, and dates, nonetheless on those occasions when its utterance is true, its truth would be physically determined" (*FE*, 249).

[22] It is also not foundationalist in any of the senses that have become such a bugaboo in recent philosophy and theology. Commenting on the metaphysical task, Post says: "From the time of Thales one such interest (that is, an interest in unification, among all the various legitimate interests we have) has been in finding some one kind of thing of which everything else is somehow a manifestation such that the way the former is determines how the latter will be" (*FE*, 210). Somewhat later he continues: "What such metaphysicians share is neither some view of mind as the mirror of nature, contrary to Rorty, nor some related foundationalist view of knowledge, nor even some theory of truth. Systematic philosophers engaged in unifying the domains in terms of a limited variety of entities are interested primarily in what there is. They can differ enormously on how we are supposed to know it, and on how truth and our knowing (if any) are related to what there is. They can even agree with Rorty and others (as I do) that all we can ever know is what-there-is-under-a-description" (*FE*, 211).

Determination commits physicalism to no more than any metaphysics seeks, and it has a clear formal superiority to many historical predecessors because it does not claim that its vocabulary for describing the ultimate unifiers enjoys an *unconditional* priority capturing *the* nature of things. It does not, in Post's phrase, "commit monopoly." "A monism of entities is compatible with a pluralism of properties, of worlds, of faces of existence, and of equally privileged vocabularies. It is compatible also with a pluralism of modes of insight and explanation expressible only in other domains" (*FE*, 212).[23] Physicalism differs only in its claim about *what* unifies, the basic physical entities of physics, and in its premise that "all truth, not just truth in the sciences, is determined by truth at the level of physics" (*FE*, 214). This premise requires neither reductionism nor the surrender of explanatory autonomy by domains outside the natural sciences.

Connections and bridges but not monopoly

Though a nonreductionist physicalism accords autonomy to domains outside physics, it must still show how they all are ultimately connected to its basic physical unifiers. As Post states the question: "How could we ever tell in practice whether particular truths in one domain are determined by truths in another, if not by way of some sort of reducibility or explainability?" (*FE*, 227). Let us note that this issue is general. Any comprehensive metaphysics must explicate a determination relation in some detail. Perhaps the major difficulty with the alternatives to physicalism is that they must posit nonphysical unifiers and then show how truths in the natural sciences are determined by nonphysical truths, something that on the surface seems patently false.[24] In this light, the enormous success that already exists *in detail* in the natural sciences cannot be overlooked; the conviction comes from the detail, not globally.

[23] For a more extended discussion of monopoly, see *FE*, 203–208.

[24] Take, for instance, the vigorous Hegel renaissance which is having a significant, sometimes subtle, influence in contemporary theology. One of Hegel's strengths as a metaphysician was the detail with which he connected phenomena through nonphysical unifiers, but surely a mark of the ultimate incoherence of his philosophy is the failure of his philosophy of nature. Process philosophy also takes nature and natural science seriously, but it is constructed out of an enormous *petitio principe* in the sense that its basic ontology is an imaginative "conceptual scheme" that is never defended except by internal coherence. That is why attempts to construe natural science in detail by process thinkers look suspiciously *ad hoc*. These often take the form, as in Hartshorne, of: "why couldn't we therefore think of it this way..." upon the basis of which enormously ambitious schemes are then erected.

Once having established the general case for nonreductive, physical determination, as above, it turns out that the physicalist's task is easier than might be expected. Post shows this is so for two reasons. First, specific intervening disciplines are already doing the actual work and have myriads of well established, uncontroversial results on hand; some of the most fruitful of this work involves determination relations across domains, as in the success of relating chemistry to physics, or physics and chemistry to biology in molecular biology or neurobiology. Often it is the effort to find such bridges that guides research, as in the effort to connect genetics with molecular biology which led to the discovery of the structure of DNA. Second, there already exist in the philosophy of science well articulated, generally noncontroversial, accounts of the formal nature of such "connective theories."

Post begins this discussion by noting that determination is transitive. This means that "if (in the same class of worlds) Φ-truth determines Θ-truth, and Θ-truth determines X-truth, the Φ-truth also determines X-truth; likewise for determination of and by reference." Yet, "such transitivity induces no hierarchy among the domains. For even though determination is transitive, it is not antisymmetric. That is, if Φ-truth determines Θ-truth . . ., then Θ-truth may or may not determine Φ-truth; if Θ-truth does also determine Φ-truth, we have an instance of codetermination" (*FE*, 215). Thus, no linear hierarchy from physics up is required, even though physics is the most comprehensive. How, for instance, Post asks, could we rank geology as compared to meteorology or anthropology as compared to history (cf. *FE*, 215–216)? Transitivity is significant because it points to connections between many intervening disciplines. "Physicalists need not shoulder the heroic, hopeless burden of describing some direct relation between the truths of anthropology, say, and those of physics, in virtue of which we may infer that the latter determine the former. Instead, they can point to a lot of intervening disciplines – such as archeology, psychology, biology, geology, astronomy, chemistry, and so on – no one of which suffices to determine anthropological truth, but only a cluster of several or all of them in conjunction." A moment's reflection reveals that we commonly relate domains by their near neighbors, and not just in the natural sciences – think of how synoptic history is in this sense. "Provided that determination holds at each step of the way, we may infer by transitivity that physical truth determines anthropological truth. Thus, the problem of establishing determination divides into a lot of local problems that concern relations between clusters of domains, clusters that in some sense are near neighbors . . ." (*FE*, 216).

Furthermore, local determination is typically inferred simply by observation: "[T]wo cells exactly alike in relevant molecular-biological respects may be observed always to be alike in some given aspect of their overt behavior." The problem is not to establish determination relations but to justify generalizations from them (ultimately to the point of: "determination of *all* Θ-truth by Φ-truth"). Again, however, a well established practice already exists for addressing this issue. Either, we "observe lots of determinations of lots of classes of Θ-phenomena by Φ-phenomena." Or, more typically and more powerfully, "we resort to theories that systematize the otherwise miscellaneous determinations across two adjacent domains," which is especially important where determination cannot be actually observed among the classes of phenomena (*FE*, 217, Post's emphasis). Such theories are called connective theories and include bridge principles connecting across domains; they are frequently used, and their nature is well understood. The physicalist's task is simply to show how they may be interpreted in terms of determination (cf. *FE*, 218). Since there is nothing especially controversial about connective theories and bridge principles, we can limit ourselves to certain consequences of Post's argument.

First, note that connective theories are customary in many disciplines, including theology. Post points out that theology often contains an internal theory about God in an entirely religious or theological vocabulary and then connects it with a secular vocabulary through bridge principles in the interest of maintaining that truths about the secular realm are determined by theistic truths. Thus, "truths about God's benevolence, for instance, are supposed to determine that human suffering, even when described in secular terms, is not pointless." In this respect, "'God created the world' may be the most fundamental bridge principle of all, in such a theory" (*FE*, 220).

The success of such theories is warranted by well accepted criteria for theory success, the logical prerequisites for truth. Post exhaustively analyzes seven of these: (i) well-formedness, (ii) nonemptiness, (iii) successful presupposition, (iv) self-consistency, (v) consistency with all other truths, (vi) truth of all the logical consequences, and (vii) objectivity.[25] Such theories should also possess other virtues such as simplicity and comprehensiveness. Assuming success with this "trial by prerequisites" (*FE*, 221),[26] comprehensiveness can be especially important because it arises concretely in the "dynamic consilence" by which a good theory explains more facts than those it was initially designed to explain (see *FE*, 221–222). From the success of a number of connective theories, the inference of determination of truths in one realm by truths in another is ordinarily made, Post points out, by "just old-fashioned inference to the best explanation, roughly what Peirce called abduction. By whatever name, it is used constantly in the sciences, in other disciplines, and in daily life" (*FE*, 225). The inference of determination follows simply when we ask what would account for the success of the happy family of theories.

According to the physicalist, the best explanation would be that the Φ-phenomena determine the Θ-phenomena. For if they do, then any two things alike in the relevant Φ-respects are of necessity alike in given Θ-respects. That is, any two things alike in their Φ-properties are alike in their Θ-properties. But then any *one* thing that has the relevant Φ-properties also is of necessity the way it is as regards the given Θ-properties; given the way it is as regards its Φ-properties, there is one and only one way it can be as regards its Θ-properties. The knowledge of this connection, together with the knowledge that some particular thing x has those Φ-properties, would enable us to understand why x is as it is as regards those Θ-properties: it has them because that is the only way it could be, given its Φ-properties. (*FE*, 223, Post's emphasis)

This latter inference, which formulates why the family of theories is successful, is nothing less than an inference of determination.

It is especially important, finally, to distinguish explanation from determination. Unlike determination, explanation is probably not transitive: "If transitivity fails for explanation, then there can be an explanation of X-phenomena in Θ-terms, and of Θ-phenomena in Φ-terms, yet no explanation of X-phenomena in Φ-terms" (*FE*, 228). In other words, there will be domains, for example, anthropology, when we are talking about the intentions of the Anasazi, where explanations of Θ-phenomena will be appropriate simply in terms of other Θ-phenomena (say, of a cultural order), *even though* we might be quite justified in inferring from *all* the neighboring local domains (from physics on up) that the Anasazi's intentions are determined by physical truths. As we saw above, even if the physicist could express the physical truths that determine the intentions, *on these terms alone,*

[26] See *FE*, 57–61.

she could not express what those intentions were; to *explain* that, explanations at the level of the intentions (and the related cultural phenomena) would be necessary. In this respect, explanation and determination are incommensurable, and there is ample room within a physicalist ontology for explanatory autonomy of domains.

Enough of Post's theory has now been sketched for us to see how a strong, coherent, ontologically forceful, yet nonreductive, physicalist naturalism is attainable today. Much hinges on the notion of physical determination. The argument turns on showing how physical determination does not entail the objectionable consequences often expected of materialism. It does not, we have seen, exclude emergent entities or properties; it is not eliminative;[27] it is not an identity theory that would require reduction; it does not violate the methodological (including explanatory) autonomy of domains outside physics; it is not dogmatic or vague about what the basic physical entities are; it is not committed to a mirror theory of truth, and it leaves open the question about determinacy of reference.[28]

Taken together these points give content to Post's paradoxical slogan: ". . . we may say that nothing but mathematical-physical entities exist, yet not everything is nothing but a mathematical-physical thing" (*FE*, 195). Unlike other materialisms, Post points out, this kind of physicalism does not claim monopoly status either for its language or its method. It is non-monopolistic in three senses.[29] It does not assert that other domains of discourse are either reducible to physics or somehow otherwise defective. Physics also enjoys no *unconditional* "preeminence or priority over all other domains of truth," for its priority is conditional: "*If* we are interested in the kind of objectivity, comprehensiveness, and explanatory power that physics pursues, then the truths of physics take on a corresponding priority, in light of which it seems significant that all other truths are determined by them. In many other contexts we remain free, and often even obligated, to be interested in other sorts of truth and to value them more highly" (*FE*, 165, Post's emphasis). Finally, it does not require that physics or any other science "describes the ultimate nature of

---

[27] "It does not entail . . . that there are no persons, minds, feelings, sensations, thoughts, freedoms, or whatever. Nor does it entail that all talk about such things is either false or meaningless or otherwise defective, or that it ought to be replaced or even someday *might* be replaced by talk about purely physical things" (*FE*, 162, Post's emphasis).

[28] For the full discussion of this list, see *FE*, 162–166.

[29] *FE*, 165–166 For a more extended discussion, see *FE*, 203–208 on "comprehensiveness versus monopoly."

existence, or the way the world is" as though there were just one face of existence. Even though all the faces of existence are "attributes of one and the same thing," as we saw above with irreducibility and the autonomy of explanatory domains, "it does not follow that this one thing of which they are all attributes is or represents the (one) way the world is . . ." (*FE*, 166).

PHYSICALISM AND THE OBJECTIVITY OF VALUE

We must now consider how religion might be placed in a physicalist world. I have emphasized that naturalism will not so much define as limit the theological construction to follow.[30] But how can we even begin to think constructively about religion from a naturalist standpoint? Theologians generally assume that Christianity and perhaps religion as such are incompatible with naturalism, and both theologians and philosophers customarily assume that naturalism is inherently hostile to religion. Neither assumption is true, but to see this we must consider how there can be a positive interface between physicalist naturalism and religion. I shall argue that such an interface is possible if religion is approached "valuationally." I shall therefore defend a *valuational theism*. Post's argument in favor of the objectivity of value as well as his discussion of "God" will be of considerable assistance for this task.

Naturalism poses a problem for religion because it seems to preclude any meaningful language about God. Naturalists find such reference either vacuous or meaningless, or they explain "God" nonreferentially by some noncognitive strategy. For Post's ontologically strong physicalism, the problem is more traditional simply because "God" is nowhere to be found in a physicalist inventory of what exists. Traditional theologians would find this unsurprising since they have always insisted that a physical inventory does not exhaust what exists. The problem is how they locate God in this alternative inventory.

The classical arguments for the existence of God can no longer serve this purpose. Contemporary philosophy has seen a revival of interest in them, and it has illuminated much of their power and perennial interest, but it has also reached a near consensus that the arguments are hopelessly flawed. Apart from numerous specific difficulties, the cosmological arguments all rely on the principle of

---

[30] Here the three affirmations discussed in the first chapter are again crucial. For a naturalist theology defined ontologically by physicalism, God cannot be a personal being and there is neither final causality nor a conservation of value.

sufficient reason, and Post demonstrates that this hoary principle is flawed beyond recovery in cosmological matters.[31] The design and moral arguments suffer even more serious, well-recognized internal problems, and they fail additionally because better explanations than God are readily available for the evidence that supports them. The ontological argument trades fatally on ambiguities in the notion of necessity. Even if it can be salvaged, it is by no means clear that its "necessary being" is the God needed by theologians. Taken individually or together, the arguments are a thin reed upon which to erect a contemporary theological prolegomena.

Beyond these considerations, however, the deepest problem facing all versions of *ontological* theism is the one already alluded to: how can ultimately nonphysical unifiers unify the sciences? Traditional theology requires such unifiers because it locates God outside a merely physical inventory. It must establish that nonphysical truths ultimately *determine* truths unifying the sciences, and this has little plausibility.[32] This technical problem illustrates broad intellectual presumptions shared widely throughout modern culture. In view of the dynamic consilience of the sciences, "the inductive evidence favors the presumption that where there is indeed an explanation to be found, it will be in natural terms" (*FE*, 331).

Getting God into the inventory by appeals to faith is no better, because even views based on faith must be coherent and must therefore pass the test of the prerequisites of truth, else they are just false. The problem of evil is only the most obvious of the problems that occur when these prerequisites are applied. The outcome of such appeals is the increasingly *ad hoc* character of so much theology in recent decades (cf. *FE*, 332).

Post observes that the contemporary theist has four logical options when faced with these difficulties. Confronted with today's pervasive

---

[31] See *FE*, 92–98. The principle of sufficient reason is basic to all cosmological versions of the arguments, and, even today, its validity is often taken for granted by both exponents and critics. The principle also plays other theological roles (as, for instance, in some varieties of process theology). But Post's critique of the principle is decisive. His analysis undermines a very great deal of traditional "rational" theology and deserves careful study by all theologians today.

[32] Post asks: "What is it that determines, say, the truths of chemistry, if not truths of physics? And as regards the latter, it is even more difficult to argue, in anything approaching convincing detail, that such truths themselves are determined by further truths. In detail, what connective theory . . . would enable one to infer that and how the specifics of quantum physics or of general relativity are determined by particular truths about the alleged unifying nonphysical entity or entities. And what *particular* truths are these?" (*FE*, 329, my emphasis.)

naturalism the theist may (1) reject theism, (2) reject naturalism, (3) show that they are after all not inconsistent with one another, or (4) attempt their synthesis (cf., *FE*, 332–334).

The first option seems theologically bleak, but it is not far from a number of contemporary theological options (for instance, some noncognitivists in analytic philosophy of religion, perhaps some "language game" theorists, and apparently various "psychological self-actualization" models derived from Jungian analytic psychology).[33] The second option to reject naturalism is the instinctive reaction of both classical and revisionary theists, and we reviewed in the first chapter how costly it is. The third option has been common in modern theology, but as Post observes, the problem is with its disjunctive form. The issue is not really that there is no inconsistency between theism and naturalism but *why*, why *in detail*, they are consistent. Failure to provide this additional step plagues all such efforts from Schleiermacher on.[34]

Post appeals to the attractiveness of the fourth option, the possibility of a synthesis between some version of theism and an austere naturalism, despite its initial implausibility for most theologians. Synthesis has ample historical precedents, not least in Augustine and Aquinas who insisted on developing their theological positions in conformity with the best science of their day. Aquinas's synthesis may

---

[33] Noncognitivist analytic theories, such as that of Braithwaite, are well known. It is difficult to see how "language game" models such as D. Z. Phillips or Paul Holmer can avoid noncognitivism. Examples of the last would seem to be the work of Charles Winquist and David Miller and others in this school, though as mentioned earlier, their positions at the interface with naturalism remain opaque because it is so difficult to clarify the epistemological and ontological status of their claims. For instance, the following statements from Miller are obscure and troubling apart from clearer conceptual boundaries: ". . . The Gods and Goddesses are *worlds of being* and meaning in which my personal life participates." "[The Gods and Goddesses] are the empowering worlds of our existence, *the deepest structures of reality.*" (Miller [1974], 61, 80 respectively, my emphasis.)

[34] This problem accounts for the finally unsatisfactory character of Langdon Gilkey's otherwise impressive efforts. Though Gilkey is really an advocate of the second option, he has tried to show that science cannot conflict with religion because of the special domain status of religious language. In order to achieve this, however, he must, in effect, construe science (and therefore its implications) merely as a perspective. Religious language also expresses a perspective, a perspective established by what Gilkey terms "a dimension of ultimacy" in experience. But throughout, Gilkey trades fatally on the ambiguity between a dimension of ultimacy in experience and ultimacy as an ontological category (with strongly referential implications). This permits him to reject metaphysical naturalism out of hand. But this rejection is plausible only if the ambiguity is eliminated by showing not merely that science and religion are not inconsistent but, in detail, the deeper nature of their compatibility. Leaving this deeper compatibility unclarified permits Gilkey to adopt the second option and to ignore the problems with ultimate unifiers we have been discussing. See Gilkey (1969), 247–413 and Gilkey (1970), 101–136.

have seemed equally unlikely in his day in view of his Aristotelian naturalism. It will be replied, of course, and correctly, that naturalism today is far more formidable than earlier philosophical accounts of nature because of the daunting problem of God's inventory status within modern accounts of nature.[35] But for two hundred years theologians have struggled to rethink traditional theological categories in light of modernity. This requirement now extends, I claim, to a world viewed in terms of an austere naturalistic physicalism. The failure to take up this challenge with real seriousness accounts not a little for the contempt for theology on the part of a broad segment of the educated public. The gains of a synthesis between a kind of "theism" and an austere ontological naturalism would be enormous. Even the attempt and failure would be instructive.[36] Fragmentary as the present work may be, it attempts to address this fourth option. Let us now see how such an effort might proceed.

Physicalism excludes traditional and revisionary theisms because it denies ontological status to "God," but another door can be opened through a consideration of value. This requires arguing that the very meaning of "God" is valuational rather than ontological. If we could establish that the values that endow "God" with meaning are true, then "God exists" would be restored to truth through a *valuational theism*. Such a theism could be naturalistic if the objective determination of valuational truth can be defended physicalistically, and Post makes this case powerfully, contrary to the weight of the Humean consensus. As for inventory status, there are ample precedents in contemporary theology denying that belief in God is justified only if God has warranted inventory status. As Post points outs, theologians often claim that "God" is "a matter not of what there is but of how we ought to talk about it and how we ought to see it" (*FE*, 330), and this is basically a value claim. Thus, there may well be a link between value and the identity of "God."

---

[35] Largely because of the implausibility of any kind of "final causality," our situation is unlike the ancient conceptions of nature in which Plato's "Good" or Aristotle's "Unmoved Mover" had immediate ontological plausibility and formed the opening wedges for the classical theisms of Augustine and Aquinas.

[36] On the issues discussed in this paragraph, see *FE*, 332–337. Note also the following from James Ross, who defends a traditional form of rational theism: "In the light of the new scientific knowledge, the formulations of belief are reexamined [by the religious person] and found to convey elements which were given undue emphasis, elements not central to the belief required and guaranteed. . . Gradually those elements are abandoned or rephrased and the original belief is recast. . . That the expression of faith should occasionally adjust itself to the achievements of science is neither unexpected nor scandalous" (Ross (1969), 88; quoted in *FE*, 335, n. 8).

Attempts to show that theism is simply a matter of how we ought to talk about and "see" God have usually resulted in reductive theories of religion. Religion is viewed noncognitively and reduced to certain functions. (Take your pick as to which ones these are.) Other efforts, inspired largely by Wittgenstein and Kierkegaard, view religion as rooted in practices, communities, "forms of life," and as a "seeing-as." These efforts are not necessarily noncognitivist – even if they inevitably dodge the deeper cognitivist issues (and are usually quite conservative). Examples are the works of D. Z. Phillips, Paul Holmer, Stanley Hauerwas, and George Lindbeck. For the moment, let us simply note this type of contemporary option and turn to Post's suggestions about a relationship between religion and value.

Arguments for the objectivity of value run head-on into the fact-value gulf that has had such a profound impact on recent intellectual culture and that seems especially intractable for naturalism. Traditional naturalism assumes that "ought" can be a function of "is" only by a term–term reduction of "ought" statements to "is" statements, and this is impossible. Valuational subjectivism is, however, much more deeply entrenched than simply among naturalists. John Mackie has recently coined an "argument from queerness" to summarize the shared assumption behind the widespread moral and valuational subjectivism in contemporary culture.[37] This is a negative argument to the effect that *objective* values must be queer things "because their relation with facts is so mysterious, being a matter neither of entailment or implications, nor of derivation, nor of reduction or definability, nor even of supervenience or 'resultance'" (*FE*, 254). Such an argument is indispensable for the subjectivist, Mackie recognizes, because disagreement alone does not justify that there are no objective values, and ordinary usages presume them. The subjectivist must hence advance an error thesis: "our ordinary usage and reasoning, entrenched for millennia, are massively in error, for there really are no objective values" (*FE*, 255).

Abstracting from value disagreements across times, societies, and cultures, the queerness argument crucially depends on the unintelligibility or inconceivability of an objective ground of value. To defeat it, therefore, the objectivist need only challenge its claim that there is no intelligible way of relating objective values to facts (that is, that the alternatives listed above are exhaustive). Post argues that the

---

[37] See Mackie (1977), 41.

determination relation applied to value can achieve such an objectivist alternative.

Post's argument is intricate, but presenting it fully is unnecessary for our purposes.[38] It is, however, worth examining the antirelativist

---

[38] For the interested reader, I here present a brief sketch of the basic argument, though this is no substitute for Post's full presentation (see *FE*, 281–283). Taking the lead from Mackie, we can overcome the fact-value gap if we can make intelligible that value is determined physically. Furthermore, from the earlier argument, it is clear that such a determination will not be reductive; it will not amount to a claim that we can either identify values with or read them off from physical entities.

The determination claim requires a realist and objective claim for the determination of truth by the world to the effect that "the world determines truth iff [if and only if], given the world and given any other world that is relevantly similar, under each interpretation the same sentences have the same truth-value in both" (*FE*, 27). The determinacy of truth follows from two further premises which are non-controversially shared by all the opposing theorists: verificationists, pragmatists, coherentists, and realists. The first is that if two "interpreted sentences Φ and Θ differ in truth-value, then there must be some further, relevant difference between Φ and Θ that accounts for this" (*FE*, 28). The disagreements are over what counts as the relevant difference, not with the principle itself. Post calls this the "Equity Principle for Truth" (EP): "Given any two relevantly similar circumstances or worlds and any interpretation-$\mathcal{T}$, Φ is true (false, neuter) under-$\mathcal{T}$ in one iff Φ is true (false, neuter) under-$\mathcal{T}$ in the other" (*FE*, 29). EP is insufficient because different theorists differ over the relevant factors that make a sentence true and can thus accord different interpreted sentences different truth values. "In this sort of case, the differing theories of truth would yield genuinely conflicting (value) judgments about the truth-value of Φ (not because they disagree about the evidence for Φ – the dispute is not thus epistemic – but because they disagree about the concept of truth, or truth's 'first principles')" (*FE*, 30). Consequently, a second, stronger premise is required. Borrowed from what Post terms "meta-ethical antirelativism" it states that not all such conflicting judgments can be correct ("where 'correct' need not mean true but can mean rationally warranted or justified" [*FE*, 30]). Depending on its account of the relevant factors, each theory will yield its own distribution, even when it is not known what the actual distribution is. This principle from meta-ethical antirelativism (MEA) can be formulated as: "One and only one of the possible distributions of truth-values (including neuter) over all the sentences of our language is correct" – "and one of the competing theories' distributions may or may not be it, the realist's included" (*FE*, 30–31).

Neither EP nor MEA *taken alone* imply the determinacy of truth. MEA means that just one distribution is correct, but determination goes further to state that "which one is correct *is* determined by something further, and in particular by the world" (*FE*, 31, Post's emphasis). Determinacy thus follows only from the conjunction of EP and MEA. MEA is not question-begging because alternative theorists (including antirealists) can accept that a piece of the world does the determination work but can then construe this part of the world to include the *beliefs* (or *consciousness*) of the theorist herself. For the realist who is a physicalist, determinacy as such is not the issue but rather *what* it is that determines truth. It must be the world *independent* of consciousness, perceivers, inquirers, or methods of verification. (A truth may be indeterminate in reference to the items on this list since given a world consisting only of consciousness, or inquirers, and so forth, and given any other such world relevantly similar, the same sentence need not have the same truth-value in each world. In other words, "such a world does not suffice to induce one and only one distribution of truth-values" over the sentence [*FE*, 33].) Therefore, MEA must be conjoined with a physicalist construal of EP to induce a physicalist determination of value.

These principles together with two further premises can now develop the argument toward the determinacy of valuation. The first premise is a supervenience principle accepted by all parties that "moral properties (or at least our ascriptions of them) supervene on natural properties in the sense that nothing can differ in its moral properties without differing also in its natural properties" (*FE*, 259). With some thinkers such as Hare, this has merely a weak sense in that the *relevant* natural difference can be defined as a *judgment* only from the point of view of *one's own moral principles*. The strongest version would have to hold that "a natural difference is morally relevant or not, independent of the moral principles one happens to hold" (*FE*, 259). An intermediate version, sufficient for our purposes, results from an extension of EP's possible worlds formulation: "For any W_1 and W_2 relevantly similar as regards natural properties, an act A has a certain moral status for person P in W_1 iff A has that same status for any relevantly similar P^* in W_2; and a substantive moral rule, principle or first principle R is true (or at least correct or to be followed) in W_1 iff R is true (or correct or to be followed) in W_2," (*FE*, 260), and the same principle may be extended for value in general (*FE*, 266).

The second premise follows from a strong assumption "that given a moral judgment and its denial, one or the other should be given assent by both parties (whether they know it or not) and in that sense is correct" (*FE*, 261). This is related to our common assumption that when two persons genuinely conflict over the same moral judgment, no one should assent to both of them. The assumption does not require the even stronger assertion that our moral judgments are true, only that we treat them as though they are for the purposes of argument. This weaker position is permissible because we can defeat the queerness argument simply by showing the *possibility* of an alternative. So, the valuational version of MEA becomes the second premise: "If we pretend our moral judgments are true or false, and distribute those values over the totality of the moral judgments, then among all the possible mutually conflicting such distributions, only one is correct" (*FE*, 261), and this is to be taken in the sense that "there is only one distribution allowed, and one of these distributions – ours included – may or may not be it" (*FE*, 262).

Determinacy now follows from the conjunction of these two premises. In a particular P-world (W_1) with its natural properties in which moral judgments are correct, we may pretend that these judgments are true or false. From MEA it follows that with any set of mutually conflicting judgments, only one distribution of truth-values over the moral values is correct. But let us now see whether we could coherently suppose another P-world (W_2) in which all entities have the same natural properties as in W_1 but there is a moral judgment true in one but not in the other. It would still be the case that the persons, acts, and circumstances in the two worlds are indiscernible as regards natural properties. It follows from applying the equity principle that we *could not* make the above supposition (and its contrary is what must be shown). Note what follows when we apply the equity principle (EP):

But if W_1 and W_2 are relevantly similar, then according to EP, (i) an act has a certain moral status (of being obligatory, permitted, wrong, etc.) in W_1 iff it has that same status in W_2 (because both the persons who perform the act and the circumstances in which it is performed are relevantly similar, however relevance is defined). Hence (ii) the persons in W_1 have the same obligations as those in W_2 to act and to be treated in various ways. And also according to EP, (iii) a moral principle or rule is true in W_1 iff it is true in W_2, first principles included. Furthermore, every moral judgment asserts either (i) the moral status of some particular act or compound of acts, either act-tokens or act-types; (ii) an obligation (or compound of obligations) of or to some particular person or persons; or (iii) some general principle or rule, first principles included. (*FE*, 262)

Thus, contrary to the former supposition which would defeat the argument, there is after all "no moral judgment true in one of W_1 or W_2 but not in the other" (*FE*, 263).

This argument permits neither the stronger cognitivist conclusion that the moral judgments *are* true or false nor, even assuming truth, that they are true or false realistically. Regarding the latter, MEA is compatible with any theory of truth (see *FE*, 264–265). As for the former, though not cognitivist, the conclusion is quite strong, for, "given the purely natural properties of people and things, whether or not the moral judgments are true or false, if we pretend they are and distribute those values over them, there is one and only one such distribution allowed. . ." (*FE*, 264). But, though determinacy does not result from either MEA or EP alone, and though it is not yet a full physicalist determinacy, world

aspect of the argument. The argument for determinacy depends
largely on two principles. An equity principle states that in any two
relevantly similar worlds, a statement is true (or false or neuter) in one
only if it is true (or false or neuter) in the other (cf. *FE*, 29, 260–261)
(the "Equity Principle for Truth" [EP]). An antirelativist principle
states that only one distribution of truth values over all the sentences
in our language can be correct (even if we do not know which theory
would account for the proper distribution) (cf. *FE*, 30–36, 261–262)
(the principle of "Meta-Ethical Antirelativism" [MEA]). Determinacy
follows from EP and MEA in conjunction, and this defeats the
queerness argument because at issue is the intelligibility of an
alternative to queerness, and determinacy is such an alternative.
Subjectivists therefore must reject one or another of these. Since EP is
unobjectionable, they must reject MEA, which of course they do. It
cannot, however, be because it is unintelligible (cf. *FE*, 272–273).[39]
They must, therefore, admit its intelligibility and reject it as false. But
then they concede the *intelligibility* of the premises of the argument for
determination, and this is all that is required to defeat the argument
from queerness.

What the subjectivist really finds objectionable about the antirelativist
principle (MEA) is that it is explanatorily impotent. By asserting that
"just one member of an exhaustive set of conflicting moral judgments
is correct," MEA is fatally implicated in the problem that objective
values seem incapable of playing any explanatory role in our
accounts of natural events (*FE*, 272). But Post disputes this claim

determination does result from MEA and EP in conjunction, just as with truth, and it follows
that the world alone determines whatever moral truth there is.

  On the surface this may seem a quite minimal result until we remember that the queerness
argument can be defeated simply by showing the *possibility* of an objective grounding for
value. (Physicalist grounding then simply becomes a further intramural debate within the
overall objectivist position.) Stating a determination relation does defeat the queerness
argument. Based on premises EP and MEA, which are intelligible and unqueer, it *is* an
alternative to the above attempts at relation between facts and values. Neither EP nor MEA
are circular or question-begging. They would be if they were assumed as true. But the
queerness argument is simply a case against intelligibility. (That is why in the above
presentation of the argument, we need only *pretend* or *treat them as though* they are true.) So EP
is not assumed to be true but only acceptable or warranted for purposes of argument: EP is
acceptable "as a premise in an argument for the acceptability of the conclusion that whether
or not the moral judgments . . . are true or false, if we pretend they are and distribute those
values over them, then there is one and only one such distribution allowed by the facts" (*FE*,
270). MEA is also not assumed as strictly true or false. The question is whether we are entitled
to it. Here the analysis returns to the text.

[39] Subjectivists merely deny what MEA asserts; but the denial of an unintelligible assertion is
itself unintelligible.

outright in that we can in fact defend uniquely correct judgments involving moral properties that do play explanatory roles, again challenging the root of the queerness argument. "There do seem to be real regularities in the world that are identifiable only by appeal to moral properties construed as realized or not, independently of our principles [that is, independently of whatever ones we *just happen* to hold, the bugaboo of the subjectivist]. Such regularities include honesty's engendering trust, justice's commanding allegiance, depravity arousing condemnation, and so on. In this way the moral virtues and vices figure in many of our best explanations. . . Since the moral properties involved evidently are irreducible, the explanations in which they appear evidently are ineliminable" (*FE*, 272). The point is that the argument about explanatory impotence cannot be used unequivocally to reject MEA, which in turn is reinforced by the analysis just given. The argument from queerness could not itself be used to reject MEA, for it "would succeed only if the argument for determinacy failed, and the latter would fail only if MEA were false . . . So basing the rejection of MEA on the argument from queerness would beg the question of whether MEA is true. And independent of the arguments from queerness and for determinacy, the weight of the evidence, including various facts about actual moral reasoning and other usage of moral language – including the explanatory – weighs heavily in favor of MEA" (*FE*, 272–273).[40] Since the queerness argument is the only ground for subjectivism (apart from mere difference or disagreement which will not do the job), defeating it leaves "the presumption of objectivity undefeated and in full force" and "we are free to treat various facts about actual moral reasoning and other usage of moral language, including the explanatory, as powerful independent evidence against subjectivism and in particular against the subjectivist's rejection of MEA" (*FE*, 273). We may thus presume the determinacy of value (moral values included). Since EP and MEA may also be accepted regarding truth and since these permit a realist conception of truth, we may go on to presume a full-fledged physicalist account of value determination, that it is the world in the sense of the basic physical entities that determines value.

Such determination does not mean "reading off" values from descriptions at the level of the sciences. Determination by nonvaluational fact does not require that values are derivable from, or entailed by, or

----

[40] Post notes that even Mackie concedes the last point.

identical with physical fact.[41] Domain and explanatory autonomy are still maintained. Indeed, beyond the argument for physical determination of value, the real work must be done at the level of substantive moral theory on its own terms, for we must still define what the morally relevant factors are. "It is only by means of such theories . . . that one can hope to specify what a given moral truth corresponds with, by spelling out what count as the relevant things and natural properties in virtue of which what the judgment is about has the moral status it has" (*FE*, 279).

With these arguments Post settles the is-ought problem insofar as the issue is ontological: "what *is* the case is related to what *ought* to be the case by nonreductive determination." This leaves open the epistemic issue of how they are related; we still want to know how "ought might be derived from or reduced to or otherwise . . . justified by is" (*FE*, 274).[42] The determinacy of valuation is not, however, without significance even here. Once determination is clarified, then the way is opened for the specific epistemic work of observing determination or establishing it by connective theories. In value theory the main achievement is to guarantee "that an important sort of epistemic enterprise is not doomed from the start" (*FE*, 274).[43] Post

---

[41] As Post says, "the existence of objective values is a matter not of extra entities but of there being a truth of the matter as regards the correctness or incorrectness of our value judgments, a truth of the matter determined by objective natural fact. If the physicalist is right that natural fact in turn is determined by physical fact, it follows that the correctness of our value judgments is determined ultimately by truths at the level of physics" (*FE*, 252).

[42] Post points out that in ethics "determination" or "grounding" typically has concerned problems of "discovery" and "justification," not surprising given "our frequent doubts and disputes about what to do when, on the basis of what principles" (*FE*, 258). These concerns, however, slant the notion of "determination" in ethics toward an epistemic meaning, whereas its crucial sense in the present context is semantic or ontological. To say that one thing determines another in this latter sense "we mean that given the way the first is, there is one and only one way the second can be" (*FE*, 257), and this ordinary meaning of determination can be formulated nonreductively in technically precise language by the modal use of possible worlds, as we have seen. Once we have achieved objectivity conditions contrary to the queerness argument, then we are still faced with the epistemic issues of discovery and justification which have to be developed autonomously within the domain of substantive moral theory.

[43] On the force of his strategy, it is worth quoting Post at length: "It follows that if we can undermine the argument from queerness by showing the falsity of one of its assumptions, then not only is the presumption that there are objective values undefeated and in full force, but we are free to treat ordinary usage and normal moral reasoning and explanation as powerful independent evidence against subjectivism, and in particular against its thesis that a couple of genuinely conflicting moral judgments can be equally correct, there being no real truth of the matter in the first place. If we can undermine the argument from queerness by showing how an objective ethics is possible, we need not worry so deeply about irresolvable moral disagreements and the occasional seeming irrelevance or impotence of moral explanations of various admitted facts. Without the argument from queerness, or something very like it,

shows how correspondence with the facts can be formulated, how it can be construed to make truth-claims, and how there can be confirmation by way of descriptive phenomena, and we have already seen that there is a fact of the matter as regards their correctness (see *FE*, 275–277). He concludes that "it seems ever more strained and artificial to withhold strict truth and falsity from value judgments. . . A distinction between judgments for which all this holds (and more) and judgments which in addition are strictly true or false looks like a distinction without a difference" (*FE*, 277).

We need not pursue these matters in detail since we now have enough for our purposes. We now have the possibility of an objective account of value on physicalist terms, surprising perhaps, but very powerful. Contrary to the entire modern tradition, as Post concludes, "if all descriptive truth is determined by truth at the level of physics, as physicalists contend, then the objective world of matter in motion exhibits an element of value after all, in that the physical truths about the world determine the correct distribution of truth-values over the value judgments. A purely scientific description of us and the world is not ethically neutral, despite long tradition to the contrary, and we are free to regard nature and value as ontologically reunified. Although values seemed banished forever from nature, they were always there" (*FE*, 283).

A VALUATIONAL THEISM: PLACING RELIGION IN A PHYSICALIST WORLD

This objective account of value now offers a way to construe religion naturalistically. We have noted that a respectable position in contemporary theology asserts that the existence of God should not be a matter of what is but of how we ought to talk about and see what is.[44] Construing God-talk as a matter of what there is, these thinkers

---

subjectivism has little to be said for it" (*FE*, 255). In contrast to much contemporary paralysis, it is significant how much support has emerged in recent philosophy for a renewed investigation of the rational objectivity of moral and other values in the spirit of this statement by Post. See, for instance, the vigorous, though much less technical, defense of this course in Taylor (1991). And, see also Reiman for a powerful and technically sophisticated substantive moral theory defending just such an option.

[44] Examples are, broadly construed, such thinkers as R. B. Braithwaite, John Wisdom, Paul van Buren, D. Z. Phillips, Paul Holmer, Stanley Hauerwas, and George Lindbeck. The tendency toward conservative theological positions among these thinkers arises from the influence of Wittgenstein, who permits them to take the position that a language in use is in "good order."

claim, is a kind of category mistake. God-talk has its own truth and should take precedence in appropriately qualified contexts to any ontological or metaphysical implications. In effect, they are arguing that the truth status of theistic language belongs in a valuational domain. The problem is that such positions usually end in noncognitivism. There is no reason in principle, however, that they should require noncognitivism. Physicalism excludes "God" from ontological inventory status. But parallel to these theists it also permits a valuational, yet naturalistic, approach to "God." Surprisingly, such an approach is by no means noncognitivist, and it also permits us to avoid the theological conservatism typically found in these positions.

Such positions arise from the question forcefully pursued by analytic philosophy about whether "God" refers. The responses usually end either critical of religious discourse or, as with Braithwaite, in noncognitivism. If "God" does refer, we have all the problems of inventory status, and Occam's razor is very sharp. But, if it does not refer, it would seem that such discourse could not be true (or false), hence, the temptation to move to some kind of noncognitivism. Such problems form the background against which "valuational theists" insist that "the question of God is not a question to which Occam's razor could apply, indeed not strictly a question of extra entities at all" (*FE*, 345–346), though they are not always explicit about the consequences of reference failure. The advantage of this move is to emphasize that the proper home of religious discourse is in articulating a form of life and a practice. Such a form of life includes, broadly speaking, a complex valuational matrix (including but not exhausted by moral values) combined with a "seeing-as." A seeing-as is required because seemingly referential language is used to constitute the religious form of life and must somehow be accommodated. Such a form of life, as attested in the Apostle's Creed for instance, includes *seeing* heaven and earth *as* made by a loving God who is the Father of our Lord and Savior Jesus Christ. The problem with this approach, to repeat, is that it seems destined for noncognitivism – even on the part of valuational theists such as D. Z. Phillips or George Lindbeck (and perhaps Stanley Hauerwas) who do not espouse noncognitivism but leave the underlying issues blurred. As Post puts it: "how could this seeing-as be correct, or based on fact, if it is not *true* that God made heaven and earth?" And "how can the latter be true if 'God' fails to refer" (*FE*, 346).[45] Such "cognitivist valuational

---

[45] These valuational theists are cognitivists because they seem to intend both that "God is the maker of heaven and earth" is a way of seeing heaven and earth as made by God *and* that

theists" usually just evade this issue. After all, to take it up would require showing that after all "God" does refer by being in the metaphysical inventory of what is. The consequence of the evasion is to make it difficult to distinguish their positions from form-of-life relativisms.

The issue is how we might take the valuational, seeing-as approach and still claim that discourse about God is true, all the while that "God" has no referent. The value objectivity permitted by a nonreductive physicalism provides a way. It is elementary that an assertion may be true even if its subject term does not refer. As Post explains, giving some of the classical counter-examples: "There are no point-masses, frictionless surfaces, objects free of all perturbing influences, or other ideal objects. Yet many a truth in physics mentions such things, as do text-book paradigms like 'A perfectly smooth elephant of negligible girth is rolling down an inclined plane ...' Nor need there by any entities called duties, rights, virtues, or the Good, over and above persons and their natural properties and relations. Yet it can be true that a certain duty is painful, or a certain right inalienable, or the Good unattainable, and so on" (*FE*, 346–347). In the same spirit, "God-talk" could be true even if its subject term does not refer, provided we could work out an alternative way to construe its truth – and irrespective of how we might scandalize traditionalists (who have problems enough with inventory status). The truth of God-talk would have to consist in something other than the subject term's possessing a property.

A first step would be to take seriously the valuational theist's insistence that we look not to claims about what exists but to a form of life and a practice to do justice to religious discourse. Comprehending religious discourse, they are saying, is a matter of seeing how, in certain circumstances (which may be rooted in a community, its

"God is the maker of heaven and earth" is true. But they evade the questions of how we are to connect these two. Certainly this is true with the ambiguities that are now familiar in D. Z. Phillips tortured attempts to confine all theological discourse entirely to a language game (see, e.g., Phillips [1976], 151–182). (An exception is his powerful book on death and afterlife in which he shows himself willing to *interpret* religious discourse about a resurrection to bring it into conformity with what we otherwise, outside the Christian language game, might be inclined to believe about the world and our deaths. But it is difficult to fit this book into the rest of his corpus (cf. Phillips [1970])). George Lindbeck's theory about doctrines as rules for the discourse of a religious community of practice simply evades the connective issues in a fashion analogous to Phillips. Stanley Hauerwas, though rooted in a kind of valuational form of life ethical analysis, falls back on a very conservative theological foundation about which he remains persistently unreflective. In effect, he takes a strongly traditional and conservative position on inventory status even though almost all of his highly creative work in ethics is done within the valuational, form of life position.

practice, and its form of life but may also, for all that, be richly extended to a seeing-as of the entire world), a particular discourse *is called for in a particular context*, and, as Post notes, this is largely a value judgment (*FE*, 339). The cognitivity issue could be addressed, then, even physicalistically, if it could be made entirely a matter of *valuation* rather than metaphysical inventory, if, in Post's formulation, the *truth* of religious discourse (including its God-terms) consists in "*the objective correctness of certain values and of a way of life*" (*FE*, 347, my emphasis). The immediate objection to this strategy, of course, is that values cannot be grounded in fact so that a seeing-as based on them will have no objective basis and will thus be arbitrary (however "valuable" to the person adopting it). This objection, widely accepted even by most theologians today, is unstoppable if the fact-value gap cannot be bridged, and the arbitrariness it implies is what undermines the valuational theists mentioned above. But for a physicalist the gap is not only bridgeable but bridged: by EP and MEA and the determinacy of valuation that follows from them. As Post says, echoing the arguments presented above, "theologians need no longer be bullied into holding that the decision to use or continue in some such language game or form of life is a matter ultimately of subjective preference or 'faith,' on the ground, say, that the decision is neither derivable from nor reducible to any totality of natural fact. Instead, they can borrow the idea of the determinacy of valuation and argue that this decision corresponds with the facts . . . , as indeed it might" (*FE*, 339).

Much of a religious form of life is entirely valuational. But what of the apparently referential God-terms which seem to anchor it? The surface grammar of "God" is obviously referential, but it is possible that like many other terms (such as rights and duties), it has a depth grammar that alone reveals its meaning, indeed the possibility of its truth. The "seeing-as" of valuational theists seems to require something like a distinction between surface and depth grammars. Since Schleiermacher, such ideas have become well entrenched among liberal theologians concerned to revise traditional theological categories, and this liberal tradition has always understood itself as a continuation of the core Christian tradition, not its elimination or evisceration.[46] The issue here simply requires a deepened sensitivity to theological literalism. Starting from the surface grammar of "God," according to

---

[46] For powerful documentation of this claim, see Gerrish.

which to assert something about God is to ascribe a property to a subject, such literalism insists that language about God can be true only if "God" refers to an entity beyond the naturalist inventory. "Subject-predicate" literalism then carries other literalisms in its train, as with language about creation, miracles, providence, and grace, even in some revisionary theisms, which presuppose that there is a being, supernatural or not, who may or may not stand outside natural causal relations, but who certainly performs causal operations within the natural world. Yet there is ample precedent within modern theology for insisting that literalism in all its forms be overcome by some such distinction as that between surface and depth grammar.[47]

Such an approach would treat "God exists" and all its cognates (such as "God is the Creator") as a kind of meta-assertion that compactly expresses a valuational matrix, a form of life and an attendant seeing-as. Thus, to take a plausible enumeration from Post, there might be predicates "that express the holiness of certain places and events, or the blessedness of certain persons and acts, or buoyant confidence in the goodness of creaturely existence despite suffering, or the redeeming power of *agape*." The seeing-as involved in such predicates along with the God-terms they ultimately involve can be construed (and theologically interpreted) by some such subjunctive form as: "would be that way (or would be like that) for an appropriately religious person in appropriate circumstances" (*FE*, 338). These circumstances, as Lindbeck and others emphasize, often include a further, reflexively subjunctive qualification to the effect that such predicates are appropriate precisely as the rules that constitute the experiencing, the valuing, the form of life, and the seeing-as involved in the basic subjunctive form: "would be that way if this term is taken as . . ."

God-talk can be construed as a set of meta-assertions at both of these levels. Thus, at the first level, the content of "God" as "Creator" can anchor a way of seeing the universe and ourselves as essentially good, not as meaningless and absurd, and seeing "our lives as having a certain meaning and destiny dependent not on our transient purposes but on invariant and irreducible if sometimes mysterious imperatives about faith, hope, and love" (*FE*, 350). At the second level, "God" has still other roles in terms of functions or rules that

---

[47] See *FE*, 351–354 for Post's critique of subject-predicate literalism.

constitute the seeing-as itself. The prohibition against idolatry might, for instance, be taken as such a "meta-rule." It would be a rule prohibiting the absolutization of any of our values, serving thereby as a critique of our tendency to identify "God," a value term for an absolute devotion, with any of the limited beings, achievements, or aspects of existence to which we are always tempted to give such devotion. In this sense, it not merely preserves but defines the meaning of "God's transcendence." "God's transcendence" would serve as a rule identifying the total matrix of our valuing orientation to the world (thus as the ultimate meta-rule constituting what Post above calls those "invariant and irreducible if sometimes mysterious imperatives about faith, hope, and love"). It might seem surprising to establish God's transcendence in this fashion, but this is precisely what follows from such a valuational stance in the sense that now "God is not this, not that, indeed not any*thing* – not any mere being, entity or existent" (*FE*, 346, Post's emphasis).[48]

Unlike other valuing and seeings-as approaches to religious discourse, this one permits the possibility that God-talk is objectively true. If "God exists" and its cognates are construed to express a valuational matrix, then a valuational theist can attempt to claim that the language is true and objectively so (according to a naturalist determinacy of value), that there is a fact of the matter about the values it expresses (and the experiencing, the form of life, and the seeing-as that are integral to those values) (see *FE*, 347). Post points to two conditions that would have to be met to achieve this goal. One would have to show first that the valuational matrix is the true one (or at least among the true ones), and then one would have to make a case that this valuational complex (of experiencing- and seeing-as) is appropriately expressed by a theistic seeing-as. As Post says, speaking of moral values alone, if values can be grounded by determinacy so that there is a fact of the matter about them, then "this quality of their being a fact of the matter *is inherited by whatever the moral values entail*" (*FE*, 344, my emphasis).

I shall discuss some of the difficulties in making this theistic case below, and we shall see Wieman's relevance to this position. For the moment, I want to clarify some of the implications of taking "God" as a subjunctive meta-assertion for a valuational complex. Such a

---

[48] See *SHG*, 264–265 for Wieman's powerful statement of a notion of "functional transcendence" and his claim that it is identical to the actual reality mythically represented within traditional Christianity as "metaphysically transcendent."

theism avoids many difficulties usually associated with naturalist philosophies of religion and at the same time has surprising continuities with the theological tradition. I shall extrapolate a series of points from Post's discussion of these issues.

(1) A natural objection to this approach is that it amounts "to conferring truth on 'God exists' on the dubious ground that even though there is no such thing as God, still the sentence is true because all it means is that it is good or useful for people to see the world as if there were" (*FE*, 348). This supposition is beside the point for two reasons. First, the theory does not use or even imply the relevant clause: "even though there is no God." The reason is that "God exists" is a meta-assertion that *can be true*. The theory thus does not say, "even though there is no God," but "even though God is not in the inventory of what there is, hence not the value of a variable and not a matter to which Occam's razor could apply, the God-talk is true" (*FE*, 348). Second, the theory is not pragmatic or instrumental. It does not say that it would be good or useful for people to see the world as if there were a God (even though there is not). It says, rather, that "God exists" is simply true. Such truth can be quite independent of what we might construe as good for us or in our long term best interest, as is the case with all objective truth applied to values. A valuational theism need not be treated as a pragmatic fiction (cf. *FE*, 349).

(2) There are also implications for the notion of projection. All valuing involves a certain kind of projection because of the way physicalism treats emergent properties. Such properties (for instance emotions and what it is like to be a subject, but also valuations and seeings-as) involve projection in the sense that such properties cannot be reduced to or read off basic natural fact. Because of the determination relation, however, there is a fact of the matter as regards them, *if they are objectively correct*. They need not be *mere* projections. The experiencing, the valuation, and the seeings-as defined by a theistic valuational matrix can be "matched by an objectively existing God, in the sense that the God-talk is true and indeed objectively so, via the determinacy of valuation" (*FE*, 349). The problem for the valuational theist lies elsewhere: with normative arguments that the values are correct and that they require the theistic seeings-as. Assuming hypothetically for the moment that this case can be made, then we can say with Post: "This world may be but canvas to the religious imagination, in the sense that no religious assertion about it is derivable from or reducible

to physics or any other admittedly objective discourse. Nevertheless, there are better and worse ways of spreading such imagination on external objects, and some ways correspond with the facts, while others do not... Religious names for the whirlwind ultimately are no arbitrary affair" (*FE*, 341–342).

(3) The same strategy is relevant to other predicates that accompany "God exists." These typically lead to thinking of God as a being who maintains causal relations with the world. This is certainly how creation was traditionally understood. Post convincingly argues that the "universe" is not the sort of thing that could have a creator (cf. *FE*, 128–138). Similar ideas are now widely accepted, even by most "inventory theists," and there is strong precedent today for a "symbolic" account of creation language, as in Bultmann's existentialist account or Langdon Gilkey's *Maker of Heaven and Earth*.[49] The valuational theist is committed to an alternative account that is valuational through and through. Above we saw that it might involve seeing existence as essentially good. I shall argue below that it expresses a profound trust in being which is a product of a devotional stance toward value itself.[50] Articulated as a seeing-as, creation language accords truth to "God is the maker of heaven and earth" out of the same structure of meta-assertions by which the truth of "God exists" is anchored in a valuational matrix. As Post says, the predicates that we apply within a theistic valuational matrix "could be true and could express a face of existence, one that smiles only on religious persons in response to their training in these ways of seeing and feeling. . . . Even if the things are not made or created, literally, but come to be only by chance (so far as any science is concerned), nevertheless, they satisfy the predicates if accorded the appropriate role. Even if everything is identical with some mathematical-physical entity or other . . . nevertheless, *everything is describable by some subjunctive religious predicate, and in that sense is a religious entity*" (*FE*, 338–339, my emphasis).[51]

(4) A powerful contemporary objection to religious discourse is

[49] See Bultmann (1956), 15–22, and Gilkey (1965), 23, 35, 77–78, 150, 190, 204. See also, Gilkey's more recent work on the "creationist controversy" and the Arkansas "creationist trial" (Gilkey [1985]) where he applies his more mature theory about the nature and function of religious language.
[50] Herein lies the meaning of the title of this work: *Events of Grace*.
[51] Even classically, the underlying issues in the Gnostic and Marcionite debates which led to the received Christian doctrine of creation were valuational, in the sense of affirming the goodness of the world and the dominion of God over it. In the idiom of the day there was simply no alternative to defining these issues in metaphysical (i.e., in inventory and causal) terms.

that God language is ultimately empty, "dies the death of a thousand qualifications" in that theistic language cannot be strictly true or false because it is meaningless (cf. *FE*, 344, 352). Conservative theologians sometimes turn this argument on "demythologizers," claiming that such strategies end in vague abstraction and emptiness because the "living God of history" is lost. No such conclusion need follow, for, as Post says, "God-talk could well be objectively, solidly true even when 'God' refers to nothing. But if it is thus true, then the nonemptiness prerequisite is satisfied" (*FE*, 352). It follows that far from being vague or abstract, such language will be as rich and as concrete as the valuational matrix, the seeings-as, and the form of community are rich and concrete. This is where "the living God of history" finds its content. Historical religions have claimed that their values, anchored in the relationship to God, are relevant to this world. In this sense, "God exists" makes a difference to what this world is like, and generally speaking, this "making a difference" is the substance of the "living God of history." "God exists," valuationally construed, does make a difference to this world in the precise sense that "a change in truth-value of a religious claim would change the truth-values of some nonreligious claims about the world" (*FE*, 339) for a person committed to such a form of life.[52]

(5) Because I am defending a theology based on a physicalist naturalism, it might be surmised that it must identify God with the being of nature and thus be a version of pantheism or monism. Such is not the case for reasons rooted in the fact that "God" does not refer. God is not an entity in the ontological inventory, nor is God even the universe as a whole (*FE*, 350). Among other things, this has the marked advantage of not making God the source of evil, unlike not merely all pantheisms but also all versions of classical and revisionary theism.[53]

[52] Post quotes John Hick as follows: "The *meaning* of 'God exists' will be indicated by spelling out the past, present, and future difference which God's existence is alleged to make within human experience" (*FE*, 339, n. 11; Hick [1983], 106, my emphasis).

[53] For Post's full discussion of these and a number of further issues related to a valuational construal of "God," see *FE*, 348–356. Among these are very interesting comments he makes about Ivan Karamazov's statement that "If God does not exist, then everything is permitted." A valuational theism, which asserts that "'God exists' is true," rests on the premises of a physicalist determinacy of valuation, EP and MEA. It follows that rejecting them, not treating like cases alike and accepting meta-ethical relativism (as many theologians today do), is to become an atheist. The converse of Ivan's statement then obtains: "if in either sense everything is permitted, then God does not exist." If Dostoevsky therefore meant that if God did not exist there would be no truth of the matter in morals, "then what he said is true, on any account according to which 'God exists' is implied by the meta-assertion

The proposal for a valuational theism on physicalist terms remains to this point entirely hypothetical. It is conditional on normative arguments defending the nonarbitrary character of a theistic valuational matrix, and this is a formidable challenge. Let us nevertheless recognize the enormous advantages offered by such a valuational approach to religion. In the philosophy of religion, it offers a fresh agenda by which to confront the challenges of modernity, to try, namely, to show how the truth of God-talk might be reconceived on valuational grounds.[54] The corresponding theological task would be to construe the full doctrinal and confessional structure of the tradition in terms of the seeings-as of a theistic valuational matrix. This approach makes the entire theological tradition available once again to imaginative conception. However problematic these two agendas may be, they offer an exceedingly fresh opportunity for modern theology.[55] Not only could theology reclaim its right to speak about truth, thus overcoming the rampant relativism and subjectivism

that there is a truth of the matter in morals" (*FE*, 355). EP and MEA entail "that the world's entities and their natural properties allow one and only one distribution of truth-values over the moral judgments." But this requires that there be a truth of the matter as regards description. Thus "moral realism presupposes descriptive realism." It then follows that to be an antirealist is also to be an atheist. "If what there is does not determine the descriptive truths irrespective of our capacity to know them – if in this deep sense everything is permitted, and we are the measure – then again God does not exist" (*FE*, 356). None of this is surprising within traditional theism (including the role it played broadly speaking in Western culture until the onset of modernity). But it is surprising from within an austere physicalistic naturalism. As Post aptly summarizes this discussion, "conversely, those theists ill serve their cause who abandon this objective notion of truth when their faith is threatened by the trial by prerequisites. Rejecting talk of objective truth in favor of talk of truth as subjectivity, in the manner of Kierkegaard or at least his theological descendants, is not merely to talk about truth in a changed sense, but ironically, to become an atheist. Indeed those atheists who do commit themselves to this objectivist-realist notion of truth thereby embrace notions of transcendence and mystery unavailable to antirealists who *call* themselves theists. For according to realists, there can be truths that transcend humans' capacity ever to know them even in principle, and there can thus be mysteries aplenty, even unfathomable mysteries, expressed by questions to which there is a true answer but none known or perhaps knowable by us" (*FE*, 356, Post's emphasis).

[54] Here Wieman's 1934 essay "The Need of Philosophy of Religion" is still highly relevant. See Wieman (1975b).

[55] Fritz Buri's work (1956–1978) is the best contemporary example of the richness of the theological tradition being appropriated through a radically revisionary approach. Despite the richness of Buri's interpretation of the tradition, his dependence on the thought of Karl Jaspers unfortunately leaves the underlying philosophical principles of his methodology unclarified. His basic principle of a non-objective, existential relation to "Transcendence" remains obscure, ultimately, because it makes it impossible to comprehend his position on the "reference" of God terms. Buri's entire position seems devilishly designed to evade a clear answer to this question. Furthermore, the systematic principle itself seems too narrow, too thin, and too arbitrary to support the massive "dogmatic" interpretation he erects upon it. For a deeper analysis of some of these issues, see Hardwick (1972).

that hamper its rearguard actions today, it could do so in direct continuity with modern naturalism, the most powerful intellectual force in modern culture. In addition, its claim to objective truth would offer it a secure home in the modern university. In this respect, it may provide the most promising foundation for the fledgling field of cross-cultural philosophy of religion. It offers an approach to the richness of competing religious traditions without being immediately driven into the dilemmas produced by having to treat them as making alternative and contradictory claims about inventory status. It may also offer an alternative to the subjective perspectivalism which bedevils the weak methodologies of this discipline today. Far from being a rearguard action to rescue some aspect of religion, this approach offers a way to place the philosophy of religion and theology on a new footing.

I certainly shall not make this entire case here. I shall be able only to make a beginning toward the twofold normative argument which must ultimately establish such an ambitious program. As Bultmann said when he first made his demythologizing proposal, its successful execution requires the work of an entire generation of scholars.[56] Efforts in this direction offer the most promising continuation of Bultmann's proposal, and I shall argue that his position is best developed as a valuational theism. Accepting the outlines of Post's valuational approach to religion, the next two chapters will show how Christianity can be interpreted as a valuational theism on physicalist terms. Once we see how such a position looks, it will be possible to explore some of the formidable problems surrounding the normative status of such a valuational theism.

[56] Cf. NTM, 26 (ET, 14).

PART II

Bridge principles for a naturalist Christian theology

CHAPTER 3

Existence in faith: naturalism and existentialist interpretation

I am proposing to interpret the Christian confession of faith as a seeing-as for which "God" functions as a meta-assertion expressing a theistic set of values. I shall develop a set of "bridge principles" connecting philosophical naturalism with this view of the Christian faith. These principles justify a naturalistic theism by interpreting "God" in terms of a valuing stance ("faith") articulated as a seeing-(and experiencing-) as. This stance is not a single value but a complex structure of valuing (a "religion"). We should therefore expect that these bridge principles (including the content of "God" that they articulate) will be complex, not simple. Three sets of such principles are required, and these will be the topics of this and the following two chapters.

The first principle involves Rudolf Bultmann's method of existentialist interpretation. According to this method, the content of faith is an existential self-understanding. This chapter defends the compatibility of this method with philosophical naturalism. It also shows how an existentially interpreted Christian faith is a valuational stance encompassing a comprehensive conception of human being in the world that makes a valuational claim to meet the human quest for liberation and fulfillment. The second bridging principle (chapter four) shows how Wieman's naturalistic conception of God can anchor an existentialist analysis of faith. The final principle (chapter five) explains how this existentially interpreted "valuational theism" is a seeing-as. With the argument thus completed, chapter five will also address the normative assessment of such a valuational stance. We shall then be in a position to turn to more specifically theological themes in the chapters that follow, although these bridge principles will already involve considerable attention to substantive theological material.

This first bridge principle proposes to understand faith as an existential self-understanding and to interpret it by the method of existentialist interpretation.[1] I do not claim that this is the sole method by which a naturalist view of Christianity might be developed, but, as richly elaborated in Bultmann's thought, it already has important standing in contemporary theology, and its attractiveness for a naturalistic approach to religion is evident at once. Interpreting the theological content of faith entirely as modes of existence immediately liberates a naturalist theology both from myth and from the tradition's problematic metaphysical formulations.[2] Faith can be understood entirely in terms that are relevant to human experience in the here and now. This strategy is thus suggestively parallel to the valuational approach defended in the last chapter. It also accords nicely with two formal emphases in Bultmann's own articulation of this method: his claim that an existentialist interpretation of faith should be *exhaustive* and his criticisms of objectivistic misconstruals of faith in mythology and theology.

Bultmann, of course, rejected naturalism, so there is a question whether existentialist interpretation can be compatible with it. Bultmann's responses to naturalism do not, however, touch the naturalist framework espoused here. He typically identifies naturalism with "scientific objectivity," and he objects to its monopolistic pretensions, specifically to its failure to grasp the "non-objective" structures of existence (i.e., human personhood).[3] The naturalism defended here is also critical of such monopolistic pretensions.

---

[1] Despite its awkwardness, I use the term "existentialist interpretation" rather than "existential interpretation" in order to preserve a strict parallel in English to the distinction between *existentiell* and *existential* in Heidegger. When I refer to *existentiell*, I shall use the English "existential" or "existentially." *Existential* will be rendered as "existentialist." For Heidegger (and Bultmann), *existentiell* refers to any understanding of existence actualized here and now as a mode of existing. *Existential*, in contrast, refers to the formal analysis of the structures of existence embodied in any specific "existential" self-understanding. *Existential* is thus always formal, general, and categorial; *existentiell* is always particular and concrete, given immediately "with the individual's own unique situation and responsibility" (Ogden [1960], 7). The *existentiell* dimension of existence is what led Kierkegaard to claim that an existential system is not possible. Kierkegaard is ambiguous about whether this precludes a formal (system-like) analysis of the structures of existence actualized at the *existentiell* level (the level that distinguishes *Existenz* from objects), yet a large portion of his writings imply just such an analysis, which accounts for his influence on Heidegger. (For further discussions of this distinction, cf. *SZ*, 12–13 [32–33]; *CM*, 46–48; Hardwick [1972], xxvii–xxxiv.)

[2] I do not intend to imply that either the mythological form of the biblical witness or the subject-predicate form of the tradition are to be eliminated. This remark is intended exactly in Bultmann's sense when he says that demythologizing seeks not to eliminate myth but to interpret it (see NTM, ET, 12 [24]).

[3] See Bultmann (1984), 54–60, esp. 57; ZPE, ET, 105–110 (191–195). See also, Hardwick (1987b).

Though so-called scientific objectivity has a certain priority in ontology and metaphysics, Post's physicalism is open to a pluralism of domains of discourse. In effect Bultmann rejects scientific objectivity because it seeks reduction or promotes a single, unique, and privileged vocabulary, and our physicalism is equally critical of such attempts.

Physicalism's realist conception of truth does require a strong meaning for objectivity, and the sciences (especially physics) have priority in establishing the unifying entities. But according to Post, objectivity concerns invariance in the sense of not being conditional on a perspective or a point of view, and it only comes into play with sentences that express eternal truths (see *FE*, 288–289). These requirements do not apply to all true sentences, however, and such objectivity does not imply that whatever cannot be so expressed is insignificant or nonexistent.[4] Claims to truth from other domains are perfectly compatible with the physicalist requirement that the objective phenomena, the invariants, determine that there are such truths (in the sense, note carefully, *of determining what that which they are about is and what it is like*). This is so even of subjective phenomena that may be entirely ineffable (such as what it is like to be a bat). Thus, the sciences have a priority because they offer the best guide to establish the ultimate ontological entities, but this is not a monopolistic priority that excludes other domains of discourse.

Another less specific criticism from Bultmann arises simply from his belief that naturalism, defined still largely in terms of "scientific objectivity," is inhospitable (or deaf) to religious interests. In this sense, Bultmann shares the antipathy to naturalism generally prevalent

---

[4] See *FE*, 289–291. One formulation of Post's is worth quoting: "There is a more innocent way of expressing a realist notion of truth: Φ is true iff the things Φ is about are the way Φ says they are. Yet even here trouble lurks, since the phrase '*the* way' appears to imply monopoly, and one might be tempted to conclude that realism can only be monopolistic. But this would misconstrue the role of 'the way' in this sort of truth-schema. The point is not that there is one and only one way the things can be, and Φ says they are that way. Instead, Φ says the things are a certain way, and that way is indeed one of the ways they are. Thus even though caution is required in order to formulate realism nonmonopolistically, it can be done. There is no need to go to antirealist extremes simply in order to get subjectivity back into the scheme of things entire, or to reinject the significance of time, conscience, death, and more." Objectivity is solely a logical prerequisite of truth that is objective, of "truth *period* – of what there *objectively* is. . . What [it does] *not* do, unlike its monopolistic interpretations, is make objectivity the measure of truth and reality in *other* senses as well – in the sense, say, of truth from a point of view, or of what there relatively is . . . Nor are we compelled to say that of all the members of the family, propositional truth and objective reality are unconditionally prior to others, that they are the patriarchs from which all the others are descended and by which they are 'grounded.' The relations among the members are much more complex than that" (*FE*, 290–291, Post's emphasis).

in the theological community. The burden of this book is to show that this view is mistaken, or at least unnecessary.

These points will become clearer as we proceed. For the present, let us leave Bultmann's criticisms aside and examine what can be made of an existentialist method when it is construed naturalistically. I emphasize that this appropriation of existentialist interpretation hinges on the possibility of viewing faith and its content *entirely* in terms of structures of existence. "God-terms," therefore, must derive their meaning solely from terminations in existence. Though my approach coheres verbally with Bultmann's own claim that de-mythologizing and existentialist interpretation be "exhaustive,"[5] it is not obvious that he would accept my reduction of faith's content entirely to modes of existing. Consequently this first bridge to a naturalistic theology will require an analysis of the existentialist method showing why it may be interpreted as I am proposing. As we shall see, the fundamental question concerns how the *understanding* involved in the notion of an existential self-understanding is itself to be understood. It is precisely on this issue that Bultmann's thought vacillates. The analysis to follow will show that his position can be construed in line with the approach to religion defended here.

Before we take up these challenges we must address another preliminary question. This concerns the dependence of an existentialist method on the philosophy of Martin Heidegger. The question is whether Heidegger's fundamental ontology is even remotely compatible with a physicalist naturalism. Is not Heidegger's attempt to uncover the meaning of being inherently opposed to any naturalist metaphysics?

NATURALISM AND THE ANALYSIS OF EXISTENCE: CAN HEIDEGGER BE A NATURALIST?

Being and Time is the crucial text for our purposes. Insisting on the unclarity of the question of being in the philosophical tradition, Heidegger argues that clarification requires a fundamental ontology. By this he means an analysis of human being, termed *Dasein*, the being who can raise the question of being. The very nature of Dasein is that *in its being* it has a relationship to its being which is constituted as an understanding (or *understandingly*). My being is not an object which I understand by first confronting various entities (including

---

[5] See NTM, 21–22, 26–27 (ET, 8–9, 14–15).

myself) as an apprehending subject. Rather, I myself am this being, and my understanding is given with being it. Furthermore, I am not first this being who then confronts a world of other entities; rather, I am always already in a world, a being-in-the-world, so that an understanding of this world is co-constitutive with my own self-understanding.

From this basic move, richly elaborated in *Being and Time*, much of Heidegger's and Bultmann's criticism of objectivity originates. The "distancing" stance involved in objectivity, as they construe it, fails to capture the self relation of Dasein to its own being which is basic for understanding its being, and it fails to grasp the primary way in which the world is co-present with this understanding prior to any objectification. Indeed, objectivity is a derivative, and in a sense, deficient mode that can arise only on the basis of this prior relation. *Being and Time* consists to a large degree of a series of elaborate analyses describing Dasein's structure and showing the misconceptions that result from taking a merely "objective" approach either to Dasein or to the being of entities that constitute its "world." Or, perhaps more accurately, Heidegger demonstrates again and again the presumptive character of such "objectivism" that neglects its own background which is grounded in Dasein's world orientation.[6]

This fundamental ontology in *Being and Time* is intended to make possible a general ontology. But, as is well known, *Being and Time* was never completed. Its fundamental ontology remained a fragment of the general ontology it promised, and there is much controversy over whether Heidegger's remaining writings ought to be viewed as the completion or the revision of that project. It is undoubtedly true that however the later work is taken its emphases are profoundly different from what *Being and Time* seems to promise.

Two conclusions can be drawn from this indeterminate standing of *Being and Time*. The first is that the phenomenology of Dasein's being is a major achievement in its own right whatever Heidegger came to think of it and however his later thought is to be assessed as a contribution to ontology. The second is that it remains unclear what conclusions ought to be drawn from it for a general ontology. The

---

[6] In his excellent commentary on the first part of *Being and Time*, Hubert Dreyfus interprets Heidegger as articulating a non-mentalistic form of intentionality which Dreyfus describes in terms of "'mindless' coping skills as the basis of all intelligibility" (Dreyfus [1991], 3 [cf. 12–16, 45–59]). In a footnote discussing Husserl, Heidegger says: ". . . the intentionality of 'consciousness' is *grounded* in the ecstatical unity of Dasein . . ." (*SZ*, 363, n. 1 [ET, 498, n. xxiii]).

question is whether the conception of Dasein's being in *Being and Time* is compatible with a physicalist naturalism. I believe that it is.

Applied to the analysis of human existence, Heidegger's critique of objectivity serves to deny that Dasein's being can be approached objectively. To take something objectively in this sense is to take it as an entity with properties that can be described by a neutral observer. Even when I observe my own properties, my observation is neutral with respect to me; the properties are available in principle to any suitably competent observer. Obviously I have many properties that are objective in this sense, and Heidegger does not deny this. His point is that when it comes to my being, what it is that I am, this approach is crucially deficient. It fails to recognize that my being, the "what" or the "who" that I am, is such that it is I who am at stake in it. Unlike an object, I cannot be indifferent to my being as I exist. I cannot stand over against it or be a spectator of it. Unlike objective properties, my being is in question and can only be laid hold of by the action that I take toward it – as though I am constantly trying to catch up with myself. This is not merely an interesting fact about me but characterizes my very being. Heidegger expresses this by characterizing Dasein as "existence" (*Existenz*). Dasein's being is constituted by its possibilities – but not as properties attached to a subject whose being might be characterized otherwise: "The 'essence' of this entity lies in its 'to be' ... *The essence of Dasein lies in its existence.* Accordingly those characteristics which can be exhibited in this entity are not 'properties' present-at-hand; they are in each case possible ways for it to be, and no more than that... In each case Dasein *is* its possibility, and it 'has' this possibility, but not just as a property, as something present at hand would" (*SZ*, 42 [67–68], Heidegger's emphasis).[7] It follows that my being is always my own (*je meines*), never an instance or exemplar of a species of properties; my being is such that I can, indeed must, win or lose myself. Furthermore, I am never anything other than this; I am *always* my possibilities, so that I am always confronted with the choice of myself. From this basic structure of Existence and the opposition to objectivity implicit in it, the entire analytic of Dasein then follows.

The basic argument is that *this* opposition to objectivity does not preclude a physicalist ontology. The point here is parallel to the earlier argument that physicalism is compatible with irreducibly subjective states. Heidegger is basically arguing that *it is like something*

---

[7] In the original, the last sentence reads: "*Dasein* ist *je seine Möglichkeit und es 'hat' sie nicht nur noch eigenschaftlich als ein Vorhandenes*" (see *SZ*, 12, Heidegger's emphasis [ET, 32–33]).

to be a human being. Dasein can be characterized ontologically only by an account of what it is like to be it. As we saw earlier in the discussion of Nagel, there is nothing in this claim precluding the parallel claim that facts about what it is like to be Dasein are determined by facts at the level of physics. Such facts about what it is like to be Dasein are, for instance, that "Dasein is an entity for which, in its being, that being is an issue" such that it is "an entity whose being must be defined as 'care'" and such that "care" is ultimately structured by the possibility of one's death which, in turn, is the overarching possibility that defines one's existence as possibility as a whole (*SZ*, 191, 193, 249–252 [236, 238, 293–296]). To be compatible with a nonreductive physicalism, such an account requires only that there be a fact of the matter about what it is like to be Dasein, and far from negating this claim, Heidegger's position would seem to require it.[8]

No reduction is implicit in this interpretation of Heidegger (see *FE*, 244–250). Physicalism is compatible with discourses that can never be reduced to or need be stated in parallel vocabularies from physics or other natural sciences. In this sense, Heidegger's claims about the necessity of a special discourse required to articulate what it is like *to be*[9] a person simply does not settle questions about ultimate ontological inventory status. In fact, any claim to the contrary that Heidegger's analysis of Dasein by itself could settle questions of general ontology would overstep the bounds of what is, strictly speaking, only a phenomenology of the being of Dasein. Phenomenology involves description of the phenomena of experience. In Heidegger's phenomenological ontology it involves description of the appearances of Dasein's being in Dasein's existing (that is, in Dasein's being it, in Dasein's *"to be"* [*sein*]). It would simply be a mistake to use

---

[8] By "fact of the matter" I simply mean what Heidegger means by "existence" (*Existenz*). Since what is at issue is not an abstraction or objectification about Dasein but its "be-ing" (its existing) one way rather than another in the concrete here and now, it is appropriate to say that "there is a fact of the matter" about what it *is* as existing. Heidegger and the Heideggarians may think that the self-relation co-constitutive of the being of Dasein rules this out. But the point is identical with the one we examined earlier from Nagel about irretrievably subjective points of view. Even if Dasein is inherently nonobjective, its nonobjective existing is still a fact of the matter about what it is like to be it, and, as we saw with Nagel, that there is such a fact of the matter and what it is like to be it is compatible with being determined by basic physical entities. No reduction is required. For just this reason, Heidegger's critique of the priority supposedly accorded "presence-at-hand" by naturalism is beside the point. This issue has to do with a priority accorded to expressibility and/or explanation. We saw that denying such priority does not touch the issue in which there is still a fact of the matter in question.

[9] Significantly, German uses the same word for both the noun and the infinitive of being, *das Sein* and *sein*, a parallel important for Heidegger's point about the "being" (the "to be") of Dasein but impossible to capture in English.

description of this sort to warrant claims about what is real, and this move is explicitly prohibited by the phenomenological *epoche* in any case. It would be a mistake, for instance, to think that such description could settle the mind-body problem, or determine whether ultimate metaphysical unifiers require nonphysical entities, or that the ultimate unifiers are concrete particulars or not. Heidegger's phenomenology in *Being and Time* requires him to remain strictly neutral on these basic metaphysical questions.

The analytic of Dasein appears, therefore, to be compatible with the kind of physicalism defended by Post.[10] Husserl's phenomenology was restricted to appearances to a spectator consciousness. Heidegger pushed phenomenology toward ontology by showing at a deeper level that we cannot be spectators of our own existing. By moving phenomenology behind "consciousness" to "existing," he provided an enormously powerful analysis of the structures by which we orient our being in the world. But what it is like to be the beings we are as described by this phenomenology is nevertheless consistent *both* with inexpressibility in any physical vocabulary *and* with being determined by facts at the level of physics. This account provides the basis for Bultmann's theological method. Let us turn, therefore, to Bultmann's theology to see how his existentialist interpretation is also compatible with naturalism.

DEMYTHOLOGIZING AND EXISTENTIALIST INTERPRETATION

An existentialist conception of faith is attractive for a naturalist theology because articulating faith by modes of existence avoids both mythology and the subject-predicate literalism of theism. Bultmann's analysis of the biblical witness gives this approach plausibility because he effectively shows that the witness's underlying intent is to express an existential self-understanding. The standard criticism of this method from both the "right" and the "left"[11] objects that an

---

[10] This position is also compatible with Bultmann's claims about the "right" philosophy for purposes of theology. By this he simply means a philosophy that articulates the nature of human being as Existence, namely, as pertaining to a being for whom its own existence is at issue (see ZPE, ET, 105–110 [191–195]). For Post's discussion of Heidegger, cf. *FE*, 288–293.

[11] By the "right" I mean the conservative reaction to the demythologizing proposal of which Barth is probably the most notable example. This response usually insists on preserving the "surface" of biblical mythology in combination with some form of classical theism (cf. Barth). By the "left," I mean the position that accepts Bultmann's proposal but insists on some "objective," theistic ground of self-understanding in the form of a revisionary theism. This option is developed most fully by Schubert Ogden (see, for instance, *CM*, 95–111; *RG*, 84–90, 158–161).

exhaustive existentialist interpretation will reduce faith to a simple human possibility.

This criticism can be interpreted in different ways. One is that the method roots faith in mere human possibility rather than in God's grace. We shall see that Bultmann effectively addresses this concern, and we shall share his position. A more powerful interpretation concerns the question of "God-terms," for, so this criticism goes, an existentialist method must convert statements about God into nothing more than statements about human existence, expressive of nothing more than certain possibilities of existential self-understanding (cf., *RG*, 159). This criticism does apply to noncognitivist strategies, all of which bear some similarity to the method of existentialist interpretation. It is not so evident, however, that it applies here. The present position has a stake in conceiving the content of faith entirely in terms of modes of existence. But neither "God-terms" nor the seeing-as through which these existential modes are expressed are noncognitive or "non-objective" in any straightforward sense. To see this, we must examine what kind of *understanding* is involved in an existential self-*understanding*. I want to show that an existential self-understanding should be interpreted entirely as a mode of existence, but I shall argue that its "understanding of God" can have "God-terms" that are cognitive yet not "objectively" metaphysical. To make this case, we must carefully examine Bultmann's position.

Bultmann's demythologizing proposal entails a twofold method-ological claim: (1) that the underlying meaning of all religiousness is existential; and (2) that theology's content should itself be entirely existential. Theology's task is the interpretation of faith, and faith is nothing other than an existential self-understanding. This implies that the content of faith contains nothing that does not belong to our present experience and ways of being in the world. Articulating this method through the analysis of mythology in his programmatic essay, "New Testament and Mythology," Bultmann says that "the real meaning of myth does not present an objective world picture but instead expresses how man understands himself in his world," and he concludes that "myth does not want to be interpreted in cosmological but in anthropological terms – or better, in existentialist terms" (NTM, 22 [ET, 9]). These statements require careful attention because they are commonly construed in a fashion different from what they seem to say.

Bultmann conceives the existential "understanding" by which we "understand ourselves in the world" in terms of Heidegger's analysis of Dasein's being-in-the-world, and he carefully states that this is an understanding of ourselves *in* the world, nothing more. In contrast, some thinkers such as Ogden and Macquarrie take him to be saying that myth expresses our understanding of ourselves *and* the world (*and*, by implication, God).[12] This reading leads them simply to replace myth with some more adequate version of *metaphysical* theism suitably informed by existentialist insights about human existence. Why is there a problem here?

Apart from the fact that Bultmann does not says this, the problem lies with the way it forces us to construe his criticism of myth. Bultmann criticizes myth for distorting faith. It takes the content of faith to be "objective" states of affairs that are in principle independent of any present experience, and for Bultmann, no such objective content *in any form* can represent the content of faith. The contrasting interpretation takes him to be saying that the real content of myth expresses our understanding of ourselves *and* the world *and* God. This makes his criticism of myth equivalent to criticizing it for its inadequate metaphysics in favor of a more adequate objective metaphysics. This reading seems an implausible way to construe Bultmann's alternative to mythology, given his commitment to conceive faith entirely existentially. This much, I think, is clear.[13] But it is admittedly difficult to determine precisely how references to God can be contained by and limited to existential modes of being. There are problems with any reading of Bultmann's position. Further analysis will make these difficulties apparent.

Bultmann specifies "the real intent [*Sinn*] of myth" by three features, each of which fails adequately to express "how man understands himself in his world." Myth, first, involves an awareness of transcendence. It expresses an existential awareness that the familiar daily world is limited by powers that lie beyond it: "Myth talks about the power or the powers that we think we experience as the ground and limit of our world and of our own action and passion . . . What is expressed in myth is the faith that the familiar and disposable world in which we live does not have its ground and aim in itself but that its ground and limit lie beyond all that is familiar and

---

[12] See *RG*, 209, and Macquarrie (1955), 70–81, 172–184, 241–243; Macquarrie (1960) 127, 240–242.

[13] As I shall argue in the following, an exhaustively existentialist interpretation is also supported: (1) by Bultmann's interpretation of biblical symbols, (2) by his criticisms of theologically false "objectifications," and (3) by his treatment of "God" references throughout his theology.

disposable and that this is all constantly threatened and controlled by the uncanny powers that are its ground and limit" (NTM, ET, 9–10 [22]). Second, myth expresses our awareness that we are not masters of ourselves or our lives, that we are dependent not only on powers within the familiar world "but that we are especially dependent on the powers that hold sway beyond all that is familiar" (NTM, ET, 10 [22–23]). Finally, it expresses the confidence that through this latter dependence "we can become free from the familiar powers" (NTM, ET, 10 [23]). The problem in each case is that myth inappropriately objectifies the transcendent reality that it intends to express, treating the ground and limit of the world as though it were a disposable object within the world.[14]

The question is how "transcendence" qualifies the existential content of faith. Bultmann concludes this discussion by saying that myth itself contains the motive for criticizing its objective images [*Vorstellungen*], for "its real intent to speak of a power beyond [*von einer jenseitigen Macht*] to which both we and the world are subject is hampered and obscured by the objectifying character of its statements." He then immediately continues: "Hence the New Testament mythology should not be interrogated as to the objectifying content of its images but with respect to the understanding of existence that expresses itself in these images. What is at stake is the truth of this understanding of existence. This is the truth affirmed by faith so that it need not be bound by the New Testament's world of images" (NTM, 23, [ET, 10]). Bultmann's point here is clearly the central issue. But how is it obvious that the real intent "to speak of a transcendent power [*von einer jenseitigen Macht*] . . ." can be *appropriately* identified with the expression of "an understanding of existence," with "how man understands himself in his world"? Why is "transcendent power"

14 This is far from a complete presentation of Bultmann's characterization of myth, but the issue of objectivity is central throughout. Ogden's superb analysis shows that the full conception contains three features: (1) an inadequate objectification of the nonobjective reality experienced as the ground and limit of our existence; (2) an etiological function explaining both the origin and goal of the world and of unusual phenomena within it, but again by speaking of this "beyond" as though it were a part of the world – also a problem with objectification; and (3) a narrative form which amounts to a history of the gods, again, derivatively, a form of objectivity. I am also assuming Bultmann's arguments for why this mythological world picture is unacceptable for modernity. These reasons are basically of two sorts: myth conflicts, one, with the world picture implicit in modern science, a closed and lawfully regulated unity, which forms the deep background of all modern conceptions of the world and, two, with the modern person's self-understanding "as a unified being" who "attributes his experience, thought, and volition to his own agency, not to divine or demonic causes" (*CM*, 35; see 24–27 and 31–37).

appropriate here but not in mythology? The immediate answer is that myth inappropriately objectifies this power. This response has two problems.

Bultmann's strongest articulation of the issue is to say that *"myth objectifies the beyond as part of the world . . . [der Mythos objektiviert das Jenseits zum Diesseits]"* (ZPE, 184, Bultmann's emphasis [ET, 99]). Or again: "Mythology is a form of representation in which the unworldly and divine [*das Unweltliche, Göttliche*] appears as worldly and human, or the beyond appears as worldly [*das Jenseitige als Diesseitiges*] . . ." (NTM, 22, n. 2 [ET, 42]). The problem with these formulations is to imagine how any speaking of God could be otherwise. This problem is not unique to mythology but is simply the classical problem of analogical predication, which recognizes that any predicates applied to God must be drawn from this world and therefore qualified. Or, if it is formulated in Bultmann's language of "ground and limit," then it is simply the Kantian problem of applying phenomenal categories to a world beyond experience, a problem not solvable on Kantian terms. If this is what is objectionable in mythological expressions, it is difficult to see how "an understanding of existence" could make any improvement.

Even if we could solve this problem, it is difficult to see how the solution would be identical with "man's understanding of himself in the world in which he lives." How does an existential self-understanding *properly* include reference to a "beyond" that is improperly expressed in mythology (and, we should also add, improperly expressed in the entire objectivistic theological tradition)? Here the question is not, as in the former, how an understanding of existence can solve the problem of reference "beyond" the world, but why we should think an existential self-understanding should include such reference at all.

These problems make clear that there are cross-currents in Bultmann's basic notions of *existential self-understanding* and *objectivity* which make it difficult to understand the full dimensions of his theological method. Let us examine the cross-currents associated with each of these notions.

(1) According to Bultmann, faith is a mode of existing (an existential self-understanding) the theological content of which may be understood entirely as a matter of the present experience of the believer. Faith is, in Heidegger's terms, authentic human existence, and the language of faith, both mythological and theological,[15] is to

---

[15] Mythological speech is, of course, itself a theological interpretation of faith.

be interpreted entirely in terms of the existential modes of being which constitute authentic existence and its opposite. Most of Bultmann's actual interpretations adhere to this conception of theology.[16] They show how faith is exhausted by its existential content. The first cross-current, as we have seen, is that "man's understanding of himself in his world," an existential self-understanding articulated by a description of modes of being, includes a reference to transcendence. How is this so? The following is an interpretation that adheres strictly to Bultmann's existentialist method. Taking my "understanding of myself in my world," first entirely formally – that is, apart from any *existentiell* modes by which it is actually realized – my self-understanding is a concernful attempt to actualize my life within the practical world of my everyday dealings and in view of my existential awareness, however inchoate, that I live but once and then no more for all eternity.[17] My *existentiell* understanding of myself involves, in this sense, a kind of ultimacy and transcendence. I not only raise and give answers to final or ultimate questions about the meaning of my life, I also respond in terms of the world in which I realize my destiny, for instance, in terms of my confidence that the world supports my projects or, perhaps, in terms of resentment or bitterness at the hand destiny has dealt me. This understanding is entirely *existentiell*; at this level it can be interpreted entirely in terms of ways that I exist. In this sense, my *existentiell* self-understanding is an *understanding* of both myself and my world. Or stated more accurately in terms of Heidegger's analysis of being-in-the-world, my understanding of myself always already includes a "world-structure" in which I and my projects are disclosed and brought to focus by my "care",[18] and this "world-structure" is the "transcendence" basis for my self-understanding. At a material level, the actual *existentiell* realizations of my existence moment by moment are an answer I give to these issues of ultimacy, and they may be interpreted in terms of Heidegger's two formal possibilities of authenticity and inauthenticity.

"Transcendence" and "ultimacy" here correlate strictly with the idea that the "understanding" in an existential self-understanding occurs entirely in our "ex-ist-ing." The problem is whether this interpretation accords with Bultmann's apparent claim that this self-understanding includes an understanding of a "ground and limit" of my world that somehow, and in principle, lie "beyond" it. It would seem that I could only construe it in this way by stepping

---

[16] Even Ogden acknowledges as much. See *CM*, 56–64 and NTM, 17–22 (ET, 15–20).
[17] See Reiman (1989), 43–49.   [18] See *SZ*, 72–76 (102–107), 191–196 (235–241).

beyond the understanding that is strictly given with "my *existentiell* understanding of myself in my world." It might be claimed that this is exactly what Bultmann is doing and, moreover, that he is entitled to do so. He is giving a theological *interpretation* of what is *implicit* in the *existentiell* self-understanding. But this is what mythology does also. This interpretation would, therefore, take us back to the idea that the real issue involved in mythology is simply adequate versus inadequate ways of speaking about ground and limit, not, as seems Bultmann's deepest intention, with the contrast between mythology and "expression of existential self-understanding." To make this move, we must step beyond a self-understanding and provide interpretations of something not strictly given in it as such. As soon as we do this, we are doing something more than presenting the existential understanding we have of ourselves in our world. We then also run into the question concerning how any such interpretation can avoid the objectivity which occasioned the problem with mythology to start with. So, this cross-current in the notion of an existential self-understanding brings us back to Bultmann's criticism of objectivity.

(2) With objectivity we can again identify two cross-currents. One is myth's inappropriate objectivity. It speaks of a transcendent power "beyond" the world in objective statements that represent it as another part of the world. The second is connected with the notion of an existential self-understanding. It claims that treating such an understanding "objectively" will fail to capture the self-relation (the *Jemeinigkeit*) of existence. Broadly speaking, this criticism has the force of criticizing objectivity for its detachment. In this sense, a theological statement can be criticized if it fails to capture the existential involvement of faith, and, in contrast, an adequate theological statement must reflect this involvement. The *true* intent of myth is to express this kind of existential involvement. Heidegger's distinction between "categories" and "existentials" makes it possible to articulate an existential self-understanding so as to capture this "self-involving" feature,[19] and Bultmann takes over this procedure exactly on Heidegger's terms.[20]

[19] See *SZ*, 44 (70). Heidegger says here: "All *explicata* to which the analytic of Dasein gives rise are obtained by considering Dasein's existence-structure. Because Dasein's characters of Being are defined in terms of existentiality, we call them '*existentialia*.' These are to be sharply distinguished from what we call '*categories*' – characteristics of Being for entities whose character is not that of Dasein" (Heidegger's emphases). The notion of a "self-involving" language is from Evans. Evans's analysis is quite different from the existentialism of Heidegger and Bultmann, but the phrase "self-involving language" is a happy one for capturing what is also at stake in their work, and a great deal of Evans's contribution could easily be transferred into the idiom of existentialist analysis.   [20] See HMF, 92ff.

This latter problem of objectivity accounts for Bultmann's reluctance to make direct statements about God. He insists that we can speak of God only by speaking of faith, that is, of the modes of existence involved in the self-understanding of faith. Such reluctance lies behind his notorious statement that because for Paul "every assertion about God is simultaneously an assertion about man and vice versa," his theology "is, at the same time, anthropology."[21] Other instances of this reluctance could be multiplied,[22] and of course, it is this approach to God language that lends support to the attempt here to interpret the self-understanding of faith entirely existentially. But, as we now can see, the cross-currents in his position make it difficult to give an unambiguous interpretation on this issue.

Let us now examine how these two meanings of objectivity are related. This issue is but another version of the earlier one about how inappropriate reference to transcendence in mythology justifies thinking that a legitimate reference is all at once included in the notion of an existential self-understanding. We might claim that the problem with mythology is its objective form. Its form becomes particularly troublesome with the rise of a scientific view of the world, because, expressing its intention in objective terms drawn from inner-worldly phenomena, myth appears linguistically similar to scientific statements and therefore cannot avoid scientific criticism that makes it increasingly implausible. We might then argue that the real intent of myth is existential and proceed to interpret it, as I am proposing, through existential modes of being. By so doing we would be giving a perfectly coherent rendering of the claim that the real intent of myth is to express "man's understanding of himself in his world." Such a method could lay powerful claim to being the appropriate approach to myth because it could render the issues of ultimacy implicit in myth, but entirely in existentialist terms, as suggested above. It would also be consistent with almost all of Bultmann's actual practice. It would thus unify the two different issues we have examined with objectivity. The first meaning would provide the grounds for the criticism of myth. The second, the detachment problem, is already incorporated in the existentialist understanding of faith and myth, for as Bultmann says: "existentialist analysis points so to speak beyond itself, by showing . . . that an

---

[21] Bultmann (1951), I, 191.
[22] See, for instance, the powerful statement of this position that does not include the ambiguous "vice versa" in ZPE, 198 (ET, 113), and note the entire discussion that accompanies it, ZPE, 197–202 (ET, 111–117).

existentiell self-understanding occurs only in an *existentiell* enactment that is my very own [*sich nur als je meines im existentiellen Vollzuge ereignet*]" (ZPE, 201 [ET, 116]).

The problem with this reading is that for Bultmann, myth's *intent* to refer to transcendence should not be eliminated (though its false objectivity should), and this makes it difficult coherently to connect the two meanings of improper objectivity. If the first meaning says that the problem of myth lies in improperly speaking of the ground and limit of our being (a conception that is already metaphysically loaded), it is difficult to see why speaking of existential modes of being is a solution *to this problem*. Even if we could answer this question, we are still left to ask why, given the general and "objective" character of any reference to "the beyond," existentialist categories provide a solution.

The conclusion to be drawn from this analysis can be stated directly. The tensions in Bultmann's conception both of self-understanding and objectivity arise from his attempt to include a reference to transcendence directly in the real intent of myth. As soon as he does this, he steps beyond an existential self-understanding and makes a claim about what is *implicit*, at one step removed, in the real intent of myth conceived as an understanding of existence. He wants to claim two things: (a) that the real intent of myth is to express an understanding of existence in the world *and* (b) that it seeks to express dependence on a "beyond" that is the ground and limit of the world. But he can combine these only by stepping outside what is strictly given in an intent to express an understanding of myself in my world. I am questioning the legitimacy of this step beyond a strictly existentialist method. It falls outside what can fairly be claimed if the real intent of myth is existential. It is, if you will, an interpretation of the real intent of myth in *metaphysical*, not existentialist, terms, and it would have to be supported by independent metaphysical arguments that could not be drawn directly from an existentialist analysis. If, for example, one wanted not merely to describe myth's real intent but to claim, as Bultmann does, that its intent contains *truth* that can be preserved by an existentialist analysis, one would have to show (1) that such metaphysical references were implicit in an understanding of existence (in this sense already going beyond existentialist analysis alone) and also (2) that such notions as "the beyond" or "ground and limit" are themselves coherent, metaphysically adequate, and expressible in our language.

The difficulty is caused by Bultmann's attempt to combine two, not one, expressions of the real intent in myth. This is a serious problem because it obscures the cogency of the move to an existentialist method. In addition, as we now see, it occasions two problems: (1) how any reference to a transcendent reality is possible at all (given the terms of his criticism of myth) and (2) why an existentialist analytic should give more adequate grounds for including it.

Bultmann, of course, resisted all efforts to interpret his proposal as though it eliminated "God" or was a reduction to human subjectivity alone, and I emphasize that the present position must also avoid these charges. Bultmann himself was clearly a "classical" theist in some sense, never surrendering belief in an "objectively" existent God who is "absolute," strictly transcendent, and the ground and limit of the world. At the same time, as a Lutheran, he was so deeply committed to the radical implications of justification by faith that he was reluctant ever to separate any speaking of God from faith itself. Hence, his work suffers from the cross-currents we have examined and from the ambiguous status of "God" throughout his theology.

Bultmann's most explicit attempt to address these issues occurs in the longest of his rejoinders to his critics.[23] There he responds to the critical question whether the notion of an act of God is mythological in principle, and he makes a nascent attempt to develop a doctrine of analogy. He acknowledges that the primary fear about demythologizing is that existentialist interpretation "would make it impossible to talk about the act of God or that it would allow such talk only as a pictorial way of designating subjective experiences." He then asks: "For is it not mythology to talk about the act of God as an objective occurrence that encounters me?" (ZPE, 110 [ET, 196]). Elsewhere he categorically denies that the Christian confession is mythological as such. The non-believing critic who makes this charge, using "myth" in a looser sense, is ignoring that a demythologized gospel is not made "easier" but is as much "scandal" as ever.[24] In the response to his critics, he answers the rhetorical question about an act of God, by asserting that "if *talk about an act of God* is truly to be meaningful, *it cannot be pictorial, 'symbolic' speech* but must intend an act in the fully real and 'objective' sense" (ZPE, 196, Bultmann's emphasis, [ET, 110]). However, he

---

[23] ZPE, is the original of this essay. A translation of its second half appeared as "Bultmann Replies to His Critics" in Bultmann, *et al* (1961a). Unaccountably, this translation fails to include the first half of the original which contains his longest discussion of the problem of objectivity. The full essay in an improved translation by Schubert Ogden appears as Bultmann 1952c.   [24] Bultmann (1948b), 123–124 (104).

immediately qualifies this statement in his characteristic fashion: "If
. . . God's act may not be understood as a phenomenon in the world
that I can perceive apart from being existentially affected by it [*abgesehen
von der existentiellen Betroffenheit von ihm*], then it can be spoken of only by
talking about myself at the same time as the one affected by it. *To talk
about God's act means to talk at the same time of my own existence*" (ZPE, 196,
Bultmann's emphasis, [ET, 110]).

This *existentiell* encounter with God's action leads Bultmann to
introduce a concept of analogy. He proceeds: "Since human life is a
life in space and time, the encounter with God for human beings can
only be an event that takes place in a specific here and now. Such an
event of being addressed, questioned, judged, and blessed by God
here and now is what is meant by speech about an act of God.
Therefore, to speak of God's act is not a pictorial, symbolic manner of
speaking but for all that is *analogical* speech. For in such speaking, we
represent God's action as analogous to human action, and we
represent the communion between God and human beings as
analogous to our communion with one another" (ZPE, 197, Bultmann's
emphasis, [ET, 110–111]). He expands this solely by contrasting
God's action with the mythological notion of miracle. Portraying
God's action as one that "invades the continuum of natural,
historical, or psychic life and disrupts it," miracle "*objectifies the divine
action and projects it onto the plane of worldly occurrences.*" The transcendence
[*der Jenseitigkeit*] and non-worldly character of divine action can only
be preserved if such action is visible to the eye of faith alone and
therefore only "if such action is represented not as something that
takes place *between* worldly occurrences, but as something that is
actualized *in* them, so that the closed continuum of worldly events
that offers itself to objectifying view remains inviolate" (ZPE, 197,
first emphasis mine; [ET, 111]).

In the remainder of this essay, Bultmann responds to the charge
that his method eliminates God by reducing God's action to
representations of subjective experience. Twice he insists that though
we can speak of God only from the vantage of faith (an *existentiell*
encounter with God), it does not follow that God is not independent
of the believing act.[25] But he develops no further the implications of a

[25] ". . . it follows not at all that God is not real apart (*ausserhalb*) from the believer [*des
Glaubenden*] or the act of faith [*des Glaubensaktes*]" (ZPE, 198–199 [ET, 113]). "That God is
not visible outside of faith does not mean that God is not real outside of faith" (ZPE, 114 [ET,
199]).

kind of speaking that might capture this independence of God. Instead, he emphasizes how an existentialist conception of faith neither reduces faith to an idea nor subjectivizes it to "consciousness" or intra-psychic processes. To the extent that the concept of analogy is implicit in these discussions, it is not used to develop analogical ways of speaking about God but to show how other existential processes (such as experiences of loving and being loved) also arise out of real events of trans-subjective experience and are misunderstood if interpreted as "intra-psychic." An encounter with God, too, may be conceived analogously as real (i.e., trans-subjective) but not objective (and thus "worldly" in *this* sense).

These efforts to address the problem of God do not really remove the tensions analyzed above. On the one hand, by "God," Bultmann unquestionably means the absolute, personal ground and source of all being intended by the tradition. But he fails to show why any speaking about this reality would not fall prey to the same problem of "objectivity" for which he criticizes myth. He also fails to show why an existentialist notion of faith conforms to this conception of God's independent reality or why such a notion would somehow permit speaking properly about God. On the other hand, the existential character of faith does permit him to claim that we cannot speak about God apart from faith, but now the emphasis is on the type of concern that faith involves – an *existentiell* decision in which through encounters with my world, I take up ultimate issues of authentic or inauthentic modes of existing. God is encountered only in this way and, thus, it is appropriate to speak of God's actions only in connection with such *existentiell* decisions. This still fails, however, to show why I have to do here with something transcendent in the *metaphysical* sense Bultmann seems to require. If this could be shown, it would then fail to show why I could not speak of this reality independently of the *existentiell* decisions in which I encounter it.

These problems have led Schubert Ogden to develop Bultmann's concept of analogy in an explicitly metaphysical direction that seems consistent with Bultmann's position (and perhaps with his intentions). Ogden exploits Heidegger's distinction between two types of understanding appropriate for an analytic of Dasein. One is an *existentiell* understanding realized in Dasein's actual existing, or, in the language I have been employing, realized in and as modes of existing actualized by the decisions in which I take upon myself the task of "ex-ist-ing" who I am. Such an understanding is properly "non-objective" since it cannot be detached from the moment by moment acts and decisions of being it, and it is this type of understanding realized in faith *as lived* that Bultmann terms an existential self-understanding. But Ogden defends another kind of understanding, an *existential* one, that is "objective" yet appropriate to a formal analysis of the *structures* of existence that are realized in acts of *existentiell* self-understanding. Heidegger's entire analysis in *Being and Time* depends on this kind of distinction.[26]

To call an existentialist analytic "objective" obviously introduces a new level of complexity, but the meaning is actually quite intelligible. Generally speaking, something is objective when it falls within the subject-object correlation of theoretical cognition. It is treated as an "object" in the world which can be viewed independently of any personal involvement by the spectator; in this sense it is "there" for any neutral observer, and statements about it can be assessed by any qualified person. Though the notion is general, scientific method is the ideal model for this kind of cognitive relation, and we appropriately speak of scientific objectivity. Mythological language is objective in this sense because it treats its subject matter as an object in the world that could be grasped in this neutral or detached manner. For the same reason, it becomes unbelievable with the rise of modern science because this manner of speaking comes to be dominated by scientific assessment and criticism.

A second, yet related, meaning of objectivity is necessary once we undertake an existentialist analytic. We recall that it describes the being of an entity whose understanding of its being is given with being it. Because of this self-relation, a self-relation defined by care (*Sorge*) that is always just my own (*Jemeinigkeit*), this being is not like an "object" and no independent neutrality is possible toward it *in its*

---

[26] Karl Jaspers and Fritz Buri reject this distinction, claiming that it is impossible to speak of *Existenz* in the formal categories of an ontology. This sharply distinguishes their work from Heidegger and Bultmann. But their rejection of this approach results in the extreme emptiness of their specifications of existential acts. Ironically, in each of them, it results in a far more extreme air of formality, of material emptiness, than is to be found in Heidegger or Bultmann. It often appears that conceptual, or linguistic, or "objective" articulation for them can serve only as an indirect language which creates a kind of clarification or "clearing" in which the call for an existential act can be heard – an appeal, if you will, from *Existenz* to *Existenz*. The result is that they speak repeatedly of the realization of personal existence by acts of responsible decision (*existentiell* acts in Bultmann's sense), but they are incapable of specifying the content of such acts.

being qua realization. Now, however, the distinction between *existentiell* and *existential* understandings comes into play, for though this being is always realized *existentiell* as just my own, an altogether general and neutral conception of its structures is possible. These structures are not themselves *existentiell* realizations but are the general formal elements which account both for its difference from "objects" in the world and for its *existentiell* realizations. It is necessary, then, to say that the epistemological form of an *existentialist* analytic is "objective" (in this second sense).

The potential for confusion arises because the first sense of "objective" is a way of speaking about objects in the world. We are tempted to say that an existentialist analytic is "non-objective" because its subject matter is inherently different from such objects, as indeed it is. But an existentialist analytic is "objective" in the second sense. There is no confusion because the second meaning is identical in form to the first, and this formal identity justifies calling it objective. Just as with scientific objectivity, its results are detached and neutral *vis à vis* any particular *existentiell* actualization, and they are open to rational assessment and criticism by neutral parties.[27] What must be recognized is simply the unique ontological character to which this "objectifying" analysis is applied, a uniqueness that requires a different set of categories to describe it, categories that are, nonetheless, epistemologically objective.[28]

Bultmann clearly understands the significance of the distinction between *existentiell* and *existential* types of understanding.[29] Ogden is therefore justified to exploit this distinction as a way to clarify Bultmann's inchoate remarks about analogical predication. Noting Bultmann's statement that "every assertion about God is simultaneously an assertion about man and *vice versa*," he argues that when Bultmann concludes that Paul's theology "is most appropriately presented as a doctrine of man," it should be equally legitimate to conclude the

---

[27] Of course, neutrality here is in regard to an epistemological stance. Regarding the subject matter in question, I cannot be neutral at all. What I say about it objectively from an epistemologically neutral stance requires recognizing the peculiar kind of "object" it is.

[28] Heidegger himself almost never speaks of objectivity and non-objectivity. He avoids the potential confusions by distinguishing between the concepts used to accomplish the different descriptions, terming the one "categories" and the other *existentialia* (i.e., "existentials"), but regarding the formal epistemological features, the issues are the same (see *SZ*, 44 [70]). Ogden clarifies this second sense of "objectivity" in a similar fashion (see *RG*, 78ff.).

[29] Bultmann is, however, uncomfortable describing the existential analytic as objectifying (see *CM*, 45, n. 72 and 149).

opposite and see it as a doctrine of God.[30] It should be possible, Ogden argues, to develop a proper way of speaking about the "non-objective" being of God along lines identical to the way in which the *existentiell/existential* distinction permits a "scientific analysis of man's inner or personal life" (*CM*, 45; cf. p. 149). To do so would straightforwardly apply what Bultmann seems to mean when he says that in speaking of God analogically, "we represent God's action as analogous to human action, and we represent the communion between God and human beings as analogous to our communion with one another" (ZPE, 197 [ET, 110–111]).

We need not describe Ogden's full execution of this proposal. For one thing, he himself has not yet completed it, though in *The Reality of God* he has developed it considerably beyond his remarks in *Christ without Myth*.[31] The crucial point is that Bultmann's own reference to analogy implies a way to speak about God that is objective yet neither "scientific" nor "mythological." Ogden proposes to develop such a speaking metaphysically using Hartshorne's process philosophy.[32]

Ogden succeeds in connecting an existentialist understanding of faith with the intent of myth to speak about a "beyond." If God is not an "object" but the eminent actuality of every moment of being and if at the same time God may only be conceived analogously to the "non-objective" character of personal being, then human existence qua its *existentiell* actualization is at every moment a response to God; this response is realized as an existential self-understanding, and theology can have no other theme than faith so understood. At one and the same time, theology can be conceived existentially and yet speak fully and objectively about God.[33] Ogden thus seems to provide a coherent interpretation of the theory implicit in Bultmann's notion of analogy and at the same time to realize the latter's constantly reiterated theme that God's action "can be talked about only in that I myself, as the one affected by it, am at one and the same time talked about" (ZPE, 197 [ET, 110]).

---

[30] See *CM*, 148. The quotations are from Bultmann (1951), I, 191.

[31] In *The Point of Christology* (*PC*, 127–147), Ogden seems to propose a major revision of his earlier work. The implications of this revision are, however, still undeveloped, and though I discuss these issues further in chapter six, their import must await a complete statement of Ogden's doctrine of God. Until it appears, we must rely on Ogden's earlier position.

[32] It should be noted that when combined with Hartshorne's version of the ontological argument, Ogden can develop this position in close verbal identity with Bultmann, for he can maintain both that every statement about human existence is at one and the same time about God and that the theme of theology is nothing other than faith (see, e.g., *RG*, 209–210).

[33] See, e.g., *RG*, 178–179.

Ogden's interpretation does sort through the ambiguities in Bultmann's position, and it is a powerful position in its own right. While taking Bultmann far beyond his stated position, it attempts to remain faithful to its underlying logic. Given the "transcendent theism" Bultmann presupposes, it may be the only coherent rendering of his position that also remains faithful to the theological problems that led to his demythologizing proposal. There can be no denying the force of Ogden's proposal.

Nevertheless, from the present standpoint, Ogden's position is obviously unacceptable. The problem is not his suggestions about analogy but the theism presupposed by Bultmann and explicitly advanced by him. Not only is it strongly personalistic, but it also depends on the plausibility of process philosophy's nonphysicalist (indeed, panpsychist) ontology. I have given my reasons for believing that theology cannot start from these premises, and, apart from earlier mentioning the problems such an ontology must have with unifying the sciences, I shall leave to other naturalists the detailed critical assessment for which the process ontology begs.[34]

My concern instead is to develop an alternative reading of Bultmann's method that is consistent with a physicalist ontology. Ogden's proposal gains its support from Bultmann's apparent commitment to some form of classical theism, but the position developed here has no stake in any conceivable version of that view – though it does have a stake in rendering "God exists" objectively true. Despite the cogency of Ogden's analysis, the cross-currents in Bultmann's position make it difficult to reconcile with any one view; alternative, equally plausible ways of construing it are justified. This is all the more so because, as we have seen, it is precisely Bultmann's commitment to theism that creates one of the elements making it difficult to fit all the pieces of his proposal together. To see this, let us briefly examine several points in Bultmann's position that raise questions about Ogden's argument.

To develop his interpretation, Ogden presses Bultmann on the distinction between an inappropriate objectification in myth and a legitimate objectivity based on analogies drawn from existentialist analysis. In other words, Ogden insists that "God may also be spoken about in 'objective' but not 'mythological' terms" and charges Bultmann with inconsistency for not acknowledging this (*CM*, 149).

---

[34] Despite its brevity, one of the best such critiques still remains Wieman's review of Hartshorne's *The Divine Relativity*. (Wieman [1949]).

In order to make this case, however, Ogden also identifies the illegitimate form of mythological objectivity with the epistemological form of scientific objectivity and claims that this is the proper way to construe Bultmann's conception of myth.[35] Thus, the contrast between myth and analogy becomes a contrast between *a category mistake in myth, confusing its real intent with scientific objectivity*, and an appropriate analogical objectivity in which no such confusion occurs.

As powerful as this interpretation is in cutting through the cross-currents in Bultmann, it fails to recognize that at least in Bultmann's mind *scientific objectivity* is not the only kind of inappropriate objectivity involved in myth. He also objects to what can only fairly be termed *metaphysical* objectivity. Ogden's position requires Bultmann to be criticizing myth not merely for its false objectivity but for its inadequate metaphysics, as though, as indeed is the case with Ogden, the issue all along centered on the need for a full scale revisionary theism. There is simply no evidence *from Bultmann* that his criticism of myth is to be construed in this fashion. Again, Bultmann may simply be incoherent or inconsistent on this issue, but implicit in his criticism of myth, otherwise widely articulated throughout his theology, is that it is never appropriate to speak *about* God.[36] This position, namely, that "if one wants to speak of God, one must clearly *speak of oneself*,"[37] is deeply implicated in what Bultmann means by the method of existentialist interpretation.

At least part of Bultmann's reluctance to accept Ogden's proposal is rooted in the "understanding" involved in conceiving faith as an existential self-understanding. We saw that there are ambiguities in Bultmann's description of the real intent of myth "to express man's understanding of himself in his world," and these ambiguities open the door for Ogden's interpretation. But for Bultmann, all theological statements are statements about human beings and our possibilities of understanding our "ex-ist-ing." They are expressions of a self-understanding realized *existentiell*, and as such, their description is a description of modes of human being in the world. Statements about God, taking this notion of existential self-understanding strictly, become statements about modes of human being realized in response to God's gracious action. This action is understood as a word of judgment and promise accomplished in events of encounter in which, *qua* events, the possibility of a new self-understanding is offered (see

[35] See *RG*, 104–106, 166–167.   [36] He specifically argues this in Bultmann (1933d), 26–33.
[37] Bultmann (1933d), 28, Bultmann's emphasis.

ZPE, 199–200 [ET, 114–115]). In other words, Bultmann never wants to speak *about* God but only, if you will, *of* God's action. Such action can be entirely fused with modes of human existing when the latter are conceived in terms of Heidegger's analytic of existence, namely, as acts of self definition, continually re-enacted, as "care" in response to the world disclosed (*erschlossen*) in one's "being-in" it.

With this interpretation, we can, with Bultmann, still deny that God's action is merely a "pictorial designation of subjective experiences," and we can affirm that speaking of it "must intend an act in the fully real and 'objective' sense" (just as was the case with Luther) (ZPE, 196 [ET, 110]). We also need not qualify the "scandal" involved in understanding such events as acts of God (see ZPE, 187–188, 206 [ET, 102, 121]). Furthermore, such intra-worldly encounters account differently from Ogden for the way Bultmann continues the statements quoted immediately above: "If, *however*, God's act may not be understood as a phenomenon in the world that I can perceive apart from being existentially affected by it [*abgesehen von der existentiellen Betroffenheit von ihm*], then it can be talked about only by speaking about myself as the one affected. *To talk about God's act means to talk at the same time of my own existence*" (ZPE, 197, first emphasis mine, second Bultmann's; [ET, 110]).

The "understanding" in a self-understanding is thus an understanding of myself disclosed as possibilities of existing. It also includes an understanding of my world since my existential possibilities are disclosed in my commerce with a world of practical concern (*Besorgen*). Such is the import of Heidegger's criticism of an isolated Cartesian ego which first exists and then stands over against a world of objects. The "world" is already implicated in my self-understanding and is thus "understood," and my existential possibilities will have implications for how I "understand" and deal with the everyday disclosures of my world, as is seen from Heidegger's analysis of the two formal possibilities of self-understanding, authentic and inauthentic existence.[38]

This existentialist concept of understanding can be significantly contrasted with Ogden. When Ogden interprets Heidegger's distinction between "categories" and "existentials," he distinguishes between "internal" and "external" perception, "external" perception being equivalent to the "objectivity" that legitimates the canons of "scientific objectivity." In contrast to this type of "understanding," he claims

---

[38] See *SZ*, 220–222 (263–265).

that we have an "inner nonsensuous perception of our selves and the world as parts of an encompassing whole." This is the "understanding" illuminated by the existentialist analytic (which legitimates assertions not open to the canons of empirical falsifiability appropriate to external perception).[39] I simply note the difficulty here in comprehending what an internal (and essentially private) *perception* is. Independent of this problem, there is little reason to think that such a notion captures the kind of understanding intended by Heidegger. Far from being "internal" (or a perception), Heidegger's entire point is that the being of Dasein is constituted by a kind of disclosure that is always peculiarly "open" or "exposed" precisely to its world. There is no reason to construe this "disclosed world" as "an encompassing whole." The world is simply the world of practical commerce which has a transcendental "world structure." This world is the world of my "being-in" and is "disclosed" to me by the structure of "care." It is not "an encompassing whole" but the everyday commerce of practical concern (*Besorgen*).

The notion of an encompassing whole is crucial for Ogden. It underwrites his interpretation of Bultmann to the effect that the real intent of myth includes a reference to a non-objective "beyond" that is the ground and source of our being, that is misconceived if objectified as worldly, but that can be properly objectified when based on our internal awareness of ourselves as persons. Ogden, however, cannot base this interpretation on an existentialist analytic, for it becomes plausible only through *another* ontology, the Whiteheadian conception of experience which is *its* ontology. This is the real basis of Ogden's claim, and it cannot be gotten out of the analytic of existence without first reading it into it. This illuminates Ogden's reading of Bultmann, but it also shows another reason why Bultmann's entirely Heideggerian conception of self-understanding can be restricted to modes of human being in the world.

By this analysis, I do not intend to challenge the validity of Ogden's interpretation. Ogden's essay, "The Temporality of God," is a splendid argument for wedding Heidegger to a process conception of God,[40] and the tensions in Bultmann can support his reading. I do

---

[39] *RG*, 105; see also 114. In another context, making the same point in slightly different language, he says: ". . . there is our original internal awareness of our own existence in relation to the manifold reality encountering us, which awareness in some modification is the most distinctive feature of our being as men, as selves or persons" (*RG*, 74).

[40] *RG*, 144–163. It should be noted that Ogden supports this argument differently from the interpretation of the "understanding" involved in an existential self-understanding presented above.

claim, however, that those same tensions equally support another reading, one that binds existentialist interpretation much more closely to possibilities of existence. When so construed, the method of existentialist interpretation has a clear-cut attractiveness for a naturalist theology. It does require, however, that we interpret somewhat differently what Bultmann means by analogy and by the real intent of myth.

We have seen that myth for Bultmann intends to refer to a kind of transcendence, and we have examined various difficulties this occasions. Other aspects of myth express an awareness of our dependence and our desire for liberation. If we hold to a strictly existentialist account of the summary phrase, "to express man's understanding of his existence in his world," then we can construe these notions of "beyondness," "transcendence," "dependence," and "powers" in reference to the *existentiell* awareness of our being-in-the-world. They function as existential responses to what Heidegger terms our "thrownness."[41] This construction suggests a *functional* role for "transcendence terms" in myth, with no metaphysical intent at all – *provided that we hold strictly to the idea that the real intent of myth is to express an existential self-understanding.* Taken existentially, such terms bring to expression *concrete, immediate* experiences of life that we all have. These experiences, embedded directly in our being-in-the-world, are actualized as its horizon when we encounter those "boundary situations" (death, chance, conflict, suffering, and guilt) by which we experience our lack of any ultimate control over our lives that are bounded by powers beyond our ability to determine or even existentially to understand. Transcendence terms express our existential self-understanding in response to these concrete experiences of life.

These terms function as an aspect of what Heidegger calls the "world structure" which determines our practical commerce with the concrete things and persons "in" our world. This world structure and "being-in" the world denote an existential relationship, not an objective (i.e., spatial) one. The world structure discloses my world in its "concerns" (*Besorgen*) because its "disclosedness" is structured by the comprehensive existential relationship that defines my being (and thus my existential self-understanding). This comprehensive relationship is termed "care" (*Sorge*) because it is determined, overall, by my existential awareness of my finitude, by my "thrownness" which is a "being-toward-death." Transcendence terms may thus be interpreted

---

[41] See *SZ*, 134–138, 179, 284–285 (172–177, 223–224, 329–331).

as expressions for certain types of ultimate existential relationship realized at the horizon of a "world structure." They articulate its horizon because they express the ultimate terms of "care." As such, they may be viewed entirely existentially, not metaphysically at all.

This, then, would be a functional, entirely existentialist account of myth's intent to refer to a "beyond." Such transcendence terms, and their existential relations, express existential responses (possibilities of self-understanding) to the limiting questions of our existence. In this sense, the "Christian myth" or the "Christian witness of faith" is the expression of a particular possibility of existence realized in encounter with the horizon of one's world structure. It is also possible to comprehend the "Christian witness" as the *offer* of one such existential possibility.

It is important to emphasize that this interpretation of myth does not prejudice additional questions about God or about the metaphysical reference of the Christian witness of faith. It is simply an attempt to render Bultmann's notion of the real intent of myth in fully existentialist terms. How existential transcendence terms, or the Christian conception of the offer of a new self-understanding, might be further construed is left open. It is consistent with Bultmann's own apparent theism and even with Ogden's interpretation of Bultmann. What it does provide, however, is an interpretation of Bultmann's claim that theological statements are statements about human beings and their possibilities of understanding their existence. It thus seeks the content of theological statements entirely in modes of human being in the world, and this opens the door for a naturalist reading of Bultmann's method.

An alternative reading of Bultmann's concept of analogy is also possible. It is generated by adhering closely to the way he qualifies analogy by insisting that we cannot speak *about* God but only of ourselves as encountered by God. First, note the definition once again: "Therefore, to speak of God's act is not a pictorial, symbolic manner of speaking, but it is for all that *analogical* speech. For in such speaking, we represent God's action as analogous to human action, and we represent the communion between God and human beings as analogous to our communion with one another." Immediately prior to this statement, after he has admitted that God's act must be "fully real and 'objective'," Bultmann qualifies this admission, as already noted, by stating that we can speak of God only by speaking of ourselves at one and the same time (ZPE, 196, Bultmann's emphasis, [ET, 110]).

This qualification becomes still clearer when he rejects the criticism that his position is simply a version of pantheism. Pantheism, he says, is a world-view consisting of an *anterior* conviction [*vorausgegebene Überzeugung*] about God and the world to the effect that everything is the work of God. Unlike pantheism, Christianity does not identify God's action straightforwardly with every occurrence. *Because it springs from the experience of God's grace*, Christianity "believes that God acts on me, speaks to me, in each particular situation" (ZPE, 111 [ET, 197]). Unlike pantheism, therefore, it does not simply identify God with all events. But it is also incompatible with pantheism because it is incompatible with any world-view. Being an anterior view of things, a world-view is a set of beliefs that can be possessed, whereas faith in God's gracious action must be constantly renewed in the *existentiell* events in which God does indeed act (see ZPE, 197–198 [ET, 111–113]). This is one of Bultmann's clearest and most explicit rejections of *metaphysical* objectivity, and it makes apparent that one cannot immediately translate his willingness to speak of analogy into an endorsement of a metaphysics based on analogies.

Another reading of analogy is suggested by the following statement from the same context:

It becomes clear from all this that the world loses its character as a closed continuum for my existential life, which is realized in decisions in face of encounters. Put differently, in faith the closed continuum presented (or produced) by objectifying thinking is sublated – not of course in the manner of mythological thinking, so that it is thought of as disrupted, but in such a way that it is sublated as a whole when I talk about God's act. *Actually, it is already sublated when I talk about myself; for I myself, in my authentic being, am just as little to be seen and established within the world as is the act of God.* When I look upon worldly occurrences as a closed continuum, which I have to do in the interest not only of scientific understanding *but also of my daily life and work*, then, indeed, there is no room for God's act. (ZPE, 112–113 [ET, 198], my emphasis)

Entirely different from Ogden, the analogy supported by this passage is between a conception of God's transcendence which emphasizes God's indisposability and non-objectivity (not God's metaphysical otherness) and a dimension of human existence similarly transcendent. On this reading, Bultmann is not speaking about God at all, but about human beings. There is a dimension of human existence which cannot be objectified like a worldly phenomenon but, as clarified by Heidegger, is one in which the reality at stake can be grasped only by one's concernful engagement with it, since what is at stake is one's own being being at stake. The analogy is between *our* "transcendence" and non-objectivity *vis à vis* the world and the indisposability and non-objectivity of *God's action*, and it permits us to relate God's action *to this realm of human agency or personhood*. The analogy is appropriate because the questions of God and of God's gracious action deal with this existential dimension of our lives. The analogy is not metaphysical; instead, it warrants *the independence* of God's action exactly analogously to the "independence" or "transcendence" of our own existential actions. This "transcendence" of our existential actions does not make them "subjective," for we are still engaged by a world. In this sense they should be understood, in Bultmann's language, "historically," not "psychologically," that is, as involving our full, yet non-objective, engagement with events in a world independent of us (see ZPE, 197–198 [ET, 111–113]). Analogously, God's action is entirely existential, yet not for that reason "subjective" or lacking independence from those encountered by it. In the following, I shall term this existentialist account of God's action *events of grace*.

I conclude, therefore, that Bultmann's proposal to treat theological statements as statements about human beings and their possibilities of self-understanding can be understood entirely in terms of modes of human existing. This interpretation does not qualify Bultmann's assertion that "from the statement that only a faith which knows itself encountered by God can speak of God so that when the believer speaks of God's action she can only be speaking of herself, it simply does not follow that God has no reality outside the believer or the act of faith" (ZPE, 198–199 [ET, 113]). What it does do is give a better account of Bultmann's resistance to metaphysical objectivity. Of course, the question remains open how this independent reality of God's action can be rendered naturalistically. That is a question to be taken up in the following chapter. For the present, I shall close this chapter with an existentialist account of faith. I shall base this account on Bultmann's own incomparable description of the "life of faith" and "life outside of faith," but I shall be at pains to emphasize its compatibility with a naturalist version of existentialist interpretation.

THE EXISTENTIALIST INTERPRETATION OF FAITH

In the New Testament, the opposition between "unfaith" and "faith" is presented as "bondage" or "enslavement" versus "freedom" or "liberation." According to Jewish apocalypticism, human beings have fallen into bondage to "objective" powers (the princes, prince, or god of this world) that rule "this world" or "this evil aeon." Bultmann assumes that the language of "this world" or "this aeon" is borrowed from Gnosticism, and he articulates the distinctive character of New Testament anthropology by contrasting it with the Gnostic myth of redemption.[42] The crucial difference is that Gnosticism presents human destiny as a cosmic fate. The condition which predetermines the self's earthly fate is a pre-existent self that is brought into bondage by entrapment in matter, "the material and thus sensual body of human beings" (NTM, 27 [ET, 15]). Despite this mythological, cosmic terminology, the New Testament differs from the Gnostic myth on two other counts. It assumes that God is "the creator of the world, including human life in the body," and it always attributes human bondage or sin to freedom and responsibility (NTM, 27 [ET, 15]). Because Gnosticism assumes a connection between human bondage, fate and matter, these differences give an entirely different accent to the New Testament understanding of enslavement to "this world" and "this evil aeon."

These differences are especially important for Paul's identification of the sources of sin and death with the "flesh." New Testament scholarship makes clear that when Paul speaks of "life after the flesh" he does not mean matter or our sensual nature. "Flesh" means, rather, a total life orientation. As Bultmann describes it, the flesh is "not what is corporal or sensual but rather the whole sphere of what is visible, available, disposable, and measurable, and as such the sphere of what is transient. This sphere becomes a power over us insofar as we make it the foundation of our lives by living 'according to it,' that is, by succumbing to the temptation to live out of what is visible and disposable instead of out of what is invisible and nondisposable . . ." (NTM, 16 [ET, 28]). In other words, "life after the flesh" is not a cosmic fate but results from human freedom. The "flesh" does not first control us, but our decision to live "according" to it transforms it into "this world" which comes then to have a fate-like power over us.

[42] See NTM, 27–28 (ET, 15–16), and Bultmann (1956) 189–208. Throughout his writings, Bultmann assumes that the conceptual background of much Jewish apocalypticism and of much of the New Testament was a Gnostic world of ideas in circulation at least two centuries before the turn of the common era. Later work on these sources and on newly available Gnostic materials has cast doubt on these assumptions, and the matter is now controversial, some scholars maintaining that Gnosticism does not pre-date the New Testament. The issue is an important historical one, but it does not fundamentally affect Bultmann's interpretation of faith and unfaith. Whether Gnostic or not, the background is a cosmic dualism presented in mythological form.

Yet this "fate" or "bondage" is always simultaneously guilt. In this sense, there is already an implicit demythologization at work in Paul's and John's conception of "this world." A cosmic dualism is transformed into a dualism of decision.[43]

If the human problem is already implicitly existentialized in this fashion, then two questions arise: what is the motive for life after the flesh and why is it enslaving? For Paul the source of a life devoted to the "sphere of what is visible, available, disposable, and measurable" is care or anxiety. We find ourselves insecure and try to secure ourselves by centering on what lies within our power of control, the objectively visible, or tangible, or manageable. The crucial issue here is the illusion of a kind of control. It can manifest itself as "flesh" in terms of sensual pleasures, but the "flesh" can also come to expression in refinement, nobility, and achievement, hence Paul's analysis of the pride of achievement in the works of the law. The result is that "the natural person expresses her care in the effort to secure her life. Corresponding to her possibilities and successes in the sphere of what is visible, she 'puts confidence in the flesh' (Phil. 3:3–4), and the consciousness of security finds expression in 'boasting'" (NTM, 28 [ET, 16–17]. "Pride" or "boasting" result from the existential assumption that the conditions of one's "care" or "anxiety" lie within one's power of control.

This interpretation of enslavement is integral to the entire New Testament anthropology and is rooted in the fact that human life is not secure at all. This insecurity and the enslavement it produces are also intimately connected with the New Testament conception of God. To live according to an illusion of mastery, which Paul terms "pride" or "boasting," is not merely illusory but is, existentially, to live as though one's mastery could secure one's life. One lives as though one were the source and ground of one's life and thus effectively as though one were one's own creator. This is to deny and indeed to revolt against God who is the true source of life. Bultmann says:

The world, which could be God's creation for us, becomes precisely through this attitude "this world," the world opposed to God. Precisely this attitude is what allows the "powers" upon which we are dependent first to arise. Because they now appear as powers over [*gegenüber*] us, they can be represented as mythical entities. What is visible, disposable is what is transient, and consequently, whoever lives out of it falls under [*ist verfallen*] transience and death.[44]

[43] See Bultmann, (1951) II, 15–21, 40, and Bultmann (1956) 178–195.
[44] NTM, 28 (ET, 17). Cf. Bultmann (1960a), 82–83.

Reinhold Niebuhr comments in this same vein that the biblical notion of sin is fundamentally religious, not moral, because it takes the ultimate nature of sin to be unbelief.[45] Sin is always both idolatry and revolt. At one and the same time, sin refuses to trust in the source of one's being, and it centers life on a false center of value. Because the source of this false center is one's insecurity, the ultimate nature of the false gods that are thereby worshipped can be traced back to the self. At the root of idolatry is always the self's own self-idolization. For the same reason, sin or "life after the flesh" in Paul's analysis always has the character of "boasting" or "pride," in the sense of "self-elevation."[46]

The same analysis accounts for the close relationship between sin and "death" and sin and "hatred" in Paul. Though Paul sometimes traces sin and death to Adam's fall, he is clear that "death came to all human beings since Adam 'because they all sinned' (Rom. 5:12), a statement which cannot be harmonized with the Adam theory" (NTM, 28 [ET, 16]). Sin and death are connected, as above, by the fact that "life according to the flesh" seeks security in that which cannot finally give it, a world of transience and death. Bultmann clarifies what this means as follows: "Because man understands himself in terms of what he accomplishes and produces, because he thus takes his god*less* being to be his authentic, his ultimate being, he is punished by death – i.e., the death to which the whole of his present existence is subject – also acquiring for him the character of something authentic and ultimate."[47] In other words, Bultmann existentializes "death." One seeks life from what is dead, and in so doing one becomes enslaved to that realm. But "death" has a double meaning here, for in seeking to secure one's life from what is dead (transitory, subject to corruption, tangible), one's "care" and "anxiety" permit death to rule one's living. In this sense, "death came into the world through sin" and "the wages of sin is death" (Rom. 5:12; 6:23). As Bultmann continues: "Because he tries to cling to his provisional being he slips away from himself. If, however, he could once again understand himself as provisional and could surrender his provisional being, *then death also could once again become something provisional for him.* But if, instead, he clings to the provisional, he is always already past.

---

[45] Reinhold Niebuhr (1941), I, 179, 183.
[46] For this entire analysis, cf. Reinhold Niebuhr (1941), I, 178–188. Niebuhr's discussion of sin as pride is closely related to Bultmann. See, for instance, Bultmann (1960a), 82–83.
[47] Bultmann (1960a) 82, Bultmann's emphasis.

The unfaithful are dead in their sins (Col. 2:13; Eph. 2:1, 2:5)."[48] Death can become provisional because its domination over our living can be broken – by God's grace, we shall see. Its provisionality is not supported by any sort of survival of death. Indeed *that* kind of provisionality would assume that we ourselves had not become provisional by surrendering our provisional being. In other words, any such conception of faith and its grounds would itself be "fallen," based on "life after the flesh."[49]

The connection with "hatred" also follows from an existential account of "life after the flesh." When I try to secure myself by what I can control, then every other person becomes either a threat to my control or an object of that control itself. The self-regard, which is at the center of this attempt and which ultimately defines "life after the flesh" as idolatry, leads to disregard for the needs of others – or worse, to their subjection to one's own concerns. A pervasive attitude of lovelessness runs through the center of one's existential orientation to life. This "war of all against all" is ameliorated only by a desire for mutual security which gives rise to minimum standards of mutuality and justice (cf. NTM, 28 [ET, 17]). Yet these are only compromises and adjustments of conflicting interests that mask the underlying self-seeking, "envy, anger, jealousy, and the like." As a consequence, they themselves become a new source of anxiety produced by our attempt to control the conditions of life. They paper over the conditions of conflict and create "a pervasive atmosphere which already always surrounds each of us, guiding our judgments, an atmosphere that each of us always acknowledges as justified, so that each of us participates in the way it reconstitutes itself ever anew. From it grows the slavery to anxiety which oppresses us (Rom. 8:15).

[48] Bultmann (1960a) 82, my emphasis. This thoroughgoing existentialization of death will be of fundamental importance for the analysis of eschatological symbols in the last chapter.

[49] Jaspers distinguishes "existence" (*Dasein*) and "Existence" (*Existenz*) and makes the latter equivalent to "authentic existence." This permits him to capture the existential reality of death better than Heidegger, though with a somewhat different accent from Bultmann's conception of how death can rule our living. Note, for instance, the following statement: "An *existence coupled with the nonbeing of Existenz* raises the specter of an endless life without potential, without effect and communication. I have died, and it is thus that I must live forever; I do not live, and so my possible Existenz suffers the agony of being unable to die. The peace of radical nonbeing would be a deliverance from the horror of continual [*dauernden*] death" (Jaspers [1932], ET, 199 [227]). Note that in this densely metaphorical passage, Jaspers's reference to "living forever" no more assumes life beyond biological death than Bultmann's notion of death's provisionality. It means that if one does not actualize the existential possibility of living (*Existenz*), so for all eternity will one *have been*. (For an excellent analysis and comparison of Heidegger and Jaspers on these themes, see Westphal [1984], 95–102.)

This anxiety leads us to hold fast to ourselves and to what belongs to each of us, in the secret feeling that everything, including our very lives, is slipping away" (NTM, 28–29 [ET, 17]). According to Bultmann, this union of lovelessness and an anxious regard for conventional standards is also what John means by being "of the world," which carries the same existential weight as Paul's "life after the flesh."[50]

For Bultmann, Paul's and John's incipiently demythologized conceptions of "life after the flesh" or being "of the world" are comprehensible for modern persons because their content is identical with the "inauthentic" self-understanding described by Heidegger. Similarly, the "life of faith" is open to an existentialist interpretation in terms of "authentic" existence (cf. NTM, 33–36 [ET, 23–26]). Its content is more or less the exact obverse of "human existence apart from faith" (NTM, 27 [ET, 15]), and its mythological terms admit of the same existentialist interpretation.

Thus, "a genuine life would be one lived out of what is invisible and indisposable, a life in which all self-contrived security was surrendered." Such a life becomes possible out of faith in the "grace of God" (NTM, 29 [ET, 17]). To understand this terminology about "invisible, indisposable" realities it helps to recall the opposition between objectivity and the "invisible" and "the beyond" in myth. In contrast to "life after the flesh," a "life based on what is invisible and indisposable" simply means "the abandonment of all self-contrived security" (NTM, 29 [ET, 17]). Such life is possible if I can trust that I *always* receive my life as a gift, that it is never something I can secure but is something I can always receive as a gift and not a threat. Such confidence is what is meant by "the grace of God," for grace *"means* trust that precisely the invisible, the unfamiliar, the indisposable encounters us as love, *gives us our future and signifies not death but life for us"* (NTM, 29, my emphasis; [ET, 17]).

Bultmann captures this reality existentially with the distinction between "bondage to the past" and "openness to the future." He explicitly asserts that what faith *means* is "to open ourselves freely to the future" (NTM, 18 [ET, 29]). The anxiety from which "life after the flesh" arises is, if you will, a fundamental mistrust of the way our contingency is configured toward time. It is a mistrust of the future, and it leads to the enslavement that the New Testament calls sin. The

[50] See, e.g., Bultmann (1933a), 135–142.

New Testament claims that we can trust the way the future comes to us because it comes as a gift. Existentially interpreted, this is what "the grace of God" *means*: to receive the future as a gift. To reject this possibility is to mistrust the gift of one's being, to seek to secure oneself from the future by one's achievements, and thus to live according to the past.[51]

The situation is more complicated, however, for "the grace of God" is not merely an attitude toward one's contingency but the event or process by which one is actually liberated to become open to the future. And, "bondage to the past" is not simply the opposite of an attitude of openness to the future but an enslavement by which one actually does not have a future. "Life after the flesh" is enslaving. Every effort to free oneself is based on the same self-regarding anxiety by which one seeks to secure one's existence. In this sense, it is truly bondage to the *past*, to one's own past efforts to define the terms of existence for oneself in mistrust of the future. In this more precise sense, one truly does not have a future, a new possibility of living authentically.[52] Bultmann therefore objects to Heidegger's notion of "resoluteness" as though it were a simple choice to be authentic: "What faith and theology say and show is that in this possibility of being (which in its ontological character is not in dispute) there is always present in fact a *necessity of being*, insofar as in every actual choice in which man chooses a possibility of existing authentically he in fact always chooses what he already is – that he never gets rid of his past and therefore is never free" (HMF, 107, Bultmann's emphasis). Thus, openness to the future is actually an event by which one is given a future. The "grace of God" has two closely related senses here. It is to be open to the future, to receive the future as the gift of God's love,[53] and it is the event by which one is opened to be free for the future.

The existentialist interpretation of the "forgiveness of sin" is particularly significant. Bultmann says:

The grace of God is *the grace that forgives sin*. This *means* that it frees us from the past which holds us in bondage. That human disposition by which we seek to secure ourselves and therefore grasp after what is disposable and cling to what is perishing, indeed to what has already always perished – just this

---

[51] See Bultmann (1952b), 71 (81).

[52] See Bultmann (1960a), 82 for the connection with death.

[53] This is also the meaning of Bultmann's existentialist interpretation of the doctrine of creation when he says that its fundamental intention is "not the statement of a cosmological theory that seeks to explain the origin of the world, but rather man's confession to God as his Lord . . ." (Bultmann [1956], 15; taken from Ogden's translation, *CM*, 54).

disposition is sin *because it amounts to closing ourselves against the invisible, against the future that God gifts to us [gegen Gottes sich schenkende Zukunft]*. Those who open themselves to grace are forgiven of their sins, that is, *they become free from the past*. "*Faith*" means nothing but this: to open oneself freely to the future. (NTM, 29, first and last emphases Bultmann's; [ET, 18–19])

"Forgiveness," then, is not so much a transaction with a divine subject as events through which we are "offered" a new self-understanding which frees us from the repetition of our bondage. However theistic Bultmann's understanding was, the point is that here "forgiveness" and "love" are defined entirely in terms of a possibility of existence, being open to the future, and the appropriateness of the language of "forgiveness" arises entirely on these terms. I am offered a new possibility of existence that is liberating in the precise context of my having rejected it in my living and having bound myself by that rejection. Clearly there is a question whether this possibility of existence and therefore this conception of "the love of God" can be conceived apart from something like Bultmann's (and Ogden's) theism, and we shall have to consider this issue in later chapters. For now, it is sufficient to see how entirely existentialist Bultmann's analysis is.

The life of faith brings "liberation" or "freedom" from enslavement to "this world." This notion of freedom is best captured by Paul's dialectic of "as though not" (1 Cor. 7:29–31), of being in but not of the world. At a first level, such freedom is the freedom of openness to the future. As such it is freedom *from* the world. It expresses itself in an attitude of inner detachment from all "available, disposable objects" through which "life after the flesh" seeks to secure itself (NTM, 28 [ET, 16]). Its content is identical with faith since "openness to the future" and commitment to God are one and the same. Such faith means

to surrender all security, to renounce establishing one's worth, one's life, on the basis of one's own efforts, to renounce trusting alone in oneself, and to resolve to trust solely in God. . . It is radical submission to God, which expects everything from God and nothing from oneself, and it is the *detachment* thereby given *from everything in the world that can be disposed of*, and hence the attitude of being free from the world, of *freedom*. (NTM, 29, Bultmann's emphasis; [ET, 18])

Yet, Bultmann emphasizes, faith is not asceticism, especially not the Gnostic's opposition to the world by the devaluation of "sense" and "matter." In its spirit of inner detachment, it is also a freedom *for* the world. Because "the world" is no longer the anxiety driven source of my attempt to command it for my security, I can be open to it in its own right. In Paul's words, "all things are lawful for me, but I will not be brought under the power of any" (1 Cor. 6:12; cf., 10:23–24) (see NTM, 29–30 [ET, 18–19]). One is, in particular, opened to the claim of the other, the neighbor, who no longer confronts as a threat. Thus, freedom for the world is preeminently the service of love, and this is the content of God's demand upon us – just as the content of this demand is nothing other than the claim of the other. Faith may, therefore, also be described as "working through love" (Gal. 5:6) (see NTM, 31 [ET, 20]).

Jewish and New Testament eschatology are also demythologized, as captured by Paul's concept of the believer *already* being a "new creature" (II Cor. 5:17) and John's notion of *already* having passed from death to "eternal life" (John 5:24). Bultmann, therefore, makes faith synonymous with what he calls "eschatological existence,"[54] and he roots this existentialist interpretation of eschatology in the New Testament itself. The crucial difference from Jewish apocalypticism, a difference already present in the preaching of Jesus, is that "the day of salvation has already dawned for believers and the life of the future has already become present." The elimination of apocalyptic eschatology is especially marked in John, for "the judgment of the world is not a cosmic event that is still to happen but has already happened in Jesus's coming into the world and issuing the call to faith (John 3:19; 9:39; 12:31). Those who believe already have life and have passed from death to life (John 5:24, etc.). Outwardly, nothing has changed for believers, but their relation to the world has changed: the world can no longer concern them; faith is the victory that overcomes the world (1 John 5:4)" (NTM, 19 [ET, 30]). Faith is eschatological existence because it is life in the "end." In the New Testament, the "end" is God's judgment which even now is judging the world in Christ's coming (John 3:19; 9:39; 12:31) and which demands the decision for life or death.[55] Thus, the "end" occurs precisely in the existential event of God's grace. As the offer of a new possibility of life, it is also judgment on one's past life and in this sense is "the judgment of the world." Eschatology has the same *existentiell*

---

[54] See NTM, 30–31 (ET, 19–20). See also, Bultmann (1951) I, 144, 278–279, 328–330, 335–339; II, 75–92.

[55] See NTM, 30 (ET, 19). Bultmann's ability to render the underlying meaning of New Testament eschatology existentially is supported by Heidegger's analyses of the "ecstasies" of existential temporality and, in particular, of "the moment" (*Der Augenblick*). See *SZ*, 337–338 and n. iii (387–388 and n. iii) where Heidegger distances himself from Kierkegaard.

content as the other mythological terms through which faith is expressed.

Equally important is the distinction from Gnostic eschatology. Like the New Testament, its appeal was rooted in offering "true life" as a present reality. It conceived this, however, as an ontological guarantee of one's final destiny. One is given a new nature in the sense that one's pre-existent nature is emancipated from its entrapment in matter, and in this way, "the journey of one's soul to heaven is assured" (NTM, 30 [ET, 19]). Gnostic eschatology is thus consistent with the Gnostic tendency to treat soteriological issues objectively in terms of fate or a condition that can be possessed.[56] The New Testament's emphasis on freedom and responsibility mean that faith cannot be possessed at all. Bultmann articulates this by saying that faith for the Gnostic can be expressed exclusively in indicative terms as a given condition [*Zustand*], whereas for Paul and the rest of the New Testament, "the imperative must be used immediately with the indicative, which is to say that the decision of faith is not made once and for all but must be confirmed in each concrete situation by being made anew. In fact, it is just by being genuinely made anew that faith sustains itself" (NTM, 30 [ET, 19]). New Testament eschatology is thus existential through and through. For this reason, Bultmann insists that the language of "obedience," and not merely that of "offering," must constantly be used with its conception of faith.

The relationship between "indicative" and "imperative" is especially illumined by Bultmann's analysis of Paul's notion of the "Spirit" and of "life in the Spirit." Because Gnosticism regarded the "Spirit" as a new nature to be possessed, it saw evidence of the Spirit in ecstatic possession and other pneumatic phenomena. Though not rejecting them outright, Paul refused to take such phenomena as proof of the Spirit. He does speak of the spirit mythologically "as a power that operates like a natural force" and "as a mysterious something in us whose possession guarantees resurrection (Rom. 8:11)" or otherwise as "a kind of supernatural stuff (1 Cor. 15:44ff.)" (NTM, 30–31 [ET, 20]). But whenever he speaks of the "fruits of the Spirit," "it is clear that at bottom he understands the 'Spirit' as the factual [*faktische*] possibility of a new life disclosed in faith. The 'Spirit' does not operate as a natural force, nor does it become a possession of the believer. Rather, it is the factual possibility of life that must be seized by resolve" (NTM, 31 [ET, 20]). This is the significance of Paul's

---

[56] See Bultmann (1956), 202–208.

paradoxical injunction of Gal. 5:25 (one of Bultmann's favorite indications of the existential content of faith): "If we live by the Spirit, let us also walk by the Spirit." In the same vein, "'Being led by the Spirit' (Rom. 8:14) is no natural process, but the enactment of the imperative not to live 'according to the flesh' . . ." (NTM, 31 [ET, 20]). It follows that Paul's catalogue of the fruits of the Spirit ("love, joy, peace, patience, kindness, goodness, faithfulness, gentleness, self-control" [Gal. 5:22]) is entirely consonant with an existentialist view of both indicative (liberation from enslavement to "this world") and imperative (obedience to God's claim). Thus, Bultmann concludes, "in this manner *the concept of the 'Spirit' has been demythologized*" (NTM, 31, Bultmann's emphasis; [ET, 20]).

This is a brief but basically complete existentialist interpretation of the Christian view of our fundamental possibilities before God. I have attempted to emphasize its entirely existentialist form. Bultmann assumed that these possibilities were anchored by a personalistic theism, but we have seen that he resisted all efforts to talk about it except in terms of the *existentiell* possibilities I have discussed here. It is commonly assumed that what Bultmann means by "openness to the future" is only theologically coherent if strongly ontological, and thus referential, meaning along theistic lines is attributed to such notions as the "love" and "grace" of God. In subsequent chapters this assumption will be challenged. For the present, the case has been made, largely on Bultmann's own terms, for an exhaustively existentialist conception of faith. Since this conception is compatible with naturalism, we have achieved our goal of establishing a first bridge principle for a naturalist theology.

CHAPTER 4

Grace and the knowledge of God

A second bridge principle concerns a naturalist conception of God. The last chapter proposed an entirely existentialist account of theological statements. Yet I have projected an approach to religion in which "God exists" can be objectively true. As a meta-assertion for a valuing stance (a seeing- and experiencing-as), "God exists" can be true because determined by physical fact. This "theistic valuing stance" can be cognitivist and can also avoid reducing theological statements simply to statements about human subjectivity. I shall argue that Wieman's naturalist conception of God furnishes such a non-subjectivistic account of theological assertions.

How can theological statements be interpreted entirely existentially without surrendering all possibility of conceiving of God independently of human subjectivity? Wieman's "valuational theism" addresses this puzzle by redefining what the question of God is. It is not about the existence or non-existence of a being with certain attributes but a question about our orientation to "the source of human good." This argument links Wieman's conception of God to an existentialist method which interprets theological statements as expressions of an *existentiell* self-understanding. If understood from the outset in terms of its *religious*, not theological, origins, Christian theism, I shall hold, is precisely such an *existentiell* self-understanding valuationally oriented to God as the source of human good. The claim to truth that Christianity makes rests on the specific content of this self-understanding, and this content is the subject matter of theological interpretation. We saw in the last chapter that the modes of existing that structure this self-understanding are not merely subjective but are constituted crucially by the "world." "World" here is not an "objectively" described "world" but the events of practical encounter which constitute an *existentiell* response. "God," then, may be interpreted existentially (that is, tightly bound to modes of existing) in terms of such events. The Christian claim, which is in principle falsifiable, is that there is a normative valuational stance in relation to such events which is definitive of human authenticity.

Linking Wieman's valuational theism to an existentialist method requires an indirect approach to God. Rather than asking about God directly, we must ask how the valuational orientation which is the content of "God" arises. In Bultmann's language, we must ask how there is a possibility of authentic existence. Within its Christian framework, this is the question of grace. Thus, the question of God must be addressed indirectly by asking what it means to speak of God's *grace*. This indirect approach is a version of what Tillich calls the theological circle: because the content of theological assertions are matters of concern, of *existentiell* self-understanding, their meaning requires already standing within the circle of that concern.[1] Similarly, the cogency of a naturalist version of Christianity cannot be detached from presenting a particular valuational stance. In this chapter, I argue that the theological articulation of God hinges on seeing the question about God as a particular kind of existential concern. That concern, however, is already structured by the Christian way of seeing it which itself is articulated by the notion of grace.[2] This point will become clearer as we examine how Bultmann binds assertions about God existentially to the question of grace.

GRACE AS EVENT

Bultmann's demythologizing program is attractive for a naturalist theology because salvation and the human problem to which it responds are described in a fashion entirely compatible with modern conceptions of ourselves. As Schubert Ogden cogently argues, the content of salvation is nothing other than our "original possibility of authentic existence,"[3] and, as we saw, salvation for Paul can be

---

[1] See Tillich, (1967) I, 8–11.

[2] The point here is quite similar to Bultmann's treatment of natural theology. His dependence on Heidegger's analytic of existence as well as his presentation of "human existence outside of faith" bears similarity to traditional natural theology. Yet Bultmann rightly insists that the portrait of the natural man is dependent upon the subsequent point of view of faith. In the language used here, the cogency of the Christian conception of life in general depends on the cogency of the valuational stance and the seeing-as from which it is viewed and cannot be defended independently of a presentation of that stance. In Bultmann's case as here, the conception of faith which makes this argument possible is decisively connected with the notion of grace. See HMF, 98–102 and 305, n. 19., and Bultmann (1933c), 311–312.

[3] *CM*, 146; see also pp. 112–116.

described simply as "openness to the future," when the full weight of this notion is grasped existentially. Yet this very attractiveness also raises a host of difficult theological questions, for if salvation is simply authentic human existence and if the possibility of such existence is our original possibility as such, then what need is there of such theologically loaded notions as "God," "grace," and "sin" – or even the notion of "salvation" itself?

The Christian response is that however much authentic existence is our original possibility, our actual condition is a "fallen" one in which this possibility cannot be grasped directly. It is this "fallenness" that requires notions of "grace" and "God's action." But this answer raises new questions. It is one thing to assert a "fallenness" from which we cannot free ourselves, but it is quite another thing to give a demythologized account of it. The burden for any existentialist account, but especially for a naturalistic one, is to show how a plausible conception of "bondage" or "fallenness" can be rendered in existentialist terms alone. Demythologizing must describe "fallenness" as a fundamental human condition that does not already illicitly require any theological terms to interpret it. To be sure, there is a circle here, for, as we shall see in the next chapter, the normative case for a Christian seeing-as cannot be made apart from the full account of human being in the world which that seeing-as represents. But this simply means that such a normative case hinges on showing how "fallenness" can be demythologized and rendered entirely in non-mythic and existentialist terms.

Bultmann himself asks about the need for any theological language at all once one has provided an existentialist account of faith, and his argument rewards careful scrutiny. The issue, as he poses it, is whether the event of Christ, in the sense of a specific historical event of the datable past, is necessary for faith, as the New Testament seems to assume. This amounts to the question whether the content of faith can be discovered independently by a suitable philosophical method (see NTM, 31–32 [ET, 21–22]). Bultmann discusses such thinkers as Karl Jaspers, Wilhelm Kamlah, and, of course, Heidegger, and he goes a considerable distance toward conceding that these thinkers adequately describe authentic human existence as an original possibility of human being as such (see NTM, 32–36 [ET, 22–26]). The decisive issue, however, is not whether authentic human nature can be discovered apart from the New Testament but whether it is achievable simply by its becoming known (NTM, 34–35 [ET, 24–25]). Here philosophy and theology part ways because philosophy assumes that simply showing authentic existence is sufficient to bring us to it (NTM, 35 [ET, 25]). To be sure, philosophy sees that our common condition is that we are not what we ought to be, and Heidegger even adopts the theological notion of "fallenness" to describe this condition.[4] Bultmann concedes that theology cannot mean that fallen persons do not know that they are not what they ought to be, for our concern for our authenticity already reflects such awareness (NTM, 27 [ET, 36]). Furthermore, in contrast to Gnosticism or to any substantialist misconception of essential human nature, the existentialist philosophers agree with the New Testament that our "authenticity does not belong to us like some natural property over which we dispose," for they "know that authenticity must constantly be grasped by resolve" (NTM, 36–37 [ET, 27]). The difference, as Ogden nicely puts it, is that philosophy believes "that knowledge of one's authenticity already gives one the power to realize it" (*CM*, 73). Bultmann claims that this is to confuse a factual (*faktische*) possibility with a possibility in principle (*eine prinzipielle Möglichkeit*) and asserts that, according to the New Testament, "human beings have lost the factual [*faktische*] possibility so that indeed their knowledge of their authenticity is falsified by being bound up with their belief that they have control over it" (NTM, 37 [ET, 27]).

Bultmann explicitly sees that the issue here is about how to understand fallenness.[5] The New Testament claims that "we cannot free ourselves from our factual fallenness upon the world but can be freed from it only by an act of God" (NTM, 35 [ET, 26]). The question turns, then, not on fallenness as such – which philosophically can simply be phrased as knowing that one is not what one ought to be – but on the "totality" of the fall (see NTM, 35 [ET, 27]). Bultmann recognizes that a nonmythological description of "sin" is required that will account for this bondage. His argument is extremely compact and requires very careful attention. The argument is perhaps too informed by New Testament vocabulary (which of course is precisely what needs explaining) and thus not sufficiently phenomenological. Nevertheless, a careful analysis will show that he does indeed provide a kind of phenomenological argument for an existential account of fallenness.

[4] See *SZ*, 175–180 (219–224).
[5] NTM, 36 (ET, 27), Bultmann's italics. In his language: "*Es handelt sich um das Verständnis der Verfallenheit des Lebens, in der sich jeder Mensch zunächst vorfindet . . .*"

The crux of the argument involves two assertions. The first is simply that "*in the condition of fallenness our every movement is a movement of ourselves as fallen*" (NTM, 37, Bultmann's emphasis; [ET, 27–28]). This is the condition that Paul describes as "life after the flesh." It is constituted by "willfulness" (*Eigenmächtigkeit*). As we saw, existentially interpreted, this life binds itself to the past by "willfully" seeking to control its own ultimate conditions. The alternative would be to surrender all securities by unreservedly opening oneself to the future, which is the existential content of opening oneself to God. The nature of this binding arises directly out of the assumption "willfulness" makes, namely, that I must and that I can seize ultimate control over the final conditions of my life. Such willfulness is the meaning of the "boasting" which Paul attributed to the Jews in the striving for "righteousness" (*Gerechtigkeit*) and "justification" (*weil sie durch die eigenen Werke "gerechtfertigt" werden*) and to the Gnostics in their striving for "wisdom" (NTM, 37 [ET, 27–28]). Apart from the fact that such "willfulness" can inform even the noblest and most righteous life, the important point is that from within this existential condition even the effort to achieve "self-surrender" is a willful act. This is the profound meaning of Jesus's statement that he who would save his life must first lose it (Mark 8:35). Far from being merely a paradoxical wisdom saying, Jesus's statement already compactly contains the entire Christian conception of sin: every effort to save one's life by losing it is in fact not losing it but an effort to continue to control the conditions of saving it, even as one sees what those conditions are. As Bultmann says, "if genuine life is a life of self-surrender, then it is missed not merely by *those* who instead of living out of self-surrender seek to live by controlling what is controllable (*aus dem Verfügen über das Verfügbare*) but even by *one* who sees self-surrender itself as a controllable goal. . ." Or again, "that *our fundamental condition is willfulness (Eigenmächtigkeit)*, becomes evident precisely in those who, even while recognizing self-surrender as our authentic being, try to draw it within our own control (*in die Eigenmacht einbezieht*), and thus finally end in self-contradiction" (NTM, 37, Bultmann's emphasis; [ET, 27–28]).

The claim that "in the condition of fallenness our every movement is a movement of ourselves as fallen" may be disputed, but that is not at issue here. What we are trying to discern is whether it can be made intelligible, whether a plausible phenomenological account can be given of the "totality" of human fallenness, and this Bultmann's account achieves. Given the existentialist analysis of how our being-in-the-world is shaped by "thrownness," "anxiety," and "care," Bultmann effectively shows how it is possible to be locked into a condition of "willfulness." Even when one sees the nature of authentic existence, one's every effort to achieve self-surrender is an effort to *achieve* it by controlling its conditions. The truth of this account is, of course, dependent on the entire conception of human being in the world that supports the Christian valuational stance. But Bultmann's analysis makes clear that it can be made intelligible within a plausible, nonmythological account of human existence.

This becomes even more evident with the second assertion about the totality of fallenness. Bultmann has claimed that one may recognize authentic existence as the surrender of all security in openness to the future and yet not be able simply to achieve it. What would it take to "achieve" it? The issue again turns on whether the notion of "sin" is merely mythological, whether "self-assertion" and "self-boasting before God" are merely "unnecessary mythological interpretations of an ontological proposition." For these to be nonmythological, the "guilt" involved in self-assertion would have to be rendered nonmythologically as "that responsibility before God that human beings have simply as part of their humanity" (NTM, 38 [ET, 29]). What would such a rendering be? Here Bultmann says, quite significantly: "What is clear is that self-assertion is worthy of being called guilt only if it can be understood as ingratitude. If the radical self-assertion in which we close ourselves to the possibility of authentic life as self-surrender is to be understood as sin, *then it must obviously be possible for us to understand our existence generally as a gift.*"[6] Bultmann introduces this statement by saying that the question of whether sin is mythological or not will hinge on how radically one understands St. Paul's questions to the Corinthians: "What have you that you did not receive? If then you received it, why do you boast, as if it were not a gift?" (1 Cor. 4:7).

Clearly the notions of "gratitude," "ingratitude," and "giftedness" are, in Bultmann's mind, related to a transcendent divine being, as

---

[6] NTM, 38, my emphasis; (ET, 29). Though Fuller translates the last word as "gift of God" (see Bultmann, *et al* [1961b], 31.), Bultmann simply uses the word "gift." In other words, despite the theologically loaded language Bultmann often uses, it would appear that here he is attempting simply to give a phenomenologically adequate rendering of the *existential situation* in which it becomes appropriate for an existentialist interpretation to introduce language of "God," and the overall context in this paragraph supports this reading, as I have indicated in the text.

when he says that "language about sin ceases to appear mythological there where we encounter the love of God *as the embracing and sustaining Power* which upholds us even in our self-assertion and fallenness . . ." (NTM, 38, my emphasis; [ET, 29]). One might assume, therefore, that his statements quoted above simply beg the question by introducing theological notions that are themselves hermeneutically obscure. Correctly understood, however, Bultmann makes possible the same kind of phenomenological illumination we found with the first assertion.

Bultmann himself sees that the issue about the mythological character of sin cannot *first* be addressed with explicitly theological claims. If we attend very carefully to what he actually says, it becomes clear that such notions as "gratitude," "ingratitude," and "gift" are not at first theological notions but ideas of general phenomenological import, as are also the supporting statements from Paul (see NTM, ET, 29 [38]). Furthermore, existentially considered, "receiving one's life as a gift" is identical with radically opening oneself to the future, and the latter is the existential content of God. Alternatively, it is quite faithful to our existential situation, thus phenomenologically legitimate, to speak of "self-assertion" or "life after the flesh" as "ingratitude." This simply recognizes how we subvert the "receptive," "passive" element in our being that is given *prior* to our efforts after control and security. As long as we are clearly aware that we are trying to define ways of being in the world, then such metaphors seem quite appropriate. Bultmann's use of God-language can thus be made hermeneutically transparent by rigorously adhering to the type of existentialist interpretation upon which I have been insisting.

We can conclude that a phenomenologically transparent account of "fallenness" and "sin" making evident the Christian understanding of bondage is available. But this account only sets the stage for the argument. We must understand how the transition from "unfaith" to "faith" is made, for it is this transition that justifies speaking of God's grace. In any case, to this point we can see why Bultmann opposes the philosophical view that simple knowledge of authentic existence is sufficient to achieve it. For him, authentic life becomes a factual possibility "only *when we are delivered from ourselves*" (NTM, 39, Bultmann's emphasis; [ET, 30]).

At this point Bultmann introduces language of God's act. He says, for instance: "there where man is incapable of acting, God acts for him, has acted for him"; this is the significance of the New Testament notion that God has acted in Christ (NTM, 39 [ET, 30]). The content of this action is an *encounter* with "the love of God," for it is just this love, "the embracing and sustaining Power which upholds us even in our self-assertion and fallenness," that validates us as other than we are and by so doing, in an actual *encounter*, "delivers us from ourselves" (NTM, 38 [ET, 29]). As we shall see more fully below,[7] Christ *means* a transformative encounter *now* with "the love of God." What I want to emphasize here is Bultmann's insistence that an actual event of "action" or "encounter" must occur. He says, for instance:

> *The event that happens in Christ is thus the revelation of the love of God* which delivers us from ourselves; an existence for ourselves becomes possible because it delivers us for a life of self-surrender in faith and love. Faith as freedom from oneself, as openness for the future, is only possible as faith in the love of God. But faith in the love of God remains self-assertion so long as God's love is wishful thinking (*ein Wunschbild*), an idea, so long, that is, *as God has not revealed his love*. Christian faith is therefore faith in Christ because it is faith in the revealed love of God. (NTM, 39, first emphasis Bultmann's; [ET, 31])

This notion of an event of encounter is finally what distinguishes the New Testament from the philosophical view, for the former "speaks and Christian faith knows about *an act of God that first makes possible surrender, faith, love* – in short, authentic life" (NTM, 40, Bultmann's emphasis; [ET, 31]).

Clearly I shall have to show how language about "the love of God" or "God's act in Christ" can be understood existentially and naturalistically. We can already see, however, that if openness to God has the existential form of openness to the future, yet if we must be delivered from ourselves in order to achieve it, then it will be existentially appropriate to speak of an encounter with the love of God. In fact, it will be appropriate to speak of the love of God both as a synonym for openness to the future and as the event by which we become open. Since such an event is what Bultmann means above by "God's *revelation* of himself," it also provides the foundations for a Christology. I shall discuss these topics in greater detail later. Here, let us confine our attention to Bultmann's emphasis on an *event* or an *encounter*, for on this issue Wieman's thought will be especially illuminating.

We can pursue the idea of "eventfulness" further by considering

---

[7] See chapter six below.

how Bultmann's notion of the kerygma advances our understanding
of existentialist interpretation. The Greek word *kerygma* became a
technical term in twentieth century theology through form criticism
which tried to identify the earliest layer of oral tradition in the New
Testament. *Kerygma* has come to refer to this earliest version of the
Christian proclamation – which probably took form as something
like: "Jesus is the Lord" or "Jesus is Christ [i.e., the Messiah come]."
Theologically, the term has been broadened to mean the normative
content of the Christian message *as a proclamation* or a *gospel* rooted in
the earliest New Testament tradition. "Kerygma" therefore has a
twofold force in contemporary theological usage. *Normatively* it refers
to the *content* of the earliest Christian message, which may be specified
as God's eschatological act in Jesus Christ. But it also has a *formal*
meaning, which refers to the nature of this message as a proclamation
of God's action. In this formal sense, the weight falls on the kerygma's
event character.

This double meaning is relevant to Bultmann's argument about
the nature of myth because he criticizes previous efforts at demythologizing for failing to preserve the kerygma as kerygma.[8]
Unfortunately, he tends to collapse the two meanings of kerygma
together. For instance, in a characteristic statement about liberal
theology and the History of Religions school, he says: "Here too they
fail to speak about a decisive act of God in Christ proclaimed as the
event of salvation [*Heilsereignis*]" (NTM, 26 [ET, 14]). This ambiguity
raises a fundamental question about which of the two possible
meanings of kerygma is lost. Is it the action of God in a series of
specific events some two thousand years in the past that is lost (i.e., the
content of the kerygma)? Or is it the *event* character of what is
proclaimed as action of God that is lost?

This question drives straight to the center of the controversy over
Bultmann's demythologizing proposal. At issue is whether demythologizing requires giving up the idea of God's special, unique,
and constitutive action in specific past events. Bultmann's criticism of
liberal theology seems to imply that preserving the kerygma means
not surrendering this idea. But this would make demythologizing
incoherent, for, on the one hand, Bultmann sees that demythologizing
must be exhaustive, yet, on the other hand, this position seems to
insist on a content for the kerygma that is patently mythological.

---

[8] See NTM, 23–26 (ET, 11–14).

Through the powerful analyses of Fritz Buri and Schubert Ogden, this problem has come to be known as the "structural inconsistency" in Bultmann's position.[9] This critique implies that the Christ event itself must be demythologized. Assuming this conclusion, we can see why the notion of kerygma has implications for the method of existentialist interpretation. Despite the ambiguity in his formulation, there are good reasons to understand the force of Bultmann's criticism of liberalism in terms of the second, formal meaning of the kerygma, namely, as the proclamation of an event (which has the content of God's action of redemption). Three considerations support this interpretation.

First, after the statement quoted above directed at failed attempts at demythologizing, Bultmann continues:

> The decisive question, therefore, is whether precisely this salvation event, *which is presented in the New Testament as a mythical event [Geschehen]*, or whether the person of Jesus, *which is conceived in the New Testament as a mythical person*, are nothing but mythology. Can there be a demythologizing interpretation that discloses the truth of the kerygma as kerygma for those who do not think mythologically? (NTM, 26, my emphasis; [ET, 14])

Bultmann thus admits that his own phrase for the kerygma, "decisive act of God in Christ," has a mythological form, and this implies that, undemythologized, it cannot be identified with the kerygma lost by other efforts at demythologizing. It further implies that this phrase does not determine the *content* of the gospel but is intended *formally* to designate the character of the gospel as kerygma, as *present event* offering the possibility, *existentiell*, of a new self-understanding. Or, perhaps better, it implies that the content of the kerygma, mythologically expressed as "decisive act of God in Christ," must itself be determined by the formal character of the kerygma as *existentiell* event. "*Decisiveness*" therefore has an entirely existential meaning. Second, in criticizing past attempts at demythologizing, Bultmann repeatedly insists that what was lost is the "*event* through which God has wrought our salvation" (NTM, 25, Bultmann's emphasis; [ET, 13]), and for Bultmann this cannot be an event of the distant past (or any past event, for that matter). What is at stake, in other words, is the *event character as such* of the kerygma as a present proclamation. Finally, nothing could be clearer than Bultmann's insistence that the decisive issue in the proclamation of the kerygma is an event of God's

---

[9] See Buri (1952) and *CM*, 111–126.

redemptive action that happens solely in the present, not in the past –
regardless of his apparent attachment to an undemythologized Christ
event.[10]

What is really behind Bultmann's demythologizing proposal is this
notion of God's action in the present. At stake is not the metaphysical
character of God but the event character of God's action. Myth
makes such present action unintelligible. Other demythologizing
efforts reduce the content of Christianity to ideas or ethical principles
and thereby surrender the notion of God's redemptive action in
present life. The theological objection to philosophical attempts to
describe human existence is not that their description fails. Rather,
they fail to see that we cannot make the transition from inauthentic to
authentic existence without an event by which we are liberated to
choose authentic life.[11] In other words, the real force of the kerygma is
its event character, which points to God's redemptive act in the
present, and it is this that divides Christianity from its alternatives.

The mythological phrase, "the decisive act of God in Christ,"
must, therefore, be so interpreted as to elucidate this formal character
of the kerygma as present event. Furthermore, its character as event
must determine the content of "decisive act of God in Christ"
because, if the formal character of the kerygma as present event is
decisive for thinking about *any* "act of God," then no simply past
event can ground or constitute its intrinsic character as present event.
The *content* of the kerygma, the content of the phrase "decisive act of
God in Christ," is not historical events of the distant past, however
interpreted, but the formal character of the kerygma which, through
proclamation, becomes an event of redemption in the present. Thus,
the question of the kerygma's truth[12] is not about the truth of some
past event but concerns whether an act of God or an event of
redemption is necessary at all for human existence to become
authentic.[13]

The formal, event character of the kerygma is absolutely crucial for
contemporary theology because it places at the very center the
question of God's action (or the question of how God makes a
difference in the world). Bultmann's thought is cardinally important

---

[10] See, e.g., NTM, 45–47 (ET, 37–40). The same also applies to Bultmann's interpretation of
the resurrection.   [11] See NTM, 35–40 (ET, 25–32) and HMF, 107.

[12] See, e.g., NTM, 23 (ET, 10).

[13] Bultmann's claim, as analyzed here, also provides further support for the argument that
what is at issue in the critique of myth is not a false versus a more adequate metaphysics.

here because he makes so clear that God's action can never be anything other than a *present* event in the life of the believer. It is through the *present* proclamation of God's action in Jesus Christ that *God's* action becomes an event. But how can this possibly be so, or rather, how can such a claim be made nonmythologically transparent in conformity with an existentialist and naturalist analysis? This is a truly difficult issue. We have seen that, given our existential condition, we cannot deliver ourselves from fallenness, and this establishes the necessity of an event that liberates us. But how can an event of *proclamation* be such an event, especially if, with Bultmann, we clearly recognize that such an event cannot simply be the communication of ideas?[14]

Another problem is very tightly bound to this one, and the two must be addressed together. This concerns Bultmann's (and Ogden's) emphasis on freedom and responsibility. Bultmann insists that part of the situation calling for demythologizing is the modern understanding of ourselves as unitary beings who can win or lose ourselves only by free and responsible acts of our own agency.[15] Furthermore, one reason why demythologizing is a demand of faith itself is the "peculiar contradiction that runs throughout the New Testament: on the one hand, human beings are cosmically determined, and, on the other hand, they are summoned to decision; on the one hand, sin is fate, and, on the other hand, it is guilt . . ." (NTM, 11 [ET, 23]). Existentialist interpretation demands the reality of freedom because it sees faith as our original possibility of authentic existence requiring the decisions through which we constitute our being-in-the-world, and it understands the offer of faith as the offer of a new self-understanding for which we must decide. Consequently, for all the emphasis on God's action, Bultmann also describes that action as presenting a possibility for which we must decide,[16] and he sometimes speaks of inauthentic existence as simply a rejection of such a possibility when it is offered.[17] Ogden is even more emphatic, constantly emphasizing that Christian proclamation is the summons to a new self-understanding and that faith is a decision laying hold of this possibility.[18]

The question this raises is whether proclamation does anything

---

[14] See, e.g., Bultmann (1952a), 6–7, 14–17 (6–7, 17–19).   [15] See NTM, 18–19 (ET, 5–6).
[16] See, e.g., NTM, 38, 43, 46 (ET, 28, 35–36, 39); Bultmann (1951), I, 302–303; Bultmann (1956), 200–208.   [17] See, e.g., NTM, 46 (ET, 39).
[18] See, e.g., *CM*, 85, 86, 88, 89, 121, 136, 140.

other than present the idea of an authentic self-understanding and then demand that we accept it. Such an interpretation would conflict with our entire analysis. It would account neither for sin as a kind of bondage in which one cannot simply *achieve* authentic existence, nor for God's action as an event which actually liberates. Yet if faith (i.e., openness to the future) is an *original* human possibility belonging to our existence as such, why is not the proclamation of this possibility merely the presentation of å new idea? Or, at most, why is its event character not simply the event of acquiring an illuminating insight – like an "Ah, Ha!" discernment experience.[19] It would then be just the event of coming to see something we could always have seen, leaving us with the task of appropriating it into our lives through resolve. Clearly we need an understanding of proclamation *such that the offer of a new self-understanding in proclamation is actually an event of encounter which actually constitutes the possibility for deciding in its favor.* Related to this is the subsidiary issue of freedom and responsibility, for we also need a clearer conception of how the offer of a new self-understanding can require our full, personal, "decisional" response while at the same time having a passive or receptive dimension of *being* liberating.

To clarify how our freedom can be involved in liberating events, Bultmann draws on analogies from personal selfhood, especially encounters of friendship or love. Central here is Heidegger's notion of the "historicity" (*Geschichtlichkeit*) of human existence. "Historicity" for Bultmann means that human possibilities are constituted as possibilities by events of encounter with a world independent of us which elicit our *existentiell* responses. Such encounters are "nonobjective" because they cannot be "subjectivized" or "psychologized" into "objectively" present intra-psychic processes; they thereby become, as we have seen, the analogical basis for speaking of encounters with the love of God. Some events actually present possibilities by *making* them possible without in any sense violating our freedom and responsibility, as for instance, when I am confronted with my mendacity, or a word of forgiveness is uttered to me, or a loving act makes it possible for me to respond lovingly. Thus, Bultmann says:

What *encounter* means generally can be clarified simply by reflecting on our historical life. The love of another person encounters me and is what it is only as event, for it can be perceived as love not by an objectifying view but only by me myself, the one who is engaged by it. Observed from outside it is not

[19] See Ian Ramsey (1957), 18ff.

visible as love in the genuine sense but only as a psychic phenomenon or one of human spiritual history which is susceptible to various possibilities of interpretation. Naturally, the reality of the love with which someone loves me does not depend on my understanding and reciprocating it. (Indeed, this is precisely what I know when I do respond with reciprocating love.) Even when I do not understand it, even when I do not open myself to it, it still calls forth a (so to speak) *existentielle* reaction; ignoring it is such a reaction, as are closing myself to it and hate. In all these cases, I am qualified through the encounter. Yet this in no way alters the fact that it is visible as love only through an encounter.[20]

Though we are no longer the same after such encounters, the fact that they *change* us or, indeed, that we might not have changed or even been unable to change apart from them in no way diminishes the involvement of our freedom in the total situation. Drawing on the distinction between "knowledge about" and "knowledge of," Ogden makes the same point with the example of a father's seeking to forgive a disobedient son: "The father's purpose in speaking is not to talk *about* his forgiveness and the new relationship it makes possible, but rather to speak *of* his forgiveness or to bestow it, so as actually to establish such a relationship."[21]

We are in much need of a more complete phenomenology of such existential situations. We need a more adequate account of the phenomenological richness of *transformative* events that liberate us. Such events actually constitute possibilities *as* possibilities for us while at the same time engaging our freedom and responsibility. There is thus no reason to question the general adequacy of Bultmann's and Ogden's claims here. The existentialist concept of "historicity" makes it possible to combine the notions of bondage and liberation with freedom and responsibility – though Bultmann's and, especially, Ogden's relentless usage of the language of "decision," "summons," and "laying hold of" surely requires some qualification.

This solution, however, simply returns us to the prior questions about proclamation. It is evident that encounters with persons or even with structured situations that may not have specifically personal characters (such as physical objects or surroundings) can be constitutive of our *geschichtliche* existence, in the sense of "offering" us possibilities of self-understanding. Such encounters can take linguistic

[20] ZPE, 199, Bultmann's emphasis; (ET, 114). See HMF, 99–100.
[21] *CM*, 162. Ogden is also correct to assimilate the "knowledge about/knowledge of" distinction to at least one dimension of Heidegger's and Bultmann's distinction between *existential* and *existentiell* understanding.

form, as when a *word* of forgiveness can shape a new possibility of self-understanding.[22] All such events assume an encounter with some situation shaping reality. Either the event simply is the reality or, if it is linguistic, the word is "of" that reality, as a "word" of forgiveness actually bestows forgiveness. But how is there a reality in the proclamation that both "offers" and "opens up" the possibility for openness to the future? The proclamation cannot be simply *about* such a possibility. The proclamation is "of" God's action, and it is precisely in the proclamation of it that "God's action" occurs. What is this reality that constitutes itself in the proclamation of it? Only by answering this question can we avoid reducing proclamation to information (the *idea* of an existential possibility) or insights (experiences of discernment), and only thus can we account for it as a liberating *event*.[23]

Bultmann's answer to this question follows the analogy of personal encounter we examined above; especially important for him is an encounter with an unconditional love which, by freeing us from ourselves, makes love possible. Just as the "word" of love can manifest the *reality* of a person's love, so the word of proclamation speaks of God's self-giving love. But in the latter case, what is the reality which this word is "of"? Bultmann's answer follows the traditional Christian claim, namely, that there is such a reality because God has actually given himself in Jesus Christ:

[22] Even when such possibilities are offered by events that are non-personal and/or non-linguistic, it is often appropriate to use linguistic metaphors to describe them. The reason is that such *existentiell* situations involve our inmost being which in certain respects is already profoundly linguistic.

[23] This issue is what makes Ogden's thoroughgoing usage of the language of resolve, decision, responsibility, demand, summons, and "laying hold of" misleading. Ogden is clear that faith is possible only because of God's self-giving love (see *CM*, 72–75, 121–123), and he insists that theology must give an account of the *fides quae creditur* (see *CM*, 138–140, 146–149, 158–162). He always speaks of both the *gift* and the demand God's love (see, e.g., *CM*, 140, 153). But such statements as the following, which are entirely characteristic, seem to place the emphasis more on the demand than the gift: ". . . this means that for the first believers, just as for those of every succeeding generation, Jesus's saving significance was visible only to the eyes of faith, or, in other words, was a matter of *existentiell* decision in face of a more or less explicit summons to believe" (*CM*, 88). "The premise of this conclusion . . . is that man is a genuinely free and responsible being, and therefore his salvation is something that, *coram deo*, he himself has to decide by his understanding of his existence" (*CM*, 136). Ogden clearly asserts that "I am always confronted by the event of God's forgiveness and so always have the possibility of accepting it" (*CM*, 123), but the language of resolve is so prominent in his thought that it is difficult to see how the event of God's forgiveness differs merely from the presentation of a possibility of understanding myself before God which I must *resolve* to accept, as, for instance, is suggested by the phrase, "and so always have the possibility of accepting it." Precisely what is the *gift* that *transforms* my possibilities?

The event that occurs in Jesus Christ is thus the revelation of the love of God which frees us from ourselves to become ourselves by freeing us for a self-surrender in faith and love. Faith as freedom from ourselves, as openness for the future, is possible only as faith in the love of God. But faith in the love of God is always self-assertion [*Eigenmächtigkeit*] as long as God's love remains merely a wish [*ein Wunschbild*], an idea, so long, that is, as God has not actually revealed his love. Christian faith is consequently faith in Christ *because it is faith in the revealed love of God.* Only those who are already loved can love; only those to whom trust has been gifted [*geschenkt*] can trust; only those who have experienced surrender [*Hingabe*] can surrender themselves. We are freed to surrender ourselves to God in that God has surrendered himself for us. "In this is love, not that we loved God but that he loved us and sent his Son to be the expiation for our sins" (1 John 4:10). "We love because he first loved us" (1 John 4:19). (NTM, 39–40, first emphasis Bultmann's; [ET, 31])

The reality present in the proclamation is a reality of God having given himself in love. This is the traditional way of stating the issue, but, of course, for Bultmann this formulation is obviously mythological. God's having acted in a specific past event could not account for the efficacy of that event in a *present* proclamation. To be sure, the tradition tried to account for a present efficacy by claiming that the past event was somehow *ontologically constitutive* of new possibilities which are then proclaimed (as, for instance, in quasi-Gnostic notions of Christ's cosmic significance, or in theories of substitutionary or propitiatory sacrifice). But apart from the fact that they conflict with other emphases in the biblical tradition (chiefly surrounding the doctrine of creation whereby we are *always* constituted by God's love), the theories by which such accounts are given are themselves mythological. So, Bultmann is obliged to render the traditional claim in a different, demythologized and existentially interpreted, fashion. Yet his own reformulations are either equally problematic or circular.

On the one hand, Bultmann creates the structural inconsistency in his thought when he claims that authentic historical existence is factually possible only because of God's action in the past historical event of Jesus of Nazareth. This claim is effectively mythological, and it bases faith on an event whose very nature cannot be rendered in existential terms. But it is also problematic because it fails to explain how God's act of self-giving *then* can constitute a *reality* present in the proclamation of that event *now*. Since Bultmann rejects the traditional, mythological accounts of its constitutive character, his thought is simply opaque at this point.

Ogden makes clear, on the other hand, that Bultmann does in fact demythologize the Christ event in his actual interpretative practice (see *CM*, 76–90). In this case, however, "the event of Christ" becomes identical with the event of God's gracious action. As Ogden powerfully shows, Bultmann's statement that "'Christian faith is faith in Christ because it is faith in the revealed love of God' can be true only if 'Jesus Christ' and 'the revealed love of God' are merely two ways of saying the same thing" (*CM*, 121–122). But regarding our question, this now makes Bultmann's position circular. We are asking what the *reality* of God's love is in the proclamation. We are told that it is God's self-giving love in the event of Jesus Christ. But this latter event turns out, now, simply to restate the event of God's self-giving love. It does not help us to identify what *that* reality is in the proclamation.

Ogden clearly sees that to explicate the meaning of Jesus Christ, we must explicate "the revealed love of God" in such a way that it is neither confined to nor defined by the past historical event of Jesus of Nazareth. We must give an independent account of "the revealed love of God" such that we can then say why "faith in Christ" has the same content. The necessity of such an account is central to Ogden's effort to sort through the structural inconsistency in Bultmann's position. Thus, for instance, Ogden objects to Bultmann's claim that those who reject the exclusivity of the past event of Jesus Christ must deny radical human fallenness: "It is at least conceivable that what makes authentic existence everywhere factually possible is not that man is not completely fallen, but that, in spite of his fallenness, he is everlastingly the object of God's love, which is omnipresently efficacious as a redemptive possibility." Even if such fallenness consists in closing oneself against this possibility, "the first conclusion to be drawn from it is not that man needs Jesus Christ, but that he needs a new self-understanding in which his fallenness is overcome by laying hold of this possibility of life in God's love" (*CM*, 121).

In the same vein, from the argument that faith cannot be belief in an idea or a timeless truth but must be an event of personal existence, it does not follow that it can only occur through the message of the church about God's act in Jesus Christ.

Could I not always have accepted it, with or without such encounter, *provided only that I am always confronted by the event of God's forgiveness and so always have the possibility of accepting it?* . . . Although we may agree that faith must indeed be an event of *existentiell* decision, rather than the intellection of timeless truths, Bultmann completely fails to show that such a requirement has any necessary connection with what he takes to be the distinctive Christian claim. So far as his argument goes, all that is required is *some* event in which *God's grace becomes a concrete occurrence and is received by a decision of faith*. (*CM*, 123, first and last emphasis mine)

The same outcome results when Bultmann recognizes that if faith does not involve some mythological, supernatural quality, then it must be an original possibility of human existence as such. This implies, however, as Ogden effectively shows, that

Christian existence is always a "possibility in fact" as well as a "possibility in principle." This may also be expressed by saying that the specific possibility of faith in Jesus Christ is one and the same with a general ontological possibility belonging to man as such. The difficulty with the second statement is that it may mistakenly suggest that the possibility in question literally "belongs" to man, in the sense of something he possesses independently of his relationship with God, and so is able to dispose of as he pleases. The truth is that this possibility is not man's own inalienable possession, but rather is constantly *being made possible for him* by virtue of his inescapable relation to the ultimate source of his existence. To be human means to stand *coram deo* and, by reason of such standing, to be continually confronted with the gift and demand of authentic existence.[24]

Though Ogden does not discuss the circularity identified above,[25] his argument here shows that something like it can only be broken by identifying "the love of God" independently of special reference to "Jesus Christ." Additionally, his statement that what is "required is *some* event in which God's grace becomes a *concrete occurrence* and is received by a decision of faith" (*CM*, 123, first emphasis Ogden's), shows that "the love of God" must be so identified that it can become a reality in proclamation.

Apart from some brief remarks near the end of *Christ without Myth*, which we shall examine in a moment, Ogden's essay, "What Sense Does It Make to Say, 'God Acts in History'?," is his most extensive effort to address this issue. This essay is one of the most ambitious efforts in contemporary theology to deal with the problem of God's action,[26] but it will become evident that it suffers from difficulties parallel with those we have found in Bultmann. Relying on Hartshorne's dipolar conception of God, Ogden develops Bultmann's conception

---

[24] *CM*, 140, Ogden's emphasis; see *CM*, 112–114, 117–119.
[25] He simply assumes that "the love of God revealed in Jesus Christ" has an independent *identifier*. He fails to see, as the analysis which follows will show, that *this* "love of God" lacks a specific identifier *in the proclamation itself*, though, in effect, his further work on "the action of God" is an attempt to provide one.
[26] See Thomas (1983) for a good collection of essays on this fundamental contemporary topic.

of analogy to speak of God's action. He begins by clarifying human
action. Here he makes a distinction upon which he then relies heavily.
Human action may ordinarily be taken to mean the words or deeds
"whereby, through the instrumentality of the body and its various
members, the self undertakes to carry out its particular purposes or
projects" (*RG*, 176). A more primary or "essential" kind of action, as
illuminated by Heidegger and Hartshorne, is that

> whereby the self as such is constituted. Behind all its public acts of word and
> deed there are the self's own private purposes or projects, which are
> themselves matters of action or decision. Indeed, it is only because the self
> first acts to constitute itself, to respond to its world, and to decide it own inner
> being that it "acts" at all in the more ordinary meaning of the word; all its
> outer acts of word and deed are but ways of expressing and implementing the
> inner decisions whereby it constitutes itself as a self. (*RG*, 177)

These essential actions are either authentic or inauthentic (in
Heidegger's sense). The self can either "open itself to its world and
make its decisions by sensitively responding to all the influences that
bear upon it, or it may close itself against its world and make its
decisions on the basis of a much more restricted sensitivity than is
actually possible for it," and these two possibilities of what we may
call "essential self-constitution" may be defined as "love" or "hate"
(*RG*, 177).

God's love is analogous to the second, essential, kind of human
action in God's own essential self-constitution: "I take [the Christian
confession of God as 'pure unbounded love' (Charles Wesley)] to
imply that the primary meaning of God's action is the act whereby, in
each new present, he constitutes himself as God by participating fully
and completely in the world of his creatures, thereby laying the
ground for the next stage of the creative process" (*RG*, 177). It is not
necessary for my purposes here to develop Ogden's full dipolar
analysis. It is relevant, however, to examine how Ogden relates what
he terms the indirect, existential meaning of God's action to this
direct, essential, self-constitution. He does this through the Christian
confession of God as Creator and Redeemer:

> On this conception, to say that God acts as the Creator is not merely to say
> that both I and my world are utterly dependent on his power and love and
> that I am bound to be obedient to his will as it pertains to myself and my
> world. That this existential meaning is the *indirect* meaning of the statement is
> to be readily granted. But what it *directly* says is that the ultimate ground of

every actual state of the world is not just the individual decisions of the creatures who constitute its antecedent states, but rather these decisions as responded to by God's own decision of pure unbounded love. In a similar way, to say that God acts as Redeemer is to say more than that I now have the possibility of that radical freedom from myself and openness to my world that constitutes the authentic existence of love. It is also to say – and that directly – that the final destiny both of myself and of all my fellow creatures is to contribute ourselves not only to the self-creation of the subsequent worlds of creatures, but also to the self-creation of God, who accepts us without condition into his own everlasting life, where we have a final standing or security that can nevermore be lost. (*RG*, 178–179, Ogden's emphases)

In both its indirect and its direct senses, this quite powerful conception of God's action still fails to help us define how God's action is specifically present in proclamation, or for that matter, in any other event by which we are transformatively offered the possibility of a new self-understanding. Ogden does provide a conception of God's action, *but it is indifferently relevant to every event as such.* Ogden himself acknowledges this by recognizing that to this point God's action is not an action in history at all.

Although his action as Creator is related to history – indeed, is the action in which all historical events are ultimately grounded – his creative action as such is not an action *in* history, but an action that *transcends* it. . . Likewise, God's action as the Redeemer cannot be simply identified with any particular historical event or events. As the act whereby he ever and again actualizes his own divine essence by responding in love to all the creatures in his world, it is an act that transcends the world as the world's ultimate consequence. (*RG*, 179, Ogden's emphases)

The dipolar conception of God's "*eminent* historicity" counters the objection that God's action is timeless and unhistorical, for God both constitutes and is constituted by every moment of the world's passage (see *RG*, 179–180). But this offers no help with the problem of God's *particular* action. Ogden admits as much by the way in which he formulates the first, ontologically primary, form of God's historical action:

. . . we may say that every creature is to some extent God's act – just as, by analogy, all our bodily actions are to some extent our actions as selves. There is, to be sure, a certain freedom on the part of the creatures so that they are the result not only of God's action but also of their own; in part, at least, they are self-created. Still, this creaturely freedom has definite limits ultimately grounded in God's own free decisions, and in this sense every creature has its basis in God's creative action. Although the acts whereby God actualizes his essence are his acts and not the acts of the creatures, each creature is what it is only by partly reflecting or expressing in its being God's free decisions. (*RG*, 180)

This conception *can* make sense of God's "pure unbounded love." But it does so only by interpreting this claim in terms of the way eternal objects are made available and relevant to the ongoing passage of *every* event, by the way, that is, that God's primordial being provides the ground of ordered passage through the responses of his consequent nature. It does not show how God's love is made *specifically* available, precisely as love, in any particular events, and especially in those *present* events by which God's love is transformatively *active* as a grace that is a *concrete occurrence*, as, for instance, in proclamation.

For just this reason Ogden turns to a second sense in which God may be said to act in history. Here he defends a nonmythological way to say that God has acted decisively in Jesus Christ. The argument turns on seeing that human beings are preeminently creatures of meaning. Having the capacity for consciousness and self-consciousness, we not only exist but know and understand that we exist. Thus, part of what it means for us to exist is to express an understanding of ourselves symbolically by the way we make sense of our lives. Such symbolic expressions of the ultimate meaning of our lives constitute the religious dimension of culture. Some of these symbolic expressions will be more adequate than others to the actual reality that does truly define the ultimate meaning of our lives. The Christian claim that Jesus is the Christ – a claim identical to "the revelation of the love of God" – is just such a symbolic expression of the ultimate truth about our lives.

Here God's action turns on another analogy from human action. Though all our actions in word and deed express our essential self-constituting action, some of these actions are particularly "decisive." With special clarity, they give paradigmatic expression to our innermost character, that is, to the self-understanding by which we existentially constitute our being in the world. This is the sense in which Jesus Christ is God's decisive act. It is not that God has acted specially in Christ and nowhere else; rather, in the symbolic word and deed that Jesus who is the Christ *is*, God's essential action in all events is manifested with full transparency. In this sense it can be said that God has acted decisively in Jesus Christ. What is manifested here is nothing other than a "transparent means of representing a certain possibility for understanding human existence" which Ogden defines as follows: "[Jesus's entire history in word and deed is] a single witness to the truth that all things have their ultimate beginning and end solely in God's pure unbounded love and that it is in giving ourselves wholly into the keeping of that love, by surrendering all other securities, that we realize our authentic life" (*RG*, 186). Ogden intends this analogy strictly. We saw him argue above that in a certain respect "every creature is to some extent God's act" (*RG*, 180). It follows from this, given the centrality of symbolic meaning in human life, that a human being "can, at least in principle, also re-present or speak for the divine. Insofar as what comes to expression through his speech and action is the gift and demand signified by God's transcendent action as Creator and Redeemer, he re-presents not only his own understanding of God's action, but, through it, the reality of God's action itself" (*RG*, 181), and this is true despite, or perhaps better, because it is also true that "any event, whether intended by anyone as symbolic or not, can become such an act of God insofar as it is received by someone as a symbol of God's creative and redemptive action. Because man is distinctively the creature of meaning, there is no event he experiences that cannot become for him such a symbol" (*RG*, 183).

The problem is that this argument is simply the obverse of the circularity in Bultmann. For Bultmann, the event of Jesus Christ is identical with the revelation of the love of God, but when we try to give content to what the love of God is, we are simply referred back to the event of Jesus Christ. Ogden's position is not correspondingly circular, but it has a similar problem. He specifies what the love of God is, and therefore, he can also say what is revealed decisively in the words and deeds of Jesus (and articulated symbolically in the church's proclamation of the Christ). Insofar as such words and deeds are decisively "re-presented," then, given God's transcendent essential action as such, they also may be understood as God's action. But now what is decisively revealed in Jesus Christ simply restates God's action that is *indifferently characteristic* of *every* event. We can now specify the content of "Jesus Christ," unlike in Bultmann, but now it loses any specific content in terms of our concrete encounter with the world.

Ogden succeeds in defining both God's action and the content of God's love. The problem is that these have absolutely general ramifications. This has two damaging consequences for the issue I am trying to address here. First, a careful examination of what Ogden claims as the content of the Christian confession of God as Creator and Redeemer shows that I can *understand* myself in terms of them only by understanding something like Hartshorn's metaphysics. *What* I then understand is that *every* event that occurs, without any differentiation, is *equally* an expression of God's love. This has the consequence, second, that what is revealed decisively in Jesus Christ is just this *general* understanding. It is suspiciously difficult to see where, and specifically *as what*, I have an encounter with God's transformative grace by which I am liberated to adopt as an existential self-understanding what Ogden terms the indirect content of God as Redeemer, namely, "that I now have the possibility of that radical freedom from myself and openness to my world that constitutes the authentic existence of love" (*RG*, 178). True, I can understand everything that occurs in such a way that it would be appropriate (perhaps) for me to adopt an existential self-understanding of openness to the world. How is this different, however, from simply having an idea or an insight which I may then resolve to incorporate as my existential self-understanding? Where is the *existentiell encounter* with the gracious love of God by which my self-understanding – my very being in Heidegger's sense – is *transformed* by God's love, in some sense active upon me, into openness toward the future which I then obediently take upon myself? Ogden fails to provide an account of God's action in this sense. Yet, as we have seen, his and Bultmann's notions of fallenness and of the "event-fullness" of God's grace require it. Ogden gives us an account of God's loving action that is exactly the same in those events to which I respond by binding myself to "life after the flesh" as in those which *liberate* me for the "life of faith." He fails to give an account of God's *specifically* gracious and liberating action which is the *existential* content of "the love of God."

Ogden does establish God's loving relation indifferently to all events, and this might support God's specific gracious action, were the latter provided. It is at least intelligible that, responding existentially to God's gracious action by a stance of openness to the future, one would require a "background" conception of every event as grounded in God's love. Perhaps no specificity is required, and every event may be described indifferently as a manifestation of God's love – though it is worth noting that such a description will support exactly the contrary position (i.e., a God of hatred and evil). But some specificity *is* required if a new self-understanding is possible only through God's *gracious* action.

Ogden seems to see this, for he is quite clear that somehow God's gracious action must apply to *me*. Such is, indeed, implicit in everything he writes about faith as an *existentiell* self-understanding. In the essay under review, he indicates his awareness of this issue when he writes, for instance, that "an event is a decisive revelation of God only insofar as it truly re-presents the *existential gift* and demand of 'the one eternal good'" (*RG*, 185, my emphasis). I am simply claiming that an account of this action falls between the stools of his position. The analysis of God's decisive action in Jesus Christ in this essay fails to articulate just this action by which it becomes a gracious action for me. Near the end of *Christ without Myth*, Ogden seems to address the same problem with his important notion of "re-presentation."

In this context the issue is the "'objective' reality of the revelatory event Jesus the Christ" (*CM*, 158) which an existentialist interpretation must capture. He states that the entire reality of Jesus of Nazareth, not only his preaching but his acts of healing, his fellowship with sinners, and especially his death on the cross, was transparent to "the word he sought to proclaim," and he emphasizes that the content of this "word" is "an event that in its 'significance' confronts those who encounter it with a certain possibility of *existentiell* understanding" (*CM*, 159). Thus, "in summoning men to live in radical dependence on God's grace, and so in freedom from the past and openness to the future, the event of Jesus is but the re-presentation of man's original possibility of existence *coram deo*" (*CM*, 160), and we know that this "original possibility" is a way of being in the world, an existential self-understanding. By way of clarifying this notion of *re-presentation*, Ogden then states: "It belongs to the nature of a true statement that, just insofar as it is true, it is transparent to the reality that makes it true. Indeed, *this reality itself is actually present 'in, with, and under' the statement that seeks to express it.* When we say, then, that the integral significance of the event of Jesus is to re-present as a possibility demanding decision the final truth about man's existence *coram deo*, we are actually saying the reality this truth seeks to express is literally present 'in, with, and under' that same event" (*CM*, 161, Ogden's emphasis).

Now, I submit that it is not at all evident that in every true statement the reality that makes it true is actually present "in, with and under" the statement that seeks to express it. It is not even evident what this claim means. More important, Ogden's own discussion of this claim supports two different ways of taking it. On the one hand, the transparency in question may simply state the significance of Christ's decisiveness worked out at greater length in "What Sense Does It Make to Say, 'God Acts in History'?," as when Ogden says that "the reason we can speak of it as the 'eschatological event' *pro se, extra nos, sine nobis, et contra nos* is that in its deepest reaches it is nothing less than the God-man relationship that is the essential reality of every human life" (*CM*, 161). We saw above that taken this way it does not show how the truth of this "eschatological event" becomes an event of God's gracious action for me.

On the other hand, Ogden makes clear that by "re-presentation" he also means the *existentiell* encounter with this possibility that, *in the encounter*, becomes a possibility *for me*. Thus, he says, "by this is meant not that Jesus himself in his 'person' actualizes this relationship *existentiell*, but rather that the word he speaks and is, in fulfilling his 'office,' is the re-presentation *to us* of the possibility of such a relationship" (*CM*, 161, Ogden's emphasis; cf. p. 162). With this, however, the notion of re-presentation, in itself, as just noted, not terribly clear, simply restates the question. *How* is the *reality*, about which this truth is true, *present* in the encounter with Jesus Christ, especially in the proclamation which re-presents that truth? With this issue of existential import, what Ogden says above about true statements is clearly not true, for a statement carrying existential import for me can be true without its *existential truth* being evident to me at all. In this latter sense, the reality which makes it true is not at all present "in, with, and under" the statement that seeks to express it. At least part of the force of Ogden's statement about "re-presentation" is apparently intended to mediate the distinction between "objective truth" and "existential truth" (or between "knowledge about" and "knowledge of" [*CM*, 162]), but instead it simply restates the question of how a truth that may be objectively true can become an existential truth for me.

Because this problem remains unillumined, Ogden too often leaves the impression that he is speaking of the presentation of a possibility which I *can* appropriate only through an effort of "willful self-assertion." He leaves this impression even when he clearly sees the issue under review here. Thus, for instance, directly in the context where he is insisting on the distinction between "knowledge about" and "knowledge of" he says, "what confronts us in Jesus is not, in its first intention, a 'world-view' addressed to our intellects, *but a possibility of self-understanding that requires of us a personal decision*" (*CM*, 162, my emphasis). I am not disputing that *what* confronts us in Jesus is to be understood as a possibility of existential self-understanding, but Ogden fails even here to identify where and how God's grace (which makes this self-understanding possible for me) is present in this "confrontation" with Jesus?[27]

I have undertaken this discussion of Bultmann and Ogden in order to clear the ground for an examination of Wieman's notion of God's action. To summarize, existentialist interpretation requires approaching the question of God through the question of God's action. We have seen how an existentialist analysis provides a phenomenologically adequate account of fallenness, and why, consequently, a notion of the "event-fullness" of God's action is required for an existentialist theology. This analysis establishes a significant part of the second bridge principle we need to make a naturalist theology intelligible, for all of these notions are compatible with an entirely naturalist conception of human being in the world. But we have also seen the deep difficulties in Bultmann and Ogden in identifying the specific "event-fullness" of God's gracious action. This problem is the nub of the issue that now permit us to turn to Wieman.

FAITH AS AN EXISTENTIAL ORIENTATION TOWARD CREATIVE TRANSFORMATION

We have seen that the notion of faith is crucial for a naturalist theology. Though the naturalist rejection of traditional conceptions of God might seem to require rejecting religious conceptions of faith as well, this would be true only if faith is equated with belief.[28] Actually, the biblical tradition as it received its normative expression in classical Protestantism refuses to accept this equation. Thus, for instance, in the *Large Catechism* Luther states that "the trust and the faith of the heart alone make both God and an idol. . . For these two belong together, faith and God. That to which your heart clings and entrusts itself is, I say, really your God."[29] The same idea lies behind

---

[27] See Robinson and Cobb (1963) and (1964) for discussions of "language-event" theology which attempt to address some of the issues surrounding the "event-fullness" of grace. Raschke (1979) also addresses these issues, but his constructive proposal concerning a "freedom of language" in I-Thou encounters is weakly conceived and simply restates the issues discussed above (see pp. 81–89). Evans's discussion of "self-involving" language also makes an important contribution to these issues, though he is far too bound to an "objectivistic" conception of religious meaning.

[28] See Hardwick (1987a) and (1988).   [29] Tappert (1959), 365.

Bultmann's existentialist interpretation, and significantly, for Wieman faith corresponds directly with this normative Protestant meaning.

Both conceive faith as essentially practical, not theoretical, with only a tangential relation to belief. Faith is not made up of objectively entertained beliefs which may or may not be true or justifiable by rational criteria. Rather, faith is trust, commitment, devotion, and loyalty, a way of being or doing. Though any instance of faith will contain beliefs, faith itself is not constituted by entertaining them. Wieman understands this perfectly. "The notion is prevalent," he says, "that faith can survive only when knowledge is inadequate. This would be true if faith were a belief sustained by less evidence than is required to lift the belief to the status of knowledge. But such is not the case. Faith is not essentially belief at all, although faith generally has a belief. Religious faith is basically an act – an act of giving one's self into the keeping of what commands faith, to be transformed by it, and to serve it above all" (*SHG*, 46).

This conception of faith is warranted by Wieman's understanding of both God and the religious problem. As we saw, God may be formally defined as that reality upon which human abundance is dependent.[30] That there is such an actually operative reality is evident since human existence and the goods of life are not something brought about by human effort alone. It must be an actuality within nature because we have no way of warranting claims about any reality beyond our experience of this world. For the same reason, we can discover the nature of this reality solely through an empirical examination of its actual operations and of the conditions that enhance or inhibit them.[31]

These simple formulations already provide the basic ingredients of Wieman's empirical naturalism. Simple as they are, they suggest the same relevance to contemporary theology that we found with Bultmann.[32] Two features of this approach to God are especially relevant for a naturalist theology: (1) its formal and (2) its functional character. It identifies God formally and thus without predetermining the content of his reality, yet in such a way that God can be both the "object" of an absolute devotion and also concretely actual within the world. We saw how this was achieved by redefining the very question of God in valuational terms, a position I have been calling a

---

[30] See RESM 9–10; *SHG*, 23–26, 44–48; *MUC*, 11.   [31] See *SHG*, 31–37.

[32] See Wieman (1975b) for an analysis of the contemporary religious problem that is surprisingly similar to that of Bultmann.

"valuational theism." Such a formal approach has enormous relevance for a naturalistic interpretation of religion for, though it need not be naturalistic in and of itself, it is compatible with naturalism precisely because it prescinds from the question-begging ontological absolutes of traditional theism (which are often identified with religion or the religious interest *tout court*).[33] At the same time, this approach is not empty because it identifies God in terms of functions that can be understood to apply universally within human experience.[34] The attractiveness of this combination of formal and functional approaches to God within the contemporary hermeneutical situation supports the appeal of a naturalist theology. They provide the foundations for a naturalist conception of God, especially since its functional aspect can be specified more concretely by an existentialist method.

This attractiveness remains incomplete, however, unless it is connected with a view of how the human situation is religiously problematic, with what the theological tradition calls sin.[35] In the first chapter, we looked briefly at how Wieman develops a concept of sin out of his valuational theism. Now we need to examine this view more carefully, for it is closely related to the existentialist analysis already established as foundational for our approach to God. According to that analysis, sin is a failure to orient oneself to God when this orientation is conceived as openness to the future. We now need to see how closely Wieman's view both of God and of the human situation before God is related to this existentialist analysis.

Naturalistically conceived, the religious problem lies in the tension between the human drive for fulfillment and resistance to that very drive. Fulfillment consists in the fullest possible actualization of human potentialities. Wieman understood this fulfillment in terms of the richness of experience which he termed "growth in value."[36] By this he meant not simply intensity or a quantitative accumulation of experience but its qualitative enhancement through the development of capacities for sensitivity, complexity, differentiation, and integration. He took as axiomatic that fulfillment requires continual transformation within experience and its structures. Being constantly transformed, experience and its richness reflect our dependence

---

[33] See Hardwick (1987c).
[34] See, for example, Smith (1982) and Tremmel (1976), 40–72.   [35] See Smith, (1982).
[36] Wieman understood the richness of experience through a sophisticated conception of processes that are essentially communicative and interactional in character. The present account interprets this richness through Bultmann's existentialist interpretation and therefore largely ignores this aspect of Wieman's thought.

upon processes that we do not ultimately control but that are creative within us.

Equally as prominent as this drive for fulfillment is our resistance to it just because it is transformative. This tension is best captured by the distinction between "creative good" and "created good."[37] Creative good is synonymous with the formal definition of God because it refers to those actual processes in nature which produce value and its growth.[38] Creative good produces value by novel arrangements of already existing entities in nature; value is produced by transformations which result in new structures of value. Creative transformations, in other words, are sedimented into structures which are either new material objects (a new molecular structure, for instance) or new arrangements of relationships within or between already existing objects (new, richer forms of experience, for instance, with their material bases in the brain and nervous system). Such products of "creative good" are Wieman's "created goods." All forms of value in human experience are created good in this sense because they are mediated by already existing structures such as language, culture, historical memory, education, and, most especially, by the human brain.

The problem is that human beings are inclined to define their fulfillment by the good as they know it, to seek the growth of value according to value as created good already appreciable within experience. But, Wieman argues, this destroys the conditions for the growth in value and thus for the fulfillment of human life.[39] Such resistance occurs in several ways: through limits of imagination; through clinging for security to known versus unknown orders of life; or in more sinister ways through egocentricity, arrogance, and the will to power.[40] In each case, the possibility for human fulfillment is limited, distorted or destroyed. The way to human fulfillment lies in giving oneself to the real source of this fulfillment, namely, to the

---

[37] See *SHG*, 16–26.

[38] Wieman would want to say that this is also true of traditional, non-naturalist conceptions of God. Even if God's working is not identified with natural processes, the *religiously* significant interest in God is formally identical with "creative good," he would say, because it is an interest in *the source* of human good, an essentially valuational concern, whatever else the classical theologians want to say. It must be identified with natural processes, Wieman claims, simply because we can *know* about nothing else, again despite the mystifications of theologians. See *SHG*, 31–33 and Wieman (1968).

[39] In a time when technological development gives unprecedented power, Wieman also considers such an orientation enormously dangerous for the human future (see *SHG*, 24–25, 28–29). His argument bears similarities to the critique of the doctrine of progress by Niebuhr and others to the effect that increase in human power brings no increase in human virtue (see, e.g., Reinhold Niebuhr [1941], II, 168–169, 206).   [40] See *SHG*, 23–29, 44–46, 87–93.

"creative good" or God, and such devotion is what Wieman means by faith. Stated positively, then, the religious problem is simply a specification of the functional meaning of God. Hence, the God question, to quote Wieman, is the question: "What operates in human life with such a character and power that it will transform man as he cannot transform himself, to save him from the depths of evil and endow him with the greatest good, provided that he gives himself over to it with whatsoever completeness of self-giving is possible for him?" (*MUC*, 11).

These entirely naturalist concepts of God and faith permit construing the human problem as a problem of the orientation of a devotion and thus as fundamentally religious. The parallel with an existentialist account is striking. According to both, faith and sin are valuing stances, and these may be understood as orientations toward God when God is conceived valuationally, as in Wieman's notion of "source of good." Existentially it is the "love of God" that makes "openness to the future" possible, and "openness to the future," existentially conceived, is nothing other than devotion to God, a valuing stance. In a moment we shall see how close to one another "source of human good" and "openness to the future" are.

We should note again that both Wieman and Bultmann stand within a major strand of the prophetic tradition which conceives the basic human problem as idolatry, the worship of false gods. The orientation to created goods amounts to absolutizing them as an alternative to devotion to the one true God upon whom we are dependent as the creator of the goods of life, and, existentially interpreted, "life after the flesh" amounts to worship of the creature, and ultimately, as is shown existentially, the elevation of the self to the functional role of "God." "The gravest peril that men have to face," Wieman says, "resides in the way . . . created good . . . can arouse an absoluteness and supremacy of loyalty which only its source, creative good, the generating event, really commands" (*SHG*, 24). Wieman (and Bultmann) would agree with Reinhold Niebuhr's astute observation that "Christian orthodoxy has consistently defined unbelief [in the sense of false devotion] as the root of sin."[41]

There is thus a surprising continuity between Wieman's naturalist concept of faith and the biblical tradition. Nevertheless, the theological content of faith remains relatively undeveloped in Wieman's thought.

---

[41] Reinhold Niebuhr (1941), I, 183.

Fully to appreciate its fruitfulness for a naturalist theology requires that we amplify it in two directions. To begin with, Wieman tended to regard faith merely instrumentally, simply as a concept to promote devotion to God. He consequently never exhibited the specifically religious (or intrinsic) values of faith. This issue is connected with a second one having to do with the distinction between creative good and created good. The problem is that value *increases* solely through transformative processes in nature (the creative event), but it *exists* or terminates in experience as created goods. Faith can be an intrinsic value, then, only as a created good, yet as a created good, it seems to suffer from the same distortion it is supposed to resolve. More subtly, though faith is instrumental to achieving greater value *in created goods*, it seemingly cannot itself be a value since it is committed to their perpetual *transformation*.

It is difficult, then, to see how faith can be a religious value in its own right. Yet assimilating Wieman's naturalism to existentialist interpretation hinges on giving such valuational content to faith. I have made a case for a strictly existentialist account of salvation, and we have seen why this is attractive for a naturalist approach to religion. That account requires, however, that we conceive faith or salvation – openness to the future – as a kind of abundance. We must show, therefore, how Wieman's conception of faith admits of intrinsic value. Significantly enough, resources from existentialist analysis will permit us to address this issue. Correlatively, this deepened conception of faith will permit us to resolve the obscurities in contemporary theology concerning God's gracious action.

It is altogether too easy to think of faith as a series of specific practical acts, thus suggesting that faith is simply one created good (or a series of such goods) among others. In order to address the difficulties discussed above, however, it will be important to think of faith not as a set of singular acts but as an *orientation* or a *framework* for activity. This idea is compatible with created goods because such goods, the concrete values within experience, are themselves either structures or are configured in structures. The existentialist idea of self-understanding is also closely related to the notion of an orientation. We order our lives through an overall context of meanings by which we configure our being in the world. Though we do not determine the values within experience just as we wish, an element in the overall structure of experience arises from our answer to the general question of who and what we are within the world. We answer this question by acts of reflective subjectivity that run deeply into the constitution of our selves and our worlds. Our being in the world is not primarily an intellection but a mode of *existing*; yet it also involves an *understanding* because, by giving our lives a certain configuration in interaction with the objects and persons encountered in practical concern, we order our lives by an overall and very deep-lying response to meaning.[42] Such self-determining acts pertain not to this or that good but to the way we have goods at all. The existentialists refer to "existence" rather than to "experience" here because these acts constitute our very being and are not just experiences that we undergo. This existential dimension is therefore an overall act of *self-understanding* by which we constitute the frame within which any experiences at all (and therefore any created goods) are the experiences they are for us.

Obviously, and contrary to some existentialists, we determine neither existence nor experience totally *de novo*. But at the level in nature reached by reflective, finite subjects, the way value is had is constituted by the existential angle taken toward it. This implies that in some instances the actual content of what is or is not a created good in experience is also constituted by this act of self-understanding: some created goods would not occur in a particular world of experience if there were not an angle on that world to start with – though clearly no angle can constitute all created goods because any angle is itself taken up only because of some goods already given. Hence, the particular created goods in a world of experience are partially a product of the structure produced by our answers to existential questions about the meaning of our lives. Thus, the "absolutization" of created goods, the crucial element in Wieman's analysis of the human problem, in its most fundamental sense means the absolutization of *the entire way goods are had* (and not simply the absolutization of this or that good).

We can now amplify this point by carefully examining Wieman's description of faith as a transformation. The movement of faith, he writes, is "the reversing of the order of domination in the life of man *from* domination of human concern by created good *over to* domination by creative good" (*SHG*, 269, Wieman's emphasis). By referring positive value solely to creative good (to devotion to God), this statement would seem to eliminate value entirely from created goods.

---

[42] Heidegger marks the depth of this understanding by finding it most profoundly disclosed in mood (*Befindlichkeit*) (see *SZ*, 172–188).

But this cannot be Wieman's intention. As a naturalist, he must not only affirm that human fulfillment, or, religiously speaking, salvation, occurs solely within the present world; he must also insist that salvation is an actual achievement within experience. If so, however, it must occur as created goods since value can occur in experience only as the created goods precipitated in experience by God's creative activity. This is all the more true if faith itself is a value, for then the intrinsic values it realizes precisely as faith can only occur as values within created goods. The problem is to see how faith can have intrinsic qualities within created goods and yet also be the *reversal* characterized above. The solution lies in seeing faith as an existential self-understanding so that the reversal becomes a reversal in an overall orientation.

With this in mind, let us note how crucial the notion of *transformation* is in Wieman's description of the movement of faith as a reversal.[43] Although faith can be described as an act, an act of commitment or devotion, its actual movement is something *undergone*. This permits the movement of faith to be understood as an actual operation of the creative event, and this provides the seeds for a solution to the problem of God's specific gracious action that we examined above. This element of undergoing suggests that both the movement of faith and the operation of the creative event must be understood in some more complex way than as one act among others in a linear series. This suspicion is confirmed by Wieman's description of the transformation as a *reversal* in an *order of domination*. The movement of faith is not a singular act, one of a series, but involves a structure *within* which singular acts occur. Only this could justify the language of domination which suggests that we cannot simply step into or out of faith. These notions of transformation, reversal, and domination bring Wieman's analysis very close to the existentialist account of sin and bondage.

Parallel to that earlier analysis, Wieman's language also suggests that faith and unfaith are correlative. Just as in Bultmann, then, it will be helpful to approach Wieman's conception through its opposite, unfaith, understood as devotion to created goods. Describing such devotion as a "domination" already implies that unfaith is not merely a series of particular values but an orientation in the sense of a false center of life. Furthermore, as already noted, Wieman identifies this

---

[43] Wieman makes this clear in the full context. See *SHG*, 269–279, esp. 272, 275, 279.

devotion to created goods with the biblical notion of idolatry; it is thereby congenial with "life after the flesh" which is itself idolatry in the sense of an egoistic orientation to the creature rather than to God. This proximity of his demythologized version of "God" and "faith" to the existentialist conception of idolatry lends support to my argument that his notion of faith can be construed as an orientation, that is, an existential self-understanding.

We have already seen that unfaith is not the intellectual refusal to affirm the truth of certain propositions but the existential refusal to trust God. The human problem is rebellion against God, a refusal to recognize our dependence upon God and to acknowledge his claim upon us. This rebellion becomes, in effect, an attempt to usurp the place of God by making ourselves the center of existence, existentially configuring our lives as though we could be the source of our own being. Unfaith, thus, ends in an overall orientation to life that has the content of idolatry. This is particularly evident in the existentialist interpretation of the doctrine of Creation. As Bultmann argues, the doctrine of Creation simply means to acknowledge God as Lord, and its existential content is openness to the future.[44] The opposite existential stance rejects openness to the future in an effort to secure life by acting as though it is in one's control.[45] Such "life after the flesh" is to treat oneself, existentially, as one's own creator, the source of one's being, and thus has the existential content of idolatry.[46]

This approach to the human problem lends itself to rich descriptive analyses of the human situation which have been exploited most powerfully in our time by literary figures and the existentialists. This is important for a naturalist theology because it permits translating such hermeneutically opaque notions as "rebellion against God," "usurping the place of God," and "placing oneself at the center of existence" into existential descriptions of the human attempt to control the vicissitudes of fate and to secure ourselves against or even to deny our fundamental contingency, finitude, loneliness, and insecurity.

In sum, Wieman's "domination by an order of created goods" may

[44] See Bultmann (1956), 11, 16, 18.
[45] In Bultmann's words, it is to live "in terms of controlling that which lies within one's powers of control" ("*aus dem Verfügen über das Verfügbare*") (NTM, 37 [ET, 28]).
[46] See also, Reinhold Niebuhr's analysis of "unbelief" as a rebellion which elevates self into the place of God. Thus, the ultimate content of the worship of false gods is always, finally, self worship (Reinhold Niebuhr [1941], I, 179, 183, 186, n. 1). The same analysis is made somewhat differently but also very powerfully by Paul Ramsey (1950), 295–301.

be seen as an existential self-understanding that seeks to secure existence by controlling an already given structure of value. This is idolatry and rebellion against God, the creative event, because it mistrusts the sole source of human "security, welfare, and increasing abundance" (*RESM*, 9). Existentially, it is the attempt to "usurp the place of God" by dictating the abundance of life from an angle already given in experience.

Interpreting Wieman's "order of created goods" as an existential orientation now permits us to expand his notion of a domination that can be reversed only by an event of transformation. An idolatrous existential self-understanding is fittingly characterized as one of hatred and death because it creates conditions in which the self must regard every "other" as a threat to its powers of control.[47] But from within this existential structure, every effort to free oneself from its convoluted circle of self-concern simply replicates the same structure. Wieman's notion of "transformation" thereby captures the biblical paradox that "whoever would save his life will lose it" (Mk 8:35). Every effort to escape domination by created goods recreates that domination so long as it arises out of the existential structure which centers the self on created goods. Elaborating Wieman's notion of domination by an existentialist analysis shows that behind such an orientation is an existential background of anxiety and care. His position can accommodate this refinement because, on the one hand, his "domination by an order of created goods" requires reformulation as an existential orientation, and, on the other hand, an existential self-understanding is ultimately a valuational ordering of life and thus entirely compatible with Wieman's philosophical vocabulary.

It follows that one must be freed from an entire existential stance, not from domination by this or that created good. Consequently, the reversal alters the very center out of which one lives. Since this center is a structure for the very *having* of appreciations and thus the center out of which we think and act, its radical alteration is quite strictly a transformation. Borrowing Heidegger's and Tillich's language, we may call it an ecstasy, a standing outside ourselves.[48] Through such an ecstatic, transformative event, even if only momentarily (but momentarily again and again), we experience a new center for the very having of experience, a transformation of the horizon of our experience as a whole.

[47] See NTM, 28–29, 31 (ET, 17, 20).
[48] See *SZ*, 323–331 (370–380); Tillich (1967), I, 111–114.

Unfaith as "domination by an order of created goods" is thus an existential orientation for the having of created goods. This allows us to see how the movement out of unfaith is a transformation. We must now examine how this analysis of unfaith permits us to understand faith also as an orientation. The orientation of faith will be a structure, and its description will be of the interior quality of faith as a religious value in its own right. At the same time, because faith is a transformation, we can conceive of God's gracious action as an event. As emphasized earlier, an existentialist theology must tie the knowledge of God closely to the way God is present to faith. Because for Wieman God is present to faith as an event of creative transformation, God is known in the events where he is creatively active. God is known, therefore, solely in events of grace.

EVENTS OF GRACE AND THE KNOWLEDGE OF GOD

Parallel with Bultmann's notion of faith as openness to the future, I now propose to describe the interior structure of faith as *readiness for transformation*. I shall approach it by dividing faith according to two modes: the movement of faith and the life of faith.

The movement into faith is a transformation reversing the orientation by which created goods are had as goods. This movement has two sides, a "freeing from" an "order of domination," which existentially interpreted is an order of "hatred," "defeat," "despair," and "death," and a "freeing for" an alternative. Both moments have intrinsic quality. The first and less interesting is simply the relief in being liberated from a self-defeating order of life. This moment is important, though, because it is the basis for understanding the transformation as God's gracious action. More difficult to comprehend is the character of the second moment, the "freeing for" or the change to a new configuration. It is, however, much the richer and provides a more important basis for understanding God's action. It also accords strikingly with Bultmann's claim that because God is nonobjective, we can speak of God only by speaking of ourselves.

Let us remember that "God" for Wieman refers functionally to those processes upon which we are dependent for the abundance of life. If we understand the notion of transformation entirely formally, then the *character* of God is always simply creative. This means that *God is known only as creativity*. Unfaith is an orientation dominated by created goods. This domination arises because we imagine that life takes on its greatest abundance within an order of created goods. This amounts to saying that unfaith is an orientation in and through which we are blinded by our refusal to recognize the character of God because within this orientation God's activity as creativity cannot occur. This refusal thwarts God's activity within certain crucial domains – much as traditional theology says that human freedom limits and displaces God's purposes. The orientation of unfaith makes it impossible for the creative event to be fully creative since it is precisely through creative transformations that such processes can occur.[49] Finally, we now see the movement into faith as itself a transformation. This transformative movement is a movement to commitment to God. We have just emphasized that, strictly speaking, God is known in this commitment only as creativity.

Two things follow from these points. The first is that the movement into faith *is* the experience of God. The movement from unfaith to faith is always a transformation, a reversal of orientation. The character of God is strictly creative. God can, therefore, be experienced only in a moment of creative transformation which, because it breaks an orientation to created goods, becomes the very movement of devotion to him. Faith is "readiness for transformation," but this is never a state or condition. Readiness for transformation is *always* itself a transformation, a product of God's continuing, ever renewed, gracious action upon and within us. Surprisingly, no modern theologian can celebrate God's gracious action more powerfully than the naturalist Wieman!

It follows, second, that God *as God* can only be known in a movement which recognizes God's character, namely, as transformatively creative. God is known only as grace and in events of grace. The movement of faith is not conceptual but existential. True, the theological interpretation of God as loving and gracious conceptually recognizes God's character as a creativity known solely in transformative moments. But now from a deeper existentialist framework, we see that this conceptual recognition contains a content that acknowledges its own transformative quality. Faith acknowledges God *as God* and this means as creatively transformative. But since God can only be known

---

[49] Wieman makes this point in two ways. (1) As openness toward the creative event, faith acknowledges the creative event (God) as the ground for the growth of value (and thus of abundance). (2) The operations of creativity are not seriously affected by human beings until they acquire real power through science and technology to affect how any creative advance into the future occurs. They do this by their orientation toward the created goods by which they seek to guide that advance (see *SHG*, 23–26, 37–39, 44–48; *MUC*, 9–18).

as creativity in a transformative moment, the content of what is recognized (God *as God*) is identical with the very moment of recognition (the transformation). Since God is creativity, God can be known properly only in a moment that is creative, and such a moment is a transformation. God cannot be known merely conceptually, or "objectively," for then God is not truly known. The knowledge of God always occurs as the movement of faith. Though the interior structure of faith is readiness for transformation, faith must always be described by a formula that says that faith is *transformation* to readiness for transformation. The "achievement" of readiness for transformation is itself *always* – that is, in every moment – transformative.

These same points may be explicated in terms of the traditional categories of creation and redemption. At a relatively trivial level, "God" is "creator" as the source of value, and is "redeemer" as the reversal in the movement from unfaith to faith. But conceiving faith as a transformative movement in existential orientation makes possible a much more textured account. On Wieman's terms, to acknowledge God is to recognize our dependence on the creative event as the source of value in experience. Faith as "readiness for transformation which is itself always a transformation" now permits us to say that the form this acknowledgment takes *directly in experience* is the capacity to experience our very givenness as itself a value. It is, if you will, the capacity to experience the givenness of our givenness. To undergo just this value requires a particular openness in which we can acknowledge and therefore trust precisely our dependence, the givenness of our givenness – the *"thatness"* of our being given – and this is exactly what we cannot do from within the existential structure of unfaith. Wanting such openness, unfaith is a structure of mistrust because it lacks a basic receptiveness to our very givenness. On the other hand, to acknowledge our dependence, in Wieman's sense of opening ourselves to it, simply is to undergo the givenness of our givenness as the value of a gift. That is why a certain kind of openness that can only be called trust is required.

Thus, the first moment of faith is the transformative moment by which God is Redeemer, and this is the action by which we come to acknowledge God, existentially, as Creator. Only in faith is God known as God in a fully experiential sense, and this is to know God as Creator in the theological sense. It follows that in the order of existential knowing, the knowledge of God as Redeemer precedes and is required for the knowledge of him as Creator. Thus, as in the tradition, but now existentially, what it means to live in unfaith is nothing else but the failure to acknowledge God as one's creator. The existential force of this refusal is to live as though one were the source of one's own being and the ground of one's own security. On naturalist foundations, therefore, we can say quite literally that the content of redemption is nothing other than the recognition of God as God. As defined above, this means recognizing God as creativity in a moment that is always itself a creative transformation. This recognition is a value in its own right because its content as a transformation is the capacity to trust our givenness. Actually, it is the capacity *to have* the experience of givenness, thus to experience our givenness as given, for unfaith is nothing other than the evasion of this experience.[50]

The movement into faith is, thus, the creative enactment of an existential openness to being. Bultmann's "openness to the future" becomes interchangeable with "readiness for transformation." But the latter formulation makes the connection with God and God's gracious action more transparent than the former. The movement into faith has this character because devotion to the order of created goods, life after the flesh, has the underlying structure of an attempt to secure our lives on our own terms. Readiness for transformation involves, therefore, a kind of openness and trust: readiness for transformation is openness experienced as a continual transformation to openness. In this sense, faith always has the experiential character of a gift. But its gift character also has giftedness as its content, for what we receive in faith is the giftedness of our being itself. "What have you that you did not receive? If then you received it, why do you boast as if it were not a gift?" (1 Cor. 4:7). This is why faith confesses God as Creator. This giftedness is what the experience *existentiell* of our givenness as given means and as such it is the experiential content of the recognition of God as God, that is, as Lord or Creator.

This interpretation of Wieman's creative event hinges on taking with complete seriousness his notion of transformation. His "creative event" then permits us to resolve the problem of God's gracious action in Bultmann and Ogden. By analyzing faith as an *existentiell* self-understanding which is an orientation, we see that the creative event is active precisely in the *transformation* of *existentiell* self-understanding. Faith is openness to the future in which *that*

---

[50] In Heidegger's language, this openness to our givenness is, *existentiell*, *be-ing* toward death, the resolute running out ahead of ourselves toward our own *dy-ing*. In experiential rather than existentialist terms, it is permitting into our experience the actuality of our own finitude *as our own*.

self-understanding becomes a possibility of self-understanding. We resolve the problem of God's gracious action precisely in the movement of faith and at the same time give profound content to the doctrine of justification by faith through grace apart from the works of the law. Indeed, in its central thrust, Wieman's philosophy of religion is nothing other than a fully modern statement of this doctrine. God's specific gracious action is the transformation that creates faith. We do indeed receive our lives as gifts, and as gifts of God's grace – all the more when we approach the religious question through a valuational theism and understand God as the source of human good. We also capture the logic behind Bultmann's reluctance to speak *about* God, as well as his insistence that God is known only nonobjectively, in the *existentiell* act of faith where *what* is known of God is always God's gracious action.[51]

Openness to being, experienced as the movement of faith, enables us now to turn to the life of faith itself and to show how it also has intrinsic qualities. In unfaith, the existential structure that determines *how* created goods are had in experience is a form of mistrust. Created goods are valued inordinately because the self cannot trust the way time, i.e., new possibilities, the future, comes to it. Life oriented to a structure of value already achieved is an existential attempt to stave off this threat of the new. Devotion to created goods thereby becomes a form of *closedness* in experience, even when the created goods are of the highest order of nobility. We have seen that the movement into faith is readiness for transformation which involves an openness to the givenness of our being given. It is an existential realization of an openness to being. Because faith is readiness for transformation, there is another kind of openness which results from the structure of faith itself. The structure within which created goods are had is such that those goods themselves figure in experience through a kind of openness.

Before we proceed to show this, we should note that it is here in the life of faith itself that Bultmann's and Ogden's emphasis on the integrity of personal agency, on freedom and responsibility, comes most fully into play. Bultmann typically expresses this, in opposition to Gnosticism, by insisting that faith includes both indicative and imperative. His favorite support for this proposition, and incidentally, for the implicitly nonmythological character of Paul's theology, is Paul's concept of obedience captured in his statement: "If we live by

<hr />

[51] See ZPE, 197–198 (ET, 111–112).

the Spirit, let us also walk by the Spirit" (Gal. 5:25). Paul, Bultmann says, "understands the 'Spirit' to be the possibility in fact of the new life that is disclosed in faith. The 'Spirit' does not work like a natural force nor does it become the possession of believers. It is rather the possibility of life that they must lay hold of by resolve" (NTM, 20 [ET, 31]).

Personal agency is also involved in the movement into faith where God's grace is active. This is because the very notion of an orientation or existential self-understanding involves the deepest dimensions of our agency. If freedom means anything at all, then in its widest sense it is engaged in those self-constituting acts by which we define our overall posture toward ourselves and the world. For this reason, the full integrity of ourselves as persons is also involved in those trans-formative moments by which we appropriate a new self-understanding. There is, then, both indicative and imperative involved in such moments. Although I do not want to deny this involvement of our freedom in the appropriation of a new, liberating self-understanding, I do not think that such processes are well understood. This is evident in the conundrums about the action of God's grace into which Ogden's excessive emphasis on freedom lands him at this point. Simply stated, he slights the bondage which sin is, though he does this despite his otherwise careful acknowledgment of the issue. In any case, as will be evident now, it is in the life of faith, which still involves the *indicative* of God's grace, that the role of obedience, freedom and responsibility most intelligibly comes into play.

Traditionally, faith is trust because God is recognized as the source of all good. Translated naturalistically, this means that value arises not from extension of created goods but from processes of continual transformation upon which we are dependent for all abundance. The content of readiness for transformation is trust in and dependence on this source of good. Consequently, this trust issues in a kind of openness which is a letting-go of the goods that are already in experience. It is important to understand this letting-go carefully. It does not mean that those goods are not appreciated. Quite the contrary, they are had in experience precisely as the goods they are. The openness of faith creates a kind of space whereby created goods may be appreciatively experienced without the added burden of an inordinate valuation. In this sense, created goods are experienced in faith "as though not," and a person of faith is "in but not of the world." Furthermore, their appreciation as the goods they are becomes itself an appreciation. This means that the trust and openness that make possible the appreciation of created goods simply for what they are also make it possible to appreciate the having of them as a gift. This appreciation can be had only when we are "freed from" ourselves by grace for that trust and openness in which the full appreciation of the goods of life first itself becomes appreciable for us. This is, if you will, nothing other than "life in grace."

Bultmann is, therefore, exactly correct to define faith as freedom from the past and openness to the future. What he means by this is connected with the bondage of sin. Locked into that bondage, all one's actions are from within that self-understanding, and in this sense are pure past. Thus, he says:

> What faith and theology say and show is that in this possibility of being [which has the formal ontological character of resolve by which one lays hold of one's being as possibility] . . . there is always present in fact a *necessity of being*, insofar as in every actual choice in which man chooses a possibility of existing authentically he in fact always chooses what he already is – that he never gets rid of his past and therefore is never free. For this reason, however, he is also never genuinely historical insofar as historicity means the possibility of an actual, i.e., a new occurrence. (HMF, 107)

It is God's grace that grants genuine historicity by liberating from the bondage to the past in this sense. Openness to the future, then, is the consequence of this liberation from the past, from bondage. But we saw that Bultmann cannot properly account for how this action, the actual event of God's grace, occurs, and that for Ogden, despite himself, freedom becomes simply the adoption of a self-understanding based on a *view* that God is gracious.

We can now give a more textured account of openness to the future, understood not, as above, simply as the negative of "bondage to the past" but as the actual content of an existential self-understanding directed toward God. Freedom from the past is, in the first instance, simply freedom from bondage to created goods, preeminently in the sense of freedom from self. This is the meaning already implicit in Bultmann. But more important, faith involves a real temporal component. Because of the existential structure of domination by created goods, unfaith is finally mistrust of the future and thus the attempt to secure one's life by living in the past, that is, *on the terms of the past*. It is a basic refusal of our temporality when temporality is seen as the existential structure of our contingency. To live a life of faith is to live with a fundamental openness toward the future. This is the form in which created goods are experienced when they are structured by readiness for transformation, and this is a precise existential statement of what devotion to the source of human good means. The self-understanding of faith, then, is quintessentially readiness for transformation in the life of faith itself. It is an openness which comes from acknowledging our entire dependence on God, the creative event, for the riches of life.[52]

We now have a second bridge from an austere physicalistic naturalism to a naturalistic Christian theology. This bridge shows how God and God's action may be conceived naturalistically when it is first granted that faith is an existential self-understanding. We saw how faith can be conceived when the existential meaning of sin is made intelligible. This existential notion presses us to take up the question of God in terms of the eventfulness of God's gracious action, as is made evident by an analysis of Bultmann's formula that we can speak of God only by speaking of ourselves. Yet we saw that neither Bultmann nor Ogden seem able to capture this eventfulness. This makes it difficult, especially in Ogden's case, to see why faith should not be understood *simply* as the free appropriation of a self-understanding – in the light, of course, of a view of God as gracious, but not of God's actual gracious action by which bondage is *broken*. That problem led us to Wieman's concept of God, developed in terms of his notion of transformation. Transformation, conceived existentially, permitted us both to deepen the understanding of faith and to develop a naturalistic conception of the knowledge of God. We now have the foundations of a naturalist theology.

[52] See Shaw (1988) for an insightful analysis of such "openness" in cross-cultural religious perspective.

CHAPTER 5

Christian faith as a seeing-as

Taking the Christian faith as a "seeing- (and experiencing-) as" forms the third and final bridge principle to a naturalistic physicalism. Theologically, the Christian faith must be conceived as a seeing-as because naturalism undermines the traditional subject-predicate surface grammar of theism. Such a theology, must, if you will, carry demythologizing deeply into the doctrine of God. The world *is not* as it must be according to the "literal" surface grammar of traditional theism (in either classical or revisionary forms). This becomes especially evident with the three essential metaphysical assertions examined in the first chapter: that there is an absolute personal God, final causality, and a conservation of value. Hence, historical Christianity's theistic language must be construed as a seeing-as, a way of taking the world, and its appropriateness must be ascertained differently from traditional theism. It could be said that such a theology *rests upon* philosophical naturalism. But theology need not derive its assertions directly from this philosophical position; rather, though theology must be compatible with this background view of the world, it does not directly dictate theology's own positive assertions.[1] In particular, this background view constrains theology mainly in what it *cannot* say or imply – but it does so constrain at every point.[2] That is why bridging, though not direct derivation, is necessary.

At the same time, though the world is not as it must be for literal theism to be true, the theology proposed here is a genuine theism. It does not entail that "God exists" or "there is a God" are false. It is a valuational theism in which "God exists" can be true. Furthermore,

---

[1] Much in the same way, "the scientific world view" forms the background of Bultmann's demythologizing program but does not dictate its positive content.

[2] The present work grows almost entirely out of the conviction that "the modern scientific world-view" constrains theology much more seriously than is typically entertained by theologians today.

the seeing-as by which "God exists" can be true is linked, though not as traditionally, to the way the world actually is, linked, that is, to a realist, and objective, philosophical naturalism. This means that unlike most seeing-as views, this one has a strong cognitive component. It does not require us either to deny that there is a way the world ultimately is that can be known and defended or to reduce theological assertions merely to expressions of attitude. Our task in this chapter is to analyze the components of such a theistic seeing-as. The foundations for this task have already been provided by the first two bridge principles. These have enabled us to defend a thoroughgoing method of existentialist interpretation which is formally compatible with philosophical naturalism, and then to see how such a method enables us to understand the human problem, the eventfulness of God's grace, and the knowledge of God in events of grace.

Seeing-as positions are generally formulated in one of two ways. One asserts that every conceptual position is a seeing-as so that the theistic one is equally as well (or ill) founded as any other. The other is strictly noncognitive, regarding theological assertions as nothing more than expressions of attitude or dispositions to action. The distinctive character of the present proposal will emerge most helpfully by being set against these more typical positions. The first may be termed a "'categorial' seeing-as" and the second a "noncognitive seeing-as."

SEEINGS-AS IN THE PHILOSOPHY OF RELIGION

The categorial seeing-as option is effectively presented by James Hall in *Knowledge, Belief, and Transcendence*. Hall offers a highly critical discussion of traditional efforts to defend the truth of theism. His most telling point is a critique of divine transcendence for the difficulties it occasions for any rational assessment of theism (*KBT*, 74–85, 135–139). Hall then examines alternative forms of language which do not have truth conditions, unlike "reporting/asserting/describing" language which does. Here he defends a legitimate, or at least plausible, way of understanding theism as a seeing-as, or what he calls, "a way of taking" (*KBT*, 156–160, 205–221).

His view is derived from R. M. Hare's "bliks" and John Wisdom's famous parable of the garden.[3] Implicit in Wisdom's parable and

[3] See Hare (1955), and Wisdom (1965).

then systematically formulated by Hare's "blik" conception is the notion that we always have a vantage on the world, independent of any evidential check, the elements of which determine how any and all evidential claims can have the truth conditions they have. This argument implies that bliks do not make assertions and cannot be true or false since they are the conceptual frame within which assertions can be made and any assessment carried out. At the same time, *every* assertion and all truth conditions presuppose, on this view, some blik.

Hall extends Hare's and Wisdom's views in two ways. First, he develops a general category of nonassertive language use which covers what Hare has in mind with bliks. He terms such usage "categories" (and their establishment "categorizing") (*KBT*, 169–170, 183–204). According to Hall, bliks establish the basic categories by which all else gets "sorted." Every "reporting/describing/asserting" presupposes such a background of categorizing, even when it is not explicit. The world is first taken in a certain way before we can assert anything about it, and this "taking," just because it makes assertion first possible, also establishes the broad framework for assessment of truth.

Hall argues, second, that categories can be assessed in terms of "felicity conditions" (*KBT*, 170–181). What is odd and disturbing about Hare's conception of bliks is that a blik cannot be true or false. It establishes a framework for truth and falsity, but just for this reason, it cannot itself be true or false; it does not assert anything. Seemingly, it cannot be assessed, even though, given his example of a demented student who believes all dons are out to get him, Hare acknowledges that it is obviously important to have the "right" blik. But how could we ever know if our blik was "right"? Hall meets this objection by claiming that though strictly speaking the language constituting a blik does not include assertions and thus does not have truth conditions, bliks can be assessed in terms of "felicity conditions" which he regards as largely pragmatic in nature (*KBT*, 197). These are: relevance, "meshingness" (with other data and theories), coherence, theoretical fertility, simplicity, self-testing (*KBT*, 197–202).

Theism, according to Hall, is just such a categorizing which, as all such fundamental "categorizing," is a way of taking the world (or a seeing-as). If "God exists" is such a categorizing taking-as, then neither "God exists" nor God's specific content is true or false. Such "claims" are not assertions at all but a way of "sorting" the world such that *other* assertions can be made and assessed. This accounts for why "seeing-as" positions cannot be divided simply into cognitive and noncognitive versions. There is indeed a noncognitive variety as we shall examine in a moment, but Hall's version, as he himself affirms, is not properly cognitive at all (*KBT*, 206, 227). Yet, it also does not merely describe expressions of attitude. It takes the world in one substantial way rather than another, and presumably, for such a taking, the world really is this way rather than another (*KBT*, 226).

The basic content of "God exists," Hall argues, is the imposition of a purposive or telic structure on events. This is not "to say that in the basic theistic move one asserts, 'There are ends in the world to be seen, tasted, smelled, felt, or heard.' It is to sort the data, not describe them. Even as the physicalist makes his basic moves, imposing a material and causal structure upon what he observes, without suggesting for a moment that we can gather a pocket full of causes or taste a soupçon of matter, so the theist structures the world telicly without asserting the sensory discernibility of purpose 'writ large in the sky'" (*KBT*, 206). The theist takes this purposive order as the product of intention, so she also "takes the world as . . . the output of an intender" which is best conceived under the rubric of a plan (*KBT*, 207).

These are the basic elements in the theistic taking-as, but other closely related ones follow. The theist takes the world under the model of norms and values and thus brings them under judgment, which is to see events "under a pattern of appraisal" (*KBT*, 208). Because events are thus winnowed by purposive appraisal, the features of theism "meld together into a taking of life, especially man's life, as (at least in potential) 'meaningful' and 'worthwhile'" (*KBT*, 208). From this it follows that the "basic theistic move also involves taking the world as an occasion of joy," which is to say that the theist sees the pattern of life as a struggle "in which there is joy like that of an artist producing a work out of an intractable medium" (*KBT*, 209). Again, events in the world are taken as "revelatory," for they are perceived as a general disclosure of what is and of what ought to be (*KBT*, 209–210). Yet, the world is also in some deep sense "unfathomable," ultimately to be seen under the rubric of mystery as well as disclosure (*KBT*, 210). In sum, the "theist sees the world as mysterious, as disclosure, as intended, as normatively structured, as challenge and arena, and as ruled" (*KBT*, 210). The dispute between the theist and the nontheist is not a dispute about facts or events, not even about the truth or falsity of "God exists." The issue is simply about how the facts and events are to be arranged under a structure.

Hall goes some distance in evaluating the theistic "taking" in terms of his felicity conditions, but because these conditions are "soft" and *because they apply equally to every conceptual position whatsoever*, the evaluation is itself "soft" (see *KBT*, 210–221). Theism has problems, but so does every other broad taking-as. The chief problem with the theistic taking occurs, as we might expect, with the "mesh" with other theories of lesser generality, chiefly those from science and secular value theory, and with the problem of evil (*KBT*, 212–216). But none of these problems can "defeat" theism because the theist can always retreat behind the objections with *ad hoc* explanations about God's purposive ordering.

The problems with Hall's theory of religion have to do not with evaluating theism by his felicity conditions but with his whole account of categorizing as such. These problems are of two sorts, one having to do with the philosophical conception itself and another specifically with its application to the philosophy of religion. The first issue is simply whether Hall's reformulation of Hare captures what is going on in theory construction of the widest generality. His theory is similar to "conceptual scheme theory," and it suffers from the same problems.[4] Conceptual scheme theory is a theoretical bog at the present time, and it would involve a major work in its own right to sort it out here. My effort is concentrated simply in trying to delimit what we are talking about with a religious seeing-as, so I shall do little more than allude to some of the major problems in an effort to clarify this latter issue. In any case, the major theological problem occurs at another place, as I shall take up in a moment.

No thinker today can deny that assertions about facts are theory laden. This recognition is what pushes us back to the conceptual structures by which facts are taken and is what makes it seem that our theories, especially those of widest generality, must be defended by some other process than that appropriate to truth conditions. But in Hall's case and in conceptual scheme theory generally there is far too little attention given to the detailed analysis of how categorizings (or conceptual schemes) are individuated. We require much more detailed analysis of what the ultimate categories are by which a

---

[4] See, Runzo for a similar but more thorough attempt to work out the notion of "conceptual schemes" and to apply it theologically. I am examining Hall rather than Runzo because unlike Runzo, Hall sees that "conceptual schemes" or "categorizings" result in theological seeings-as. Despite its greater thoroughness, Runzo's work contains the same shortcomings I criticize in Hall. The most serious of these is an insufficiently detailed analysis of the logical structure of conceptual schemes in relation to assertions at lower levels of generality. For critical discussions of Runzo, see Proudfoot (1988), 305–306 and Hardwick (1991).

categorizing (or a conceptual scheme) is determined, and then we need to be shown, again in detail, how this ultimate order connects with categorial determinations at lower levels of generality, for only in this way could we ever be in a position to assess conceptual schemes. We need to be shown, that is, what the hierarchy of "sortings" is in a conceptual scheme by which categories of widest generality are connected with categories of lesser generality (such as those, for instance, in the natural sciences).

Were such a logical analysis of conceptual schemes undertaken, it is not so evident as Hall takes for granted that our categories of widest generality cannot be assessed according to canons of truth or falsity. Hall too easily assumes that the truth conditions necessary for assertions are exclusively empirical in character. But it is not so evident as he assumes that the movement back and forth between evidence at lower levels of generality and wider conceptual (and metaphysical) categories that account for the lower levels does not admit of arguments about these wider categories precisely as assertions about what is the case that can be true or false. It is significant that in his list of felicity conditions, the crucial one he omits from what Post terms the "trial by prerequisites" is the prerequisite of objectivity.[5]

This issue can be illustrated by Hall's notion of taking the world as having a purposive or telic order. It is crucial to recognize that the world either does or does not have such an order. A taking-as cannot make it so. *If the world does have a purposive order*, then a purposive taking-as is the correct way to unpack what it means to live in such a world. But without begging the question, a purposive taking-as cannot, in principle, inform us on the crucial question at stake. That issue can be settled only at the level of arguments about what are the true categories of widest generality, and these appear very much like assertions about what is the case. Only so, I think, can we understand any serious metaphysical debate about categories of widest generality. Our ultimate questions at this level are not merely about "sortings" but about what is the case – even as we admit that establishing such all-encompassing categories (in their truth conditional form) is among the most challenging engagements of intellect.[6]

Let me turn, then, to the second criticism of Hall's seeing-as, one

[5] See *FE*, 66–70, and for the entire discussion of assessment, pp. 53–72.
[6] See, for example, Hartshorne (1983), 19–42. It is difficult to comprehend the kind of activity Hartshorne is engaged in in this essay except as an effort to establish the truth-conditions of precisely those categories that Hall claims can have none. The same is true of Post's analysis of "Infinite Parades of Explanation" and "Ultimate Explanation," though in quite a contrary direction to Hartshorne (see *FE*, 84–106).

that has directly theological ramifications. Hall's approach to theism as a "categorizing" completely short circuits any revisionary program (such as demythologizing) which many theologians assume to be a necessary condition for practicing theology today. Either Hall must assume that his theism in place is in good order as such and must be taken whole as it is, or he must assume that a taking-as can be improved. But on his terms, a sufficiently ambitious mythology (such as biblical Christianity) is itself a categorial taking-as. It either is or is not identical with theism. If it is identical, then it must be taken whole. But suppose he wants to argue that theism and the mythology (take your pick as to which one) are not identical. Then he must engage in some sort of argument about which categories *among theistic categorizings* are correct for defining the *theistic categorizing*. Now, however, the issue is not between a theistic and a nontheistic categorizing but between two ostensibly theistic ones. How could such issues possibly be resolved on Hall's terms? It would seem in principle that he cannot deal with adjudication at this level.

This question again runs up against the issue that Hall's taking-as cannot handle, namely, that the world is one way or another independently of a taking-as. What we want when we take the world as something is to take it as it is. Hall gives the following example of a descriptive claim within a religious framework: "At the ringing of the bell, the host transubstantiates into the mystical embodiment of the body and blood of Christ" (*KBT*, 224). He recognizes that this claim is either true or false, but according to his assumptions, he must also assert *that it can be weighed only by criteria that are germane to the frame of reference in which the claim occurs* (*KBT*, 224–225). But this is either absurd or it trivializes the Roman Catholic claim. Of course the host transubstantiates according to the Roman Catholic frame of reference. But adopting the frame of reference cannot make it so. Either the host transubstantiates or it does not, and this issue is independent of any taking-as. What we *and the Roman Catholic* want to know is whether the frame of reference making it possible to say that the host transubstantiates is true or false. This fundamental type of question is impossible on Hall's terms. And just for this reason, his position evades the revisionary or demythologizing challenge. Only if we push these questions back to the level of ultimate categories can we engage the proper hermeneutical questions. According to my position, for instance, the host does not transubstantiate in the traditional Roman Catholic sense. It does not follow, however, that the sacrament has no intelligible existential meaning.[7] But to undertake the hermeneutical exercise of showing its existential meaning, we must be able to get the demythologizing program off the ground to start with, and it is short-circuited by Hall's approach to the seeing-as issue.

Let us turn, then, to the second, explicitly noncognitive seeing-as which is far the more interesting view. Its most substantial formulation is Paul van Buren's *The Secular Meaning of the Gospel*. Van Buren's argument is really an extended application of R. B. Braithwaite's *An Empiricist's View of Religious Belief*, but van Buren is more helpful because, unlike Braithwaite, he formulates the full range of a noncognitive Christian seeing-as.

Van Buren takes the pervasive character of what he terms modern "empirical attitudes" or the "empirical spirit of the age" (*SMG*, xiii–xiv, 68, 104, 106) to render meaningless for modern persons all reference to God or transcendent realities.[8] Appealing to Braithwaite, and making some use of Hare's notion of bliks, he argues that there are other usages of language apart from the assertive and cognitive ones (see *SMG*, 85–86, 92–96, 145). In particular, he appeals to usages which express attitudes or behavioral dispositions (see *SMG*, 85–106). Though noncognitive, such usages can express an overall perspective on the world that guides attitudes and behavior.

---

[7] See Bultmann, (1933b), 167; NTM, 47–48 (ET, 41); ZPE, 206 (ET, 121); and Ogden, *CM*, 63–64, 89–90, for existentialist interpretations of the church and its sacraments.

[8] Van Buren has been criticized for confusions in his definition of empirical attitudes. This confusion is particularly striking in the following statement: ". . . the heart of the method of linguistic analysis lies in the use of the verification principle – that the meaning of a word is its use in its context. The meaning of a statement is to be found in, and is identical with, the function of that statement. If a statement has a function, so that it may be verified or falsified, the statement is meaningful, and unless or until a theological statement can be submitted in some way to verification, it cannot be said to have a meaning in our language-game" (*SMG*, 104–105). Van Buren clearly confuses the original verification principle with the later development of ordinary language analysis. The verification principle attempted to be a criterion of *meaning* and cannot be identified with later language-game theories which reject the verification principle by insisting that meaning is context dependent upon various language usages. What van Buren is really doing is appropriating this later model for *meaning* while insisting upon the empirical, verification (or properly, falsification) principle as a criterion of *cognitive* meaning. He wants to say that if a statement asserts something, it must be empirically verifiable, but there are other legitimate non-assertive, non-cognitive usages of language that are meaningful in expressing moral, attitudinal, and behavior stances. Because some of these usages are quite broad, encompassing overall expressions of how one gives shape to an entire life, they may be called "perspectives." A "historical perspective" like the gospel is is such a perspective formed in direct association with particular historical events and personages. Despite his confusion in stating what he terms "a modified verification principle" (*SMG*, 15), I do not believe it undermines his position. He explicates his historical perspective in terms of noncognitive linguistic usage, and it is clear enough that he uses a verificationist understanding of cognitivity to anchor what he means by contemporary "empirical attitudes."

Van Buren is concerned solely with the Christian faith as a gospel or kerygma and has no interest in establishing a general theory of religion. He claims that the Christian gospel is a distinctive "historical perspective" (*SMG*, 135–145) that is compatible with modern empirical attitudes when it is interpreted in terms of noncognitive expressions of attitude and moral stance. This approach has the advantages of taking seriously those New Testament assertions that do have empirical content, of according a proper place to the historical elements in Christianity, especially the historical particularity of Jesus, and, according to van Buren, of properly weighting the reality of Easter in the Christian story, which he claims Bultmann and Ogden neglect (see *SMG*, 68–74, 145–156). His claims about Christianity and the gospel are modest, as he thinks is appropriate for our contemporary situation, for he makes no pretense to dictate for others what religion can be or to show why Christianity should be an evangelical faith for nonbelievers. He wants only to show how the contemporary Christian can understand himself within the empirical attitudes that define his secular life.

The key move in van Buren's argument for a Christian "historical perspective" concerns the link between the historical Jesus and the event of Easter. Van Buren acknowledges the difficulties in reconstructing a life of Jesus. The New Testament documents are through and through kerygmatic, representing a response to the event of Easter (*SMG*, 114–116). Easter is central because Jesus was seen from the point of view of that event, and, indeed, seen in a new way. Yet, van Buren insists, though a response to the kerygmatic preaching of Easter, the gospel is, nevertheless, oriented to the man Jesus (*SMG*, 116–117). Jesus is crucial because his life gives content to the Christian perspective. The historical character of van Buren's perspective is, therefore, both ineliminable and perfectly amenable to modern empirical attitudes. Relying on the "new quest for the historical Jesus" that claims some knowledge of Jesus rooted in the kerygmatic character of the documents themselves,[9] van Buren describes Jesus as "a remarkably free man" (*SMG*, 121). The records manifest this freedom through parables, sayings, teachings, and incidents. Because of this freedom, peculiar "authority" was attributed to Jesus (*SMG*, 121–123). It was especially evident in his freedom from anxiety and from the need to establish his own identity as well as

---

[9] See *SMG*, 119–121, and also J. M. Robinson, (1959).

in his compassionate freedom for his neighbor without regard for himself (*SMG*, 123). This freedom accounts both for Jesus's attracting a following and for his death (see *SMG*, 123–124).

Yet such historical knowledge of Jesus does not constitute faith. Taken straightforwardly as an historical account, Jesus's ministry, as teacher and as example, seems to have been a failure. Above all, he did not produce sufficient freedom in his disciples to survive the events of his death. As van Buren says, "his freedom was his alone; at best it was shared only in the most fragmentary and fleeting way by a very few men at certain times" (*SMG*, 125). The decisive question concerns how faith is related to this historical picture. Though its historical reference is essential, faith cannot be read off the historical figure of Jesus. The answer to this seeming conundrum is the event of Easter, "which stands between Jesus and the believer, as indeed it stands between Jesus and the New Testament witness to him" (*SMG*, 126).

But the event of Easter seems utterly alien to modern empirical attitudes. Van Buren addresses this apparent problem at two levels. There is a factual statement simply of what happened. In accordance with respectable New Testament criticism, he emphasizes the New Testament language of "appearance," not of resuscitation of a corpse, and claims that the appearances must be understood in terms of "sense-content" statements. Such statements are about subjective mental images that, by their very nature, "are not common-sense or empirical assertions" (*SMG*, 129). Of the resurrection appearances we can say only that the apostles had certain mental images "on the mirrors of their minds";[10] there is no way to establish their "objective" correlates, if any, but it is not really important that we should do so. There is another kind of empirical test for such reports, however, for we can examine whether "the words and actions of the person who makes the statement conform to it" (*SMG*, 129).

The "appearance" accounts were followed by the assertion, "Jesus is risen," and this does seem difficult for our empirical attitudes. Yet according to van Buren, this difficulty comes from the linguistic oddity of the expression, not from its assertion of an objective physical fact. The New Testament evidence, he claims, does not support that the apostles intended to attest Jesus's physical resuscitation (see *SMG*, 130). "Jesus is risen" oddly juxtaposes words from different language-

---

[10] The image is van Buren's, though I have changed the phrasing slightly to fit the present context (see *SMG*, 129).

games. The proper name functions like any proper name to identify a certain historical personage. The "is" links not with "Jesus" but with the verb which belongs in the context of Jewish eschatology. Thus, "the assertion 'Jesus is risen' takes the name of a historical man and says that he was of the realm of 'the end'" (*SMG*, 131–132), and this transforms the statement into something quite different from an empirical proposition.

According to van Buren, "end-words" which point to "the end and goal of all existence" are not empirical or referential at all. Their function is "to inform the hearer of, or to commend to him, a certain attitude of the speaker" (*SMG*, 131), and their empirical content, or verification, would be found in the conduct of the persons asserting them. It follows, and is the crucial step in van Buren's argument, that "the statement 'Jesus is risen' . . . does not signify a movement from a sense-content statement, 'He appeared to me,' to an empirical assertion. It is a movement to an 'end-word' statement which is verified by the conduct of the man who uses it" (*SMG*, 131–132). This analysis thus provides the basis for interpreting the Easter event.

It seems appropriate to say that a situation of discernment occurred for Peter and the other disciples on Easter, in which, against the background of their memory of Jesus, they suddenly saw Jesus in a new and unexpected way. "The light dawned." The history of Jesus, which seemed to have been a failure, took on a new importance as the key to the meaning of history. Out of this discernment arose a commitment to the way of life which Jesus had followed . . . *Easter faith was a new perspective upon life arising out of a situation of discernment focused on the history of Jesus.* (*SMG*, 132, my emphasis)

Two things were important about this discernment. Jesus was seen in a new way, true, but of greater significance was that those who saw him anew found that they shared in the freedom that had been his. "One might convey better the tone of the disciples' words if one said that on Easter they found that Jesus had a new power which he had not had, or had not exercised, before: the power to awaken freedom also in them" (*SMG*, 132). Van Buren uses the word "contagion" to capture this discernment (*SMG*, 133, 154).

Van Buren argues therefore that the Easter event transforms the account of an admirable and tragic man into a gospel. The Easter event is nothing other than a situation of discernment in which, observing the life, teachings, and death of Jesus, something of his freedom is conveyed to one who responds, and one's entire life comes to be patterned on that of Jesus. Furthermore, "contagion" identifies the kerygmatic and even gracious reality of this discernment, for it is not something that we simply accomplish, but something that happens to us (see *SMG*, 133, 136 f.). Van Buren thus captures both the historical and the kerygmatic nature of the gospel. "For the disciples . . . the story of Jesus could not be told simply as the story of a free man who had died. Because of the new way in which the disciples saw him and because of what had happened to them, the story had to include the event of Easter. In telling the story of Jesus of Nazareth, therefore, they told it as the story of the free man who had set them free. This was the story which they proclaimed as the Gospel for all men" (*SMG*, 134).

What van Buren terms a "historical perspective" is simply a noncognitive seeing-as. Hall's "taking as" is also a perspective. Even though, according to Hall, it is a category mistake to speak of it as cognitive, it has genuine cognitive import, for claiming to "take" the whole of things as it truly is, it establishes the frame for cognitivity and in this respect is cosmological in scope. Van Buren strictly avoids any such wider, cognitive implications. Cognitive issues are entirely settled by empirical attitudes. Framed by such empirical attitudes, questions having to do with Christianity – and thus with religion, were his approach to be extended beyond the gospel[11] – are issues about attitudes and patterns of behavior. As such, the language of Christianity asserts nothing and can be "verified" only by empirically observing the fit between a person's stated attitudes and intentions and that person's actual behavior. It is, nevertheless, a perspective because it is a framework encompassing the entirety of a person's attitudes and intentions. In this respect, it provides reasons why a person lives as she does.

Before evaluating van Buren's position, let us examine several ways in which he fills out the gospel's historical perspective. Take for instance expressions about God, the meaning of which are already suggested by the discussion of "end-words." Thus, when the disciples asserted that God had raised up Jesus as Lord, they were saying that something had happened to them that affected their outlook on the entirety of life (*SMG*, 133). Or again, that Jesus was Lord over the entire world "indicated that their perspective covered the totality of life, the world, and history, as well as their understanding of

---

[11] Although van Buren demurs from any such extension – here his Barthian background with its opposition between religion and Christianity shows through – the logic of his position unavoidably contains implications for a wider theory of religion.

themselves and other men" (*SMG*, 133). The divine reference to the work of the Holy Spirit indicates "that the new freedom and perspective are received as gifts by the believer and that they are of fundamental importance to him" (*SMG*, 133). Indirectly it also indicates the singular importance of Jesus for this historical perspective. Protestantism made this especially clear by tying the operation of the Holy Spirit to the proclamation of the Word (*SMG*, 136–137). It also shows how conversion and the expression of faith on the part of later believers are logically and historically connected with the apostolic witness (*SMG*, 137). In effect, God-terms are reduced to Christology – not at all an unusual move in modern theology – a point which van Buren makes forcefully in connection with John's statement that he who has seen Jesus has seen the Father (John 14:9). The whole issue of God is here transposed. For those who have found their own freedom in the freedom of Jesus, "whatever 'God' means – as the goal of human existence, as the truth about man and the world, or as the key to the meaning of life – 'he' is to be found in Jesus, the 'way, the truth, and the life'" (*SMG*, 147). There is no need to look further for the identity of God, and this is especially convenient, but also thoroughly Christian, for persons who must understand the gospel within modern empirical attitudes. "Since there is no 'Father' to be found apart from him, and since his 'Father' can only be found in him, the New Testament . . . gives its answer to the question about 'God' by pointing to the man Jesus. Whatever men were looking for in looking for 'God' is to be found by finding Jesus of Nazareth" (*SMG*, 147). This same transposition is suggested by the statement that Jesus is "in" the Father and the Father "in" Jesus (John 14:10).

Even more forceful is van Buren's interpretation of Paul's words: "in Christ God was reconciling the world to himself" (II Cor. 5:19) which assert that God has acted in some special way in Jesus. This is especially difficult because it is so exclusively a "'God'-statement." But it may be taken in another way, for "does it not suggest that the history of Jesus, including the event of Easter, is the history of a reconciliation of a peculiar sort?" (*SMG*, 149.) For Christians, reconciliation will always be related to the freedom for which Jesus has set them free, especially with freedom for the neighbor. This freedom will have consequences of such breadth as to extend to the entire world, which means that

the Christian understanding of reconciliation has no limit to its application
. . . Wherever he sees at work in the world any reconciliation at all like that
which characterized the history of Jesus of Nazareth, he will support it, and
he will rejoice over signs of such reconciliation accomplished, however
partially, as much as he rejoices over the reconciliation with his neighbor
which has been made possible by his having been set free for his neighbor.
(*SMG*, 149)

But what of the past tense in Paul's statement or the New
Testament claim that God's action occurred through Jesus's dying
for our sins? Paul's statement that through Christ "God . . . did not
count men's trespasses against them" (II Cor. 5:19) makes no sense as
an empirical statement, but we can imagine "how we should treat
others if we regarded them as pardoned and accepted in some 'final'
sense which qualifies all human judging and forgiving. . . This is
another way of expressing the Christian's historical perspective,
which leads him to take sides with reconciliation, mercy, and
forgiveness and to oppose enmity, retribution, and revenge" (*SMG*,
150). We may understand Jesus's death for our sins in a similar
fashion. Jesus's whole ministry demonstrates his solidarity with other
persons, marked especially by his proclaiming forgiveness to "sinners."
In such a way he inspired their confidence and "convinced them
that they were released from the burden of guilt and the consequences
of their acts" (*SMG*, 151). In the New Testament, the "cross" and
Jesus's death in general are regarded as summary ways of speaking of
his whole history. Consequently, since his entire history was one of
solidarity with humanity in mercy and compassion, it is not surprising
that his death came to be spoken of as "for us," or that the
contemporary believer will be inclined to say, "He died for me, for
my forgiveness and freedom" (*SMG*, 151). The New Testament
claim that he died "for the sins of the whole world" (I John 2:2) is
but a way of saying that Jesus was free for all persons, not just those
who acknowledged him, and that the Christian historical perspective
includes all humanity, not just Christians (*SMG*, 152).

Finally, there are themes of exclusivity and universality. The
language of faith contains an exclusive element simply because its
historical perspective is formed in reference to the unique history of
Jesus. There may have been many free men and women, but the
gospel is the good news about a specific free man who has set others
free, and this has happened again and again in history as this gospel

has been proclaimed (*SMG*, 137–138). Christians say they are "in Christ" because "their understanding of themselves and their lives and all things is determined by their understanding of Jesus. They are a 'new creation' in that this orientation to the whole world is new for them" (*SMG*, 138). This exclusiveness does not deny that something of this sort might happen in reference to someone else but is simply – almost tautologically – a reference to how it has happened for Christians. For just this reason, it expresses the firmness of the Christian's conviction (*SMG*, 137). At the same time, the traditional exclusiveness claimed that something of universal significance happened in this particular history, and the tradition used the language of eternity, absoluteness, and divinity to say this. Despite the patristic doctrine of the incarnation, the New Testament asserts such claims simply with the confession "*Jesus* is Lord." The universal dimension of this confession says that faith is an historical perspective on self, humanity, history, and the entire world that has its norm in the history of Jesus and in Easter (*SMG*, 140). Its universality becomes evident in the subordination of all lesser loyalties to the norm of service (*SMG*, 142). Because the Christian "sees not only his own history but the history of all men in the light of the one history of Jesus of Nazareth and Easter, he will not rest content when his nation, family, or church seek to live only for themselves; he will try to set them in the service of others" (*SMG*, 142), and van Buren especially emphasizes how integral this "public" dimension is for the Christian historical perspective (*SMG*, 142, 149). It is also the source of "eschatological" hope for the Christian, for his historical perspective contains the conviction, though not the prediction, "that the freedom which the believer has seen in Jesus and which has become contagious for him, and the reconciliation which he sees to be associated with this freedom, will prevail on this earth among men" (*SMG*, 154).

Van Buren's theological contribution is extremely impressive. Though his restriction to "empirical attitudes" prevents him from taking up the wider metaphysical issues which I believe must come into the picture, his noncognitive seeing-as bears certain striking similarities to the present position and is a response to the same theological constraints. Though his method is not existentialist, the content of his Christian historical perspective is closely related to the content of faith as openness to the future. The existential way of being in the world, which I have argued provides both the content and criterion for a valuational theism, forms a valuational seeing-as closely related to the attitudes and dispositions of van Buren's historical perspective. Furthermore, as I shall show in the next chapter, modern biblical scholarship provides resources for Christological reflection that permit a similar orientation to the historical Jesus. Despite these similarities, however, van Buren's position suffers debilitating problems, and it is in reference to them especially that the seeing-as proposed here will become evident.

These problems center on the centrality he gives the Easter event. For him, the Easter event is the discernment situation which transforms the believer's blik into the Christian historical perspective. He uses the "contagious" aspect of Jesus's freedom to speak, if you will, of the "causal" power both of Jesus's freedom and of the church's proclamation of the gospel. The problem is that the notion of "contagion" only names something but does not account for it. It simply says that Christians have become Christians. But how, and for what reason? Part of the problem, as other commentators have noted, is that "contagion" is so thin an explanatory notion.[12] The problem here is simply an extreme example of the need throughout contemporary theology for a deeper account of the transformative character of events of existential involvement, especially linguistic ones conveyed through personal encounter. Even, however, if van Buren could give such an account, there would remain a much deeper problem with his notion of contagion. This has to do with its utter arbitrariness and the arbitrariness which it attributes to the Christian gospel in general. Why should we care about the freedom of Jesus? Why should we care about the general attitudinal and dispositional stance to which it leads? This problem has several dimensions.

One concerns the notion of bliks. Van Buren admits the arbitrariness of Hare's bliks (*SMG*, 143, 155). This actually justifies the exclusiveness of the gospel, for even if other persons should find the key to a historical perspective in other pieces of history, "the fact remains that the history of Jesus is not the same as the history of the Buddha, the Communist Revolution, or Henry Ford" (*SMG*, 155). This is true enough. There is something historically particular about Jesus (and every other piece of history), and a historical perspective wedded tightly to it will certainly have distinctive characteristics

[12] See, e.g., Gilkey (1964), 240.

that cannot be separated from it. Van Buren speaks of the inability to "prove" the uniqueness of Jesus's history and then says:

Christians have never been able, however (and when they were at their best have not tried), to *prove* the "superiority" of their historical perspective over other perspectives. Claims of "finality" are simply the language appropriate to articulating a historical perspective. The logic of these claims can be illuminated by setting them alongside the statement "I'm I." (*SMG*, 155, van Buren's emphasis)

In the sense of "superiority" van Buren has in mind here, he is certainly correct. But Christians have always been concerned to think out and to share with others, including non-Christians, grounds for the *normative* content of their gospel, and this does not necessarily have to be an argument for "superiority" at all. It is simply what "giving an account of one's faith" has always meant, even if today we judge some of these efforts to have been tendentious, self-righteous, or question begging in the extreme. But van Buren can give no account at all. All that he can say is: "I *just happen* to find myself 'caught' by this historical perspective and not another," or "It *just happens to be the case* that Jesus's freedom has been contagious for me." This problem then touches every other aspect of his notion of historical perspective.

It raises the question, for instance, as van Buren himself notes, of the possibility that other historical personages, such as Socrates, might also be free persons who set others free. Van Buren simply admits this possibility and uses it to mark the distinctive (in the sense of different and unique) character of Jesus's history. But this is a mark of every historical pattern. If we ask the Christian why it has been Jesus rather than Socrates, he or she can only say: "Well, that's just the way it happened to have happened to me; I'm I." How on this count is the Christian to respond to much more "negative" or "demonic" historical possibilities, such as, for instance, Hitler, who also had the power to "set men free" within the context of the Nazi historical perspective?

This question touches on another, related, issue which undermines van Buren's notion of history. For we can also ask why we need some historical personage at all. Why would a fictional story, or image, or pattern not be sufficient for an historical perspective? Why do we need the actual *history* of Jesus? If we knew that it was just a story and nothing more, why would that not be enough? Van Buren will reply that for this historical perspective it is simply not a story but an account of a real historical personage. But again, this is so with the Christian gospel because *it just happens* to be so in this case. The tie to a history upon which van Buren places so much emphasis, turns out to be utterly arbitrary, and seemingly dispensable. For instance, suppose we thought that we could "improve" our historical perspective in some way; van Buren could give us no reason why we could not dispense with the *actual* history by simply "improving" the story to make it better conform to our "improved" gospel.[13]

All of these problems come together with the claims to normativity that van Buren in fact makes. He begins his description of the gospel, for instance, by saying: "The Gospel, the 'good news' of the apostles concerning Jesus of Nazareth and what happened on Easter, was proclaimed as news of an event *which it was good for men to hear*" (*SMG*, 135, my emphasis). He contrasts the universal aspects of the gospel with loyalty to a nation and says of the Christian, simply as a mark of his distinctiveness, "that Jesus has become his point of orientation, with the consequence that he is freed from acknowledging final loyalty to his nation, family, church, or any other person and is liberated for service to these other centers of relative loyalty" (*SMG*, 142, cf. p. 141). The Christian's historical perspective shows one how to treat others as though "we regarded them as pardoned and accepted in some 'final' sense which qualifies all human judging and forgiving" such that the Christian is led "to take sides with reconciliation, mercy, and forgiveness and to oppose enmity, retribution, and revenge" (*SMG*, 150). Or, in reference to Jesus's election as "called by God" and his "obedience," such statements "speak of Jesus as one with a history which is different from that of any other man, and of Jesus as one who is 'set apart' from all the others and for all the others" (*SMG*, 154). Finally, the eschatological hope of Christians is that Jesus's contagious freedom and the reconciliation associated with it should prevail "on this earth among all men" (*SMG*, 154). Though this is not a prediction, it is such a deep commitment to a policy "that one would die rather than abandon it. It indicates the unqualified, undebatable aspect of the Christian's historical perspective" (*SMG*, 154–155).

Such statements could be multiplied many times. Usually they indicate the unconditional and life-forming character of the commit-

---

[13] Van Buren could not, of course, specify what counts as "improvement," but that is a problem with his terms, not with the example.

ment. The commitment, however, is not in question. He also speaks
of norms in the sense that the pattern of Jesus's freedom is normative
for the Christian historical perspective, and this also is not problematic.
But as the above examples show, van Buren cannot articulate the
content of the gospel without time and again either including or
implying some normative character for it. The gospel would scarcely
be interesting were this not the case. But on his own terms he can
give no account of this normativity. Why is the gospel something
good for human beings to hear? Why *should* I want Jesus's freedom to
become contagious for others and for the reconciliation associated
with it to prevail throughout the world? It may be that something in
Jesus, described as "freedom" (scarcely a nonnormative word), is
conveyed to others, but why should I regard this as *liberating*, either
for myself or for others?

One might respond that the attitudes, dispositions, and patterns of
action in the Christian historical perspective are so attractive that
their normative character is self-evident. Yet even if this were the
case – which I doubt – it would be so only with specific elements in
the perspective, whereas the perspective that contains them, contains
them as a unity. Given this overarching characteristic of the perspective
as a perspective, and also given the fact that at this level there are
indeed contrasting, alternative patterns for historical perspectives
(which might contain some of the same elements), surely *some*
account of the normative character of the Christian historical
perspective is required. Yet given van Buren's conception of it as a
blik, he is blocked in principle from addressing the issue. Secular
men and women, whom van Buren takes as his point of reference, do,
in philosophy and other disciplines, address the overall valuational
and normative questions about what the best human life might be,
and also address the questions about how it might be justified. How
ironic that van Buren has constructed a picture of the gospel which
prevents the Christian in principle from sharing in this discussion.
The Christian can only say: "This *just happens* to be the way I see and
value things."

This problem of arbitrariness is related to another problem for
which Ogden has criticized van Buren. As one would expect, Ogden
criticizes him for so readily surrendering the objective character of
language about God. He correctly challenges van Buren's claim of a
philosophical consensus on the verification principle as a criterion of
cognitivity (see *RG*, 84–90). The overall point, however, is that no

Christian theology can dispense with some sort of cognitive reference to God. Van Buren's noncognitive approach makes his account of the gospel little more than a "disguised comparison" (*RG*, 87). Though I disagree with Ogden's alternative, I share his concern that van Buren makes it impossible to speak of the *fides quae creditur*. For the present theology, this constraint arises as much from the nature of sin as it does from the doctrine of God. Or, alternatively, the doctrine of God first arises from the existentialist analysis of faith and unfaith. But I share Ogden's insistence that, properly understood, faith does have its appropriate "object" or ground, apart from which the claims that the Christian gospel wants to make about the human condition cannot be stated. Van Buren can only articulate this "object" by appealing to a blik which arbitrarily just happens to capture the person of faith. Whatever that blik is in reference to, it is not "God" in any conceivable sense.

Let us now see how Hall and van Buren help to delineate the present seeing-as position. The most obvious differences are with Hall. His theistic "categorizing" defines the inventory status of the ultimate ontological unifiers – or, if not a first-order language, it must imply an ultimate inventory position. Though Hall defends a seeing-as, *what* that seeing-as is about involves a "taking-as" of ultimate ontological and cosmological scope. Hall simply denies that this taking-as can be rationally defended except by soft felicity conditions. In contrast, my naturalism is of ultimate ontological and cosmological scope, but it is not a seeing-as. As argued above, that *upon which* a naturalistically religious seeing-as "sees" must be located differently than at the level of inventory status: "God" is not in the inventory of what ultimately exists. Thus, in the sense defended by Hall, the position here is not a seeing-as at all, but rests upon a nonperspectival physicalistic naturalism.

The present seeing-as has a more complicated relationship to van Buren's perspectivalism, but the differences are no less important. This may be brought out by asking about what van Buren's perspectivalism is a seeing-as. It is a perspective on a form of life. This is what gives it its noncognitive character. To the extent that God-terms function at all, they function reflexively to express the unqualified character of the commitment the Christian has made to her historical perspective (cf., e.g., *SMG*, 133, 154–155). This perspective receives its only grounding in the historical person of Jesus. Even Easter, upon which van Buren rests so much, refers simply to the conversion experience of the original apostles and then to later believers by way of saying that Jesus's freedom has become communicable. Easter is self-referentially defined by the fact that the Christian just happens to have an historical perspective to which he finds himself deeply committed. The form of life involved in this seeing-as is thus entirely unarguable.

The present seeing-as has similarities to van Buren's position because it too makes strong reference to a form of life. This is because a valuational theism is rooted in a valuational stance. It will articulate a form of life appropriate to its seeing-as, the "life of faith" in contrast to "life after the flesh." Furthermore, because it is grounded in events of grace, the Christian form of life will have a strong kerygmatic (i.e., transformational) form, rooted similarly to van Buren in the event of Easter.

After these similarities, however, differences emerge. First, a valuational theism presupposing a physicalistic naturalism requires support from a normative account of value. It will not be enough simply to assert such a stance as a blik formed, howsoever may be, by reference to something contagious in Jesus. We shall want to know, if you will, why we should care about what is contagious about Jesus. Such a normative account is necessary because "God-exists" is a meta-assertion expressing a valuational matrix. This valuational stance must have a normative component, else it is simply arbitrary. But then, second, assuming such a normative account, "God exists" can be true, though this will require a further argument connecting a theistic seeing-as with a normative account of value. "God exists" can therefore have cognitive value. Thus, despite the similarity with van Buren's form of life, the present seeing-as seeks to have cognitive content. This means among other things that traditional language about God, suitably qualified, unlike van Buren's almost total exclusion of such language, can be readmitted to the theological enterprise. It also means that theology is something other than a blik.

But in reference to *what* will this seeing-as "see"?[14] The immediate answer is that it will be in reference to a form of life (the "life of faith") constituted as a valuational matrix. This answer follows from

---

[14] Van Buren answers this by seeing the gospel as an historical perspective in reference to a form of life qualified by Jesus's freedom and Easter. To the extent that God-terms play any role at all, "God is 'X'" could always be translated in some form of, "the Christian sees her life as . . ." Thus, for van Buren, to confess "God as Creator" means that from the historical perspective of the gospel, "the Christian sees her life affirmatively" (see *SMG*, 176–177).

the arguments for construing faith existentially as grounded in events of grace. Presupposing an analysis of the human predicament calling for the grace of God, faith is understood existentially as openness to the future. Faith then becomes a form of life which *sees* the source of human good (events of grace) *as* God. This statement may be reversed as well: faith sees *God* as the source of human good. The two together are simply condensed statements of the entire argument to this point. Though faith "sees God as . . .," the primary reference is to the valuational matrix rooted in events of grace. Existentially interpreted, this valuational matrix constitutes a form of life defined as openness to the future. This valuational matrix makes it appropriate to see God as events of grace, and seeing God as events of grace makes appropriate a valuational matrix expressed in a form of life. Once we see the linkages among "God exists" as a seeing-as, a valuational matrix, and a form of life, then the content of the gospel need not be noncognitive, though the cognitivity issue will be settled in a valuational and not an ontological context. For this reason, as the last chapter suggested, it is possible to defend a strong version of the *fides quae creditur* which is left so vacuous in van Buren. Let us turn, then, to some of the issues involved in defending the normative status of such a theistic seeing-as.

THE CASE FOR A THEISTIC SEEING-AS

The prior two chapters showed how the Christian gospel can be rendered in naturalist terms as a valuational matrix rooted deeply in the human condition. A last bridge to naturalism has shown that the theistic seeing-as involved in this view of the gospel also permits cognitive values for "God exists," in contrast to other seeing-as options in contemporary philosophy of religion. We must now examine the issues surrounding the question of truth (or cognitivity). As Post shows, a case for a valuational theism requires two kinds of normative argument – if, at least, we want "God exists" to be true.[15] We must show: (1) that the values in question are the correct ones and (2) that they require a theistic seeing-as.

This double normative issue poses a formidable challenge indeed.

[15] See *FE*, 347. Without this latter check, we can, of course, have any valuational stance we want, as is implicit in van Buren's bliks, and with sufficient artful dodging, we can probably make "God exists" apply to it as well. Only if the issue is truth are more severe constraints implied both for a valuational stance and for "God exists."

Despite sympathy for the effort to develop a valuational theism within a physicalist ontology, Post remains agnostic about whether any such effort could be successful.[16] Part of the problem lies simply in knowing how such normative questions should even be framed. We presently lack sufficient planetary, cross-cultural resources to know

[16] Post asserts, on the one hand, that the relevant issues for a renewal of theism on physicalist grounds will be valuational: "the judgment that some particular religious discourse is the one called for on a given occasion clearly is in large part a value judgment." He encourages theologians to cease being "bullied into holding that the decision to use or continue in some such language game or form of life is a matter ultimately of subjective preference or 'faith,' on the ground, say, that the decision is neither derivable from nor reducible to any totality of natural fact." Instead, theologians can, he says, "*borrow the idea of the determinacy of valuation and argue that this decision corresponds with the facts . . . as indeed it might*" (*FE*, 339, my emphasis). Despite the difficulties in any such argument, he notes in another context that "at least the crucial assumption is a normative one, requiring normative argument to the effect that the objectively true value judgments include the theistic ones." This normative assumption "is perfectly consistent with the minimal physicalist theses and, when conjoined with them, forms a synthesis of physicalism and theism *in which each enriches the other while correcting the other's occasional extremes*," and he simply leaves open whether "the crucial normative assumption" [the assumption, note carefully, not about the objectivity of value but about the legitimacy of a valuational theism] can survive (*FE*, 337, my emphasis; cf. 332). [See also *FE*, 332–335, where Post discusses the attractiveness of a synthesis between naturalism, especially physicalism, and some version of theology (or theism) in our contemporary intellectual culture against the background of several historical precedents for such syntheses, especially Thomism with Aristotelian naturalism – all the while noting how much more daunting such a synthesis must be in our present circumstances (*FE*, 333–334).]

On the other hand, Post recognizes that a valuational theism does not *follow* directly from minimal physicalist principles. It follows only with the additional normative assumption that "the objectively correct values *include* certain theistic values . . . together with the theistic ways of seeing and experiencing that they give rise to" (*FE*, 336, my emphasis), and a significant portion of his chapter on "God" (*FE*, 327–365) is a discussion of "the *possibly* insuperable objections to [making this additional assumption]" (*FE*, 337, my emphasis; see also 345–356).

Post admits that the normative assumption is very difficult to defend on the grounds of a traditional theism that depends on "subject-predicate literalism" and requires that God be found in the *ontological* inventory (see *FE*, 336–337, 351–352). Nevertheless, he recognizes that the entire program will necessarily be revisionary, thus not really a version of traditional (or even neoclassical) theism at all (*FE*, 335; see 332–337), and his entire discussion of "the possibly insuperable objections" is oriented to overcoming them. Personally, he confesses that his interest in this project arises from no "irreversible commitment" to some form of theism but rather simply from a "dispassionate" philosophical curiosity about whether such a conceptual program can be pulled off (*FE*, 336). Still, all in all, Post is fundamentally sympathetic to the program and repeatedly encourages the theologian to try. His sympathy is well captured by the following statement: "Far easier said than done, of course, but the obligation merely to try and, failing, to try again and again has been neglected for so long that it is no longer seen as an obligation, only as a quixotic ideal. . . Yet there is no more powerful way for the theologian to proceed, and a faith that seeks understanding would be well advised to seek its understanding, in this day and age, within some such framework of science and philosophy. Even the true believer probably should be satisfied with no less. The reason is that the most illuminating and long-lasting theologies of the past – Augustine's, say, or Aquinas's – were achieved not by denouncing or ignoring the best science and philosophy of their day, or even by presenting a theology merely not inconsistent with it, but by incorporating it into their rational theology as a framework within whose confines they could interpret and support the central theistic claims" (*FE*, 334).

how to do this. Furthermore, the problem is not restricted to religious persons, but will arise for any ambitious attempt to articulate valuational issues of broad scope. In other words, the nontheist, the atheist, or the secularist face identical problems with any sufficiently broad valuational conception.

Though I cannot hope to settle these normative issues definitively in this work, some progress can be made in delineating them. It is relevant to remember the position this project occupies within contemporary theology. I have argued, taking up Post's challenge, that the most attractive theological option today is seriously to explore the possibility of a synthesis between theology and a strong version of philosophical naturalism. This task could not be accomplished quickly or easily, but it is one that needs to be essayed. However flawed the present reflections might be, they are intended to contribute to what will remain a genuine, ongoing theological task. I also point out, very much in the spirit of Wieman, that at no other point more than this one can the outlines of an authentic and fruitful research program be discerned for theological reflection of the future. With these reservations in mind, I shall attempt to make an initial contribution to these normative questions.

Our task naturally divides into two normative issues: a normative argument supporting the Christian valuational stance and another normative argument for its linkage to a theistic seeing-as.[17] The discussion, we shall see, will be more significantly advanced if we take these up in reverse order, examining first the linkage to a theistic seeing-as and only then addressing the more difficult issue of the normative status of the Christian valuational stance itself.

The first issue concerns the warrant for linking a valuational stance (in this case, the Christian one) to theism. How does this valuational matrix *require* a *theistic* seeing-as? What precisely is the nature of the "requirement" that must be shown? Most seeing-as positions in the philosophy of religion assume that it must be quite tight. They assume, that is, that a seeing-as expressed theistically will simply take over the language of the theistic tradition unreconstructed.[18] This is

---

[17] See *FE*, 336–337, 340–343, 347–355.
[18] It is no accident that most contemporary seeing-as positions have been developed within Wittgensteinian analytic philosophy of religion and are quite conservative in spirit and outcome. W. H. Walsh notes that such views generally reflect a "Burkian" conception of language to the effect that any language "in use" may be assumed to be in "good order." The result, Walsh tellingly shows, is to exclude *theoretical* questions that might undermine the cognitive efficacy of the language itself (as, for instance, with alchemy or astrology). See Walsh (1963), 130–132.

even true with Post. Though his proposal is clearly revisionary, his examples do not probe the question of what makes such a seeing-as *theistic* but simply take over the language of theism as such. This may be seen in the following statement where Post proposes how the theologian might defend the necessity for a theistic seeing-as in reference to a normative conception of moral value: "A correct and sufficiently subtle morality requires a certain sort of 'seeing-as,' according to the theologian, a seeing-as that involves, among other things, seeing us and the world as created, for a purpose, by a loving and transcendent God" (*FE*, 344).

Without a prior revisionary reflection, such formulations block direct critical reflection on what makes the theistic terms of a theistic seeing-as *theistic*. In a certain sense, of course, Post is not to be faulted because any theistic seeing-as, even a radically revisionary one, will terminate in directly theistic language. But lacking a theological reflection showing precisely how it deserves to be theistic, such language remains opaque, and this is especially true if we assume from the outset that the underlying program must be revisionary. A naturalist wants to know precisely what all the crucial terms in "seeing us and the world as *created*, for a *purpose*, by a *loving* and *transcendent God*" mean. Existentialist interpretation especially demands such examination, for it seeks to translate them into modes of human existing. So, we cannot merely appropriate a theistic seeing-as without critically reflecting upon the nature of theism itself.

Bringing this issue into focus requires seeing that a fully naturalist theology requires rethinking the very question to which the religious response is an answer. This is because a naturalist theology qualifies or even eliminates many of the ontological terms of absoluteness and ultimacy which traditional theism, both classical and revisionary, assume are necessary to anchor the language of faith. In this sense, a naturalist theology amounts to a revision of what "God" means in human life. I believe that Wieman should be seen as engaged in just this enterprise. He is not merely redefining God as "the source of human good" but, in effect, trying to recast the entire religious question to which God is an answer. Thus, the plausibility of a significant number of my proposals depends upon entertaining, sympathetically and imaginatively, a revisionary reflection on this question. It is true that many of the ontological references theologians make are compromised by this effort. But the day is very late for Western theism, and those references are already deeply compromised anyway. Furthermore, quite apart from the construction I have given it, the wide acceptance of existentialist interpretation among theologians today means that much of the "ultimacy" language of the witness of faith is already understood existentially and thus valuationally, not ontologically or cosmologically.[19]

Once one sympathetically embarks on rethinking the religious question, then it is significant how much of the tradition a valuational theism readmits – but from a different angle of vision. Take, for instance, the conception of religion itself. It is widely assumed that the religious question requires answers that place our lives against the widest ontological background, and this is typically the way "ultimacy" is construed. Tillich's definition of religion as ultimate concern, perhaps the most influential conception of this sort in recent theology, is a case in point. Despite the existential force Tillich gives ultimacy, he also means that an authentic ultimate concern must concern what is genuinely ontologically ultimate.[20] Ogden's distinction between "faith" and "religion" is helpful here because it roots the discussion more clearly at the existential level. Thus, by "faith" Ogden means the ultimate confidence in the worth of life that all human beings express in their very existing. By conceiving "religion" as a question of faith in this sense, he distinguishes between authentic and inauthentic forms of faith. "Religion" (in the narrower sense), in contrast, is one form of culture among others by which this basic existential faith, presupposed by all cultural forms, is expressed in beliefs, ritual, and forms of social organization. Yet despite this existential footing for "basic faith," Ogden never doubts that its adequate expressions must be conceived in terms of "*the ultimate nature of reality* as it presents itself to that faith."[21]

The entrenched character of such assumptions about religion militate against a naturalist theology from the outset, for, from the perspective of naturalism, the ultimate *ontological* unifiers probably do not support the values religious affirmations otherwise express. But, apart from their ontological ground, these religious issues are entirely valuational, as Ogden's distinction between "faith" and "religion" has the merit of identifying. If we change our angle of vision and cease

---

[19] Even Schubert Ogden agrees with much of this, as is evident in his interpretation of creation, which, despite his insistence on a metaphysics of ultimacy, has strong existential footings and is certainly not what a great deal of the tradition meant. See *RG*, 17, 178–179, 213.

[20] See Tillich (1957), 8–12, and Tillich (1967), I, 14.

[21] Ogden (1972), 2 (my emphasis). For this entire discussion, see Ogden (1972) and *RG*, 21–43.

to assume that religious concerns can only be satisfied by a universal and ultimate ontological ground, then ultimacy returns in valuational dress. This is the merit of Wieman's attempt to understand God valuationally in terms of the source of human good. The religious question becomes the valuational question about a final devotion or loyalty. Since, as we have seen, Wieman's position can be restated existentially, it also may be rephrased exactly in terms of Ogden's conception of faith, but now without begging the question of what satisfies our ultimate confidence in the worth of life.[22]

Admittedly, such a change in the nature of religion may disappoint some of the needs religion has expressed for millennia, but such changes are by no means uncommon in the history of religion and account for some of its most profound alterations, as is made evident, for instance, by Santayana's distinction between "natural" and "ultimate" religion or Bergson's between "static" and "dynamic".[23] Indeed, the Christian identification of Jesus as the Christ was itself just such an alteration in the question a "Messiah" was taken to answer.[24] All that is required is a willingness to entertain the question with a sympathetic imagination (along with an admixture of the courage that high religion has always required). And as I mentioned earlier, the day is late for Western theism.

Another such alteration concerns the predicates of divine absoluteness that are eliminated by an austere naturalism. They reappear in a valuational theism, but from a changed angle of vision. Wieman's argument for the "absoluteness" of the creative event is a case in point.[25] This argument has been almost entirely neglected by students of Wieman, perhaps because it has seemed artificial, more a "term of art," developed against the background of classical theism, but incompatible with his "empirical" bent. But if his thought is viewed as an attempt to redefine the religious question itself, then this argument becomes much more relevant.

The claim is that God, creative good, is absolute good. The argument depends on viewing absoluteness valuationally rather than ontologically. This in turn requires the weight of absoluteness to fall on Wieman's notion of "creative *transformation*." As transformative event, God's absoluteness means that the creative event is good "under all conditions and circumstances." It "remains changelessly

---

[22] See Hardwick (1987c).   [23] See Santayana (1968), and Bergson (1935).
[24] See Neville (1991), 38 for a nice statement of this.
[25] This entire discussion is from *SHG*, 79–82.

and identically the same . . . so far as concerns its goodness," hence not relative to time or place or to human need, desire or belief. It would continue as good even if human beings ceased to exist, and it remains good even when it "runs counter to all human desire." Yet it is also good "when desired and when working in the medium of human existence." A second mark is that it is unqualified good. From every standpoint, its goodness remains unchanged and self-identical, unlike created good for which there is always some standpoint from which its value can be qualified.

Three final features are more specifically religious and bring God's absoluteness close to the Bible's "living God of history," as this is especially qualified by the biblical critique of idolatry. Thus, a third mark is that demands of the creative event are unlimited. Its goodness is absolute because "it is always good to give myself, all that I am and all that I desire, all that I possess and all that is dear to me, into its control to be transformed in any way that it may require." Closely related, fourth, is the infinite value of creative good. "Its worth is incommensurable by any finite quantity of created good," for "the created good of the past sinks into oblivion when not continuously revitalized by the recurrent working of the creative event." Finally, it is entirely trustworthy. "We can be sure that the outcome of its working will always be the best possible under the conditions, even when it may seem to us otherwise."

These last three features are especially helpful in clarifying how transformation, existentially interpreted as openness to the future, is to be understood theistically. Openness to the future, taken simply as an existential structure, is indeterminate as to value. But when openness to the future is interpreted as God in reference to events of grace and thus understood as readiness for transformation, then readiness for transformation can be understood valuationally in terms of this conception of the absoluteness of God's goodness. Openness to the future, readiness for transformation, is the formal valuational structure appropriate to the absoluteness of God's goodness as grace. The absoluteness of God's goodness thereby permits us to shift our angle of vision and understand trust in being valuationally, not ontologically. In Ogden's terms, our basic faith in the worth of life is made normatively transparent by the absoluteness of God's goodness. Furthermore, again in Ogden's terms, our need for *reassurance* about this basic confidence (served by the symbolic expressions of religion) are also addressed by this conception of God's absoluteness, though from an altered, valuational angle of vision, and thus much differently than Ogden would have it.[26] Wieman's analysis, for instance, can readily support Ogden's statement that "religious assertions can serve to reassure us only because they themselves are the re-presentation of a confidence somehow already present prior to their being made" (*RG*, 32). But the changed angle of vision is crucial. Otherwise we are straightaway driven into thinking that naturalism has no resources for addressing these most profound religious issues of human living.

A final example concerns monotheism. Wieman has been criticized for having an insufficiently determinate way to identify the unity of God.[27] The implication is perhaps that Wieman's conception of God is henotheistic. The criticism is certainly well taken if the issue is understood ontologically. God for Wieman is *whatever* events or processes it is in nature that produce value, and he remained blithely unconcerned about their ontological identifiers. From the standpoint of physicalism, these processes seem certainly not to share an ontological unity since they are differently determined physically in different domains of nature and since, at the level of intentional states and other emergent properties, the same states and properties can be determined by non-identical physical states, especially by different brain states.[28] Wieman thus seems to compromise monotheism. But again, the angle of vision is crucial. When we take the issue valuationally, the problem disappears, for God concerns an absolute devotion. Valuationally considered (as events of grace), it has the same unity that monotheism has always affirmed, and existentially conceived, it permits an equally powerful criticism of the worship of false gods.[29]

The purpose of these comments is to show that a naturalistic theology cannot uncritically appropriate traditional theistic language but must undertake a revision in the nature of theism itself. A major barrier is thereby lowered for connecting a theistic seeing-as normatively to a valuational stance. Once the religious question is transformed, a normative defense of theism is quite similar to its defense on traditional grounds. A claim is advanced that theological statements are simply the appropriate way to render a valuational stance fully transparent. Once we change our vision about what "God" *means*,

---

[26] See *RG*, 29–34.   [27] See Cobb (1969), 51–59.
[28] This is a deep problem in neuro-physiology and the philosophical problem of mind.
[29] See *SHG*, 23–26.

then we can defend theism as integral to the articulation of a normative valuational stance.

With this revisionary conception in place, existentialist interpretation now requires that we direct hermeneutical attention to precisely how "God" enters the content of faith. In terms of this argument what makes the Christian seeing-as theistic is the appropriateness of theistic language for an existentially interpreted conception of human bondage and liberation. This appropriateness becomes evident when the deepest issues regarding authentic human existence are brought to the surface. As we saw, these issues concern the transition from inauthentic to authentic existence. In that context, it becomes entirely appropriate to speak of sin, of God, and of God's action. It also becomes appropriate to understand authentic human existence, openness to the future, as the giftedness of life, trust in being, and consequently, the love of God. Of course, the context that permits us to construe the deepest existential issues of human living in this way is itself constituted by the broad theistic tradition we are trying to interpret, but this involves no vicious circularity. All that is required is to assure at every step that the analysis is compatible with naturalism. This was accomplished with the first two bridge principles which defended a phenomenologically transparent conception of human sin that in turn made possible, indeed demanded, an existentialist understanding of God as transformative action (events of grace, the love of God). The answer to our question, "what makes a theistic seeing-as theistic," therefore arises from a phenomenology of the human situation. We simply draw forth from an existentialist interpretation of faith an existentialist interpretation of God. A theistic seeing-as then becomes appropriate for expressing a normative valuational stance (authentic human existence).

This analysis requires us to reformulate our initial normative question in a more nuanced fashion. Our initial question seemed to demand that we show normatively why the "correct" valuational stance requires a theistic seeing-as. We began by asking what kind of requirement this is, and we saw that a naturalist theology demands that we revise the role of "God" (the "theistic terms" of a theistic seeing-as). We now have the outlines of such a revision, and this permits us to rearticulate hermeneutically how "God" enters the content of faith. Taking "openness to the future" as a summary statement for the Christian valuational matrix, we can defend the appropriateness of articulating such a valuational matrix with a theistic seeing-as. The question is whether such *appropriateness* is sufficient to establish normativity. This last question is important, again, because we want to claim cognitive value for the Christian form of a theistic seeing-as, namely, that "God exists" is true from within a physicalist ontology.

The really normative level for the truth of "God exists" is the phenomenological description of the human condition that describes bondage to a self-defeating order of life. Given this condition, the Christian proclamation is the offer of a new self-understanding articulated in terms of events of grace. "God exists" becomes a meta-assertion for the truth of *this* description and is a condensed summary statement for its valuational matrix.[30] A theistic seeing-as, therefore, is an appropriate expression for this normative account of the human condition. It is appropriate but is not itself normatively *necessary*. The normative account arises, rather, from the description of the human condition.

This loosening of the normative requirement for a theistic seeing-as is imposed by the content of the gospel itself (including its critique of idolatry). When Christians have best understood themselves, they have wanted to say that the love of God is shed abroad upon all humankind, not merely upon those who use Christian (i.e., in Post's sense, "theistic") language or adopt a specifically Christian form of life. The emphasis in the gospel is upon the *reality* of God with which human beings have to do, not upon their special languages. This same point is also implicit in the existentialist method we have used to interpret the gospel. This existentialist analytic is entirely neutral as to theism. The content of faith is simply authentic human existence, and theologically we must avoid claiming that only Christians or only users of certain languages can have authentic life. According to the present account, the deepest existential reference for what the gospel *means* by God is simply openness to the future as this is constituted by transformative events (events of grace). God is the gift of openness to the future. In "knowing" openness to the future, the Christian "knows" God, and the Christian must be prepared to say that anyone who understands herself existentially in such a way as to be open to the future "knows" God. Instead of saying that a form of life actualized as openness to the future requires a theistic seeing-as, the theologian will say that wherever openness to the future is realized, it

[30] See *FE*, 348.

is realized in reference to that reality Christians name as God. This puts us in the position to advance the further claim that the language of theism (a theistic seeing-as) is the normatively superior account to render openness to the future fully transparent. But we must be careful not to claim exclusive privilege for Christian language or even for the specifically Christian form of life, something to which Post's formulation of the "requirement" would seem to doom us.[31]

These arguments address, at least in outline, the second of Post's twofold normative challenge, the linkage between a valuational matrix and the necessity of a theistic seeing- (and experiencing-) as. Though Post suggests that this theistic linkage is the most difficult part of the argument to make, further analysis of the "requirement" shows that it is well within reach. This becomes even more evident when one sets the theologian's task beside the challenges confronted by other, perhaps nontheistic, attempts normatively to defend a broadly conceived valuational matrix. From this perspective, the theologian's "theism" is simply one hermeneutical component of a complex valuational matrix. I conclude therefore that this part of the normative argument can be successfully met by an existentially conceived, naturalistic valuational theism. In this way Wieman's transformation of the religious question into a valuational one supports the argument in favor of a theistic seeing-as. It makes possible a cognitively strong theology on naturalist terms. Though "God" is not in the *ontological* inventory – not really new for naturalists – "God exists" can be cognitively true if it expresses the truth of a valuational matrix, articulated as a seeing-as. If the Christian witness of faith may be interpreted existentially, then a new

---

[31] I hasten to add that these remarks are presented at the level of theological reflection and do not propose any fundamental alteration in the language of piety by which the Christian witness of faith articulates itself. Here I share Bultmann's conviction that the task of demythologizing is not to eliminate but to interpret the mythological language of the witness of faith (see NTM, 24 [ET, 12]). Even van Buren takes this position (see *SMG*, 198–200), and the same is true with Ogden's revisionary efforts (see *RG*, 117–119). In his criticism of van Buren, Ogden goes so far as to admit that, formally considered, van Buren is not to be faulted for demanding "a radical 'reduction' of what have traditionally counted as theological statements." This alone does not distinguish "his proposal from the position fairly widely shared by contemporary Protestant theologians. Once one grants that theological thinking and speaking cannot be objectifying in the sense for which modern science provides the paradigm, the extent of what can pass for theological statements *is bound to be reduced* – mythological statements, for instance, no longer qualifying as properly theological" (*RG*, 85, my emphasis). In other words, it is quite common in contemporary theology both to accept the language of piety and yet to make far reaching proposals about how that language is to be interpreted in its deepest sense. The present proposal is made extreme only by its footing in naturalism, but it intends no less to be an interpretation of the Christian witness of faith.

way is opened to conceive the *truth* of Christianity that is consistent
with an austere physicalistic naturalism.

THE NORMATIVE CASE FOR THE CHRISTIAN
WITNESS OF FAITH

We must now turn to the second dimension of normative evaluation.
As Post says, the only way to justify language about God from within
an austere naturalism is to show that "ultimately its truth consists in
or at least is based on the objective correctness of certain values and a
way of life." Granted that there is a fact of the matter "as regards
values and forms of life," then there is "a fact of the matter as regards
the kinds of seeing-as entailed by them," but "one would . . . have to
argue that the theistic values and form of life are indeed among the
true ones," and "one would still have to show that they require a
theistic complex of experiencing and seeing-as" (*FE*, 347). We have
seen that this latter case can be made – provided we qualify Post's
constraints as in the prior section. Far the more formidable task is to
address the first normative dimension, to justify the theistic values
and form of life as among the true ones. At the same time, I have
pointed out that the theologian is not alone when it comes to
justifying the truth of any comprehensive valuational outlook. The
problem concerns how even to frame the required arguments in the
cross-cultural framework demanded today by an emerging global
community.

The task becomes somewhat more manageable if we make the
obvious distinction between strictly moral values and values of a more
comprehensive sort. We then can ask how strictly moral values might
be justified and what relationships they might have to a theistic
valuational stance. This still leaves us with the problem of the wider
valuational stance, but it narrows the task, and it might provide clues
for the further argument. The issue admits of three divisions: (a) the
justification of strictly moral values, (b) the relationship between
them and a theistic seeing-as, and (c) the justification of the latter
valuational stance itself.

I suggest this threefold division because it seems evident to me that
strictly moral values must receive their justification through reason
alone, and this is a philosophical undertaking. It is also one that has
been generally accepted among theologians since Kant established
that moral values cannot be grounded *directly* in God. Though the

claim to ground moral values in reason alone is controversial today, I am made bold to take this position because it seems obvious that if strictly moral values are truly to be *justified*, then their justification can only finally be by reasons all human beings can share with one another, and this requires that they be justified solely on grounds of rational transparency.[32] But I am also made bold because I think this issue has largely been resolved by Rawls and by Jeffrey Reiman's *Justice and Modern Moral Philosophy* which, building on Rawls, offers a more thoroughgoing rational foundation for Rawls's principles of justice.

Furthermore, I also assume that the primary moral values at issue concern those of justice. This is not to say that justice encompasses all moral values, but it is to say that justice is primary among them. Justice takes primacy because it concerns the justification we can give under conditions of moral conflict when we require others to submit to our moral judgments or policies of action (and these conditions concern matters that, of course, go far beyond issues of merely personal moral disagreement). In this respect, justice is, in Reiman's phrase, "moralizing's morality." As he explains:

Moralizing is morality as a real active human enterprise. But if justice is the opposite of subjugation, then justice determines generally the morally permissible terms under which people can rightly require anything of others, and these include the morally permissible means by which holders of some moral belief can get others to adopt or conform to that belief. Thus justice necessarily has authority over other moral beliefs because its task is to determine the things that can be done in the name of other moral beliefs. . . Where the usual approach in moral inquiry is to ask the moral requirements, the approach of justice is to ask for the requirement of moral requiring. Justice's authority over other moral ideals is, then, not a matter of its alleged higher worth, like the authority of noble over commoners, but of what is necessary to its unique function, like the authority of a police officer over other citizens. The analogy is apt because justice polices the border between might and right. It has authority over all moral ideals because anyone urging moral ideals must keep to the right side of this border to be moral at all.[33]

This position leaves open whether religious values may illumine, enrich, deepen, and perhaps even transvalue moral values grounded strictly in reason. One can presume that they will since the Christian valuational stance entails a form of life. Such enriching can then be conceived along lines suggested, for instance, by Stanley Hauerwas's

---

[32] This is why I believe that an ethics of virtues based on communities or historical traditions, very popular today, can finally not address the deepest issues of moral justification, however much they may otherwise illuminate ethical issues.   [33] Reiman (1989), 8.

illuminating attempts to conceive virtues and character, and their moral requirements, from within the demands of the Christian form of life understood as "conforming our lives in a faithful manner to the stories of God."[34] Hauerwas, however, refuses to address the wider issue of the relation between the Christian form of life and the rational grounding of moral values as such. Unlike him, I am assuming that if the Christian form of life can instruct about strictly moral values, it must do so under the same norms of rational assessment that all such reasoning must meet, particularly as regards the framework of justice within which it must be conducted.[35] In any case, to the extent that the Christian (or any other) valuational stance can illuminate strictly moral values, it will do so with reasons that are continuous with moral discourse itself, else it falls outside the bounds of justice, the border between might and right. This is one kind of relationship between strictly moral values and the Christian valuational stance, but it is unproblematic. It falls under one of the primary tasks of Christian ethics in so far as it engages in moral discourse at all, and it is well understood and well practiced by many Christian ethicists today.

The deeper issue concerns the relationship between moral values and the Christian valuational stance in so far as strictly moral values are informed by wider values that are not strictly moral at all. In theology, for instance, this question arises when one asks about the relationship between "the love of God" and *any* forms of life or policies of action that are taken to follow from it, as, for instance, the norm of love between persons that Christians enjoin. This relationship is by no means obvious in traditional theology, and it is a question in need of deeper attention on the part of contemporary theologians. Why should I be loving because God has loved me? How should we link distinctively religious values (e.g., "God's love") with their contribution to strictly moral values by way of illumination, enrichment, deepening, and transvaluation? Provide the link, and the contribution can be made to follow, but how do we make the link itself? All too often

---

[34] Hauerwas (1981a), 96. See also Hauerwas (1974), Hauerwas (1977), and Hauerwas (1981b).
[35] See, e.g., Hauerwas's remarks about refusing "to posit a 'story of stories' in order to provide a foundation for 'morality'." He asserts that any such attempt is "radically misconceived" because it posits "a moral order and rational community that simply does not exist" (Hauerwas [1981a], 97). But this is beside the point (and pretentious as well) because the rationality that justice requires of us when we require others to subordinate themselves to our moral beliefs and actions (as Hauerwas, willy nilly, must be prepared to do if he is serious about the moral issues he investigates, since even his position must involve sanctions) has to do with the nature of rational discourse, not with whether we can find a rational community somewhere.

theologians simply assume the link by vague references to the Kingdom of God or to other eschatological ideas that either beg the question or, again, vaguely assume some continuity of life beyond death.[36]

In so doing, however, they violate the theological norm for any acceptable modern theology assumed by most theologians today, namely, that any contemporary theology must make itself comprehensible within the *present* importance of human life. As Ogden puts it, it is "our affirmation of life here and now in the world in all its aspects and in its proper autonomy and significance."[37] This stance, of course, is deeply at home in the present position, but it is one enjoined upon contemporary theology as a whole.[38] Thus, even if made by way of an eschatological promise of faith, any such conception must conceive the relationship between distinctively religious values and moral ones in such a way that that relationship is made evident in the present experience of value.

Actually, contemporary theology is by no means without resources for addressing this issue. An initial clue is provided by a suggestion of Post's. Commenting on the attempt to ground strictly moral values in a theistic seeing-as, he notes that it "is not at all clear that theistic seeings-as are required in order to do justice to the uniqueness of each individual life, to the tensions between duty and happiness, to love and forgiveness, to the felt objectivity of these and other imperatives, and so on" (*FE*, 347). Granting this difficulty, however, and having conceded that there still might be distinctively religious values, he asks at another point: "Which domain of truth – which vision of the world – ought we to employ if we are to see each other from a correct and sufficiently rich moral point of view? The theologian believes that only a theistic vision of the world and us can do justice to the uniqueness and sanctity of each individual life, to the tensions between duty or virtue and the pursuit of one's own happiness, to the necessity of love and forgiveness, and to much more, including not least the felt objectivity of these and other imperatives" (*FE*, 347–348). Christian theology has been especially

---

[36] Hauerwas, for instance, remains persistently unreflective on these boundary questions raised by his own approach to theological ethics. See, for instance, his important "Memory, Community and the Reasons for Living: Reflections on Suicide and Euthanasia" (Hauerwas [1977], 101–115) where the problem with the linkage between the ethical position and his theology is especially striking.   [37] *RG*, 20; see *RG*, 6–12, 44–52.

[38] See, for instance, Gilkey's splendid discussion of Augustine's and Calvin's views of divine providence in Gilkey (1976), 159–187.

acute at identifying this interface between strictly moral values and a wider valuational context. I shall mention two possible avenues by which the issue might be addressed, one influenced by Reinhold Niebuhr, the other by Ogden, though both reflect a wider theological tradition.

Niebuhr's position is based on the close relationship between sin and idolatry. As I have mentioned before, Niebuhr suggests that Christian doctrine has always understood sin to be rooted in unbelief.[39] We have seen how richly this idea can be developed existentially. Niebuhr also notes that sin is basically pride and that pride has both a religious and a moral dimension. Religiously, pride is self-elevation or "glorification" in rebellion against God. Existentially interpreted, the self puts itself in the place of God.[40] But it is also directly connected to a moral dimension, for the insecure self attempts to secure itself by subjecting other selves to its own projects. Thus, sin in its primarily religious meaning is intimately connected to injustice, as the prophetic tradition has always recognized.[41]

Though this linkage does not negate the autonomy of strictly moral values, it does suggest how the Christian valuational stance is related to them. Any philosophical account of morality must ground (or presuppose) an interest in adherence to the moral demands it rationally defends. The issue here is not whether moral values can be rationally defended or even whether they can be rationally motivated; the emphasis falls rather on the wider framework of values that might motivate such rational adherence itself. Any serious philosophical defense of a moral point of view must at least presuppose some position on such a wider valuational framework. Typically, either a natural human sociability or mutual self-interest is assumed. Niebuhr, however, powerfully shows that mutuality alone is insufficient to guarantee the moral enterprise, even when its autonomy as regards rational justification is fully accepted. Human insecurity always leads to subversion as the self elevates itself and even uses its rational capacity to justify its subordination of others to its own interests. It is only when the self recognizes (in the sense of existentially actualizing) its security as grounded beyond itself in the love of God that a space is

[39] Reinhold Niebuhr (1941), i, 183.
[40] For this reason, idolatry (idolatrous self-love) is the basis of all sin, thus accounting for why the first commandment is first and is the ground and framework for all the others.
[41] See Reinhold Niebuhr (1941), i, 179, 186–191.

created wherein the full force of the moral point of view can come into play.[42]

However it is developed in detail, such an argument clearly provides the linkage between a wider valuational framework and strictly moral values hinted at by Post's remark quoted above, and it has the virtue, at least within the Christian faith, of connecting this wider framework intimately with the moral context. At the least, it provides a motivational account for the moral point of view, though this would be no small achievement. But it provides more, for it roots moral concern in a wider account of human being in the world. By so doing, it suggests how this wider account can itself contribute to the illumination, deepening, enrichment, and transvaluation of the moral sphere mentioned above.[43]

This is made evident by another perspective contributed by Ogden, one that, as Ogden would agree, is closely related to Niebuhr's analysis. In a passage clearly influenced by Wieman's radical empiricism, Ogden significantly reformulates Heidegger's and Bultmann's authentic/inauthentic distinction. Speaking of the "two basic possibilities for understanding itself in relation to its world" which always confront the self, he says:

Either it can open itself to its world and make its decisions by sensitively responding to all the influences that bear upon it, or it may close itself against its world and make its decisions on the basis of a much more restricted sensitivity than is actually possible for it. *In other words, man can act either as a self who loves and thus participates as fully and completely as he can in his own being and in the being of others, or he can act as a self who hates and thus is estranged both from the more intimate world of his own bodily life and the larger world of fellow selves and creatures.* (*RG*, 177, my emphasis)

This is one of the few instances in contemporary theology where the love of God is linked directly to the wellsprings of the Christian conception of love in human life. When it is connected with Niebuhr's view of what I have termed the wider conception of human being in the world, it provides an even stronger linkage between strictly moral values and the Christian valuational stance.

Despite Niebuhr's and Ogden's anti-naturalism, the outcome in all

---

[42] See Reinhold Niebuhr (1941), II, 81–90.
[43] See Niebuhr's illuminating comments on "the problem of moral dynamic" in Reinhold Niebuhr (1935), 203–220.

three of our views is very close.[44] I have claimed that, interpreted strictly existentially (and in light of the human problematic), the love of God means the offer of authentic existence, openness to the future. God's love is instanced in the giftedness of life, when, grounding an existential self-understanding, giftedness arises from transformative events received ever anew. In this sense, authentic existence is grounded in justification by faith conceived entirely in terms of life here and now. Events of grace make possible that openness toward being by which the self is motivated in the widest sense as one who loves and who thus, as Ogden puts it, "participates as fully and completely as he can in his own being and in the being of others" (*RG*, 177). The Christian conception of love is thereby indeed rooted in the love of God. In this way, the love of God can link a wider conception of human being in the world and strictly moral values.

A naturalist theology can thus draw on powerful theological resources to address the relationship between strictly moral values and a wider valuational stance. In all of these instances, however, the argument assumes a normative status for that wider valuational stance, and it is to this issue that we must now turn at the conclusion of

[44] Though Niebuhr was vehemently opposed to naturalism, it is surprising how much of his account of the human situation before God can be rendered on naturalist terms, including his account of justification by faith (see, e.g., Reinhold Niebuhr [1941], II, 98–126). Such a reading breaks down, however, because Niebuhr grounded the relationship between security in the love of God and the agapeistic "ideal" of the Christian form of life by an essentially unclarified appeal to eschatological symbols (a "final consummation of history" that "lies beyond the conditions of the temporal process") (Reinhold Niebuhr [1941], II, 291). He clearly regarded eschatological concepts symbolically, not literally. But what do these symbols mean? Emil Brunner identified the problem with discomforting precision: "It would be difficult to determine just what Reinhold Niebuhr means by his . . . crucial concept of the Biblical 'eschatological symbol.' . . . [W]hat kind of reality lies hidden beneath these symbols? Is it an everlasting life, for which we should hope in the hour of death? Is it the fulfillment of the biblical expectation of the kingdom of God? . . . [D]oes one not have a right to expect of every thinking Christian – and *a fortiori* of every Christian thinker – that he be cognizant of what he has to hope for in Christ? To what extent there stands behind Niebuhr's 'eschatological symbols' a *reality*, and what kind of reality – or whether perhaps these eschatological symbols are merely 'regulative principles' in the Kantian sense – these are questions on which we should like to have him make a definitive pronouncement" (Brunner [1961], 31–32, Brunner's emphasis).

Unfortunately, Niebuhr fails to answer these questions in his writings. Yet this is also what makes a naturalistic reading of his thought so intriguing. Niebuhr's sensitivities to the ambiguities of history would have prevented him from endorsing any conception of a historical realization of the Kingdom of God. For this reason, also, "love" as the norm of the Christian form of life, except on the limited scale of the relation between persons, functions for him mainly as a regulative ideal. It is tied down, in other words, not directly in the context of moral reflection, where the principles of justice reign supreme in his thought, but in the background of a valuational stance as it relates to the moral point of view, exactly as I have suggested and as is implicit in mine and Ogden's existentialist interpretations.

this chapter. We should note again why this is necessary.

The truth of "God exists" hinges on a theistic seeing-as which expresses a comprehensive valuational stance. Truth in this respect is grounded by the determinacy of value. As Post says, "there is a fact of the matter about [values], and we may speak of the particular facts with which a [moral] judgment corresponds. And this quality of there being a fact of the matter is inherited by whatever the [moral] values entail."[45] Thus, a naturalistic valuational theism requires assessing the normative status of the wider valuational stance upon which such a theistic seeing-as rests. I have argued that formally stated, this wider stance is openness to the future understood as an existential mode of being. Comprehending God's grace existentially as transformative events permits this summary formulation to be developed with great richness. But how is the normative status of this valuational stance to be assessed? How, in Post's words, can we assess "the objective correctness of certain values and a way of life" (*FE*, 347)?

In moral value theory there exist substantive moral theories that serve to focus normative questions. These theories identify the relevant moral factors that support our principles, values, and obligations, thus, serving as connective theories tying moral values to the relevant matters of fact. The present position is partially self-referential because a theistic seeing-as will be formed by the values it itself makes possible. This need not be damaging, for in the case of parallel moral theories, as Post notes, without violating the physical determinacy of value, "the facts that just suffice to determine the principles [of a comprehensive moral theory] could easily prove to involve our conception of the person and the social role of morality, rather than some Platonic or other independent moral order known by rational intuition."[46] These moral theories are most controversial, however, precisely where they identify what counts as the morally relevant factors, that is, in specifying what gives just those factors their *moral* force. If that issue can be resolved, then a positive account of the physical determinations, the "purely descriptive facts about the universe (ourselves included)" that determine the correctness of moral judgments, is relatively accessible.[47]

---

[45] *FE*, 344. Post is speaking of specifically moral values, but he concedes that there can be other objectively correct values of a nonmoral sort, so, on the decisive issue, this remark applies to them as well (see *FE*, 347–348).

[46] *FE*, 282. On this issue with respect to values other than moral ones, see *FE*, 266.

[47] *FE*, 282. For a powerful account along exactly these lines that justifies what is moral and why it is fully rational for us to believe so, see, Reiman (1989), 43–63, 141–153, *et passim*.

Controversial as these problems are in moral theory, there at least exists a rich and deeply nuanced history of their discussion that, in the modern period, is also largely naturalistic. In the wider realm of nonmoral values, including the theory of religion, no such history of substantive theory exists. Theories that do exist in religion are narrowly focused along empiricist lines, or they are questionably reductive, all the while assuming that religion is constituted by belief in the "supernatural,"[48] or they beg the question of inventory status.[49] So there is little history of research that can aid us in assessing the normative status of wide valuational stances. This is not merely a problem for the theologian or for the cross-cultural student of religion. Even the nontheist must address normative questions of wider valuational breadth, and the relationship between such wider valuations and strictly moral values is closer than is normally recognized by philosophers.

It would seem that one could address this question, both religiously and nonreligiously, only by defending some broad conception of human being in the world. This is precisely what is involved in the Christian valuational stance, as my arguments about sin and the life of faith have shown. In this respect, the normative status of the Christian valuational stance, naturalistically viewed, is simply on all fours with any competing theory. The problem, however, is that Post articulates the criterion for valuational assessment in seemingly "exclusivistic" terms: in two worlds identical in every respect as regards the world, there can be one and only one distribution of truth values across two sets of conflicting values.[50] This "exclusivism" is appropriate for morality because moral value theory engages normative questions at a generalized level appropriate to obligation or what ought to be the case (i.e., in terms of universalizability). With wider, nonmoral values, however, it is not so clear that we can speak of

---

[48] This assumption is fundamental, for instance, for both Wallace (1966), and Stark and Bainbridge (1987).

[49] This is the problem with Mircia Eliade's contribution to the history of religion. Eliade claims to be doing phenomenology, but he leaves the ontological status of the sacred hopelessly mired in ambiguity. This ambiguity permits him, when he wishes, to treat the "sacred" very much like an ontological category (see Eliade [1959], 162–215). If such an ontology is challenged, the same contexts require that the "sacred" be a valuational category along the lines of a "form of consciousness" or a "sensitivity to a domain of experience" which he believes has been lost in the modern world and should be recovered. But if the latter is his true position, then he cannot so forthrightly reject naturalism, and his relationship to a naturalist outlook emerges all over again and should be dealt with forthrightly. The issue cannot be evaded.

[50] See *FE*, 253–254, 265–266.

"what ought to be the case" in this "exclusivistic" fashion. The problem is that religious valuations (and the traditions and forms of life through which they are expressed) are irretrievably particular and historically contingent in the nonmoral values they articulate.[51] This means among other things, as we have already seen, that because all the terms in such broad views are valuational, their claims to normative status are already constituted by the valuational stances themselves. It is very unlikely therefore that we can approach normative assessment cross-culturally in an exclusivistic fashion.

We must either abandon hope that religious values can have objective purchase or we must find a way to distinguish between valuational levels, between a level at which normative assessment is possible and the historically contingent articulation of this more general level in a particularized form of life. A starting point for such considerations is a suggestion from Robert Neville's *Behind the Masks of God* which is an impressive contribution to cross-cultural philosophy of religion. Neville argues that cross-cultural religious issues require some common frame of reference that first makes it possible even to identify comparisons across significantly different and historically contingent cultural domains. He suggests that such a common frame should be "a speculative ontology and cosmology" articulated in a highly abstract fashion that in its very vagueness (hopefully) prescinds from too much historical contingency.[52] Neville's proposal is non-naturalist and conflicts with the valuational approach to religion advanced here. Nevertheless, his distinction between formal and historically particular levels seems unassailable. I want to suggest that Heidegger's fundamental ontology can provide the same kind of foundation for comparative assessment when religion is conceived valuationally.

Heidegger's fundamental ontology is a phenomenological description of the structures through which Dasein's being is disclosed in its being-in-the-world. It results in a general conception of human existence (of what it means to have distinctively human being) that is the formal framework for every particularized self-understanding actualized by concrete existing. According to my earlier argument, religion expresses a way of existing, and any particular religion may be interpreted as a concrete articulation of Heidegger's formal

---

[51] This historical contingency forms the basis of Ricoeur's extensive argument in favor of the necessarily hermeneutical character of a reflective philosophy. See Ricoeur (1970), 20–56, 419–458.   [52] See Neville (1991a), 13–21, 85–106.

structure. In Heidegger's technical language, a particular religion will be an *existentiell* modification of a general *existential* structure of human possibilities. From the standpoint of existentialist interpretation, Heidegger's fundamental ontology establishes the formal structure needed for comparative analysis and evaluation, in this sense playing the same role for a valuational theology as Neville's "speculative ontology and cosmology." The question of truth would be addressed by normative assessment of *existentiell* modifications of human possibility within the framework of the formal structure of human possibility as such described by Heidegger's fundamental ontology.

Here it is worth recognizing the special correlation between Heidegger's fundamental ontology and Post's physicalist naturalism. It is important to recall what Heidegger means by a fundamental ontology. Though its formality gives it cross-cultural reach parallel to Neville's proposal, it is a phenomenology limited to the being of Dasein. Strictly speaking the phenomenology of Dasein takes place within the *epoche* (phenomenological bracketing).[53] The ontology of *Being and Time* is limited, therefore, to a phenomenology of Dasein's being and cannot, taken simply on its own terms, dictate any conclusions at all about the general character of being. It simply lays out the phenomenological ontology of Dasein that any general account of being must ground. Heidegger's own anti-naturalist bias overlooks the rather obvious interface with a physicalist general ontology suggested by his phenomenology. From Post's physicalist standpoint, we can say that if the phenomenology of Dasein's being is credible, then this phenomenology is *determined* to be *what* and *as* it is by the ultimate physical unifiers. Here the ontological character of this phenomenology becomes crucial. Heidegger argues that consciousness is not ontologically primitive. Phenomenology must become ontological because the being of this entity cannot be captured as an appearance to an intending consciousness. It is not a matter of consciousness at all but is a disclosure in the very being (in the sense of

---

[53] Here I am assuming, against many commentators, (a) that the fundamental ontology of *Being and Time* cannot step in and go proxy for this general ontology and (b) that Heidegger's work after *Being and Time* cannot in any simple manner be regarded as supplying the general ontology missing from *Being and Time*. I would argue that insofar as Heidegger thought that his later work could be regarded as such a general ontology, then, about the character of being in general, he was simply mistaken. It seems to me that the overly anthropomorphized character of being (or of the appearance of being in human being) is warrant enough for this claim. See Post, (1987), 288–292, esp. p. 292.

the very *existing*) of this entity.[54] This is the significance of Heidegger's insistence that Dasein can never catch up with itself: *that which appears here* (what Heidegger calls *Existenz*) is never an appearance to an intending consciousness that can hold this appearance over against itself, but is its very being in the sense of its "to be" (its *Sein*).[55]

If Heidegger's phenomenology is ontological in this sense, then he is claiming that "it is like something" *to be* Dasein, and the fundamental ontology *qua* phenomenology describes, formally, what this is like. This kind of claim is compatible with a certain kind of physicalism, for it is simply about a level of determination that any nonreductionist and noneliminativist physicalism must recognize: that with some entities there exists an ontological threshold such that it becomes like something for them to be. It is significant that Heidegger's phenomenology (*qua* ontology) requires that such a determination occur in the ontology (not twice or even thrice removed in consciousness or otherwise in the epistemology), and this is exactly what would be expected from a physicalist determination relation. There is, therefore, surprisingly, a direct continuity between Heidegger's strategy in *Being and Time* and a non-eliminative physicalism. The determination relation is in the being first and only secondarily in consciousness or epistemology.[56] Heidegger has shown, if you will, what it is that it is like for Dasein to be determined physically. Post's determination relation makes possible, therefore, an existentialist method within a physicalist naturalism.

Let us return, then, to the normative question within Christianity. I have suggested that a comparative framework for normative

54 In his recent commentary on the first part of *Being and Time*, Hubert Dreyfus refers to this as a non-mentalistic form of intentionality and speaks of "'mindless' coping skills as the basis of all intelligibility" (Dreyfus [1991], 3 [cf. 12–16, 45–59]). In a footnote discussing Husserl, Heidegger says: ". . . the intentionality of 'consciousness' is *grounded* in the ecstatical unity of Dasein . . . ." (*SZ*, 363, n. 1 [498, n. xxiii]). (Heidegger also says, however, that this claim [which in Husserl involves saying that the intuition of consciousness is a "making present" (*Erkennen ist Gegenwärtigen*)] will be "shown" only in that part of *Being and Time* which was never completed.)
55 In German there is no distinction between the substantive and the infinitive form of "being" (*das Sein* and *sein*), and it is certainly Heidegger's intention to exploit this ambiguity. It is extremely difficult, however, to duplicate this verbal ambiguity in English. "Being" in the case of Dasein is never a static substance but always a "to be."
56 Adapting Post's response to Nagel, we can say that Dasein is *determined physically* in "the fourfold sense of determining (a) that there are such phenomena, (b) which ones there are, (c) what it would be like to experience them, and (d) what their (other) properties are" (*FE*, 245). There is no room within Heidegger's phenomenology *qua* phenomenology to take exception to this claim.

evaluation can be supplied by the formal character of Heideggers's analytic of human existence. Very generally this structure describes human existence as disclosed in a finite directedness toward an open future which situates its finitude but provides no certainty or ground for "taking a stand" within it. In this sense, Heidegger describes the formal structure of human being as a kind of finite openness without determinate ground, and "authentic existence" is to be "resolute" precisely in terms of this indeterminateness, not, that is, to foreclose this openness by any determination that would undercut its irretrievable openness.[57] Specific religions are concrete, *existentiell*, articulations of this structure. Existentially interpreted as a valuational theism, the Christian *existentiell* articulation affirms that *taking our lives as gifts is the best way to take our lives* in their indeterminate openness. This is the sense of openness to the future by which Bultmann defines faith. Normativity can now be seen to arise at several different levels once we have this structure in place.

In line with the interpretation presented in the last chapter, this "taking" is the existential content of the doctrine of creation (its traditional content being the sovereignty of God and the goodness of being). This existentialist interpretation of the doctrine of creation is normative in two senses. It makes a normative *existentiell* claim about the "best taking," given the formal structure of human existence. Evaluation of this normative claim would require engagement through existentialist interpretation with other *existentiell* "takings" in the history of religions. At a more theologically reflective level, it possesses another kind of normativity because the Christian wants to claim that this *existentiell* "taking" conforms to the formal ontological structure of human existence. "Taking our lives as gifts" is no simple, straightforward taking but comprises a constantly renewed affirmation of giftedness implicit in "taking as a gift." "Giftedness" holds open and does not try to evade, deny, or overcome the indeterminate openness implicit in the formal ontological structure of human existence. This is precisely the existential meaning of "trust in God." For this reason, Bultmann can claim that the Christian *existentiell* articulation of the formal ontological structure conforms to "authentic existence."[58]

---

[57] See Scott (1990), 94–124.
[58] See ZPE, 187–189 (ET, 101–104). The force of Bultmann's criticism of Heidegger concentrates not on the latter's analysis of existence as such but on the role resoluteness plays in his understanding of authentic existence, that is, on the role of "sin" in human existence

The essence of the Christian affirmation is contained in the doctrine of creation and is relatively simple and straightforward. In contrast, grace affirms that "taking as a gift" is not simple, not a simple human possibility, but is dialectically complex and dense. As we saw in the last chapter, grace restores the content of creation (thereby giving the doctrine of redemption priority over the doctrine of creation). Given the normative claim about "taking as a gift," the doctrine of grace is an interpretive recognition of the donative quality of this very taking. This density about giftedness requires a full interpretation of human being in the world. This depth of the superficially straightforward taking of our lives as gifts requires the doctrine of grace to articulate a full account of the human conditions that explains why such taking is problematic. Because of this problematic character, there is a receptive dimension (not simply an active "taking") at the existential depths of the doctrine of creation. Grace shows how the "taking" in "taking our lives as gifts" itself involves a donative element. Because it involves this full interpretive account of human being, including an account of human sinfulness, it is the doctrine of grace, not the doctrine of creation, that generates the full valuational matrix that we term the Christian faith. Nevertheless, it is important to recognize that the valuational essence is contained in the doctrine of creation. Given the latter's valuational character, the further development of the Christian perspective in the doctrine of grace is a largely empirical, not valuational, matter.[59]

I have attempted to articulate the center of the Christian self-understanding explicitly in valuational terms. The formal ontology of human existence does not dictate any ontologically grounded way of being. Rather, it articulates the ontological structure that conditions every such way, and it shows why every such way is a "taking." The Christian faith is a genuine "taking," not something that is grounded in or otherwise legitimated by a general account of being independently of this taking. Nevertheless, this taking does not construct giftedness,

(see NTM, 37–39 [ET, 28–30] and HMF, 104–110). See Scott (1990), 94–124 for an unusually sensitive discussion of the problem of "authentic existence" in Heidegger. He sees as few commentators have that Heidegger must conceive "authentic existence" as an *existentiell* articulation of the formal existential structure (since the latter can be articulated in no other way), and yet, that to be authentic, this articulation must hold itself open to the indeterminate openness of the formal structure. All the problems of historical contingency and cross-cultural normative evaluation are contained in this delicate balance of an *existentiell* articulation that holds itself open to its own formal structure.

[59] Neville straightforwardly recognizes the largely empirical character of the Christian doctrine of sin. See Neville (1991b), 87.

and the taking is not subjectively arbitrary. The valuational claim Christianity makes is normative. It claims that the most appropriate taking, given our finitely thrown openness, is one that views life as a gift (which involves receiving the future as a gift[60]). This claim involves a further normative claim about why "taking as a gift" is founded on events of grace.

The truth question involves assessing these normative claims in cross-cultural perspective.[61] Actually making this assessment involves a much larger project than I can undertake here. My concern is to show how a valuational conception of religion must address normative issues. Parallel to Neville's cross-cultural proposal, I am claiming that the comparative basis for such assessment is provided by Heidegger's formal account of human existence. The religious truth question requires, in effect, an existentialist and therefore valuational interpretation of the *existentiell* modification of this structure in every religion. This approach requires normative engagement at two levels. The broadest level will assess these modifications for the adequacy with which they conform to Heidegger's structural finite "openness" (i.e., to authentic existence). At a more historically contingent and culturally particular level, they can be compared and assessed for the adequacy with which they construe the human condition. At this level, it is likely that different *existentiell* articulations can mutually correct and illumine one another.[62]

---

[60] This is the existential content of the doctrine of providence.

[61] In his recent *The Ethics of Authenticity*, Charles Taylor attempts to show how there can be normative assessment and rational adjudication among valuational stances that are themselves rooted in radical affirmations of human freedom. See Taylor (1991) 31–53, *et passim*.

[62] Neville's comparative program distinguishes among (a) a speculative ontology (a comprehensive level), (b) a primary cosmology (a "dimensional" level), and (c) a culturally and theologically specific level (a thematic level). The purpose of these distinctions is to establish different levels at which comparative engagement and clarification (and, in some instances, mutual enrichment) can occur. Neville convincingly argues that cross-cultural normative assessment among the religions becomes hopelessly muddled unless different levels of comparative engagement are clearly established. The fruitfulness of the first two levels requires defining them by abstracting as much as possible from historically contingent and culturally particular categories. (The third, thematic, dimension is the level of specific theological assertion.) One advantage of Neville's methodology is that what at first appears to be irreconcilable religious difference across cultures can be eliminated, reconciled, or softened when the apparent oppositions are first located by and then compared in terms of these differences in level. (See Neville [1991a], 9–50, 73–84, 98–106.) In the alternative program I have proposed, Neville's first level (the speculative ontology) is replaced by Heidegger's fundamental ontology, and what I have termed "different *existentiell* articulations" is his third, "thematic" dimension. A full development of this program would require something like Neville's second, dimensional level because the thematic is too culturally particular to admit of cross-cultural comparison apart from more abstract organizing categories. Indeed, Neville's own primary cosmology might serve this purpose well (if it is articulated independently of the metaphysical assumptions with which he develops it).

Once we have separated levels of comparison, it becomes possible to reexamine Post's "exclusivistic" formulation of the criterion for valuational assessment. Today it is very unlikely that cross-cultural comparison can result in "exclusivistic" judgments about religious options. This is all the more true given the role that "historicity" plays in the formal existential structure of human existence.[63] But from the fact that no one religion can claim exclusive normative truth for its forms of life, it does not follow that no normative assessment can be undertaken. Thus, we have already seen that the formal existential structure of human existence which serves as the general framework for cross-cultural comparison itself implies a criterion of adequacy: an adequate *existentiell* articulation must conform to the indeterminate openness of *Dasein*'s ontological structure (conforming roughly, that is, to Heidegger's notion of authentic existence).[64] On the other hand, at a more concrete level (the level of *existentiell* articulation) there is remarkable consensus among various religions that religious self-transformation involves freedom from self in the form of narrow egoism. There is much unity in the judgment that such freedom is

---

[63] See *SZ*, 372–403 (424–455).

[64] See *SZ*, 42–44, 53 (67–70, 78–79). Heidegger claims that authentic existence is not a material ideal of existing. It applies, rather, to a formal structure which is meaningless apart from its *existentiell* (therefore historical and contingent) embodiment. The issue is whether such embodiments are faithful to their underlying structure or, instead, attempt to deny or evade it. When he introduces the distinction between authentic and inauthentic existence, Heidegger insists that the terms are to be taken in a terminologically strict sense (*SZ*, 43 [68]). The distinction is derivative from the formal characteristic that existence is always my own (*jemeinig, Jemeinigkeit*): " . . . in each case Dasein is mine to be in one way or another. Dasein has always made some sort of decision as to the way in which it is in each case mine. That entity which in its Being has this very Being as an issue, comports itself towards its Being as its ownmost possibility. . . [B]ecause Dasein is in each case essentially its own possibility, it *can*, in its very Being, 'choose' itself and win itself; it can also lose itself and never win itself; or only 'seem' to do so. But only in so far as it is essentially something which can be *authentic* – that is, something of its own – can it have lost itself and not yet won itself. As modes of Being, *authenticity* and *inauthenticity* . . . are both grounded in the fact that any Dasein whatsoever is characterized by mineness" (*SZ*, 42–43, Heidegger's emphases; [68]). The terminological strictness follows directly from a formal feature of existence that is tightly captured in the German (*Jemeinigkeit* and *Eigentlichkeit*) but is lost in the English translation. The normative question at this level concerns not a material ideal, which must always be an *existentiell* articulation, but conformity of *any* such ideals with the underlying structure of human existence. Ogden attempts to address the difficult issue of how Heidegger can employ such apparently normative terms as "authenticity" and "inauthenticity" without implying a material ideal by distinguishing between the "what" and the "how" of action and then arguing that the "'how' in which all action ought to take place" is nonetheless normative (*CM*, 70). Generally speaking, Ogden's position here conforms to the position I have taken. It also seems to be implicit in Scott's much more nuanced discussion of these difficult issues (see Scott (1990), 94–124). Bultmann himself accepts a similar distinction between "what" and "how" (*HMF*, 104) and then applies it along lines parallel to the one I am suggesting (see *HMF*, 105–107).

made problematic by the human condition, especially in the form of attachments that close off the kind of formal openness that Heidegger terms "authentic existence." If I am correct about these intuitions, then there is much room for normative assessment in religion today that does not have to assume exclusivity. What is important is to see that such normative assessment is at least as open to a valuational theism as to those that require a transcendent metaphysical ground.

PART III

Further elements of a naturalist Christian theology

CHAPTER 6

The point of christology

The foundations for a naturalist Christian theology are now complete. Though I have not covered the full range of theological topics, the outlines for such a task are clear. I defer the larger task, however, for more substantive reasons than limitations of space. A naturalist systematic theology is indeed possible. It would simply require an existentialist interpretation of the traditional dogmatic loci. Fritz Buri's *Dogmatik als Selbstverständnis des christlichen Glaubens* is already a superb existentialist theology, and its approach could easily be framed naturalistically. But an existentialist method requires that we ask whether the traditional doctrinal format is any longer pertinent. Existentialist interpretation expects the point of every theological assertion to be strictly existential. Once we see how frequently the existential point of doctrines has been missed, then both the range and the organization of traditional theology become a fresh theological topic. Thus, though traditional doctrine can be interpreted along naturalist lines, one must question whether this organization is any longer requisite. The question of theological organization is not new in modern theology, but it is raised with new force by the point of view I have defended here.[1] In any case, because this entire issue must be rethought today – and not merely from the present perspective – I have no hesitancy in leaving it for another day.

Accordingly, in these last two chapters, I shall cover only a selected range of topics that seem especially relevant to the theological task today. In this chapter I shall deal with christology and in the next

[1] The classic example of theological reorganization is Schleiermacher's relegation of the doctrine of the Trinity to an appendix in his *Glaubenslehre* (since it was not a direct inference from the Christian "God-consciousness") (see Schleiermacher [1986], 738–742). Buri has confronted similar reorganizational issues with unusual self-consciousness and equally radical results. Among other things, he powerfully argues in favor of reorganizing the traditional doctrines of human nature and grace and for placing the doctrine of God at the end of the theological system (see Buri [1962], 19–27, 38–41 and Buri [1978], 19–38).

with broadly eschatological issues. Whatever one says about theological organization, every Christian theology must deal with the meaning of the essential Christian confession that salvation has been wrought by God through Jesus Christ. Yet, no part of the Christian confession of faith would seem more problematic for a naturalistic theology, for in its traditional claims about the person and work of Christ, particularly with its doctrine of the incarnation, the Christian faith seems especially alien to a naturalist perspective. For a number of reasons, this impression is mistaken.

In the first place, the tradition, even in its classic form, has actually been quite indefinite in giving final dogmatic form to its confession of Christ. John Hick states this indeterminacy well in his remarks about the orthodox doctrine of the God-man:

What we receive from our tradition is a broad imaginative motif together with a history of attempts to spell it out. . . But when we turn from the general motif and its creative elaboration in art, to theological science, we quickly observe that there is nothing that can be called *the* Christian doctrine of the incarnation. Indeed, the long history of the christological debates is the story of the church's failure to achieve a clear and agreed spelling out of the broad imaginative conception that God was incarnate in Jesus the Jewish Messiah . . . [W]e have the officially adopted metaphysical hypothesis of the two natures, but no accepted account of what it means for an individual to have two natures, one human and the other divine. . . [T]he centuries-long attempt of Christian orthodoxy to turn the metaphor into metaphysics was a cul-de-sac.[2]

Second, since the nineteenth century, questions of christology have been decisively reshaped by the historical-critical study of the New Testament witness. Perhaps the decisive consequence of this work has been to highlight the implicit Docetism of all classical christologies and to bring the humanity of Jesus into christological reflection more forcefully than at any other time in theological history. Less specifically, historical-critical study has simply demanded a full scale reexamination of the entire christological endeavor.

Finally, most important, and largely as a consequence of this historical-critical work, it is now evident that no other topic than christology more powerfully requires us to ask for the point of theological affirmations. Schubert Ogden's *The Point of Christology* addresses this issue with unusual force. This work is certainly the most important contribution to christological reflection in recent decades

[2] Hick (1979), 47–49.

and is one from which I gratefully borrow the title to this chapter.[3] By going behind both traditional and modern revisionary christological preoccupations to ask about the point of christological assertions, Ogden has clarified the issues in a fashion that requires a thorough revamping of the entire christological discussion for any theology of the foreseeable future. I shall follow Ogden closely in the discussion that follows. Though my naturalism leads us to differ about the implications of an existentialist method in theology, there is scarcely any disagreement concerning the point of christology. Once we see how Ogden has clarified the whole question, we shall see that a powerful christology, in agreement with the underlying traditional issues, is also possible within the bounds of a naturalist theology.

THE QUESTION CHRISTOLOGY ANSWERS

Before examining Ogden's argument, it will be helpful first to look at an earlier, somewhat similar way of opening the christological discussion. I have in mind Reinhold Niebuhr's discussion of Christ as Messiah in *The Nature and Destiny of Man*. Niebuhr begins the second volume of his great work by asking for the conditions under which a Messiah is expected.[4] Earlier he makes an important argument that "atonement," not "incarnation," should define christological reflection.[5] Focus on the incarnation has fatefully skewed Christian thought into thinking that religious questions essentially concern the relation of time and eternity, actually the overcoming of time by eternity, and this has contributed to the otherworldliness of much of the Christian tradition. Niebuhr argues, in contrast, that the prophetic center of Christianity is the problem of sin; the real locus of christology must, therefore, lie in the doctrine of atonement, not incarnation. In the later discussion, he makes good on this claim by tracing the historical development of messianic expectations in Hebrew thought.

Such expectations were generated out of the interplay of God's election of the people of Israel, his promises rooted in his righteousness, and the disastrous political history of Israel in the first millennium before the common era. Originally expressed as a nationalistic-political redeemer, more or less on the model of the kingship of David, increasingly transcendent, supernatural, and apocalyptic conceptions of the Messiah figure developed from the disappointment of the

---

[3] See also, Ogden (1975).   [4] See Reinhold Niebuhr (1941), II, 6–7, 15–34.
[5] Niebuhr (1941), I, 136–149.

nationalistic expectations. Throughout this entire development, however, the notion of a messianic redeemer was closely tied to conceptions of faithfulness and obedience on the part of the Hebrew people, even if only on the part of a purified remnant. Under the pressure of increasingly universalistic prophetic ideas and the still outstanding fulfillment of God's promises, the meaning of human righteousness before God was deepened until it led to the terrifying question: what if there are none at all who are righteous?

According to Niebuhr, this question burst the bounds of traditional messianic thought, even as it grew out of its most penetrating development. If there are none who are righteous, then there appears to be no solution to the problem of the relation between goodness and power in history. As Niebuhr says, "the problem of the meaning of history according to prophetism is how history can be anything more than judgment, which is to say, whether the promise of history can be fulfilled at all."[6] This unresolved problem of the relation between God's wrath and mercy accounts for why the early Christian attribution of messiahship to Jesus was a transformation of the very conception of messiahship. The problem was no longer, even remotely, a messianic overthrow of the powers of evil by the power of righteousness, but the questionable character of human righteousness itself. This problem could only be addressed by a heretofore un-messianic power in weakness capable of overcoming the bottomless lack of righteousness on the part of all humanity. From this conception of the transformation of messiahship, Niebuhr then develops his analysis of salvation as justification by faith, which effectively becomes his christology.[7]

The context of Niebuhr's position was twentieth century dialectical theology. Initiated by Barth's *Commentary on the Letter to the Romans*, dialectical theology contained many diverse strands. But as Van Harvey has observed, all the dialectical theologians "understood themselves to be engaged in a thorough exploration of the significance of the principle of justification by faith for all aspects of man's life" (*HB*, 132). They shared Barth's insight that faith "may not be identified with belief, religious feeling, morality, religion, or any other aspect of man's experience" (*HB*, 132). Faith is to be understood in terms of the crisis in all human attempts at self-salvation, and grace, according to the early Barth, is not a bridging of the "infinite

[6] Niebuhr (1941), II, 27.   [7] See Niebuhr, (1941), II, 35–67, 98–126.

qualitative distinction between time and eternity" but an exposure that it exists (*HB*, 132). In this sense, faith arises "in the awareness of the total ambiguity of the human situation," and revelation is a crisis exposing all human aspirations (*HB*, 132–133).

This profound ambiguity of all human righteousness led the dialectical theologians to recover a radical notion of justification by faith because it meant that God's grace confronts humanity as pure gift precisely at the deepest and most ambiguous points of human pretension (where, just because it confronts humanity there, it also confronts as judgment). Despite the surface appearance of unrelieved negativity, the dialectical theologians were really saying, according to Harvey, that "the way to a genuine and nonidolatrous *affirmation of human life* is through the way of negation, through the crucifixion of the self" (*HB*, 133, my emphasis). This notion of justification was radical in yet another way because the early Barth expressed it non-exclusivistically: "The decisive and once-for-all nature of Christ consists in the fact that 'in Jesus we have discovered and recognized the truth that God is found everywhere and that both before and after Jesus, men have been discovered by Him'."[8]

The present work has been conceived in continuity with these notions of faith, revelation, and justification. I have sought to show that an equally radical conception of justification by faith can be captured on entirely naturalistic grounds. Especially noteworthy is how dialectical theology approaches the point of christology through the radical questionableness of the human situation. In a parallel fashion, I have shown the possibility of a naturalist theology by making naturalistically plausible an existentialist interpretation of human bondage to sin. This foundation then makes possible a radical conception of justification by faith. Interpreting the love of God in terms of the giftedness of life, God's grace becomes the transformative moment, received itself as a gift, whereby this giftedness is appropriated as openness to the future. Ogden is also indebted to Niebuhr and the dialectical theologians. By insisting that clarity about the point of christology must precede christology proper, he goes even further in supporting my argument that religious concerns are strictly and alone existential concerns.

The modern period has seen numerous revisionary christologies, many of them generated by the implications of modern historical-critical

---

[8] *HB*, 133 (quoted from Barth [1933], 97).

scholarship. Ogden's is also a revisionary christology, but he finds the "revisionary consensus" about the point of christology deeply problematic (*PC*, 14, 18, 20). There are three elements in this revisionary consensus. It should be observed that revisionary christologies are remarkably similar to classical ones concerning the basic christological question, however different their actual answers are. (1) In conformity to the tradition, it is agreed that the basic christological question is "'Who is Jesus?' understood as asking about the being of Jesus in himself, as distinct from asking about the meaning of Jesus for us" (*PC*, 15–16). The prior question about the point of christology is scarcely asked at all, the assumption simply being that christology must deal with the person of Jesus who is the Christ. The tradition identified Jesus as the God-man, the classical doctrine of the incarnation; modern efforts, in contrast, typically speak of some distinctive feature of Jesus's humanity, such as his perfect relation to God. But it is still assumed that christological assertions concern the person of Jesus (*PC*, 16). (2) The second element in the consensus concerns the *subject* of christological assertions, how this Jesus is identified. It is assumed that this subject is "none other than the so-called historical Jesus, in the sense of the actual Jesus of history insofar as he can be known to us today by way of empirical-historical inquiry using the writings of the New Testament as sources" (*PC*, 16–17). Revisionary theologies have therefore generally defended both the historical possibility and the theological necessity of a quest for this historical figure, even granting the enormous differences between a late twentieth century and the nineteenth century understanding of the historical sources upon which such a quest may be based. (3) Finally, there is consensus about the conditions that must be met to assert a christological predicate of this subject, to say that Jesus is "the Christ." These conditions, of course, presume success with the historical quest since it must uncover *what* in the historical person deserves christological predication. Here the consensus agrees that Jesus is the Christ only if *in his personal life* he perfectly realized whatever is taken to be the perfect presence of God in human life (*PC*, 17). This is the modern version of the traditional sinlessness of Jesus, but traditionally it had been implicit in the incarnation, whereas here, as Ogden puts it, "the claim for Jesus's human perfection stands alone. One might even say, in fact, that it is so far from being the effect of the incarnation as to be its cause" (*PC*, 18).

Ogden develops a powerful critique of all these elements in the revisionary consensus. His argument is profoundly important because he shows how much confusion has existed about what the topic of christology ought to be about. An adequate revisionary christology demands that we first clarify the point of christology before setting about to make it. Ogden's analysis of these issues is so fundamental for any future christological endeavor that I shall simply present it in schematic fashion, reserving a discussion of my departures from it for the next section of this chapter.

The constitutive christological assertion

The decisive unreflected issue in the christological tradition, both classical and revisionary, concerns what Ogden terms "the constitutive christological assertion." By this he means "the assertion about Jesus, however formulated, that constitutes christology as such" in distinction from "any particular christological formulation that makes or implies it" (*PC*, 21–22).[9] The "constitutive christological assertion," concerns the underlying question to which christology gives its answer. The christological tradition has assumed that this question is "Who is Jesus?" directed at the being of Jesus in himself. Ogden considers a number of New Testament christological formulations which, on the surface, seem to support this inference (*PC*, 23–28). Classic here is Peter's response in Matthew 16 to Jesus's, "But who do you say that I am?," to which Peter confesses, "You are the Christ, the Son of the living God" (Matt. 16:15–16), or John 1:18: "No one has ever seen God; the only Son, who is in the bosom of the Father, he has made him known," both of which, of course, seem to make claims about the being of Jesus.

Ogden convincingly argues that the real situation is considerably more complex than this initial appearance would suggest. Peter's response, for instance, is a confession and "therefore *implies* the christological assertion rather than actually makes it" (*PC*, 24). It also implies that this prior issue has to do in some sense with Peter who says it and is not solely about the subject about whom it is made. Or differently, with John's statement, if Jesus reveals God, the question presupposed is not merely "Who is Jesus?" but "Who is God?," for

---

[9] Note that Ogden's very formulation here shows that he is undertaking a revisionary christological program. Though such a program is untraditional, its warrant is to be found in Luther's principle of the "canon within the canon," and the latter, it may be argued, is itself rooted in the prophetic background of the New Testament kerygma.

the question about Jesus presupposes this prior question (*PC*, 25). Similarly, John's "I am" sayings such as "I am the bread of life" (John 6:35) can equally well be translated, "The bread of life – it is I," and this implies not one question, "Who is Jesus?," but a prior question, "What is the bread of life?" (*PC*, 16).

In each case, and indeed throughout the New Testament, the question is not merely "who is Jesus?" but also (a) "who am I?" (or better, "what is my authentic existence?") and (b) "who is God?" The latter questions, furthermore, are logically prior to the question about Jesus, and the three questions together have a complex structure (*PC*, 28). In effect, the question about Jesus is about Jesus's meaning or significance for us. The other two questions are logically prior to it (a) because one would have no concern about Jesus unless one were concerned about the ultimate meaning of one's own existence (and unless that meaning was problematic in some sense) and (b) because an answer to this question concerns that ultimate reality upon which the meaning of our existence depends. Indeed, these are not separate questions but two aspects of one question which Ogden formulates as either "the existential question" or "the question of faith." It is an "existential question" because it asks about the ultimate meaning of our existence as persons. And it is "the question of faith" because it already assumes a basic confidence in the value of our lives, presupposed in all our activities as persons, and thus asks about the justification of this confidence. Implicitly, therefore, it asks about what ultimate reality must be like so as "to authorize some understanding of ourselves as authentic, just as, conversely, there is some understanding of our existence that is authentic because it is the self-understanding authorized by ultimate reality."[10]

"The existential question" and "the question of faith" may also be understood as "the religious question" if, with Ogden, we understand religion as that aspect of culture which explicitly addresses these questions (assumed in all cultural activities). Carrying this analysis into the religious realm discloses the complexity of the relationship between the question of God and the question about our own authentic existence. Relying on Clifford Geertz's analysis of "ethos" and "world view,"[11] Ogden shows that religion always involves both a moral ("ethos") and a metaphysical ("world view") dimension in

[10] *PC*, 30. For Ogden's argument that "the question of faith" presupposes a basic confidence that our lives are worthwhile, see *RG*, 21–43, 120–143.
[11] See Geertz (1973a) and Geertz (1973b).

close relationship, for what religion seeks to affirm is the normativity of a certain way of life as grounded in the ultimate character of reality itself. In religion, these dimensions do not function separately from one another. Unlike metaphysics *per se*, the metaphysical dimension does not ask about the nature of ultimate reality itself, but about its meaning for us, and the moral dimension does not ask specifically about our relations with others *per se* but about the authentic understanding of our existence as such in relation to ultimate reality; it is this latter relation that then authorizes a certain form of life in relation to others (see *PC*, 33–35). Ogden, consequently, prefers to see them as two aspects of the single existential question: ". . . there is an overlap between the two questions that speaking of them simply as two fails adequately to take into account. In asking about the meaning of ultimate reality for us, one asks about ultimate reality only insofar as it authorizes authentic self-understanding, even as one asks about authentic self-understanding only insofar as it is authorized by ultimate reality" (*PC*, 35).

In the biblical christological contexts, the question of ultimate reality is the question "who is God?" In the properly religious (not metaphysical) sense, this is the question of the meaning of God *for us*. Yet, it can also occur that the meaning of God for us can itself be in question, as it is biblically where christological concerns emerge. The evidence for this is the different answers in theistic religions to the formally identical religious question of God. Thus, "the same term that functions in one respect to *answer* the existential question can function in another respect only to *ask* it, the meaning of God for us having become the very thing that is in question" (*PC*, 37, Ogden's emphasis). It is therefore also common for theistic religions to "develop other concepts and symbols, the whole point of which is to answer their question about who God is by explicitly identifying someone or something that decisively re-presents God" (*PC*, 37). This is the decisive function of the christological symbols in the New Testament. Of course, an enormous range of such symbols have been used to re-present God in the metaphysical sense. But this just illustrates the difference between the metaphysical and religious senses of the question of God. Despite these differences, in a particular religious context such designations can re-present the same authorizing source of authentic existence when they are seen to respond to the religious not the metaphysical dimension of the question. Actually, even these re-presentations can become questionable and just as with

God can be used to ask who and what they represent as much as to answer it. The significance of the christological assertions, then, is to clarify both of these kinds of questionability: (a) to identify the meaning of the various christological predicates precisely by reference to Jesus, (b) but in so doing also to answer the question of God, the question lying behind their use (see *PC*, 37–38).

Ogden concludes that the constitutive christological assertion intends to answer an *existential-historical question*. This implies that both traditional and revisionary christologies have failed to identify the point of christology. They take the christological assertion to be about the being of Jesus there and then. We now see that it concerns more than a reference solely to Jesus. It concerns the significance of Jesus for us *here and now in the present*, an issue that cannot possibly be identified in the traditional and revisionary formulations. Questions about Jesus as he was *there and then* may be designated *empirical-historical*, and these are sharply different from the existential-historical one.

This is an enormous clarification of the fundamental christological issue, but it must be carefully formulated. Unlike the traditional and revisionary approaches, the issue is not empirical-historical. But it is also not simply the existential question abstracted from all historical experience. The existential-historical question does respond to the existential question but by reference to the specific historical experience of Jesus. As such it answers to two questions: "Who is God?"; but then also, "what is the content of the re-presentations of God?" (as, for instance, "who or what *is* the 'light of the world' or 'the bread of life'"), when these re-presentations are themselves in question. The christological assertions respond to this questionability by reference to Jesus. Thus, though the constitutive christological assertion is not only about Jesus, it *is* about Jesus. About Jesus, however, it is not an empirical-historical assertion but an existential-historical one (see *PC*, 39–40).

The constitutive christological assertion answers an existential-historical question, not one about the being of Jesus, and not even one about Jesus alone at all. The question rather is about (a) the decisive re-presentation (b) of God, understood (c) as "a very specific way of asking the existential question about the meaning of ultimate reality for us" (*PC*, 39). Though the christological question has a historical dimension, the existential dimension is basic, and "it is precisely what the christological assertion asserts . . . about ultimate reality and ourselves that is fundamental to what it asserts about Jesus" (*PC*, 42). It follows that candidates for the subject and the predicate of this assertion must themselves answer an existential-historical question. This is fundamentally to transform the point of christology.

The subject of the christological assertion

The subject of the christological assertion now becomes crucial because "if the answer to my existential question about what I myself am authorized to be by ultimate reality is the answer decisively re-presented through Jesus ... then obviously everything depends on determining just who Jesus is" (*PC*, 42). Initially this issue concerns *how* Jesus is to be identified. It is just here that the revisionary consensus is vulnerable, for it takes this subject to be the historical Jesus *as available to empirical-historical enquiry*. Throughout the modern period (and very commonly today) revisionary efforts typically assert both the theological necessity and the historical possibility of such historical reconstruction. The problem is that both of these are extremely problematic.

The problems surrounding a recovery of the historical Jesus are now well recognized.[12] As form criticism showed, the original materials do not permit us to reconstruct a life of Jesus. Reflecting religious, not historical interests, the early forms of the tradition are forms of kerygma, forms "of bearing witness to Jesus as of decisive significance for the present, rather than reporting historically what he had said and done in the past" (*PC*, 47). This conclusion, which has informed all twentieth century New Testament scholarship, itself became the basis of "the new quest for the historical Jesus" in the fifties. The new quest sought to make inferences behind the kerygmatic sources themselves to a more original historical witness. The new quest succeeded in establishing a continuity between the "Christ-kerygma" and an earlier tradition of witness to the life and teachings of Jesus (what Willi Marxsen terms a "Jesus-kerygma"[13]). The advocates of a new quest have generally assumed that this continuity licenses inferences about Jesus himself. The problem with this claim concerns what Marxsen, following earlier doubts by Bultmann, calls "the form-critical reservation" to the effect that the documents themselves never permit anything more than inferences about an

---

[12] Apart from Ogden's analysis here (*PC*, 44–55), see Harvey and Ogden (1962), and *HB*, 164–200, 265–281.   [13] See Marxsen (1969).

early testimony to Jesus, not inferences about Jesus himself.[14] The sources simply do not permit reaching the empirical-historical Jesus *in any sense*.

Both quests for the historical Jesus assumed that a quest was historically possible because it was theologically necessary. Extremely dangerous in itself, this assumption has now proved impossible on historical grounds. Ogden convincingly shows, however, that there is no theological necessity for such a quest in any case, quite independently of the historical possibility. The reason follows from the constitutive christological assertion, for its subject is not the empirical-historical Jesus at all but the existential-historical Jesus to which the earliest tradition bears witness.

Ogden clarifies this point with H. Richard Niebuhr's comparison of Lincoln's appeal in the Gettysburg Address to the bringing forth of "a new nation, conceived in liberty, and dedicated to the proposition that all men are created equal" to the description of the same event in the *Cambridge Modern History*.[15] Lincoln is clearly referring to a past event prior to and independent of his own patriotism, yet he means it in Ogden's existential-historical sense, as is made evident by its difference from the *Cambridge Modern History*. His appeal is to the "authorizing source" of his and all other

---

[14] See *PC*, 51. Though Ogden's intention in endorsing this "reservation" is clear, even he does not express its cutting edge sharply enough. Speaking of the "Jesus-kerygma" as the earliest witness the sources permit, he says that "strictly speaking, all we can ever hope to talk about is not what Jesus said and did, but what Jesus was *heard* to have said and *seen* to have done by those on whose experience and memory of him we are utterly dependent." Quoting Marxsen, he says that "what is historical in the earliest Jesus-tradition is 'not an isolated Jesus, whom one could assert to be the ground of faith independently of one's own faith,' but rather 'the testimonies to Jesus as the ground of faith by the earliest witnesses'" (*PC*, 53–54, Ogden's emphasis; see also *PC*, 67; but for contrasting formulations where the ambiguity is not so evident, see *PC*, 54–55., 111). Marxsen's is surely the more trenchant formulation, for ultimately form criticism leaves us simply with an early tradition of witness. We have no control permitting to determine that what *it* reports is in fact something that Jesus was heard to say or seen to do. Strictly speaking, Ogden must formulate the gap between Jesus and the earliest testimony to Jesus even more sharply: "all we can ever hope to talk about is not what Jesus said and did, but what Jesus is *represented* as having said or done." We have no way of knowing whether this reports what he was *heard* to have said or *seen* to have done. We have no control, among all such reports that purport to report what he was heard and seen to do, for separating those that do truly report what he was actually heard and seen to do (on the part of some witness of faith, that is, some spokesperson of the Jesus-kerygma) from those which *may* report what he was heard and seen to do when he was not in fact heard and seen to do any such thing, the report itself being constituted by the interest of the witness in formulating the significance of Jesus for us. This is not at all to say that the latter instances are unfaithful to the content of what Jesus was truly heard and seen to do. It is just that we have no way to control even the interpretative discrimination that Ogden's remark implies.

[15] *PC*, 56–57. The reference is to H. Richard Niebuhr (1941), 6off.

American patriotism. Analogously, the original New Testament witness does indeed appeal to an event prior to and independent of its own witness, but the meaning of this event is existential-historical, re-presenting it as

at once the decisive revelation of God and the primal authorizing source of all that is appropriately Christian. Thus the referent of the name "Jesus" in any such formulation as "Jesus is the Christ" is not someone whom we first come to know more or less probably only by empirical-historical inquiry back behind the witness of the apostles as well as the witnesses of the New Testament. Rather, "Jesus" refers to the one whom *we already know most certainly* through the same apostolic witness as well as all other witnesses of faith insofar as they are conformed to the witness of the apostles. (*PC*, 57, my emphasis)

Yet the original witness that we can recover does clearly intend to speak of the Jesus to whom it bears witness by what appear to be empirical-historical claims about him; "they not only seem to assume that Jesus proclaimed or taught certain things or acted in certain ways, but also that he had a certain understanding of himself and his ministry that led him to confront his hearers with an extraordinary claim" (*PC*, 58). The issue here, however, is to distinguish between what in this witness really is intended in a strictly empirical-historical sense and what is a way of bearing witness to Jesus's significance. Ogden distinguishes between what the witnesses *assume* about Jesus and what they *assert* about him (i.e., as the subject of the constitutive christological assertion) (*PC*, 58–59). The earliest witnesses made many such assumptions, as for instance that Jesus claimed an extraordinary significance for himself and his words; they do therefore intend to speak of the empirical-historical Jesus. But such assumptions were not what the witness *asserted* of him in the sense of the constitutive christological assertion. Though they even used such assumptions in *asserting* what they did about Jesus, those *assertions* themselves were not empirical-historical claims about what Jesus had said or done but assertions

about what *God* had said and done and was still saying and doing precisely through Jesus, and thence through their witness of faith. In other words, whatever their assumptions about the being of Jesus in himself as a figure of the past, their assertions all had to do with the meaning of Jesus for us as he still confronts us in the present. They were all assertions about Jesus as the decisive re-presentation of God, and, therefore, as the one through whom the meaning of ultimate reality and the authentic understanding of our own existence are made fully explicit. (*PC*, 59, Ogden's emphasis)

The significance of this argument is, of course, that the subject of the constitutive christological assertion is the existential-historical Jesus and, therefore, that "what can or cannot be inferred concerning the empirical-historical Jesus *has no bearing whatever on the point of christology*" (*PC*, 60, my emphasis). This conclusion is particularly important in light of the new quest. The defenders of the new quest agree that the sources permit no conclusions about Jesus's christological claims concerning himself. They have nevertheless sought to ground christology by the empirical-historical argument that there is an implicit christology in the claims Jesus is said to have made about the significance of himself and his work. But this still hinges the subject of the christological assertion on an empirical-historical question, quite apart from the dubious historical evidence that is taken to support it. Ogden's analysis is liberating concerning this whole nest of issues because, as he says, "the subject of the christological assertion is Jesus in his meaning for us, not Jesus in his being in himself." Thus, "*whether he did or did not imply a claim for the decisive significance of his own person has no bearing whatever on the appropriateness of this assertion.* Whether he implied any such claim or not, the fact remains that what those to whom we owe even the earliest Christian witness mean in so speaking of him is the one through whom they themselves have been confronted with such a claim and who still continues to make it through their own witness of faith."[16]

The predicate of the christological assertion

The revisionary consensus also meets profound problems with the conditions for asserting the christological predicate, for it has always assumed that Jesus is truly the Christ *only* if he himself realized faith in

[16] *PC*, 60–61, my emphasis. There are still important empirical-historical issues at least indirectly related to the point of christology. In the first place, all of the things *assumed* by the earliest witness of faith about Jesus fall under the control of empirical-historical inquiry, even so far as the assumption that there was an individual person whose proper name was "Jesus." Second, the content of the earliest Christian witness can only be established by empirical-historical inquiry. Ogden takes this issue to be especially important because he argues that to be theologically *appropriate* a christological formulation must conform to this earliest witness. Yet, not all the various formulations of the constitutive christological assertion in the New Testament are consistent with one another. If they are to be tested, this can only be by comparing them to the normative witness of faith each of them claims to formulate. This amounts, however, not to a quest of the historical Jesus but a quest for the earliest Christian witness that is normative for christology because it is the earliest witness in which the decisive significance of Jesus is first expressed (see *PC*, 61–62).

perfect form, however differently such perfection has been conceived by various revisionary efforts since Schleiermacher.[17] This position is open to serious objections, both historically and theologically.

The obvious historical objection is one with which we are already familiar. Our sources permit us only to talk about a witness about Jesus, not about Jesus himself, and we have no control that would permit us to make inferences from one to the other. But beyond this structural one is an even deeper historical problem. Taking faith in the strict sense of the innermost act of trust in and loyalty to God, we lack enough evidence about any human being, no matter how much data we might have, to make warranted judgments about the quality of his or her faith, to say nothing of making them about the perfection of such faith throughout an entire life. Furthermore, even granting that there might be evidence permitting such judgments, the sources about Jesus are entirely inappropriate, lacking as they do any testimony at all about his inner life or development as a person (*PC*, 67–73). If christological predication depends on knowledge of the personal life of Jesus, then christology is in trouble indeed.

Theological objections, not historical ones, however, are the crux of the matter. It has never been evident how any christological warrant can be derived from assertions about Jesus's personal perfection, however this is conceived, whether in terms of his sinlessness, his perfect God-consciousness, or his openness to God in faith expressed through his life (such as, for instance, his being "a man for others"). No human being's perfection provides a basis for claims about the soteriological significance of that person, *in these respects*, for anyone

[17] See *PC*, 65–66. Ogden prefers to speak of Jesus as having perfectly realized the possibility of authentic self-understanding. The notion of faith is systematically ambiguous in both of its major theological uses. It refers, on the one hand, to the distinction between *fides quae creditur* and *fides qua creditur* (the faith in which Jesus believed, versus the subjective act by which he believed) and, on the other hand, to the distinction between the inner, subjective act of trusting in and being loyal to God and the broader sense by which such trust and loyalty express themselves in faith working through love. Ogden prefers the language of authentic self-understanding because, as he uses it, it unambiguously refers to the subjective dimension in both of these distinctions. Ogden is surely correct in making this point, but I have adhered to the looser usage because it more fairly captures the historical range actually represented across the revisionary consensus.

It should be noted that Ogden distinguishes between two types of criteria christological assertions must meet: criteria of appropriateness and criteria of credibility. Criteria of appropriateness apply to the subject of the christological assertion. Here, however, the criteria are those of credibility, that is, of truth, because the issue in this case concerns the necessary and sufficient conditions the subject of the christological assertions must meet in order to have christological predicates apply to it (see *PC*, 4, 66–67).

else.[18] This is especially true if personal attributes are understood as exemplary examples, as has been common in this revisionary tradition. Jesus's example provides no basis for christological assertions about him because his being an example cannot account for the possibility of my realizing such an example in my own life here and now. Ogden does not himself make this objection, but it serves to illuminate his elegant argument.

The New Testament nowhere supports the revisionary conception of the conditions of christological predication. Neither the gospels nor the kerygma refer to Jesus's faith. The new quest argument that the gospels *imply* such claims also lacks support. We cannot distinguish in the sources between what appear to be empirical-historical *assumptions* about Jesus and what are in fact existential-historical *assertions* about him, and this uncertainty would apply to any evidence supporting implications about Jesus's faith (*PC*, 73–74). It follows that "the faith of Jesus is so far from being the condition of the christological assertion as to be conditioned by it, in the sense that what is said or implied about his faith is not by way of grounding this assertion but simply one of the ways of formulating it."[19]

We can now say decisively that approaching christology through Jesus's personal faith so far from supporting a revisionary christology in fact precludes one. As Ogden earlier argued, the christological question arises within theistic religious controversy to identify God by identifying "the decisive re-presentation of God, whereby the meaning

[18]　As Ogden recognizes, John Hick classically formulated this objection in his criticism of D. M. Baillie's *God Was in Christ* (see *PC*, 80–81, and Hick [1958]). A more technical formulation is that no reference to a past historical event or to the qualities in the life of another person can make it possible for someone in the present to realize that same quality, unless faith is already presupposed. There is no intrinsic relation between Jesus's faith and my own unless it is presupposed, as Van Harvey says, "that the object of faith is the same and can be trusted. But this silent presupposition is precisely what is at issue in the decision of faith, and no reference to a past event can establish that." This point is especially apt with the resurrection. The resuscitation of a corpse "could be the basis for a religious confidence only if that event *were already interpreted as revelatory of the being with which one has to do in the present*. But this, again, is precisely the affirmation of faith," and it cannot warrant faith in the resurrection (*HB*, 282, my emphasis).

[19]　*PC*, 74. Ogden notes that this seems certainly to be the case with the synoptic material now normally classified as legendary (the temptation stories or the scene in Gethsemane), and the same seems evident concerning other New Testament claims about his "godly fear and obedience (Heb. 5:7ff.), his exemplary endurance of suffering (1 Pet. 2:21ff.), or his sinlessness (Heb. 4:15, 7:26ff.)." "Because the self-understanding of Jesus, like that of any other human being, could not have been experienced by those who came to believe in him and thus could not have even possibly been the ground of their christological formulations, such statements as they made or implied about his unique authenticity are themselves christological predications, not statements of their reasons for making such" (*PC*, 74).

of God for us is . . . made fully explicit" (*PC*, 75). Thus, for the New Testament, "whatever may be assumed about Jesus as he actually was, the one thing that must be asserted about him is who he truly is; and this means that, in some concepts and symbols or other, he must be asserted to be the decisive re-presentation of God, through whom God's own gift and demand become fully explicit, authorizing our authentic understanding of ourselves" (*PC*, 75–76). Despite the wide range of metaphysical differences among New Testament statements (and between them and those later used at Nicaea and Chalcedon), taken in their distinctively religious sense, they all "serve to formulate one and the same christological assertion of Jesus's decisive significance for human existence."[20]

Jesus's own faith or self-understanding can therefore be neither the necessary nor the sufficient condition for the truth of the type of claim made by New Testament christologies. It cannot be the necessary condition because "to assert that Jesus is the decisive re-presentation of God is not to say or imply how Jesus *did* understand himself but rather how everyone *ought* to understand himself or herself, even if no one has ever done so or ever will do so" (*PC*, 78, Ogden's emphasis). The truth of christological predicates is thus independent of how Jesus may have understood himself. It also cannot be the sufficient condition, for as Ogden rightly says, "it lies in the nature of any self-understanding, even one that would be perfectly authentic, that it can be authorized as authentic only by a primal source beyond itself," which is to say that its normative character stands under a criterion that it represents but does not itself constitute (*PC*, 78). We have seen that in theistic religious terms, Ogden takes christological assertions to be re-presentations of the meaning of God for us, when that identity has become questionable. Such re-presentations perform the role, in Ogden's formulation, of a primal "authorizing" source making explicit the implicit significance of "God." It follows that such re-presentations are different in principle from what could ever be derived from a perfect faith or perfectly authentic self-understanding (*PC*, 78). This means, Ogden points out, that the New Testament christologies make "an infinitely more exalted claim" about Jesus than could ever be supported by something about his perfect faith: that he re-presents the normative criterion (the "explicit primal source") that could alone "authorize" any such faith or self-

---

[20] *PC*, 76; see also *PC*, 76–77.

understanding. Thus, even if we could establish Jesus's perfect faith, it would not support the christological claim the New Testament makes of him (*PC*, 79).

In Ogden's language, the most that Jesus's perfect faith could support is that he is the "primary authority" for Christian faith. Ogden distinguishes here between a "primary authority" and "primal source of all authority made fully explicit" (*PC*, 79). I take it that by "primary authority" he means something like "exemplar" or "example," but the point is that any such primary authority must itself be *authorized* by something that cannot be identical with itself. Whether in the traditional incarnational language or the "low" christologies of the earliest New Testament witness, "the really essential difference . . . is the difference between being merely one more authority, even the primary such authority, and being the explicit primal source from which all authority derives" (*PC*, 81). Again, the revisionary emphasis on Jesus's faith cannot, in principle, provide conditions for the truth of christological predication.

We can now re-formulate these conditions. Christology answers an existential question. The christological assertion must accordingly be existential-historical. Its predicate must assert that "Jesus" is the re-presentation "through whom the meaning of God for us, and hence the meaning of ultimate reality for us, becomes fully explicit." It follows that "the only necessary and, therefore, the sufficient condition of any such assertion is that the meaning of ultimate reality for us that is always already presented implicitly in our very existence be just that meaning of God for us that is re-presented explicitly through Jesus" (*PC*, 82). We saw earlier that any answer to the existential question will have two dimensions, metaphysical and moral. The conditions of christological predication may, therefore, be formulated existentially by principles that articulate these two dimensions. Metaphysically, "Jesus is truthfully said to be Christ . . . if, but only if, *the ultimate reality that implicitly authorizes the authentic understanding of our existence is the one who is explicitly revealed through Jesus to be God*" (*PC*, 82, my emphasis). Morally, Jesus is truthfully said to be the Christ "if, but only if, *the understanding of our existence that is implicitly authorized by what is ultimately real is the self-understanding that is explicitly authorized through Jesus as faith in God*" (*PC*, 83, my emphasis). In both, we can know whether the condition is satisfied only by properly metaphysical or moral inquiry, respectively. Only insofar as ultimate reality is one way rather than another, the metaphysical dimension, can it "have the meaning for us it is re-presented as having through Jesus, who explicitly reveals it to be God." And it is "only insofar as acting in one way instead of another is how one ought to act in relation to one's fellows that ultimate reality can have the meaning for us it is re-presented as having through Jesus," and this can only be tested by inquiry into the moral dimension of that authentic existence implicitly authorized by ultimate reality.

Though these truth conditions must be tested metaphysically and morally, Ogden insists that they also have an historical aspect for the christological predicate. Christology has a "transcendental" or "a priori" dimension insofar as existential analysis will demand purely metaphysical and moral inquiry to identify the ultimate meaning of human existence. Furthermore, Ogden asserts, it belongs "to the very essence of Christian witness to attest that the fundamental option for salvation that is decisively re-presented solely through Jesus is also implicitly presented to every human being as soon and as long as he or she exists humanly at all" (*PC*, 83–84). But the specifically *christological* question and answer are not thus "transcendental"; they arise only in a particular history. The condition of truthfully asserting an answer to the constitutive *christological* question will therefore have an historical and not merely existential aspect. These empirical-historical truth conditions are not satisfied, however, by a quest for the historical Jesus, but by inquiry into the earliest Christian witness. Such inquiry seeks to establish what this witness took Jesus normatively to represent, and this is an historical question. It does not seek the being of Jesus in himself but his meaning for us as attested by this witness (*PC*, 84–85).

Ogden's analysis of the point of christology is enormously clarifying.[21] It shows immediately why a christology appropriate to a naturalist theology is readily attainable, contrary to the impression with which we began this chapter. Once it is evident that the point of christology

---

[21] Its importance becomes evident from a comparison with Hans Küng's influential *On Being a Christian* (Küng [1976]). A comprehensive presentation of what might be considered the contemporary Roman Catholic consensus on christology in light of the Church's recent openness to biblical historical inquiry, Küng's work is nevertheless deeply flawed at three points directly related to formulating the question of christology. (a) Despite being informed about the results of historical inquiry and orienting the christological questions to the New Testament sources rather than to the classical incarnational doctrines, Küng still assumes that the constitutive christological question regards the being of Jesus in himself; (b) he is altogether too sanguine about what the sources permit us to know of the historical person Jesus; (c) and, because he does not see that the point of christology is an existential point, he remains fixated on "objective" positions about Jesus's significance and about the resurrection.

is existential, then a christology on naturalist grounds simply falls into place. Because the conditions for Christian theology are existential, the christological conditions for a naturalist theology are exactly those Ogden has analyzed. The differences with Ogden arise from *making* the point of christology, not from the point itself.

MAKING THE POINT OF CHRISTOLOGY AND THE ROLE OF THE ''HISTORICAL'' JESUS

A naturalist theology will substantially agree with Ogden in making the point of christology, though I shall propose an addition that goes beyond his position but seems consistent with it. The major disagreement concerns the metaphysical question about how to understand what Ogden calls the primal source of authentic existence, the ultimate reality that authorizes authentic existence. Even here I shall maintain a surprising substantial *formal* agreement about how the fundamental issues, especially as they impinge on christology, are to be formulated. The disagreement itself is *material*, concerning my attempt to render those metaphysical principles naturalistically. Before we examine this disagreement, let us first outline the point christology makes.

According to Ogden, a contemporary christology must meet distinctively new criteria of credibility and appropriateness. He develops the criteria of credibility under the rubric of "the modern quest for freedom and the secular culture that is at once the outcome and the instrument of this quest" (*PC*, 89). The historical consciousness that has developed alongside modern science has produced an increasing awareness that human beings become the creators of themselves by creating their cultural and social orders. The quest for freedom, therefore, has become a quest by human beings to become the active subjects of "such collective self-creation and not merely its passive object" (*PC*, 90). One dimension of this modern quest has been theoretical: a centuries long struggle to free cognitive assent from appeals to authority and mere tradition by appeal to canons of evidence and rational assent available to all persons on no other grounds than rationality itself. This struggle has been waged not merely in the realm of the special sciences but also in history, society, culture, and politics. It is surely true, as Ogden remarks, that theology has experienced the primary impact of this quest theoretically. It has led theology to engage the modern challenges to its credibility largely over questions of belief and truth, as is exemplified by the demythologizing controversy in our time. Ogden emphasizes, however, that the quest for freedom also poses a *practical* challenge of credibility which has only recently entered the forefront of theological concern (notwithstanding earlier theologies of "the social gospel"). This challenge is posed not so much by the nonbeliever but by the "nonperson" in the modern world, "the one who finds the traditional christology of witness incredible, not because it is implicated in a religious world that for a small minority of men and women has now become untrue, but because it is implicated in an economic, social, political, and cultural world that for a vast majority of men and women continues to be unjust" (*PC*, 92; see also 90–93).

To formulate this dimension of credibility, Ogden draws an illuminating parallel between demythologizing and existentialist interpretation and "deideologizing" and "political interpretation." The positive side of demythologizing is, of course, existentialist interpretation. Bultmann warrants such interpretation because the New Testament writers use myth to articulate the understanding of existence implicit in the Christian witness of faith. The same relationship holds on the practical side. Understanding ideology as "a more or less comprehensive understanding of human existence . . . that functions to justify the interest of a particular group or individual by representing these interests as the demands of disinterested justice," "deideologizing" the Christian witness is required because, in the history of Christianity (and perhaps in the New Testament itself), its witness has served ideological purposes (*PC*, 94). Parallel with existentialist interpretation, such "deideologizing" warrants a "political interpretation" of the witness of faith in the interests of justice because "the primary use of ideology in the New Testament is not to justify the interests of some human beings against the just interests of others, but rather to give concrete content to Christian moral responsibility by making clear that it has to do precisely with establishing justice in human relations" (*PC*, 95).

This practical side of the norm of credibility in the quest for freedom may be termed "political interpretation" because Christian moral responsibility, especially in our world, involves an overriding interest in the achievement of justice, and this, in turn, requires a political dimension.[22] Broadly stated, this practical interest in justice means an interest in "either maintaining or transforming all the basic structures" of the social, cultural, and political order "so that each

---

[22] Ogden quotes Reinhold Niebuhr to the effect that "the very essence of politics" involves "the achievement of justice through equilibria of power" (*PC*, 95; quoted from Davis and Good (1960), 143).

person is equally free with every other to be the active subject of his or her own self-creation, instead of being merely the passive object of the self-creation of others" (*PC*, 95). This argument parallels the one from the last chapter that the moral dimension of the normative valuational question is ultimately about justice, the canons for which are developed and defended by moral philosophy, not theology. Ogden makes clear that the credibility of theology requires investigating whether its own christological witness conforms to this practical norm.

Ogden also shows that the criterion of *appropriateness* is changed by the contemporary theological situation. Appropriateness concerns the standard against which witness and theology are measured, and historically this has been the question of authority. The three classical positions are the Roman Catholic appeal to "scripture and tradition," the classical Protestant appeal to "scripture alone," and the liberal Protestant appeal to the so-called "historical Jesus." These debates have ultimately been about "the canon" of scripture and about how the process of its formation constituted an "authority," but in each case, an unquestioned assumption has been that the debate concerns the New Testament *writings* themselves. Recent biblical scholarship has now thrown this assumption profoundly into question, for we know in a uniquely new way that "every writing in the New Testament canon depends upon sources, oral if not also written, expressing a witness to Jesus earlier than its own" (*PC*, 99).

This new situation entirely undercuts the distinction between scripture and tradition that has been at issue in Protestant and Roman Catholic debates over authority and undermines any appeal to a historical Jesus to be found behind the earliest level of witness to him. This means that the question of authority, and therefore the question of how this authority authorizes an appropriate christology, must be reconceived in terms of the "apostilicity" of an early witness that is not identical with the New Testament writings as such but can only be recovered by critically examining them. Thus, the question of appropriateness must now be addressed in terms of a critically recovered primitive witness, and this creates special problems in the realm of christology which then impinge on questions of credibility.[23]

---

[23] See *PC*, 96–105. Ogden's analysis of this problem is considerably more nuanced and technical than I have suggested. It is also controversial because it involves a powerful critique of all the traditional approaches to authority and a fresh and demanding proposal for an alternative. I do not present it in full because I want to concentrate simply on its implications for christology, and these are already fully enough in evidence from the earlier argument that the "Jesus" of the christological witness cannot, in principle, be separated from the structure of this witness itself.

Ogden formulates the contemporary norm of credibility in terms of a "christology of liberation" (see *PC*, 106–108). Liberation has been a basic motif in all human religiosity, however differently conceived, and has often been voiced specifically in terms of freedom. The especially important formulations of the "Christ-kerygma" in John and Paul can be interpreted as christologies of liberation because of the Stoic notion of freedom that they appropriated. We now know, however, that neither of these christologies was primary but was an interpretive expression of an earlier tradition of apostolic witness. They themselves, therefore, must be judged as appropriate by this earlier standard, and on this score, the surface impressions are not particularly encouraging. Paul, for instance, defines freedom by participation in Christ's crucifixion and resurrection (Gal. 2:20), yet this understanding of cross and resurrection is missing from the earliest stratum of witness (see *PC*, 109–110).

The quests for the historical Jesus tried to make good on this problem. The early quest tried simply to base christological assertions on the historical Jesus himself. This approach was invalidated by form criticism at the beginning of this century, but, enabled precisely by the earlier stratum recovered by form criticism, the new quest seeks to validate Paul's and John's "Christ-kerygma" because the latter represents the same possibility of self-understanding as in Jesus's own self-understanding. We have seen, however, that this claim is open to insurmountable historical and theological objections. Nevertheless, the new quest does open another possibility. Though we cannot use the earliest tradition to reconstruct the self-understanding of Jesus, *we can use it to reconstruct the self-understanding authorized by the earliest witness's representation of Jesus*. In this way we can reconstruct a "Jesus-kerygma" – as long as we remain clear about what the reference to "Jesus" is – and compare it to the "Christ-kerygma" of a later witness. It follows that if the earliest witness to Jesus is the real norm of appropriateness, then "the Jesus to whom it bears witness" is "no mere authority, but instead the explicit primal source of all authority, including its own" (*PC*, 113). A christology of liberation is, thus, to be measured against this norm.

What we find in this earliest witness is a *portrayal* of Jesus in terms of (a) an eschatological proclamation, (b) a teaching about the will of God appropriate to this proclamation, and (c) a number of stylized actions which represent the same self-understanding as in the proclamation and teachings. Even if, as Ogden notes, Jesus's words in his first appearance almost certainly were not the exact words of

Mark's gospel, "the time is fulfilled, and the reign of God is at hand; repent, and believe in the gospel" (1:15), still Jesus was remembered "as an eschatological prophet, a proclaimer of the imminent reign of God, who conceived his own proclamation and the summons to repentance and faith that was a piece with it to be the decisive word of God in the last hour." Though the earliest witness evidences no call for faith in his person, he is portrayed as calling for "faith in his word, as itself the word of God that confronted his hearers with the definitive decision of their lives" (*PC*, 115). The same judgment is warranted throughout his proclamation and sayings, both when he is represented as pointing to the Son of Man to come as someone other than himself and when his sayings and deeds represent him as pointing to himself as the "sign of the times" (Luke 4:16–30, 10:23–24, 11:20, 11:31–32; Mark 3:27; Matt. 11:5–6) (see *PC*, 115–117). Similarly, in his teaching of the will of God he is represented as simply explicating "the demand for repentance and faith implied by the overriding fact of the coming reign of God" (*PC*, 117). Even the primacy of Jesus's eschatology submits to the same judgment, for he simply inherited the mythology of Jewish apocalypticism which itself gave a different answer to the existential question from that of Jesus (see *PC*, 117–118). Jesus's eschatology may have contained an implicit christological claim in the sense that it tied his own proclamation to the in-breaking reign of God. Still, Ogden notes, this christology remained purely formal: "All that it can say is what it served to say to his hearers – namely, that the ultimate reality by which their existence was finally determined was none other than the God whose gift and demand were already confronting them through Jesus himself with the definitive decision for or against their own authentic existence" (*PC*, 118).

The critical issues therefore concern the identity of this God and the content of the self-understanding it authorizes. Ogden's articulation, representing in his judgment "as reasonable an explanation as one can presently give of the origins of Christianity" (*PC*, 120), can scarcely be improved:

The God whose gift and demand were already made fully explicit in Jesus was the God of boundless love, from whom all things come and for whom they all exist; and the self-understanding that this God through Jesus both gave and demanded as one's authentic possibility was existence in faith in this boundless love – faith being understood in the twofold sense of trust in God's love alone for the ultimate meaning of one's life and, therefore, of loyalty to it and to all to whom it is loyal as the only final cause that one's life is to serve.[24]

Ogden concludes that "the essential point . . . is that *Jesus meant love*" (*PC*, 119, Ogden's emphasis). The coming reign of God was a "reign of boundless love, by which even then the existence of Jesus's hearers was finally determined," and his proclamation, as portrayed, for instance, in the beatitudes was that this love was freely offered to all. The will of God, then, "was nothing other than the demand that one trustingly accept the gift of God's love and then loyally live in returning love for all whom God loyally loves" as presented, for instance, in Mark's reformulation of the great commandment (12:29ff.) (*PC*, 119). Because of such radicality, Jesus's proclamation could also be understood as God's judgment, for it confronts all who hear it with the necessity of complete repentance. Yet such repentance is possible because Jesus assures all of God's prior forgiveness (see *PC*, 119–120).

From the earliest witness to Jesus, Ogden concludes that "Jesus also means freedom" (*PC*, 122). Unlike the new quest where this inference demands that Jesus perfectly actualized such freedom in his own life, for Ogden this is the meaning of Jesus for us, a strictly existential-historical assertion. Yet for precisely this reason, the existential meaning of christology is existence in freedom. On the one hand, it means that God's love is offered unrestrictively to all persons, so that "nothing can separate one from life's ultimate meaning. For this reason, to accept God's love through faith is to be freed from oneself and everything else *as in any way a necessary condition of a meaningful life.*" It follows that one is freed for all things and not merely from them, for "because God's love is utterly boundless and embraces everything within its scope, anything whatever is of ultimate significance and thus the proper object of one's returning love for God." One can be free for other persons in love "only by promoting their own freedom to be and to become fully themselves – active subjects of their own self-creation, instead of merely passive objects of the self-creation of others. In this sense, the existence of faith whose possibility is decisively re-presented through Jesus is a liberating as well as a liberated existence." Thus, a commitment to justice is strongly rooted

---

[24] *PC*, 118–119. It will not go unnoticed that Ogden's formulation here parallels that of H. Richard Niebuhr (1960), 16–23, whom Ogden cites. Especially in terms of the disagreement with Ogden over precisely how to construe this account metaphysically, which I shall voice in a moment, it should be noted that Niebuhr is much more cautious than Ogden about what ontological entailments such language has, even though neither he nor I would quibble over Ogden's otherwise exemplary formulation.

in the constitutive christological assertion about the ultimate meaning of our lives.[25]

Such are the outlines of a christology that meets the criteria of appropriateness required by the earliest Christian witness available to us. It also meets the criterion of credibility because it permits a christology of freedom. Ogden's contribution is to root the christology *implicit* in Jesus's witness not, as in the new quest, in Jesus's personal life or in his words and deeds, but in the earliest witness *to* him. This is the "Jesus" attested of the earliest witness: ". . . the significant thing is not that Jesus at least implicitly claimed to be the Christ, however probable it may be that he did exactly that; rather, the significant thing is that what the apostolic community understood by Jesus – the Jesus to whom they themselves bore witness, implicitly if not explicitly, as the Christ – was the one through whom they had experienced, and who, through their own witness, was still to be experienced as implying, just such a claim."[26]

Admittedly, even in making the point of christology, Ogden's position remains a fragment, though an essential one, of a full-blown christology, as he would be the first to admit. Though I shall not develop a full christology, I want to take Ogden's reflections a step further and suggest the direction by which such a task might be engaged. This direction is, I believe, already implicit in Ogden's analysis, and indeed, one with which he would likely agree. To develop these points, I shall appeal to certain implications from Van Harvey's *The Historian and the Believer*.

I refer to Harvey's distinctions among four levels of meaning "Jesus of Nazareth" may be taken to have. Harvey develops this analysis out of critical reservations identical to Ogden's about the inferences warranted by the new quest.[27] First, there is "Jesus as he really was." Such a notion is a limit of thought since, though there is no historical evidence warranting doubt that such a person actually existed, no person, to say nothing of Jesus, can be known in his or her full historical concreteness. Second, we can also refer to "the historical

[25] *PC*, 123, my emphasis; see pp. 148–168 for Ogden's detailed analysis of the latter entailments.
[26] *PC*, 121, my emphasis. Note that the relationship between implicit and explicit christological claims is exactly that defended by the new quest. Ogden's decisive contribution is to show that this relationship can only be justified in the *earliest witness to Jesus*; any inferences to Jesus himself are not merely historically only probable (and in this instance precariously probable at best, that is, very soft) but also *theologically* unjustified insofar as they are taken to warrant christological assertions. For this reason, I have consistently used the language of "portrayal" in describing Ogden's analysis.
[27] See *HB*, 164–200, esp. pp. 194–196; and also, Harvey and Ogden (1962).

Jesus" who is the Jesus "that is now recoverable by historical means." There is probably disagreement between Harvey and Ogden here because Harvey believes that at least some inferences about this Jesus are "empirico-historically" warranted by the new quest. In any case, these claims play no role in Harvey's analysis, and as a result of later developments in research, he might now well agree fully with Ogden's more nuanced use of the "form-critical reservation," thus treating "the historical Jesus" also as a limit of thought. Third, another level of meaning of "Jesus of Nazareth" is the "memory-impression of Jesus" as recorded by our sources and critically recovered through the analysis of the traditions lying behind them. This level conforms to Marxsen's and Ogden's "Jesus-kerygma," the earliest witness to Jesus recoverable in the traditions. Finally, fourth, there is "the biblical Christ," which conforms to the "Christ-kerygma" as presented by Ogden. It designates "the transformation and alteration of the memory-impression (or perspectival image) under the influence of the theological interpretation of the actual Jesus by the Christian community." It includes the Pauline and Johannine christologies but also "the idea of pre-existence, the birth and temptation narratives, many of the miracles, those stories which clearly reflect Old Testament prophecies, the resurrection and forty-day traditions, and the ascension." Harvey asserts that "because it is a transformation of the memory-image," it "is not a complete distortion of it," though, of course, under the pressure of Ogden's type of analysis, as Harvey himself recognizes, there must be serious question about just what kind of continuity this is (*HB*, 266–268).

The "memory impression of Jesus" or the "perspectival image" is the important level for Harvey's own christological analysis. This is the Jesus who conforms to the "Jesus" of Ogden's earliest witness of faith. Harvey distinguishes three interrelated elements in this image: "the content and pattern of his teaching and preaching, the form of his actions, and his crucifixion." We need not analyze these elements in detail, as they are familiar, and except for the last, have already been touched upon in our discussion of Ogden. For Harvey, the central motif in all these elements is that Jesus was remembered in the earliest witness as one who raised and answered "the basic human question of faith. It was this role which made him the paradigm of God's action, for he had taught them to think of God as the one whose distinctive action it is to awaken faith" (*HB*, 270). His teaching and proclamation articulated this call with a sense of urgency; "he so posed the demand

and the possibility of faith that it came to men as their last chance, a decision that could not be put off as other decisions could." That to which he called them, as the image preserves it, was "confidence and trust in that last power that is said to hold and sustain and limit men in their being and powers" (*HB*, 271). The memory-image preserves Jesus's actions in a fashion carefully designed to make the same point, "for it is precisely the relationship that defines it as revelation so far as the texts are concerned. His preaching and teaching specify how his actions are to be understood, and his actions . . . give concreteness and embodiment to . . . his teaching. Otherwise, the facts of his life, his behavior, could be, and have been, interpreted differently." All in all, both his teaching and his conduct represent "a radical reinterpretation of the concept of righteousness and of the ideas of God's power held by those who hoped to be justified by the law" (*HB*, 272), which, of course, is all of us insofar as law is understood widely to refer to all efforts to secure existence on our own terms, as indeed is already implicit in some New Testament usage.

Harvey believes it is important to include the crucifixion in this memory-image. Ogden's more rigorous and minimalist analysis of the earliest tradition (see *PC*, 115) would probably dispute this, but the disagreement does not undermine what is illuminating in Harvey's discussion. His point is that in the memory-image, Jesus's crucifixion raises exactly the same issue of faith as does the portrayal of his teaching and conduct, however much this point may have been obscured by traditional christological preoccupations to *explain* Jesus's significance by theories such as that of vicarious sacrifice.[28] The traditional preoccupations have "made no actual theological difference" anyway, Harvey notes, because even in notions of vicarious sacrifice "the same question – Is God gracious? – has been raised and answered" (*HB*, 273). However, the continuity between the crucifixion and Jesus's portrayal in words and deeds is especially important when, as in our time, the traditional theories of sacrifice and atonement have become unintelligible, for the crucifixion still raises and answers the same question of faith as does the portrayal of his teaching and conduct. The question of faith is whether Jesus's teaching and deeds or his crucifixion "are in any sense true, whether,

[28] This is consistent with Ogden in the sense that his interpretation of Paul's theology of the cross as a christology of freedom argues that Paul's particular mythological formulations may be judged appropriate when measured against the standard of the Jesus-kerygma (see *PC*, 124–125).

in fact, they constitute a revelation of anything at all except the meaninglessness of existence" (*HB*, 273), and this question is answered with the claim that "faith has to do with one's surrender of his attempts to establish his own righteousness and his acceptance of his life and creation as a gift and a responsibility" (*HB*, 280).

Harvey's conclusions are formally identical with Ogden's constitutive christological assertion. Unlike the new quest's attempt to infer christologically significant conclusions from what Harvey terms the perspectival image of Jesus, his account need say nothing, implicitly or explicitly, about "Jesus's person, sinlessness, or existential selfhood. These are understandable but unnecessary ways of protecting the truths that it was in and through Jesus's witness that Christians grasp the content of faith and that they find the proclamation of this event to be efficacious still in awakening faith. To say more adds nothing to faith," and attempting to do so "precipitates ... the collision with the morality of historical knowledge," (which simply replicates Ogden's critique of the historical possibility of such claims) (*HB*, 274–275).

Harvey's analysis of the "memory-image of Jesus" is especially helpful in regard to the full christology the point of christology suggests. Ogden grants that there is a continuity with the Christ-kerygma, particularly in Paul's version but implicitly in others including the Johannine, such that they can be judged appropriate by the primary authority of the Christian witness, but he is also sensitive to their mythological forms which have become unbelievable for us today (*PC*, 125). The same may be said of the traditional christology of the incarnation. Apart from its profound misunderstanding of the point of the constitutive christological assertion, even if it could be demythologized and reinterpreted, Ogden several times suggests his doubt that such efforts would be the best way of meeting the criteria of credibility and appropriateness.[29] Harvey also shares such misgivings,

---

[29] See, e.g., *PC*, 9–10, 66, 72–73, 77. In his earlier, less fully developed essay, "The Point of Christology," Ogden comes much closer to the classical christological theme: "Thus, what I properly mean when I assert that Jesus is 'divine' is that the possibility here and now re-presented to me in the Christian witness of faith is God's own gift and demand to my existence. On the other hand, what I properly mean when I assert that Jesus is 'human' is that I am here and now actually confronted with this possibility, that it is actually re-presented to me as a historical event and hence is not merely an idea or a general truth" (Ogden [1975], 385). There are echoes of the same idea in *The Point of Christology* when Ogden insists that even as an existential-historical assertion, the portrayal of Jesus in the earliest tradition makes an exalted claim by always putting him on the divine side of the relationship between God and man (see *PC*, 77–79), but the attempt to parallel the traditional Chalcedonian formulas has entirely dropped away.

but noting that the conditions of belief change from age to age, he proposes: "What may have been intelligible to and valid for Augustine and Francis may not be so for those of us who live after the advent of biblical criticism. And it is just this fact that enables us to consider another option, namely, that the call to faith may be made far more powerful for modern men if interpreted in terms of the memory-image of Jesus, who proclaimed the righteousness of God, associated with tax-collector and harlots, and was crucified, than in terms of the only-begotten Son who existed before all worlds, came to earth, was crucified as an atonement for sin, was raised from the dead, and exalted to heaven. . . . [F]or many of us, this same truth can best be mediated through the story of the despised man Jesus. Put rather starkly, is it not as possible to hear the call to faith through the image of Jesus as through the biblical Christ?" (*HB*, 281).

Just so, and I suggest that here is the most attractive avenue for a fully contemporary christology. This avenue is, of course, already evident in recent christologies that reflect the full impact of biblical criticism. But these are too often still wedded to the traditional incarnational terms. I am not necessarily claiming, as I shall indeed suggest in a moment, that this language may not still serve for christological purposes, only that it is problematic for theology to think simply of recovering it. The really fundamental objection, however, is that such christologies still believe it possible to ground a modern christology, whether incarnational or not, in the being of Jesus's person, and we have seen how questionable this is both historically and theologically. Thus, Harvey proposes the most suggestive direction for contemporary christology, and it is thoroughly consistent with the point of christology Ogden makes. It is precisely from the "memory-image of Jesus" or from the "Jesus" re-presented in the earliest witness that we should today draw the resources for a fully contemporary christology.

We must ask whether the point of christology is consistent with a naturalist theology. I, of course, have insisted at least as strongly as Ogden that the point of all theological assertions is existential. Consequently his argument for the existential-historical nature of all christological assertion agrees profoundly with the present position, and opens the way for a christology on naturalistic terms. But Ogden also insists that christology has a metaphysical dimension, and this would seem at odds with naturalism. I want now to show, however, that this is not nearly the difficulty it might at first appear to be. Just as we are in accord with Ogden's argument that the point of christology is entirely existential, we now shall see that the present position is in complete *formal* agreement with how that point is made, however much disagreement there is over its material metaphysical comprehension.

We saw that the question christology answers in asking "Who is Jesus?" is complex. It also asks the existential question about the ultimate meaning of our existence as human beings and the question of what ultimate reality must be such as to authorize that meaning. In theistic religions this "ultimate reality" is specifically understood as "God." Though this question has a metaphysical dimension, it is not yet strictly metaphysical since the question is about a meaning *for us*. Nevertheless, a full answer must eventually address the strictly metaphysical question (cf. *PC*, 29–30, 35–39). The two sides of the existential-historical question may be formulated in the two principles quoted from Ogden earlier: ". . . Jesus is truthfully said to be Christ, . . . if, but only if, the ultimate reality that implicitly authorizes the authentic understanding of our existence is the one who is explicitly revealed through Jesus to be God," the metaphysical side, and Jesus is truthfully said to be Christ "if, but only if, the understanding of our existence that is implicitly authorized by what is ultimately real is the self-understanding that is explicitly authorized through Jesus as faith in God," the moral side (*PC*, 82–83). These principles were made concrete by the claim that Jesus means love, namely, that "the God whose gift and demand [are] already made fully explicit in Jesus [is] the God of boundless love, from whom all things come and for whom they all exist; and the self-understanding that this God through Jesus both gave and demanded as one's authentic possibility was existence in faith in this boundless love – faith being understood in the twofold sense of trust in God's love alone for the ultimate meaning of one's life and, therefore, of loyalty to it and to all to whom it is loyal as the only final cause that one's life is to serve" (*PC*, 118–119).

The language of ultimacy in these statements is ambiguous. Regarding *the ultimate meaning of our existence as human beings*, it clearly is valuational. In contrast, *the ultimate reality* that authorizes authentic existence in the first sense is explicitly metaphysical or factual. Furthermore, the first usage is doubly ambiguous, since it is by no means obvious what "ultimacy" in the *ultimate* meaning of one's existence means.[30] Let us simply take it in Ogden's sense as the question of faith, namely, the question about that comprehensive self-understanding of oneself that most appropriately articulates one's existential faith in the worth-while-ness of one's life. In this sense, as we have been using it all along, it is the question of how one is to understand oneself authentically, "as over against all the misunder-standings that leave one to walk only in darkness" (*PC*, 26–27). It is also doubly ambiguous in its metaphysical sense, but this is an ambiguity that Ogden acknowledges. It is the meaning of ultimate reality for us, so that it is closely tied to the existential question, but it also means ultimate reality in the strictly metaphysical sense of (a) the most basic ontological constituents and (b) their most general metaphysical features.

Ogden regards these two usages of ultimacy as tightly wedded. He regards authentic existence as finally authorized by what ultimate reality must be like metaphysically. It should be evident that these two usages of ultimacy need not necessarily require this bond. They do in Ogden's case because for him the existential question is the question of faith. Because of its peculiar logic, it requires a ground in the ultimate nature of things that "no turn of events in the future has the power to annul" (*RG*, 36). Ogden assumes that the ultimate meaning of our lives can only be grounded by an ontological account of ultimate reality. It is crucial to see that Ogden's claim is *formally* identical with those I have defended. "Openness to the future" is the condensed formula for the account I have given of authentic existence. According to this account, openness to the future is indeed grounded, via the physical determination relation, in ultimate reality, in the ultimate unifiers of a physicalist ontology, and it is grounded by the determination relation exactly so as to authorize authentic existence. This is true assuming the normative status of authentic human existence grounded in physical determination. Though I have interpreted authentic existence naturalistically, my account has exactly the same content as Ogden defends.

---

[30] One could, for example, be asking about its meaning as comprehensive or all embracing, or unconditional, or undergirding, or everlasting, and each of these would have different implications about the conditions of a successful answer and about its relationship to the other meanings. See various analyses of these ambiguities in Klemke (1981), especially the essays by Kurt Baier, "The meaning of life," 81–117; Richard Taylor, "The meaning of life," 141–150; Kai Nielson, "Linguistic philosophy and 'The meaning of life'," 177–204; R. W. Hepburn, "Questions about the meaning of life," 209–227; and W. D. Joske, "Philosophy and the meaning of life," 248–261.

But what of Ogden's reference to the boundless love of God? By this claim he makes the meaning of ultimate reality for us concrete. Physical determination may warrant authentic existence, but surely it can never warrant "the boundless love of God." Yet again, however, the issue turns on the argument for transforming religious questions from ontological to valuational ones. At its existential nub, the issue of God's love is valuational, even for Ogden. In my account, of course, "God's love" is not referential, but that is scarcely the issue. The argument is that "God exists" is true just insofar as openness to the future (faith) warrants it as a seeing-as. It is warranted by events of grace. Openness to the future is the affirmation of the giftedness of life itself received as a gift; thereby, "God's grace," "God's boundless love," is understood concretely in terms of the transformative events by which devotion and loyalty to God occur.

Furthermore, by way of Wieman's argument for the *valuational* absoluteness of the creative event, "God's boundless love" receives exactly the valuational and functional significance it has for Ogden. As Ogden says in a passage quoted earlier: "Because God's love for us is completely boundless and is offered to any and every person who is willing to receive it, *nothing whatever can separate one from life's ultimate meaning*. For this reason, to accept God's love through faith is to be freed from oneself and everything else as in any way a necessary condition of a meaningful life."[31] According to my account, it is precisely by faith in God's transformative action, understood valuationally as God's boundless love (which *on its terms* cannot fail), that one receives the reassurance, of which Ogden speaks, about the *ultimate* significance of one's life that cannot be disappointed (cf. *PC*, 29–36). The difference is that "ultimacy" is conceived valuationally through and through, even as, in another sense, it is every bit as metaphysically *determined* as Ogden could require.

Actually, in a chapter on the metaphysical dimension of christology, Ogden significantly departs from his earlier position and now *formally* comes very close to the *type* of argument I have just presented. Earlier, we saw, Ogden appeals metaphysically to analogy. Analogically, "love" could be fully applied to God's metaphysical being. Terming such a position a "categorial metaphysics," Ogden now argues that such predication is untenable. This means that instead of three sorts of

---

[31] *PC*, 123, my emphasis. He, of course, grounds this assertion in the conservation of value, that is, in "everlastingness" as subjective appreciation in God (see *RG*, 206–230). I shall address this issue in the next chapter.

predication (literal, analogical, and symbolic or metaphorical), he now accepts only two, literal and symbolic (see *PC*, 132–139). Literal metaphysical terms apply to ultimate reality exactly as they apply to anything else, serving thereby to denote the general structures of reality necessary to constitute the conditions of anything whatsoever (*PC*, 136, 143). In this respect, however, "love" has no literal application to ultimate reality. Since Ogden now rejects the possibility of formulating this predication analogically, he must affirm that its reference is symbolic or metaphorical, not properly metaphysical at all (*PC*, 138; see also pp. 144–146).

Ogden claims not to have retreated from process metaphysics as the support for the basic christological assertions (see *PC*, 140, 145). But now he must warrant the *symbolic* attribution to God of such predicates as "love" *by additional arguments* that connect them, but now only indirectly, to literal metaphysical predicates that apply to ultimate reality directly. He therefore is in exactly my position. In a physicalist naturalism, "love" cannot apply directly to the ultimate metaphysical conditions; it can be made to apply only indirectly by the physical determination of "the love of God" valuationally in a valuational theism. Ogden even asserts that the primary function of such symbolic predicates "is the properly religious (or possibly philosophical) function of so expressing the meaning of ultimate reality for us as to authorize the kind of existence and action on our part that are appropriate to it. Specifically, the claim that God as ultimate reality is boundless love means primarily *that we ourselves are free to exist and act in love in relation to all our fellow creatures.*"[32] The significance of this admission is that "God's boundless love" (a symbolic attribution) must receive its content valuationally in a form of life, just as in the position I have defended. And the "symbolic" status that such references must now have for him, brings him very close to the type of "seeing-as" position I have defended.

Ogden's discussion of this change in his position is too brief to reveal its full implications. He suggests that he would make the linking argument connecting metaphysical and symbolic predicates by appeal to Hartshorneian internal relations (*PC*, 145–146). But this argument is not developed, and it may, indeed, be problematic. Ogden recognizes that rejecting a categorial metaphysics entails a

---

[32] *PC*, 144, my emphasis. In another context, he says: ". . . they function primarily imperatively, to express the meaning of reality for us, and hence to call for the kind of self-understanding and moral action that are authorized by the ultimate reality called 'God'" (*PC*, 143).

rejection (or at least a major revision) of Hartshorne's panpsychism (which requires an analogical argument), and it might be questioned whether a *theistic* form of process metaphysics is possible apart from the panpsychist ontology (see *PC*, 138–139). However that may be, this revision in his position now brings him close to something like the notion of a determination relation as regards religious predicates applied to God, and that position is *formally* very close to the one defended here. He must now say that the crucial religious predicates do not apply literally to God even though they and their appropriateness are *determined* metaphysically by whatever the ultimate metaphysical conditions are. It also means that the arguments linking metaphysical determination relations and religious predicates must be indirect and largely valuational. Thus, all that remains at issue between the two positions is the notion of *physical* determination, and I have, with Post, already given reasons why I regard it as far more attractive than Hartshorne's ontology. We see, then, surprisingly, that formally, even Ogden's own christological formulations admit of a christology on naturalist grounds, both cognitivist and ontologically secure.

CHRISTOLOGY AND CREATIVE TRANSFORMATION

The basic structure for a naturalist christology is now before us. Apart from the disagreement over ontology, all its elements are provided by Ogden's important contribution to contemporary christological reflection. I shall conclude this chapter by supplementing this basic structure with several themes from Wieman's thought. Specifically, it is in relation to christology, I shall argue, that Wieman's own conception of the creative event is best discussed. I also want to explore certain implications of the notion of creative transformation as they apply to christology.

Students of Wieman's thought will have noticed that I have made no use of his "creative event" in developing his thought theologically. In its widest sense, the creative event for Wieman is simply creative transformation in the growth of value. Though I have interpreted creative transformation differently, I have attempted to show how his philosophy of religion might more fully ground a Christian theology than anything he himself achieved, and I believe that I have remained faithful to its basic intent. I have not, however, used his conception of how creative transformation works within human value. In his mature position, he identified this by a kind of communicative interaction which he termed "creative interchange" (see *MUC*, 16, 22; see also *SHG*, 54–69).

"Creative interchange" consists of four sub-events. (1) It is, first, the "emerging awareness in the individual of qualitative meaning communicated to it from some other organism," and Wieman emphasizes that only when the capacity for language use (or some other capacity for the symbolic sharing of quality) develops is there the kind of quantum leap in value that we find at the human level of nature (*SHG*, 58). (2) The second sub-event is the process by which these newly acquired meanings are integrated with others previously acquired. This integration is "largely subconscious, unplanned and uncontrolled by the individual, save only as he may provide conditions favorable to its occurrence" (*SHG*, 59). It is at this level of integration more than at any other point that God works to "transform man as he cannot transform himself" (*MUC*, 11). (3) Following upon such integration is an "expanding and enriching of the appreciable world by a new structure of interrelatedness pertaining to events" (*SHG*, 61). (4) Finally, there is a level of operation which widens and deepens community among those who participate in the creative event. The creative event is communal because it operates only by including the thoughts and feelings of others in one's system of meanings, and conversely, it is productive of community precisely because community and the abundance of life it makes possible can exist at all only insofar as such sharing occurs (*SHG*, 64–65). In these four sub-events, the creative event is the transformation "that brings forth in the human mind, in society and history, and in the appreciable world a new structure of interrelatedness, whereby events are discriminated and related in a manner not before possible. It is a structure whereby some events derive from other events, through meaningful connection with them, an abundance of quality that events could not have had without this new creation" (*SHG*, 65).

Creative events extend much more widely into nature than the level of communicative interchange alone (see *SHG*, 66–68, 70–74). Wieman also insists that the creative event is "suprahuman" and "functionally transcendent," though not supernatural or otherwise ontologically transcendent.[33] Nevertheless, in his mature thought,

---

[33] See *SHG*, 31–37, 74–78, 263–268. This emphasis was, indeed, one of the strongest sources of Wieman's critique of humanism, especially in his early thought. The locus of value was not, finally, humanity, and human beings could not save themselves through moral striving. In this sense, Wieman's philosophy of religion was entirely God-centered (see Daniel Day Williams [1963], 76–79). Nevertheless, though he never abandoned the "suprahuman" character of the creative event, emphasis on the wider notion became increasingly muted in

Wieman increasingly focused his idea of God on the processes of creative interchange in human communicative interaction. The reasons have to do with the interests which lay behind his "empiricism." As I noted earlier, his concern in the philosophy of religion was never primarily theoretical; this also accounts for why he showed so little interest in developing a full theology. His concern was, if you will, entirely soteriological. He was passionately concerned with how value increases, especially in an age when human beings possess unprecedented technological power, the uses of which are by no means unproblematically beneficial or benign. His deepest interest, therefore, was an urgent desire to identify the specific empirical conditions to which human beings could contribute if their quest for value is not to destroy them. Increasingly, therefore, he sought those conditions where he believed they could most readily be identified, and this led him to concentrate on creative interchange.[34]

Communicative interaction is certainly one locus of creative transformation at the human level of nature. I have not developed this notion, however, because I believe it is too narrow to serve as the basis for a full theology. Its focus on a single dimension of human existence necessarily limits its hermeneutical range. Everything valuable in Wieman's position, I argue, can be appropriated theologically by reinterpreting it in terms of Heidegger's existentialist analytic. Bultmann's existentialist method then becomes a richer resource for explicating Wieman's naturalist account of creative transformation, which is the really significant dimension of his thought. Creative transformation can be applied to the full structure of what it is like *to be* the kind of beings we are. Within that structure,

his thought after he defined the fourfold structure of the creative event in communicative interaction in *The Source of Human Good* (1946). His interest increasingly concentrated on examining its significance in "creative interchange" until in his last major work, *Man's Ultimate Commitment* (1958), the wider meaning entirely drops away. It is no accident, then, that the critique of humanism also becomes muted in his later work and is entirely absent from the latter work.

[34] This focus of his concern is well articulated by the following two statements from *Man's Ultimate Commitment*: "All attempts to find what should command the ultimate commitment by peering into the depths and heights of Being outside of human life, or into eternity or the supernatural, is to seek it where it can never be found. What transforms human life toward the best possible must operate in human life and in time, where man is, not in an eternity where man is not" (*MUC*, 77). "This creativity which works between people in the form of interchange, and also within each individual, may be only a shallow, superficial manifestation of an infinite Being of mystery. It may be that this Being in its wholeness is what creates, sustains, saves, and transforms human life toward the greater good. But obviously we can make no statement about that mystery except to acknowledge it, precisely because it is a mystery. On the other hand, the creativity here under consideration can be known and studied and therefore can guide our commitment" (*MUC*, 33–34).

Mitsein or "being-with-others," which in Heidegger is the existential domain of Wieman's creative interaction, is only one element of what it means *to be* human, though, of course, it is an essential one. I emphasize, however, that this judgment requires no outright rejection of creative interchange itself. It may, indeed, be especially valuable for the empirical dimension of a naturalist theology, and it may have special relevance for more fully developing the normative valuational arguments. Hence, I now want to suggest the theological fruitfulness of creative interchange specifically in the area of christology.

Wieman's remarks about christology are brief, undeveloped, and by today's critical standards, hopelessly naive.[35] Yet concerning the point of christology, they are surprisingly on target, if one discounts the uncritical manner in which he speaks of the person of Jesus. In any case, he does not speak about Jesus's person so as to violate the theological issues involved in the point of christology. Note how his references to Jesus in the following can easily be construed in terms of the "Jesus" portrayed in the earliest witness or what Harvey calls the "memory-image" of Jesus. Wieman sees Jesus's significance in the creative interchange that emerged from association with him: "Jesus engaged in intercommunication with a little group of disciples with such depth and potency that the organization of their several personalities was broken down and they were remade. They became new men, and the thought and feeling of each got across to the others" (*SHG*, 39). Yet, this was not something Jesus did simply through his own self-conscious intentions or thought: "Not something handed down to them from Jesus but something rising up out of their midst in creative power was the important thing. It was not something Jesus did. It was something that happened when he was present like a catalytic agent" (*SHG*, 40). Thus, "the creative transformative power was not in the man Jesus, although it could not have occurred apart from him. Rather he was in it. It required many other things besides his own solitary self. It required the Hebrew heritage, the disciples with their peculiar capacity for this kind of responsiveness, and doubtless much else of which we have little knowledge. The creative power lay in the interaction taking place between these individuals" (*SHG*, 41). That Jesus was the Christ (i.e., the condition for asserting the christological predicate of Jesus) lies not in the man Jesus but in the possibility arising out of the specific history surrounding him of

[35] For a first-rate analysis of Wieman's christology in relation to the classical christological tradition, see Shaw (1981).

lifting the creative event into dominion in the lives of human beings. This is the sense in which God is revealed in Jesus:

Christ . . . is not merely the man Jesus. Christ is the domination by the creative event over the life of man in a fellowship made continuous in history . . . Through this domination Christ is the revelation of God to man, the forgiveness of sin extended to all men, and the salvation of the world. This historic consequence of events centering in the life of the man Jesus, *and not merely the deeds, teachings, and person of the man*, is the hope of the world and the gospel of Christ. God incarnate in these creative events, and not the human nature of the man, is the Christ revealing God, forgiving sin, and saving the world. (*SHG*, 269, my emphasis; see also p. 275)

The crucifixion was crucial for the release of this process. It broke the confines of the Hebrew heritage within which Jesus's impact on his original followers occurred. The background in Hebrew culture was important, for through it was established a "pattern . . . of recurrent catastrophe, with a prophet appearing in the midst of each breakdown, declaring that all created good is destroyed when not held subject to the will of God" (*SHG*, 270), but in Jesus's immediate context, it still had the form of Hebrew messianic expectations.

[B]efore the Resurrection, the disciples of Jesus were unable to undergo transformations of creative interchange beyond the bounds of their cultural heritage. What happened at the Resurrection was the breaking of these bounds, whence issued the 'power of the Resurrection' . . . When Jesus was crucified, his followers saw that he could never carry to fulfillment the mission of the Jewish people as they conceived it . . . They had thought that he would save the world by making supreme over human existence the good as seen in the perspective of Jewish culture. Now they saw that he never could do anything of the sort. He was not the messiah they had expected, and, so far as they could see, he was no messiah at all.

In the resurrection something happened to transform this situation.

The life-transforming creativity previously known only in fellowship with Jesus began again to work in the fellowship of the disciples. It was risen from the dead. Since they had never experienced it except in association with Jesus, it seemed to them that the man Jesus himself was actually present, walking and talking with them. Some thought they saw him and touched him in physical presence. But what rose from the dead was not the man Jesus; it was creative power. It was the living God that works in time. It was the Second Person of the Trinity. It was Christ the God, not Jesus the man. (*SHG*, 44)

Wieman does not make the revisionary mistake of rooting the constitutive christological assertion in Jesus's being, nor does he ground christological predicates in questionable historical references to Jesus's deeds, faith, or self-understanding. Rather, to combine Ogden's language with his, the christological predicates are warranted by God's offer of authentic self-understanding in "the domination by the creative event over the life of man in a fellowship made continuous in history" (*SHG*, 269). I now want to suggest two implications of this position that are significant for christological reflection.

The first concerns Wieman's conception of creative interchange. I have given reasons for preferring an existentialist account of creative transformation, but Wieman's version is particularly suggestive for christology. The reason is that his creative interchange locates the event of transformation in a personal structure of interaction. Both Wieman and I recognize that the creative event is operative throughout history; the transformative events are possibilities of existence as such. But in the history growing out of the Hebrew heritage and surrounding the formative events of Christianity, the "reversal in domination" signified by the deepest comprehension of God's transformative action took a form that could be "continuous in history." As Wieman says, "this lifting to domination [as it occurred in the events surrounding Jesus] could not . . . by itself alone, accomplish the salvation of man. It had to be perpetuated in history."[36] It is worth reflection, then, that it is precisely through the particular metaphors of personal interaction, both by reference to Jesus and in the kerygmatic "word" of proclamation, that this structure of reversal of domination became continuous in history.[37]

In this sense, Wieman's creative event as creative interchange can be important in establishing the *typological* significance of Christianity's basic motifs for the history of religions. Earlier I remarked that the normative argument for assessing the truth of the Christian valuational seeing-as requires recognizing that such a normative claim is itself constituted from within this valuational matrix as such. Wieman's understanding of the originating events of Christianity is precisely

---

[36] *SHG*, 42. See Ogden's remarks about a "transcendental" or "seeking" christology and one that "has found," *PC*, 83–84.

[37] See Robert Scharlemann's important remarks about the difference between auditory and visual metaphors for constituting the *form* of religious meaning. Scharlemann's remarks concern the significance of Luther's "theology of the word" in the formation of the basic Protestant outlook as opposed to the predominance of visual metaphors in scholastic theology (Scharlemann [1964], 1–27).

parallel to this claim. This point was earlier made concrete with the following arguments: (1) the very notion of God's grace as transformative event is reflexively formed within the overall valuational matrix, particularly the conception of the human problem defined as bondage to "life after the flesh"; and (2) the content of God's love is not merely the giftedness of life but the giftedness of life received as a gift, thereby justifying the notion of faith as readiness for transformation (its specific content being openness to the future). In its basic christological form, Christianity is decisively constituted by richly personal metaphors, and my suggestion now is that Wieman's notion of creative interchange offers a valuable avenue for comprehending its structure. This is true as regards the structure of the Christian witness itself, but it is particularly important for the way that Christianity's personal form supported the discovery of the deepest levels of personal being themselves within Western history.[38] In each of these respects, Wieman's notion of creative interchange is relevant to the normative valuational argument by which the Christian stance is assessed.

Though I shall not develop these personal motifs, it is relevant to mention the implications of this suggestion for conceiving God in personal terms. In the first chapter, I argued that the contemporary theological consensus assumes God's personal nature more or less uncritically. Wieman criticizes these references powerfully (*SHG*, 265–266). Yet he endorses a critically self-conscious symbolic attribution of personality to God based on his assertion that "the creative event at the level most important for human living always operates between persons" (*SHG*, 266).[39] It is natural, therefore, that "the religious man who commits himself in worship to the source of human good will most naturally think of this reality as an invisible, transcendental person who somehow pervades the universe," one "eternal in character, either in the sense of being 'beyond time' or in the sense of

---

[38] See Cobb (1967), 94–156, for an impressive analysis of how the structure of the Christian faith permitted the discovery of personal being as "spirit." A similar analysis, conceived in terms of the formation of Christian theology and culminating in the early councils and Augustine's theology of the Trinity, is Charles Norris Cochrane's great work *Christianity and Classical Culture*. Unfortunately, Cochrane seems to believe that these achievements were *necessarily* antinaturalistic, and this is false, however correct for an historical account of the development. For this reason, Cobb's more philosophically sophisticated (and philosophically neutral) account is to be preferred.

[39] Though operative between persons, creative interchange does not require their actual physical presence to one another, as such communication can occur through memory, both imaginative and historical and, in any case, is never immediate even with physical presence.

running through all time. But all this is mythical, wholesome and useful though it may be."[40] Thus, for Wieman, thinking about God in personal metaphors is a practical necessity of devotion, not a theological necessity. This practical necessity is grounded in his notion of creative interchange. This seems to me exactly the right position concerning personal attributions to God. Its power is made possible, as I noted in the first chapter, by his naturalist conception of God. I am now suggesting that such personal symbolic forms may have a theoretical dimension as well, if I am correct that the personal form of creative interchange is itself constitutive of the Christian valuational matrix within the history of religions.

The second suggestion also concerns the creative event becoming continuous in history, but now as regards transformation, not as regards its personal form. What the Christian witness of faith perpetuates in history is a structure of transformation. Since transformation, even in theistic forms and even as events of grace, is not exclusive to Christianity, the Christian structure must have a content that accounts for this perpetuation.[41] The formulas by which I have defined the internal structure of the Christian valuational matrix (and the formally similar ones of Ogden) define at least part of this content. These formulas, of course, by their very nature, make a normative claim about authentic existence and its authorizing source. In the present position, this normative content is not grounded metaphysically but indirectly by the normative claim of the valuational matrix which requires a defense of its normative status.[42] Difficult as this account is, I have made several suggestions both about the nature of the difficulty and about addressing it. I now want to suggest that this issue is clarified in christology precisely by the notion of transformation.

[40] *SHG*, 267. See Wieman (1949) for his first-rate criticism of some of these themes in Hartshorne.
[41] One way to view theology is as an attempt to comprehend this structure.
[42] The present position will likely be criticized for requiring such an additional argument to ground its symbolism. This position, however, is not really different from traditional theology. Biblical theologies (or theologies of revelation) simply ground the normative claims directly in the symbolism, but it is always appropriate to ask what constitutes this normativity, and such theologies often produce arguments answering such questions, if only implicitly, as, for instance, in Luther and Calvin. The more common approach is to ground the normativity in a metaphysical scheme, as in both the classical and the revisionary traditions (for instance, Aquinas and process thinkers). In such cases, the difficulties in assessment concern the difficulties in assessing total metaphysical schemes, as has been especially well documented by perspectival analysts such as Collingwood (1940), Hodges (1953), and Walsh (1963). I have simply moved the assessment question from metaphysics to a valuational matrix. The difficulties of assessment are formally similar to those confronted by the classical tradition of natural or rational theology.

In the present position, the constitutive christological assertion is grounded by events of grace. The condition for predicating "the Christ" is the structure of events of grace. I have argued that this structure is a transformation that is itself constantly transformative, continuously transcending itself as a transformation. For this reason I have said that "openness to the future" is based on faith as "readiness for transformation," and this is the meaning of my assertion that events of grace are the giftedness of life itself constantly received as a gift. If this structure now conditions christological predication, then it is a criterion of the normative adequacy of such predication.[43] In christology, the best suggestion along similar lines is John Cobb's theory regarding transformation in *Christ in a Pluralistic Age*.

Cobb bases his christology on analogies drawn from André Malraux's magisterial works on the history of art, *The Voices of Silence* and *The Metamorphosis of the Gods*. Malraux argues that the image of Christ has decisively influenced Western art, but the image of Christ has disappeared from this history in favor of a transcendence of all particularity in "artistic creativity as such through which the world of meaning is repeatedly transmuted by new forms" (*CPA*, 41). Malraux denies that this metamorphosis is a function of the Christ image, since he views it as hopelessly mired in particularity, and he sees the history of art as the transcendence of such particularity. Cobb disputes this, claiming rather that "as the figure disappeared there continued the creative transformation of styles for which the reality expressed by the figure had been responsible. Eventually this creative transformation itself was recognized as the specific value of art. . . [T]he power of creative transformation manifest especially in Western art is the continuation of the effects of Jesus in the Western experience" (*CPA*, 44).

Based on this analogy with art, Cobb claims that "Christ" names the power of creative transformation, not merely in art but in all

---

[43] This claim about the structure of transformation is similar to Tillich's Protestant Principle (Tillich [1948], 32–51, 162–176, 226–229 and Tillich [1967], III, 223–224). This principle reappears in his christology as the criterion of an adequate account of the "new being." Such an account must be one in which the christological symbols continuously negate themselves. Tillich finds this structure especially exemplified in Jesus's crucifixion and in his always pointing away from himself to his Father who authorizes him. Unfortunately, Tillich also claims that for the new being to become a real historical possibility, it must have been perfectly actualized in a particular historical life. Given Ogden's existentialist clarification of the conditions of the constitutive christological assertion, this element in Tillich's christology can now be judged mistaken; even on its own terms it is not particularly convincing (see Tillich, [1967], II, 123, 158–165).

domains of culture, including theology (see *CPA*, 41–61). This implies a normative claim for the specific images of christology just insofar as they contain the power to transform their own particularity toward processes of creative transformation. Yet such normative potential is crucially linked to those images themselves, even as they are transformed, thus accounting for what Wieman calls their capacity to perpetuate creative transformation historically. In this sense, "Christ" transcends all cultural values alone: "He is the not-yet-realized transforming the givenness of the past from a burden into a potentiality for new creation. Christ always means, regardless of what the cultural values are, that they must be relativized without being abrogated; that the believer lives toward the future rather than attempting to defend, repeat, or destroy the past; that each should be open to the neighbor, in whom also one meets the claim of Christ; and that the good in what is now happening is to be completed and fulfilled" (*CPA*, 59). Taking "the Christ" thus in terms of a self-transcending process of creative transformation permits analogies with the traditional Logos christology and with the theology of the incarnation. Christ is the Logos precisely as "the Christ" becomes increasingly incarnated in reality as a process of self-transcending creative transformation, even as that reality may be a secular one in which "Christ" is detached from the traditional values of "the sacred" (see *CPA*, 50–52, 62–94). "To name the Logos 'Christ' is to express and elicit trust. It is to promise that the unknown into which we are called is life rather than death. In short, it is to call for and make possible radical conversion from bondage to the past to openness to the future. This is to say that to name the Logos 'Christ' is to recognize that the cosmic Logos is love. . . We experience the Logos as demanding of us that we give up what we ourselves love, our security in our own achievements. It forces us to recognize that in fact these are not our own achievements at all but achievements of the Logos in which we have actively participated."[44]

There is no need to examine how Cobb develops this notion into a full christology of the incarnation, since his Whiteheadian ontology is

---

[44] *CPA*, 85. Cobb, of course, takes "the Logos" as a cosmic reality defined by Whitehead's conceptual scheme and thus as defined referentially by the subject-predicate grammar of "God exists," even if in revisionary form. Despite this deep difference, it is clear that his conception of Christ as creative transformation is fraught with significance for the position developed here.

far different from the present position.[45] Furthermore, there is the question whether the traditional doctrine of the incarnation need serve any longer for constructive christological statement at all – though it is significant that Wieman's and Cobb's notions of creative transformation permit such construction. Despite these differences, however, Cobb's insight into the historical dimensions of a self-transcending creative transformation is pregnant for christological reflection. It is particularly suggestive as a normative content for the Christian valuational matrix. It is thus directly relevant to normative valuational assessment of the Christian witness of faith. I have shown that one problem with this assessment is its potentially circular and question begging nature, a problem, however, which it shares with all competing candidates. The problem is that the valuational possibilities by which the normative claim is made are themselves constituted as possibilities by the valuational matrix itself. We can now see that this is exactly what is to be expected if creative transformation has the theological significance attributed to it by both Wieman and Cobb, and by the position defended here. But we can now also see that if such a valuational matrix is itself constituted by creative transformation, then the latter may provide its own self-transcending criteria for normative assessment. It also provides resources by which the Christian witness of faith may better understand itself.

---

[45] *Christ in a Pluralistic Age* is undermined by two serious problems. The first is that Cobb attempts a detailed correlation of the traditional Logos christology with Whiteheadian cosmology. Though his use of Whitehead (in contrast to Hartshorne) produces an empirical richness lacking in Ogden, this correlation also forces him into a whole series of metaphysical arguments which seem to me highly problematic and largely *ad hoc*. It also produces a relatively wooden matching of traditional with Whiteheadian concepts. But the really significant problem is that Cobb also tries to warrant his cosmological claims by quite specific accounts about the historical Jesus. In this sense, his position becomes a classic exercise in the problems Ogden has identified with revisionary christologies, for Cobb makes the strongest possible claims that the legitimacy of christological assertions depends on Jesus's perfect actualization of authentic existence and on the historical possibility of knowing so. For a detailed analysis of these latter problems, see Ogden (1976).

CHAPTER 7

The promise of faith

This last chapter deals broadly with issues of eschatology. It concerns questions of purpose and the conservation of value that were discussed in the first chapter, but it will include a broader set of issues. Eschatology, dealing with the "last" things, commonly supports the final terms pertaining to the possibility of meaningfulness in life and of hope, both personal and historical. It also includes the ideas by which faith witnesses to tragedy and the vicissitudes of life and is thus the basis for instructing the ministry in the care of souls. It is especially important for a naturalist Christian theology because theologians commonly dismiss the theological relevance of naturalism due to concerns about these issues.

I will address two topics. One concerns the assumption, frequent even among naturalists, that a naturalist conception of the world entails the absurdity of existence and the meaninglessness of life. We shall see that these assumptions are mistaken, at least for the type of naturalism defended here. By removing them we shall remove the grounds for many of the immediate responses with which theologians dismiss naturalism. The other topic concerns the actual content of faith in view of tragedy, hope, and, especially, death. Here we shall turn to the promise of faith, conceived naturalistically, and give special prominence to Ogden's important essay, "The Promise of Faith," from which, again, I gratefully take the title of this chapter. Ogden's essay is an especially trenchant examination of these issues – largely because he recognizes what theologians should not try to say about these matters.

NATURALISM AND THE ABSURDITY OF EXISTENCE

Naturalism deprives the world of both cosmic purpose and a conservation of value. Hence, it is commonly thought to entail the absurdity of things and the meaninglessness of human existence. This is especially true if purpose is conceived as grounded in intent, so that it can be comprehended only from a point of view. From another side, purpose is connected with the conservation of value, and it is thought that if our values perish with us, then our lives become insignificant and futile. From either side or both together, it seems to many that our lives must be driven by blind forces of matter in motion that are either "benign" or even "reptilian" but, nevertheless, indifferent to our ultimately irrelevant projects so that "on [us] and all [our] race" and upon all that we may hope and dream, ". . . slow, sure doom falls pitiless and dark."[1] Value and purpose, it has seemed, can only be defended anthropomorphically by some version of humanism that views value solely in reference to human projects. But given the reigning fact/value gap, which itself arises partially from the belief that value can have no purchase in nature, such conceptions of value and purpose have seemed arbitrary and parochial against the assumed background of cosmic indifference. How can anything really matter if matter does not?

In the modern period, the source of these convictions is surely the eviction of final causality or teleology from nature in the seventeenth century. This coincided with the rise of modern science and the beginnings of modern philosophy and is one of the most significant events in our intellectual history. The success of modern science without teleology has made philosophical defenses of it seem more and more labored and implausible and has left philosophy with no other task than simply to comprehend both the cosmos and human existence without it. It is no accident that some of the best contemporary theologians have recognized the theological significance of eliminating final causality and have sought ways to defend it again in its full cosmic scope and in the light of the best modern science.[2]

It is indeed no exaggeration to say that modern intellectual history as a whole is the story of the attempt to come to terms with the elimination of purpose from nature. Certainly this is the case with much of philosophy. It is even more striking in literature where the cultural consequences are more directly, and agonizingly, focused. In poets such as Blake and Goethe the rejection of teleology is assertively rejected, and romanticism as a whole may be understood as an effort

---

[1] Russell (in Klemke, ed. [1981]), 61; see Camus (1955); Santayana (1957), 22.
[2] See, for instance, Gilson (1984); Cobb (1983); Wiles (1982), 25–30.

to find a fresh way to affirm it. Its loss is agonizingly felt and appraised in many of the greatest nineteenth century novelists, such as Melville, Hardy, and Dostoevsky. Apart from an occasional thinker such as Camus or Bellow, in the twentieth century the agony about its loss is less commonly voiced; but that is because it is simply taken for granted, and much of the manic voice and experimentalism in post-modernist fiction is an ironic commentary on our situation in a world where purpose can no longer be affirmed because it cannot be found. Whatever the death of God means, it arises from the world viewed without teleology. This is surely the meaning of Nietzsche's proclamation of the death of God.

How can naturalism possibly avoid these conclusions? Do they not at last show how quixotic the present project is? Of course, anti-naturalist theologies themselves appear no less quixotic in the face of the naturalism so widely assumed in modern cultures. I want to argue, however, that a naturalist view of things is possible from which these conclusions are unnecessary. The place to begin is to recognize that assertions about the absurdity of existence or the meaninglessness of human life are by no means transparent. Disguised behind the uniformity of language about absurdity and meaninglessness is a variety of questions to which these assertions are answers. This multiplicity has been skillfully explored by any number of contemporary philosophers, as is evidenced by E. D. Klemke's collection *The Meaning of Life*. Concerned to anticipate some of the same objections as the present work, Post provides an excellent comprehensive account of this discussion, and I shall follow it closely in my own response. We shall see that the consequences commonly assumed to follow from naturalism are by no means obvious. Post analyzes seven ideas that have been taken to imply the absurdity of existence. These move from more abstract, comprehensive claims to more concrete ones. Also, the argument gradually develops, later levels of analysis building on earlier ones, until by the end a comprehensive response to the charge of absurdity and meaninglessness becomes possible.

(1) The absurdity of one's own existence is often taken to follow from the absurdity of the universe. If there is no reason, no explanation, for the universe's existence, it follows that its existence is absurd, and therefore our own as well. This conclusion follows, however, only if asking why the universe exists is intelligible as a question for which an explanation is possible (in Post's terms, an "explanation-seeking why-question" [*FE*, 318]). Only then would it

make sense to say that the universe has no "reason," so that it and our own existence are absurd. But, Post shows, a "why-question" with cognitive import assumes that an explanation is possible, even if it is not known or is unknowable, and he shows the universe is not the sort of thing to which an explanation-seeking why-question can apply (Post [1987], 75–106, esp. pp. 98ff.). This position is, of course, widely granted by theologians today (as a starting point for rethinking the doctrine of creation), as well as by philosophers and natural scientists who analyze the notion of "universe." If the universe is not the sort of thing for which we can ask an explanation, it cannot be absurd. Calling something absurd, irrational, or brute implies some standard of rationality. With ultimate explanations, such a standard has been the principle of sufficient reason, but Post shows that this standard is hopelessly flawed in cosmological matters (*FE*, 92–98), and he concludes that "to call something absurd, on the ground merely that it has no explanation, is to betray an erroneous or obsolete conception of rationality" (*FE*, 319). Thus, we cannot show that our lives are absurd because the universe has no explanation unless we establish independently that the universe is absurd, and this we cannot do.[3]

From the fact that there is no explanation for the universe, it does not follow that my existence has no reason, "neither in the sense that there is no explanation for my existence nor in the sense that my life has no point or purpose, hence no meaning" (*FE*, 319). Again, the presumption is that my explainer must itself have an explanation, and carried through to the end, this simply implies the discredited principle of sufficient reason again. Even if the universe has no explanation "something about the universe could still provide purpose and meaning" for my life (*FE*, 319). As we shall see in more detail in a moment, the determinacy of valuation is decisive here. We want the purposes that make our lives meaningful, such that we ought to adopt them, to be independent of our actual desires and decisions, to be discovered and not merely created by us, and this is exactly what the determinacy of valuation makes possible. Natural facts either about human or nonhuman nature would be sufficient for such

---

[3] Even if there were an explanation and it was absurd, it does not automatically follow that what an absurd explainer explains (namely, ourselves) is itself absurd. As Post notes, even without invoking the principle of sufficient reason, "it is doubtful that the relevant concepts of explanation entail that if x is explained by y, and y has no explanation, then after all x has none either" (*FE*, 319).

determinacy. In these senses, the universe lacking an explanation entails neither its absurdity nor our own.

(2) Because there is no personal God, or because purpose, intent, and responsiveness are not in the bedrock order of things, it is commonly assumed that nature is indifferent to us. Apparently this is threatening because, again, it is assumed that our values and purposes are not grounded in any reality apart from themselves. The values and purposes we have are arbitrary and do not overcome the ultimate meaninglessness of our lives. This is certainly the force of Camus's *The Myth of Sisyphus*. This work, however, assumes the unbridgeable gulf between fact and value. In fact, if the intellectual history of modernity is an attempt to come to terms with the elimination of teleology, much of the actual story has been told in terms of the consequences of the fact/value gap which is taken to follow from it. This is what led Max Weber, for instance, to his pessimistic appraisal of the modern future as "an iron box," and it lies behind Nietzsche's recommendation that we take the gulf resolutely upon ourselves and "transvalue values" through the will to power. "Reality is called absurd because it fails to satisfy the human demand that it provide a basis for human values" (*FE*, 320).

Just here the determinacy of valuation is strategic and shows that neither reality nor our lives are absurd, even if reality is identified with the totality of natural fact. Furthermore, let us note once again that such determinacy does not entail the deleterious reductionist consequences often assumed to follow if reality is just the totality of natural fact, for determinacy does not entail that value can be read off, defined by, or reduced to natural fact. Still it is this reality that can provide the basis for values that validate purposes "in the sense that the facts determine the truths about values. In this sense, reality is laden with value . . ., and so too therefore are lives lived in light of values thus determined" (*FE*, 320).

(3) Granting the determinacy of values which Post's physicalism makes possible, the values that lend our lives meaning are "something to be discovered, not a purely subjective matter," whether the facts are determined by facts about the nonhuman world or include facts about ourselves, our wants and needs. Physicalism is neutral about this question. The answer is a matter of empirical and valuational investigation in the relevant realms. If it should turn out that these facts include facts about ourselves, still *those* facts are physically determined, "for the facts allow one and only one distribution of

truth-values over our value judgments, first principles included, and what that distribution is is not something we may choose or create. If it were, then in view of the determinacy, it would follow . . . that we may choose or create what the distribution is over the purely descriptive judgments, which is absurd . . ." (*FE*, 320). Indeed, the approach I have taken to the normative status of a valuational theism suggests the likelihood that the values themselves will include facts about ourselves, including facts that are available only assuming a particular valuational matrix. In either case, whether with or without an account of our wants and needs (or our existential structure), Post's position shows that what is worthwhile can be physically grounded, so that value, purpose, and the meaningfulness of life can have all the metaphysical or ontological ground one could desire.

(4) It might be replied, however, that if our lives are made worthwhile for reasons provided solely by ourselves, those reasons cannot have the force of truth and therefore could not provide the meaning we require (see *FE*, 321). We have just seen that our reasons for living can have truth, even if the relevant facts are found in ourselves. "They have the force of truth in the sense that what they ought to be is determined by the facts, even though – if we assume that our purposes are found in ourselves – the determining facts must include some facts about our wants and needs" (or about our existential structure) (*FE*, 321). There are other senses in which our reasons for living might be thought to reside in ourselves. None of these, however, undercut the argument.

For instance, even if there is an objective reason why our lives are worthwhile, we must still commit ourselves to those values, and, as I have suggested, they may not even become the values they are until we make them our own. So, it might be said, "if we want our lives to be meaningful, we cannot discover the meaning; we must provide it" (*FE*, 321). The mistake, however, is in the last inference, the supposition that because we cannot discover the meaning except by committing ourselves to it (a typical existentialist ploy), such meaning could not have the force of truth. Because we must commit ourselves to worthwhile ends for them to be realized – or even because the value of some ends may not become evident until we commit ourselves, or become evident only through the process of living out such commitments – it does not follow that the ends themselves are not worthwhile independently of our commitment. One is a matter of the truth of our ends, the other a matter of committing ourselves to them. The latter may sometimes involve more than a simply moral or religious resolve, for states of depression often render a situation meaningless and place us in the "situation of seeing the truth but not acting. . . But *this* meaninglessness is a matter of our being unable to commit ourselves to anything, or being unable to make any purpose our own. It is not a matter of there being no such purposes to be discovered to which we may commit ourselves" (*FE*, 322, Post's emphasis).

This point is quite relevant to how a valuational theism will issue in a form of life. As Post says, "clearly, certain moods and emotions are better than others for enabling us to make various ends and values our own" (Post [1987], 322). Yet even passions and secondary qualities are determined by physical facts (though not reducible to them in the sense of type-identity, thus not to be read off them) (see *FE*, 308–317). Even passions can correspond to the facts in the sense that it can be true that we ought to have certain passions in certain situations. The physical determination relation, therefore, establishes a naturalist theological support for the kind of form of life ethics of character that Stanley Hauerwas has been so inventive in exploring. For example, a naturalistic valuational theism links directly with Hauerwas's arguments for a Christian's "reasons for living," out of which he develops an opposition to suicide and euthanasia. These practices are not opposed because they violate "the will of God" but because they violate the community of caring (and the formation of character) to which Christians are called by their commitment to "the Kingdom of God."[4] This kind of correspondence right down the line between a theological ethics of character, which Hauerwas develops out of very conservative, fideistic theological resources, and a naturalistic theism is extremely significant.

(5) The next two issues relate to the role often assigned to the conservation of value in theology. The first is the seeming futility of our lives if naturalism is true. A naturalist world is dominated by transience. It is nothing but an endless cycle of birth and death, ending finally with the ultimate chaos engendered by entropy. The image of Sisyphus captures this futility, for he was condemned to an endless toil whose end could never be attained. Sisyphus can be generalized because the attainment of his ends was made futile by a fact about the world, hence its seeming relevance to naturalism.

Some of our activities (such as care of the hopelessly retarded or the

---

[4] See Hauerwas (1977), 101–115.

terminally ill) seemingly partake of such characteristics. But what makes an activity futile is that its end cannot be achieved thanks to some fact about the world (see *FE*, 323). E. D. Joske observes that even Sisyphus "would have frustrated the Gods if he could have given worth to his eternal task,"[5] and as Post comments, "one sure way to do this is to replace the normally intended end of the activity with an end that *can* be achieved, such as the activity itself" (*FE*, 322–323, Post's emphasis). This is not as quixotic as it may at first appear. For one thing, it is the rational thing to do under the circumstances:[6] "treat the activity as an end in itself, to be embraced for its own sake or even regarded as just what we were put here to do" (*FE*, 323). But it may also be the morally or religiously correct thing to do, especially when other activities or suicide are an option. As Hauerwas argues, other persons may depend upon us to undertake such activities (and to avoid suicide), and this requirement upon us may be constituted by a form of life which has its own independent valuational grounds.[7] The reasons for such activities and for learning to rejoice in them for their own sake (as well as for the prohibition of suicide) may have nothing to do with the activities themselves, and grounded as they are in a full valuational matrix, such reasons may be exceptionally complex and even self-referential, as Hauerwas shows.

Richard Taylor is mistaken to maintain that overcoming futility in this fashion would render meaning subjective. Arguing somewhat analogously, he concludes that "existence . . . is objectively meaningless" because "the meaningfulness of life is from within us, it is not bestowed from without."[8] If there is the connection suggested above with a valuational matrix, there is still an objective ground, via the determinacy of value, for the judgment that we *ought* to embrace the Sisyphean activities as their own ends. Even the *rationality* of embracing an otherwise inescapable end for its own sake may be *morally* justified, if, as Hauerwas contends, a valuational matrix commits us to a form of life in which viewing our lives truthfully is itself a primary value.[9]

(6) Yet, the abyss of futility yawns in another sense because there is no conservation of value in a naturalistic world. Certainly there is no conservation of value in the sense of conserving the values achieved in subjectively experiencing them. It might seem, furthermore, that we

---

[5] Joske, "Philosophy and the Meaning of Life," in Klemke (1981), 260; quoted by Post, *FE*, 322.
[6] Post makes this observation contra Richard Taylor, "The Meaning of Life," in Klemke (1981), 144.   [7] Hauerwas (1977), 101–115.   [8] Taylor, in Klemke (1981), 144, 150.
[9] See Hauerwas (1981b), 117–120, 122–124, 126.

would not want all our activities to be their own end. Theologians often write as though meaningfulness rests on the hope that some of our activities will cast a shadow of significance over the future. For most persons, however, such hopes are doomed to frustration (except over exceptionally short cosmic epochs), and it is foolish to think that even the greatest achievements attained by a few will perdure *forever*.

This issue touches, of course, on the question of "perpetual perishing," and I shall deal with it again in the next section. For the present, consider it in connection with absurdity, futility, and meaninglessness. First, let us note that it is difficult to disengage ourselves from our subjective desires and fears long enough to determine whether there is a legitimate religious issue here at all and, if so, what it is. I have already argued that a valuational theism requires us to rethink the nature of religion. The same is true concerning the conservation of value. In his essay on the absurd, Thomas Nagel comments that it is hard to see why the significance of one's life in a million years makes it significant now, and if one's life is significant now, it is not evident how its not being so in a million years undermines its significance now.[10] It is also unclear to what extent our desire to have our lives "count" forever and against the backdrop of the entire cosmos does not simply mask Promethean fantasies. As Post says, "how human, and how banal, when ambition proves overweening, to blame something else – even the so-called absurdity of existence – rather than ourselves for absurdly Promethean intent."[11]

The objectivity of value grounded by physical determination of value provides an opening onto eternity in quite a fresh way, for objectivity is an invariant and thus has an eternal component (see *FE*, 67–70, 341). If physical truth determines the ends I ought to pursue, then they are objectively grounded, and it is *now* eternally true that I ought to pursue them and that they endow my life with meaning. And this is true even if the valuational matrix that makes these judgments true is itself historically conditioned, as it surely is, and not fated to endure forever. It is still true that under the conditions in which value is true for us now and under the conditions by which it is now possible for us to see its truth, those judgments are eternally true *now* – assuming, of course, that such a valuational matrix can be justified.

[10] Nagel (1983), 151.
[11] *FE*, 324. One should not discount, however, the religious significance of brief cosmic epochs. To live on in the memory and otherwise in the experience of others is no small thing, metaphysically or religiously (as grandparents and grandchildren experience). The hubris comes from thinking that this meaningfulness is undermined unless it lasts forever.

If this much is true, then it may not be so quixotic to affirm that our activities are their own ends when suitably viewed. This is precisely what an existentialist interpretation of the Christian valuational matrix shows. Against the backdrop of the human problem defined by bondage to sin, the end of life is events of grace: the love of God grounding an affirmation of the giftedness of life and issuing in a form of life and a seeing- (and experiencing-) as. Such a valuational matrix provides a proper support for how Christians, at least, *ought* to view their relation to the future. Rather than being preoccupied by Promethean fantasies to overcome perpetual perishing, their concern ought simply to be focused on trust in the love of God.[12] The shadow that Christians should seek to cast over the future is directed simply at concern for the neighbor and for posterity broadly construed (but narrowly focused by the Christian form of life on care for the next generation). The mandate is to do all that we can to assure for the next generation(s) the same giftedness of life that it has been our blessing to receive from the hands of God. Given the objectivity of value, this is sufficient eternity for anyone, I should think.

(7) Finally, let us return to the widest angle of vision and ask again about existence in the sense of the whole spatiotemporal universe. "If the universe is not the creation of God, or otherwise suitably related to something transcendent, isn't it absurd?" (*FE*, 324.) Even here, the conclusion does not follow, for, again, the determinacy of value makes it possible that "certain value terms are true of the universe – say, that it is beautiful, terrible, awesome, eerie, intriguing, astonishing, and more. The universe then would have meaning at least in the sense that it objectively has certain value properties" (*FE*, 324). It can also be true that it has meaning because "it is the appropriate object of certain emotions – not only, on occasion, of terror or awe but of acceptance and even reverence" (*FE*, 325). Values and meaning in both senses could not be read off any description of the universe, yet it could still be true that "the appropriateness could be non-reductively determined by the description" (*FE*, 325).

[12] Herein lies the truth in the theological point that Christian hope in the resurrection is distinguished from belief in immortality because the resurrection is not a natural condition but the gift of God. Unfortunately, as I commented earlier, this position is all too often asserted in such a way as to make no substantive difference at all about a hope for a survival of death. The radicality of faith as Christians ought to understand it is that their love of the love of God is not conditional on God saving their skins. The real test of Christian affirmation comes when we *stop* believing such things.

This line of argument even permits physicalism to attribute purpose to the universe. Take again Post's example of the solar marker at Chaco Canyon. Even if the slabs took their shape as a purely natural accident, they achieve the purpose of being a solar marker only if accorded that role by Anasazi culture. "In like manner, whether or not the universe is made, it can be accorded the role of, say, . . . the symbol and source of truth, beauty, and goodness," (*FE*, 325) as surely it is, and in no trivial way. Furthermore, Post convincingly argues that it is "the universe" that has most of the metaphysical attributes accorded to God, namely, "the eternal, immutable, uncreated, independent, self-existent, explanatorily First Cause of all that is" (*FE*, 325; see also pp. 131–158). For many persons, these points are enough to justify attributing a kind of Spinozistic divinity to the universe itself. Post shows that contemporary cosmology requires us to distinguish between "the manifest universe," as defined by the best contemporary physics, and "the universe beyond the universe" or simply "the Universe" (a boundary concept) (see *FE*, 117, 154–158). This distinction would then give the Spinozistic theist a notion of divine transcendence. In analogy with the solar marker, "we could treat the manifest universe as a kind of God-marker, representing our present best attempt to limn certain aspects of the Universe beyond the universe" (*FE*, 325).

This Spinozistic divinity is not Christian because Christianity has had sound reasons for not identifying God with the totality of things. In addition, a valuational theism such as I am proposing does not need to attribute the source of value to the whole of things, not least because of the difficulties this creates for the problem of evil. God as understood here is not the source of evil, not a small advantage over both classical and revisionary Christian theisms. What these last remarks do show, however, is that even in its widest perspective, naturalism does not entail the absurdity of existence. Naturalism does not require that we view ourselves as microscopic ants lost in the infinite indifference of dust, pursuing futile projects that mean nothing. The truth of that judgment is itself determined by natural fact, and if, from some perspectives and for certain purposes, it may be correct, "on other occasions it is completely inappropriate, as when it renders us incapable of making certain ends or purposes our own even though they are objectively worthwhile. Taking the measure of the measure of all things is no one-sided affair. The mood that comes over us when we view everything from afar does not always correspond with the facts, any more than does blinkered preoccupation with our petty aims" (*FE*, 326).

DEATH AND THE PROMISE OF FAITH

We see that a naturalistic view of things need not conclude that the world is absurd, offering no ground for human meaning and purpose. Let us now turn to the positive theological issues themselves. Taking the traditional theological virtues of faith, love, and hope, we have seen a naturalist Christian theology give a surprising account of faith and love (including the love of God which is love's basis). Our concern now is hope, the promise of faith. Surely this is where a naturalist theology must fail. Because it denies the conservation of value, it will be said, naturalism can provide no grounds for the articles of faith on death and "last things." Even here, however, the outlook is not nearly so bleak, not least because theologians themselves are by no means clear about the traditional eschatological symbols.

I begin by anticipating a likely criticism. This naturalist conception of faith and God's love, it will be said, is only for the fortunate of the world. Openness to the future, the giftedness of life, may be fine for those so blessed by the general conditions of life that they are enabled to embrace them – those, let us suppose, who enjoy the benefits of middle class life in a male-dominated American culture. But openness to the future and the giftedness of life inadequately capture the "good news" of the gospel for those made less fortunate by natural endowment or circumstance, those who must endure tragedy, loss, and unmitigated suffering, or most especially, those weary, toil-laden masses who comprise the vast majority of humankind and who are given to live out their lives with scarcely any expectation of relief from almost unthinkable poverty and oppression. For these, openness to the future and the giftedness of life are scarcely relevant, if not a kind of cruel joke on their condition.

Such a criticism may have some relevance to Wieman's notion of creative interchange, providing another reason why I have preferred to interpret his position existentially. Yet, even it would ignore Wieman's account of the creative event's absolute goodness as he understood it to be localized in creative interchange, and it would ignore his systematic efforts to show that the creative event is by no means identical with happiness or good fortune. Wieman is not in the least sentimental about tragedy or evil in the human condition.[13] His position, however narrowly focused on events of interpersonal communication, entails no rose-tinted view of faith or of those to whom it is available.

Neither does the position defended here. The existentialist interpretation of faith is based on an existentialist analysis of human existence as such, of what it is like to be human at all. Its normative claim about authentic existence applies to existence as such, not merely to some human beings who are ontically fortunate enough to exist under favorable conditions. The question of authentic existence, as indeed also the promise and the demand of the gospel, address all human beings in the condition of their existence, however they may find themselves in the conditions of life. If authentic existence involves the promise and demand understood by the Christian witness of faith, then the giftedness of life received as a gift and openness to the future under the demand of love for all God's creation is as relevant to those who suffer from tragedy, oppression, and restricted life as it is for those who suffer under the different existential burdens of good fortune. One would, perhaps, like to say that they are even more relevant for the suffering and oppressed, but Christian theology has always recognized that idolatrous worship is a temptation for all human beings, irrespective of their conditions of life. Ultimately, the giftedness of life and openness to the future have nothing to do with natural endowments or circumstances of life. As the witness of faith has always recognized, it may indeed be more difficult for those made fortunate by either – though Christianity has too often made this point serve ideological purposes that undercut the claims of justice. If the naturalist conception of faith is found wanting, it must be on other grounds than these.

There is another dimension to this criticism that must also be addressed, as it touches more directly on eschatological issues. There is a general consensus among theologians today that no change in all of Christian history is more significant than the relatively recent one in which the traditional otherworldly bias in Christianity has been overcome by an orientation toward life as presently lived in this world. It is not too much to say that such an orientation, including the demand for justice, has become a criterion by which the adequacy of any contemporary theology is to be measured. On the other hand, the traditional eschatological symbols of faith were mainly articulated

[13] See, for instance, *SHG*, 48–52, 60–65, 84–104, 121–123.

from within the otherworldly bias. That is one reason why they have become so unbelievable today.

But now, under the aegis of this criterion, let us note that descriptively the conditions of life for all human beings appear exactly the same, whether viewed from a naturalist standpoint or some other. Tragedy, misfortune, grief, death, oppression, but also the promise of faith with its eschatological symbols – all of these are experienced by human beings in exactly the same way, in exactly the same world, under exactly the same conditions of life, whether one is a naturalist or not. If theology today must in fact accept the criterion of relevance to life lived in this world, then candor requires the theologian to comprehend the promise of faith so that it makes a difference precisely in these worldly conditions of life. The time for escape hatches in a world beyond is long since passed. Theologians may continue to articulate a transcendent or eternal content for eschatological symbols, if that is still possible or relevant. But any such meaning must be much more closely wedded to the meaning of the only lives we are given to live than was the case traditionally. The time is passed when the meaningfulness of this life (or even its meaninglessness) could be justified by a meaning which could only be *realized* in a "beyond" beyond death, and this criterion applies as much to notions of some sort of "final" consummation of history as it does to ontological transcendence.

As we turn to the promise of faith itself, we shall see the relevance of both of these points. Their relevance follows from the existentialist approach to faith. The conception of faith as an existential self-understanding mandates that theological assertions be interpreted exhaustively in terms of the existential self-understanding they express. In order to make this case regarding the meaning of eschatological symbolism, I shall draw heavily on Ogden's essay, "The Promise of Faith," where he articulates the significance of existentialist interpretation for eschatological issues more effectively than any other contemporary theologian. Because I differ with Ogden's conclusions, I shall divide the presentation into two parts, one dealing with his clarification of the existential issues involved and the second with his own position. My interpretation of the eschatological symbols will develop as a response to his position.

In the first chapter, I suggested that at no other point is contemporary theology more lacking in clarity and candor than in its pronouncements about "last things." Ogden also makes this judgment (*RG*, 206–207), identifying two sources for the difficulty. One is that we simply have no basis in experience or knowledge for pronouncements about "the final destiny of man or the ultimate meaning of the natural-historical process" (*RG*, 207; see 207–208). More important, the modern outlook is so fundamentally defined by the scientific view of the world that the "mythological elements in the church's traditional eschatology have lost all clear meaning. . . Even the ordinary man in the street increasingly finds it hard to look forward to the imminent or eventual end of the world, with Christ's returning on the clouds to consign men to a final destiny in some transhistorical heaven or hell" (*RG*, 208).

The key to both of these problems, however, is the existentialist conception of faith and the understanding of theology it implies. According to that conception, "the one and only theme of all theological thinking and speaking is the theme of faith," from which it follows that theology has no other task than "to set forth the understanding of existence – of ourselves, our fellow creatures, and the God whose love embraces us all – which faith itself involves or implies" (*RG*, 209). If, then, eschatological symbols belong to faith, their point must lie solely in the existential self-understanding of faith. This, however, addresses, at least implicitly, the two difficulties mentioned above: that eschatology transcends any possible experience or knowledge and conflicts with a scientific picture of the world.

These difficulties are overcome because an existentialist account restricts us simply to the self-understanding of faith *now*. Whatever knowledge faith contains, whether of God or of anything else, resides in an existential self-understanding, which, let us remember, is a way of existing that can only be actualized in each present moment. In this respect, eschatology poses problems that are no different in principle from any other theological topic (*RG*, 209–210). This means that

the last things can never be properly understood as things that have a certain future place, proximate or remote, on the time-line of the individual's personal destiny or of the natural-historical process as a whole. Being really and truly *last* things, that is, *ultimate* things, things constituting the most essential reality of *all* places on the time-line, they are always and only matters of the present – though, of course, of every present. . . Hence, from the standpoint of Christian faith itself, none of the traditional eschatological symbols may be thought to refer to things or events in principle beyond our present experience and knowledge. This is because their real reference is always to the abiding structure and meaning of our actual existence here and now, which faith presently understands. (*RG*, 210, Ogden's emphasis)

This also removes the second difficulty, for these symbols are mythological in nature, not a disguised or inadequate kind of scientific speaking. Their meaning is to express an understanding of existence. Their very nature precludes any conflict with scientific claims about the world or with a view of the world based on such claims (see *RG*, 210–211).

Ogden recognizes that some such understanding of faith as this is widely accepted among contemporary theologians, but its full implications for eschatology are often not appreciated. He illustrates this conceptual haziness by a discussion of what might be considered its two extremes, one represented by John A. T. Robinson's *In the End, God . . .: A Study of the Christian Doctrine of the Last Things*, the other by a one-sided existentializing of the eschatological symbols.

Robinson's position is the more representative. Such positions agree, one, that eschatological symbols (and also those about creation) are mythological and, two, that their validity concerns the knowledge of God given with faith here and now. Yet, Robinson claims that such mythological expressions "are necessary transpositions into the key of the hereafter of sure knowledge of God and His relation to men given in the revelatory encounter of present historical event."[14] In effect Robinson still regards the content of creation and eschatology to deal with realities of the past or the future. This becomes apparent, Ogden shows, because "he repeatedly speaks, without the least sign of regarding such phrases as only mythical, of 'the final state of history,' 'the last time,' 'a supervening state of fruition,' 'the chronological moment of the end,' 'the climax of the world-process,' and 'the moment of consummation,' commenting in connection with the latter, 'Whether it takes a thousand years or one day is all the same to God'" (*RG*, 212).[15] In other words, though Robinson acknowledges that all theological symbols are based on a present knowledge of God given with faith, he apparently believes that this knowledge warrants claims about past and future events, and this leads simply to mystification.

The doctrine of creation has had a longer and more intense involvement with the scientific picture of the world than the eschatological symbols. It is now widely recognized that symbols of creation are mythological and serve existentially to express the sovereignty of

[14] John A. T. Robinson (1950), 35; quoted by *RG*, 211.
[15] See Robinson (1950), 36, 37, 44, 50, 69, 49.

God. What such sovereignty itself means is, of course, also an issue. The present position will not quite want to say with Ogden that the creation myth intends to assert "the sole sovereignty of God *as the ground and end of whatever is or is even possible*" (*RG*, 213, my emphasis), unless we first transpose this into valuational language. We shall examine such a transposition in a moment. But we can agree entirely with him that the "sovereignty of God" existentially illumines "the essential structure and meaning of our life in the present, and does not refer to some more or less remote event in the past" (*RG*, 214). The same should also apply to mythological symbols about the end. They too should be confessions of the sovereignty of God over all of life, including its end. In neither case are we speaking of events that stand apart from faith, either in the past or the future. Otherwise, we are in the untenable position of maintaining that *faith* somehow includes or warrants claims about a first and a last event in the cosmic process. Faith rather affirms something about "the essential constitution of *every present moment* in and under God's sovereign love," and only in this sense something about the past or the future (*RG*, 214, Ogden's emphasis).[16] We see, then, that Ogden's existentialist methodology brings the same clarification to issues of eschatology that we earlier witnessed with christology. The tendency in contemporary theology is to identify the existential issue but then to leave everything fundamentally unchanged, thus begging the question concerning events external to faith itself about which theology has no business declaiming. Such confusions are the products of a failure to fully demythologize the mythological symbols.[17]

The opposite extreme would be to existentialize the eschatological symbols entirely, especially the resurrection. Since this position seems to resemble the present one, Ogden's analysis helps to bring into focus

---

[16] Ogden identifies the issue here with beautiful precision by drawing an analogy between redemption and Aquinas's position on the doctrine of creation: "It does not belong to the idea of redemption that the world have an end of duration, but only an end of ultimate significance" (*RG*, 214). Aquinas's point, quoted by Ogden, is: "It belongs to the idea of eternity to have no principle of duration; but it does not belong to the idea of creation to have a principle of duration, but only a principle of origin – unless creation be accepted as it is accepted by faith" (see Aquinas, 82; *RG*, 213). The last qualification articulates Aquinas's belief that biblical exegesis requires faith to affirm a beginning of creation in time (that creation does have a "principle of duration" even though the concept does not require it), but this exegesis is now generally discredited.

[17] Other examples of this difficulty with eschatological symbols are to be found in the closing chapters of Gilkey (1976) and throughout Küng (1985). More broadly, John Macquarrie's otherwise exemplary expositions of Bultmann's theology (see Macquarrie [1955] and Macquarrie [1960]) also suffer from this problem.

exactly what a naturalist theology claims.[18] An existentialist conception of resurrection is justified because "life" and "death" have figurative meanings in much New Testament usage, as is now well recognized by New Testament scholars. Resurrection or "being raised up" simply re-presents the possibility of authentic self-understanding: that one realizes "the existential knowledge of God and of self and others in God which is made concretely possible by the witness of faith" (*RG*, 215). "Death" then is coextensive with "sin": an inauthentic, distorted knowledge of God. The inauthentic person is alive in the sense of having subjective participation in being, but "because he participates fully neither in God nor in himself and his fellows, he does not enjoy the fullness of subjectivity that is actually possible for him and is literally not what he might be" (*RG*, 216). A change, therefore, from inauthentic to authentic existence, is a change in the orientation of one's existence, and thus a change in one's subjective participation in being that may fittingly be described as a change from death to life, or as becoming "a new creation" (II Cor. 5:17; Gal. 6:15). Paul understands resurrection in this way, for instance, when he claims that Jesus's resurrection is also ours because, by allowing ourselves to be crucified with him and surrendering our old understanding of ourselves, we become "alive to God in Christ Jesus" (Rom. 6:11). Paul confirms the existential content of this new life with his notion of "life in the Spirit." Instead of appealing to mythological or supernatural conditions, he speaks simply of "keeping the commandments of God" (I Cor. 7:19) or "faith working through love" (Gal. 5:6).

Ogden emphasizes correctly that this approach to the resurrection captures only one of the New Testament motives. A fully existentialist interpretation may suggest that "resurrection" is *nothing more* than a

---

[18] Ogden cites such an extreme position as a misunderstanding of Bultmann, but he gives only van Buren as an example of someone actually *defending* it (though he recognizes that van Buren is no Bultmannian), and I know of no other examples, unless it is the present one. We shall see in a moment that the complete existentializing of resurrection (and other eschatological symbols) I shall defend does not fall prey to the existentialist one-sidedness Ogden criticizes. The reason is that events of grace permit a strong version of "God exists" and thus locate the ground of "resurrection" in God, not in ourselves or our attitudes, though they do this only by transforming the issues valuationally. The position Ogden describes might be thought to be that of Herbert Braun or Fritz Buri, though I know nowhere that either of them have actually developed it. Nevertheless, it might be taken to be implicit in Buri's contribution to the demythologizing debate (see, e.g., Buri [1952]). Ogden's characterization represents a fair statement of a position often taken to be implicit in Bultmann, and thus one stated mainly by his critics. As far as I am aware, then, Ogden's own description is actually the best statement of the position, and it certainly does represent one theological possibility that is present in the debate over demythologizing.

possibility of self-understanding, in the sense that it symbolizes the decision of faith and nothing more. The problem is that as much as "resurrection" *does* have this meaning, the decision of faith which it re-presents is also an act of God, as I have especially emphasized. It thus also re-presents a divine actuality and not merely a human possibility (see *RG*, 216). This becomes clear in the New Testament conception of Jesus as the risen Lord. According to Bultmann, "the cross and the resurrection are a unity as 'cosmic occurrence'. . ."[19] Neither the cross nor the resurrection are treated as independent historical events, and Jesus is never proclaimed as the crucified apart from also being proclaimed as the risen and exalted Lord. Bultmann expresses this unity by the formula that "faith in the resurrection is nothing other than faith in the cross as the salvation event, as the cross of Christ" (NTM, 39 [ET, 46]). This means that in confessing Jesus as the risen Lord, the early church *was* using "resurrection" to express an existential possibility. But this possibility is neither created nor explained simply by the decision of faith. For the decision of faith today, "just as for the first disciples, the historical event of the emergence of the Easter faith *signifies the self-attestation of the risen one, the act of God in which the salvation occurrence of the cross is completed*" (NTM, 47 [ET, 40], my emphasis). This stress on *God's action in the resurrection* has, of course, always been the traditional interpretation. The problem is that the tradition treats the resurrection, thus God's action, mythologically as an independent historical event of the past, thereby, among other things, effectively detaching it from its unity with the cross. Nevertheless, an adequate existentialist interpretation of "resurrection" must also capture this other dimension of the New Testament witness. The danger in any existentialist interpretation is either that it will so emphasize the existential character of "resurrection" that it misses the "self-attestation of the risen Lord" in it or, not missing it, will remythologize "resurrection" and God's action as an event independent of the decision of faith.[20]

The strength of Ogden's position is to capture both of these

---

[19] NTM, ET, 36 (44). Bultmann's argument about "cross" and "resurrection" at the end of the programmatic essay is extremely complex. A brief analysis suffices, however, for my argument here. For an excellent critical analysis, see *CM*, 78–90.

[20] This latter mistake is all too common among some defenders of Bultmann who still want to hang on to "resurrection" as some kind of independent, and therefore, objective miracle. See for instance, Macquarrie (1955), 185–187; Macquarrie (1960), 86, 89–95, and Oden (1964), 84–85. For one of the best treatments of the resurrection in the contemporary literature, see Scuka (1989).

dimensions, holding fast to an existentialist conception of faith, yet also insisting that this existential possibility is a response, not its own condition and ground. As he says, speaking of the resurrection:

God first raises us up, first makes us the objects of his limitless love, and only then do we have the possibility of participating in that "new creation" which his love ever and again makes possible for us and all our fellows. In a word, before resurrection is *our* decision, it is *God's* decision; and our faith does not create the risen life, but simply accepts it as already created by God through Christ and participates in it. (*RG*, 219, Ogden's emphasis)

The present position shares this strength (especially with the argument about God's action in chapter four). Though developed along valuational, not ontological, lines, events of grace, God's gracious action, ground the existential possibility of openness to the future, now understood as the reality of the "resurrection." Faith is a response to a possibility it does not simply create. For just this reason, I argued that openness to the future may equally well be conceived as readiness for transformation. The "resurrection" is an event, but not apart from the existential reality of faith. Precisely because it is a transformative event, God's reality and the knowledge of God given in the event cannot be captured separately from the transformative quality of the event. Because they are transformative, events of grace are actualities. We can agree with Ogden, therefore, that before "resurrection" is a human possibility, "it also refers, and, indeed, primarily, to a *divine actuality*" (*RG*, 216, Ogden's emphasis). In the present position, it is an actuality that can only be captured through the existential possibility which actualizes it; it is, hence, a transformative moment that continually recedes behind itself into another transformative moment.

Ogden develops his constructive position against the background of these misunderstandings. By the promise of faith, he means "the promise immediately implied in the witness of faith of Jesus Christ that we are all, each and every creature of us, embraced everlastingly by the boundless love of God" (*RG*, 220). The classical philosophical presuppositions which have dominated theology until recently make it impossible to articulate this promise. Because classical metaphysics believed perfect being excluded real internal relations to other beings, God's eternal nature could not be conceived to involve temporal structure, and this prevented theology from demythologizing the mythological symbols having to do with God's action in relation to the world. Traditional theology had no alternative but to conceive creation and eschatology as referring to supernatural events in the past or the future, "of which neither metaphysics nor, as we now realize, science enables us to form the least clear conception" (*RG*, 221). Even more fatefully, it also could not clearly state how "it is *God himself* who is the only final end, even as he is also the only primal beginning, both of man and of the world" (*RG*, 221), and therefore it could "give no clear meaning at all to the New Testament's own vision of that 'restoration of all things' (Acts 3:21) in which God himself is 'all in all' (1 Cor. 15:28)" (*RG*, 222).

Ogden believes that Hartshorne's dipolar theism now makes it possible to articulate the promise of faith adequately. Generally stated, this position is that "just as the myth and doctrine of creation affirm primarily that the one essential *cause* of each moment is God's boundless love for it, so the first intention of the myths explicated by eschatology is to re-present that same love as each moment's one essential *effect*" (*RG*, 214; Ogden's emphasis). For Hartshorne "being affected by the actions of others" is a completely general concept that admits of an eminent case, not the merely negative idea of classical metaphysics that can refer solely to the imperfection of nondivine beings. God's being may, therefore, be described as the perfect instance of *affecting* as well as of *being affected by* all things, and this means that "now we can make clear in terms of fundamental philosophical concepts why the reality of God's pure unbounded love is itself the whole substance of the promise of faith. The reason, quite simply, is that, in making each of us the object of his boundless love, God accepts us all into his own everlasting life and thereby overcomes both our death and our sin" (*RG*, 223).

The "death" to which Ogden refers here is not in the first instance the spiritual death of inauthentic existence. He gives "death" two fundamentally ontological (not existential) meanings. Indirectly these can lead to "death" in the spiritual sense, but they can be overcome only by God's everlasting life itself. Overcoming "death" in these fundamental (or ontological) senses is thus the foundation for overcoming the threat of "death" in the spiritual (or existential) sense. The first meaning is simply "that final termination or cessation of our subjective participation in being which one day overtakes each of us and of which we are each always aware" (*RG*, 223). Even as "death" in this sense may define our "care" in every present moment, it is still something out ahead of us. A second, more important sense is the "death" that takes place even now as the transience, the "perpetual perishing," of every moment of experience:

No sooner has the present moment of our participation in being achieved its satisfaction than it slips away from us into the past, whence our poor powers of memory and appreciation are unable to recall it into living immediacy. Nothing happens but it directly falls subject to this ineluctable passing away. All our thoughts and feelings, loves and hates, joys and sorrows, projects and causes are relentlessly carried away from us into the past, where, as they more and more recede from our present, they become all but indistinguishable from nothing. (*RG*, 224)

For Ogden, "death" in this second sense raises far the more serious existential problem. "Objective influence" theories of immortality are inadequate not only because posterity is as vulnerable to annihilation as we are but especially because its memory "is not even remotely able to do justice to what we have been in all its concrete richness" (*RG*, 225). Even "subjective immortality" could not address it since the immediacy (what it is like to be) of even an everlasting subjective experience would still be exposed to perpetual perishing. "What profit would it be for us to go on and on living – even to eternity – if the net result of all our having lived were simply nothing; if our successive presents in no way added up to a cumulative accomplishment such as no creature is able to provide either for himself or for his fellows" (*RG*, 225).

The process notion of God's consequent nature provides a solution to the problem of death in each of these senses, according to Ogden. Within his consequent nature, God is fully responsive to every moment of temporal passage and takes it up into his everlasting memory.

Because God's love, radically unlike ours, is pure and unbounded, and because he, therefore, both can and does participate fully in the being of all his creatures, the present moment for him never slips into the past as it does for us. Instead, every moment retains its vividness and intensity forever within his completely perfect love and judgment. He knows all things for just what they are, and he continues to know and cherish them throughout the endless ages of the future in all the richness of their actual being. (*RG*, 226)

This is a type of objective immortality, but it is grounded not in ourselves but in the very being of God's perfect responsiveness. At the same time, it accords with the existentialist understanding of faith, for what the Christian knows *in faith* about the future is nothing other than what is known about the present, and this is simply "the promise of victory over death. Faith knows that the final end or, as it were, the ultimate posterity of the whole creation is none other than God himself, who through his free decision in each moment to accept all things into his life overcomes the 'perpetual perishing' of death and all its terrors" (*RG*, 226).

The same solution offers the promise of a final victory over sin, where "sin" simply means the spiritual death of inauthentic existence. Because God's love is without limit, "faith knows that not even man's sin can set a limit to God's free decision in each new present to love his creatures and to give them to share in his own divine life" (*RG*, 226). The solution to the problem of sin must be more nuanced, however, since sin involves human freedom and responsibility. It also permits Ogden to articulate a position on the traditional questions of "universalism" and "double destination." At issue is the fact that human beings can refuse God's acceptance; God's love has the "strange weakness" of love that can never compel acknowledgment. Nevertheless, though we can decide whether to open ourselves to God's love, we cannot decide whether to be loved by God. Yet, precisely because our own freedom of response is involved, the prior reality of God's love cannot be taken to imply a "'universalism' which refuses to give any weight at all to man's decisions" (*RG*, 227).

This position suggests a meaning both for "hell" and for God's "judgment." "What we are, and so what we shall be forever in the final judgment of God's love, is just what we ourselves decide in the present through our responsible freedom. If we choose to open ourselves to God in faith and in love for him and all those whom he loves, then this is who we are, and this is who we will be known to be eternally in God's wholly righteous judgment. If, on the other hand, we shut ourselves off from God and our fellows and live the cramped, self-centered, and anxious life of the old Adam, then this, too, is who we are and who God, in consequence, will judge us to be even to the farthest reaches of eternity" (*RG*, 227–228). "Hell," then, is to be judged and known by God *forever* as one who, in refusing God's love, has lived one's subjective participation in being in the mode of inauthentic existence. On the other hand, and as the opposite of "universalism," theories of "double destination" accord more weight to human freedom than it deserves.

Although I may indeed decide to live without *faith* in God's love, I cannot live at all without the *reality* of his love. God as he is known to us in Christ creates all things for himself and takes all things into himself quite apart from any creaturely dispositions whatever. Therefore, even hell, even the anxious closure against God and one's fellows, cannot lie outside God's encompassing love. (*RG*, 228)

This presentation of the promise of faith is extremely impressive. Ogden's resolution of eschatological issues shows why most discussions are so unsatisfactory, even quasi-existentialist ones, and his own constructive position remains tightly faithful to the model of existentialist interpretation. What faith knows in the promise of faith is not information about future events, but exactly what it knows in its concrete actuality here and now. God's victory over sin and death follows directly from the presence of God's love to an existential self-understanding. My own position agrees entirely with Ogden's analysis of the existential content of eschatological categories. Nevertheless, his position is vulnerable to three damaging criticisms. These will provide a starting point for my own position on the promise of faith.

The first issue concerns perpetual perishing. Essential to Ogden's argument is that the disappearance of every immediate present into the past is overcome in the life of God: "Because God's love radically unlike ours, is pure and unbounded, and because he, therefore, both can and does participate fully in the being of all his creatures, the present moment for him never slips into the past as it does for us. Instead, every moment retains its vividness and intensity forever within his completely perfect love and judgment" (*RG*, 226). The problem is that this claim does not seem philosophically tenable on Ogden's own terms. Robert Neville has argued that according to the process conception of concrescence, the full subjective immediacy of actualized subjective aims are entirely private and unavailable even to the perfect knowledge of God. This subjective immediacy is what constitutes, in Ogden's language, our most intimate subjective participation in being, and it is the source of the terror about perpetual perishing, but this immediacy is lost upon the completion of a concrescence's subjective satisfaction. What is available for any apperception (including God's), and only what is available, is the objective presentation of the concrescence's achieved end, but this lacks subjective immediacy. This objective presentation is not subjective life *as experienced* but only the objective precipitate of subjective attainment, now presented as data for new concrescences, but in itself dead to subjective life.[21]

[21] See Neville (1980), 83–85, 90–91, 94–97.

True, there is a difference between ourselves and God. The subjective attainments in our experience gradually perish for us as their "causal efficacy" recedes into the past and is absorbed into wider and wider contexts of relevance. They are "objectively immortal," but they are lost to us, or, at least, their relevance for our subjective advance into the future become ever dimmer, and this is all the more true as they are inherited as data from one generation to another. This does not happen for God. God's perfect knowledge preserves their precise relevance forever. But what is so retained in God is their causal efficacy *as objective data*, not their actual subjective, experiential immediacy. If this is true, then one of the major criteria for Ogden's solution to our deepest existential terror is simply unavailable. Regarding our subjective participation in being, perpetual perishing holds, even on his terms.

A second problem concerns the change from a "categorial" to a "transcendental" metaphysics that Ogden introduces in *The Point of Christology*. We saw that rejecting analogy now compels Ogden to qualify Hartshorne's panpsychism. But "The Promise of Faith" seems crucially dependent on God's *consciousness*,[22] and this notion seems necessarily analogical, thus not available for his revised metaphysical position. In the former work, Ogden justifies the *symbolic* attribution of love to God because he claims that a dipolar conception of ultimate metaphysical categories makes possible the absolutely general characterization of ultimate reality as individual and relational, and this permits speaking *symbolically* of the meaning of ultimate reality for us in terms of God's love (see *PC*, 146–147). It is not at all clear that the same type of argument could work for a divine consciousness. Any symbolization of its meaning for us would have to be grounded in just that notion of consciousness. *That* notion could not itself be symbolic but would have to be either literal or analogical,

---

[22] Ogden criticizes Robinson for thinking that faith requires claims about the final stage of the cosmic process. Not only does faith not require them, but "certainly science can offer no support for them, since judgment on this type of claims lies outside the jurisdiction of a scientific mode of verification. But hardly less certain is that metaphysics also could never verify them. What could possibly be meant by a last (or first) moment of time? Does not the very meaning of "moment' require that the referent of the term anticipate its objectification in some subsequent moments (or remember some precedent moments which it itself presently objectifies)? And can one coherently conceive even a divine or necessary consciousness which would not necessarily have *some* contingent objects?" (*RG*, 214, Ogden's emphasis.) This is the sole mention of "divine consciousness" in this essay, but the whole apparatus of "memory," "awareness," "vividness," and "knowledge" in this essay would seem crucially dependent on some strong analogical sense of a "divine consciousness." For a powerful critique of this notion in Hartshorne, see Wieman (1949).

and neither of these options is now available for Ogden. Ogden's comments about the theological implications of a transcendental metaphysics are fragmentary in *The Point of Christology*, so we must simply wait for their fuller development. But it would at least seem that now a major revision of his position on eschatological symbols is required and that nothing like the solution proposed in "The Promise of Faith" is any longer available to him.

The final problem is strictly religious and, in my opinion, is the most damaging. It concerns whether Ogden's solution is a solution at all on the terms he proposes. His proposal hinges on the connection between God's boundless love and God's acceptance of all that we are and have been in his everlasting memory. That connection makes it possible for God to overcome both "death" and "sin." This is done because we are accepted into God's life by his pure unbounded love, "for whom each of us makes a difference *exactly commensurate to what he is and of everlasting significance*" (*RG*, 226, my emphasis).

What we are, and *so what we shall be forever in the final judgment of God's love*, is just what we ourselves decide in the present through our responsible freedom. If we choose to open ourselves to God in faith and in love for him and all those whom he loves, then this is who we are, and this is who we will be known to be eternally in God's wholly righteous judgment. If, on the other hand, we shut ourselves off from God and our fellows and live the cramped, self centered, and anxious life of the old Adam, then this, too, is who we are and *who God, in consequence, will judge us to be even to the farthest reaches of eternity*. (*RG*, 227–228, my emphasis)

Again, "for faith, the final truth is genuinely dialectical or paradoxical: God loves *all things* exactly as they are without condition; and yet God loves all things *exactly as they are*, and thus by his judgment of them provides their one definitive measure" (*RG*, 228–229, Ogden's emphasis).

Now, I simply ask whether "death" or "sin" are *redemptively* overcome here at all. To be remembered everlastingly in the life of God *for exactly what I have been*, to be remembered far more intimately than I can ever know myself by him to whom all hearts are open and all thoughts known, to know that *precisely* this is to be my contribution to the life of God *forever* – none of this appears redemptive at all. I have argued that a naturalist theology depends decisively on the validity of its conception of the human problem, "life after the flesh" or "bondage to sin." We recall from the discussion of Niebuhr in the last chapter that the crucial deepening of that conception came when developing messianic expectations realized that "there are none who are righteous." If this problem is appreciated at its deepest level, which I take to be Christianity's decisive contribution to our understanding of what it means to be human, there is no redemptive comfort in the knowledge that I shall be known just as I am and make just this contribution to God's ongoing life forever. In fact, far from constituting a redemptive possibility, I cannot imagine a more precise theological formulation of "hell," of "*eternal* damnation." It is precisely the existential self-understanding implicit in *this* conception of "God's love" that formed Luther's "scrupulosity," almost drove him mad, and led to his revolutionary formulation of justification by faith.

This problem is exacerbated by Ogden's conception of a final victory over sin. The structure is the same, namely, that we are accepted forever into God's life, the ground of his love "being . . . wholly in his own eternal nature to love," so that "his decision in every moment to accept his creatures takes place altogether independently of man's decisions" (*RG*, 227). But *how* we are thus accepted does depend on our own free and responsible decisions to accept or reject God's offer of love. To be sure, this decision in no way determines the reality of God's love (see *RG*, 227–228). But it does determine how we are held in that love, and, as the following quotation shows, this can be as much in judgment and therefore in eternal damnation as in a redemptive overcoming of sin:

God as he is known to us in Christ creates all things for himself and takes all things into himself quite apart from any creaturely dispositions whatever. Therefore, even hell, even the anxious closure against God and one's fellows, cannot lie outside God's encompassing love. . . it is no less true, as faith understands the matter, that hell is God's hell. As a matter of fact, the very meaning of "hell" is to be bound to God forever without any possibility of separation from him, but also without the faith in his love which is the peace that passes understanding. (*RG*, 228)

Exactly so, but given the depth of sin, how does this meaning of God's love eschatologically overcome it? To live eternally in hell under God's love is still to live in hell under the *judgment* of his love, and if the deepest Christian understanding of the status of *our own* righteousness is correct, then it would seem that our present self-understanding must be determined by the sure certainty that we shall indeed exist everlastingly in hell. This problem is simply another aspect of

Ogden's difficulties in making good on how God's love is made *redemptively* actual by God's action. Those problems, discussed at length in chapter four, led to my alternative conception of God's grace as transformative action. We saw that Ogden fails to make clear how God's redemptive action is made available *within* human freedom and responsibility. Here we see the consequences of that failure, for it would appear that it is after all our free decisions that determine our eternal destiny in God.

Despite these damaging criticisms, let us note how decisively important Ogden's clarification of these issues remains. Ogden insists on the existential reality of faith. Eschatological symbols must refer to a way of being in the present, not to events *of any nature* in the future. The promise of faith is an existential reality for us now, in every present now, or it exists not at all. This is absolutely decisive, not merely for this but for any theology, and it will determine everything now to follow. At the same time, though the promise of faith is entirely existential, Ogden correctly objects to any one-sided existentializing of its content. This means that "our resurrection is never an authentic understanding of our existence until it is first a gracious action of God, which is real quite independently of our self-understanding" (*RG*, 218–219). My notion of God's action as events of grace captures what is at issue in this point. This action is nowhere present except in the self-understanding by which it is actualized. Yet, what is present in that self-understanding is not simply created by it. The "resurrection" is grounded in the divine actuality because an understanding of oneself in the light of God's love, authentic existence, first becomes possible through God's transformative action in events of his grace.

Of course, this notion of God's transformative action does nothing to replace the conservation of value. All along, however, I have argued that we must transform the very nature of the religious question. The pertinence of this argument is especially evident now with the eschatological symbols that constitute the promise of faith. The question is whether the truth of faith is dependent on the conservation of value. An important element in Ogden's argument about the existential character of eschatological symbols was his statement: "Being really and truly *last* things, that is, *ultimate* things, things constituting the most essential reality of *all* places on the time-line, they are always and only matters of the present – though, of course, of *every* present." It follows that "none of the traditional eschatological symbols may be thought to refer to things or events in principle beyond our present experience and knowledge. This is because their real reference is always to the abiding structure and meaning of our actual existence here and now, which faith presently understands" (*RG*, 210, Ogden's emphasis). As discussed earlier, the issue is how we are to understand "ultimacy" religiously. For Ogden, and generally for the theological tradition, its meaning is ontological, as is indicated by his qualifying phrase, "things constituting the most essential reality of *all* places on the time-line." But it may also be conceived valuationally. In that instance, "last things" are also "really and truly *last* things, that is, *ultimate* things" because "ultimacy" becomes a valuational qualifier for how our lives are qualified by the source of human good. An ontological qualifier can be supplied by physical determination, but it is unnecessary because it misses the *religious* issue at stake. Once the religious issue is transformed, we may even appropriate Ogden's qualifying phrase (which I here use as a surrogate for all such traditional language), for, *valuationally*, God as creative transformation does constitute the most essential reality of all places on the time-line. The point is that a fully existentialist account of eschatological symbols may be rendered without appeal to the conservation of value.

The same point applies to God's sovereignty. Almost all contemporary New Testament scholarship insists that the doctrine of creation serves to express the sovereignty of God. The same motive lies behind the eschatological symbols. The question is whether "sovereignty" must be construed ontologically. This ontological focus is evident in Ogden when, speaking of Robinson, he says: "It is quite evident that the faith to which witness is borne in Holy Scripture has something important at stake in his insistence that not only the present moment, but the whole of nature and history as well, is of ultimate significance." Yet, neither creation nor "resurrection" require appealing to first or last stages of the cosmic process. "Both doctrines serve the identical purposes of asserting the sole sovereignty of God *as the ground and end of whatever is or is even possible*, and of denying, against all forms of metaphysical dualism, that there can be anything at all which is not subject to his sovereignty" (*RG*, 214, my emphasis). Though sovereignty does not deal with first or last stages of the cosmic process, Ogden, nevertheless, conceives it to have an important ontological and cosmic dimension.

In contrast, from the standpoint of a valuational theism, "God's sovereignty" is simply sovereignty over faith, not sovereignty over any kind of cosmic process. It would seem, then, that the motive for the tradition's ontological language could not be met by the present theology. But, granting an existentialist notion of faith, God's sovereignty even in the tradition *is* sovereignty over faith. The dispute is simply over the conditions necessary for asserting *that* sovereignty. Again, the transformation in the religious question is crucial. God's sovereignty is sovereignty over value. To confess this sovereignty is to confess that all goodness comes from God alone. In its widest sense this is formulated by the Christian valuational matrix as a whole. Its condensed formula is openness to the future grounded in the giftedness of life received as a gift. That this formula captures the sovereignty of God *valuationally* is evident because the same formula can be used to articulate the first commandment and the critique of idolatry. Receiving the gift of life as a gift, openness to the future, can be restated simply as what devotion to God means. As Wieman emphasized, at a certain level of nature, recognition of the source of value, devotion to it, is crucially relevant for its actualization; this is, indeed, the existential content of the *imago dei*. This understanding of the sovereignty of God may even in a crucial sense comprehend the motive to assert "that not only the present moment, but the whole of nature and history as well, is of ultimate significance." For devotion to God's valuational sovereignty over faith is devotion to the source of value however and wherever it may be achieved, as Wieman's analysis of the absolute goodness of the creative event makes clear. Again, the point here *can* receive an ontological statement *via* the physical determinacy of value, but this is scarcely necessary given the theological issues at stake.

Finally, there is the problem of perpetual perishing. Irrespective of Ogden's success at overcoming it, the issue is important because he asserts that it is death in this sense "that raises the really serious existential question," (*RG*, 224) and we examined at length his argument for overcoming it (see *RG*, 224–226). If anything is a value judgment, however, it is just this kind of claim about what constitutes a "really serious existential question." The problem is to know how to assess or validate such judgments. Certainly, it is commonly assumed, as we saw with absurdity, that the meaning of life is threatened if our achievements and the subjective consummations of our lives simply recede ever more dimly into the past. But is this judgment valid – rather than simply our first psychological reflex at the realization of our own subjective passing into nothingness? I must confess that

Ogden's conviction about this matter carries little weight in my own psyche and in that of many others I know, though it seems importantly relevant to others. Nothing in an existentialist analysis of human existence would seem to require it, however. Human existing is decisively qualified by our being toward death. The issue there, however, is not perpetual perishing but the *meaningfulness of having lived,* and that issue, as it appears in our very existing, is simply neutral regarding perpetual perishing.

Ogden's position smacks not a little, unfortunately, as a sophisticated version of the argument to which he objects regarding our subjective survival of death. "As it is usually put," he says, "*if* God really loves us, he will not permit the span of our years to be brought to an end." He comments that this seems "to betray a profound failure of faith, a lapse into the kind of thinking so severely treated by Paul, by which trust in God's love is made subject to certain conditions. . . It betrays, in a word, a most serious departure from the only really essential point, that there is but one faith with which the whole of theology has to deal and that this faith is directed to one sovereign God who *alone* is the ground of our own and all men's authentic existence" (*RG*, 230, Ogden's emphasis). Before commenting on this specifically, let us note that there is nothing in *this* faith alone requiring perpetual perishing to be overcome in the life of God. Ogden's proposal that it is overcome (granting that his argument succeeds, which I think is doubtful) is based on a conceptual scheme used to interpret faith. Even if it adequately interprets the witness of faith, its own truth, that is, an ontological and metaphysical truth, rests on entirely independent grounds. Even if, as I believe, those grounds are false, the question of the truth of faith is still open. Let us note, furthermore, that the existential character of our lives as we live unto death remains exactly the same, whether perpetual perishing is overcome or whether, as in the present work, it is not.

What this means, if I am not mistaken, is that *theologically considered* the question of perpetual perishing is simply a red herring. As Ogden himself says, the really essential point is that "faith is directed to one sovereign God who *alone* is the ground of our own and all men's authentic existence" (*RG*, 230, Ogden's emphasis). If the Christian claim about faith is true, then it may be affirmed even when on independent grounds we come to believe that there is no conservation of value and that in the relevant sense perpetual perishing is true. For a *valuational* theism, God's *everlasting* sovereignty over value holds regardless of our perishing. Wieman's way of making this point is worth quoting at length:

It is important to note that creative good [can be] obstructed but not destroyed; for creativity can be driven down to lower and lower levels of existence, and it can be forced to work with lower levels of created good. If all the more highly sensitive and responsive organisms were destroyed, creativity would have to develop qualitative meaning by way of more brutish organisms. If the human level were wiped out of existence, the creative process would occur only at the levels of life that still persisted. If all living organisms were destroyed, creativity would have to work at the level of matter from which the first new living organisms might once more be created. But creativity working at the lowest possible levels of existence is no less good than it is at the higher. . . . Creativity carries the hope and the potency of all the highest good that ever will be. It has this absolute character just as fully at the lowest level as at the highest.

One might speculate with the idea that everything in existence might be so destroyed or transformed that nothing whatsoever remained which could be the standing ground of creative good. If that should occur, creativity would be destroyed; but such speculation is idle because we have no more evidence concerning ultimate endings than we have about ultimate origins. All that we know is that creativity always has sprung anew from lower levels when the higher levels were destroyed. Thus, so far as we know, evil can destroy created good but can only obstruct creative good. (*SHG*, 86–87)

This kind of sovereignty, then, is all that faith is entitled to claim, and it has immediate consequences for the promise of faith. The promise of faith, that for which faith hopes, is simply the sovereignty of God. This means, existentially, that the giftedness of life can be received as a gift even unto death. The content of faith is simply openness to the future even in one's last moment, and the promise of faith, grounded in the grace of God, is that life is a gift and may be so received even in the moment when one faces death. This is the "good news" that the gospel should proclaim when it understands itself aright: the sovereignty of God and indeed of God's love even in death. To state this positively, it means that we are so given life that life is meaningful in tragedy, in suffering, in limited circumstance, and also in our dying. We might call this the courage of faith, but as Tillich showed so well in *The Courage to Be*, even the courage of faith in the face of despair and death is grounded in the promises of God by which the gift of life is ours. So it is better to call it the promise of faith unto death, rather than the courage of faith. The promise of faith is simply that we may receive this gift and affirm its giftedness in every moment of our living, including its last. And this is the ground too of our hopes by which we are committed to justice and to those less fortunate than ourselves.

What are we to make, then, of the promise that in Christ "the last enemy to be destroyed is death" (1 Cor. 15:26)? At the prophetic center of Christianity is the critique of egoism, and salvation is conceived as its overcoming. It is utterly implausible, therefore, that at its center it also promises a subjective survival of self that offers solace and encouragement to some of our most egoistic impulses. Thus, if I am correct, the "death" that is overcome is not physical death or perpetual perishing even here. This reference rather is to that spiritual death which resides in inauthentic existence and is the opposite of the life we have in faith. The latter, however, is openness to the future which becomes possible when we receive the gift that life is as a gift.[23]

This becomes evident even within the traditional claim that faith

---

[23] In an addendum to this essay, Ogden discusses subjective immortality. He notes that his position is neutral on this question, and that he remains open to having his own skepticism overturned. He makes clear that though the New Testament faith never denies survival of death, this belief is in no way "a necessary article of Christian belief" (*RG*, 229–230). He also harshly criticizes the argument that our survival of death is assured *because* of God's love. Noting that this argument has little logical force, he makes the same point I have emphasized: "..., it seems to me to betray a profound failure of faith, a lapse into the kind of thinking so severely treated by Paul, by which trust in God's love is made subject to certain conditions and we demand a 'sign,' some tangible proof, that we may give ourselves wholly into his keeping (see 1 Cor. 1:18–25) ... This may also be expressed by saying that the good news of Jesus's resurrection is never really heard unless it is heard to be as much an 'offence' or 'stumbling block' as 'the word of the cross' (1 Cor. 1:18). Indeed, rightly understood, the triumphant message of the resurrection simply *is* the word of the cross – the word that we live only by dying, and that our true life is not really our life at all but is 'hid with Christ in God,' in whose unending love for his whole creation we are each given to share (Col. 3:2)" (*RG*, 230).

Though I agree substantially with Ogden, I believe this analysis requires a somewhat different accent. Even a naturalist can remain neutral about what happens to our subjective identity at death. The only proper thing to say is that we simply do not know. Yet, we are entitled to form beliefs where evidence warrants, even if we must withhold certainty. Theologians need to acknowledge more forthrightly that *all* the evidence points to the psycho-physical unity of our subjective existence, from which it follows that subjective identity dissolves with physical death (or even with brain death). There is evidence, and of the most convincing sort, on this matter. Thus, though this is not really a departure from Ogden, it appears to me that Christian theology would be healthier (and far more credible) if it actively asserted that there is no survival of death and then worked out its theological affirmations *from* this position. It is indeed *logically possible* that we survive death subjectively. Many theological discussions of this issue start from this logical possibility (and the logical impossibility of knowing) and proceed to treat it as an actual possibility. Then taking these possibilities, possibilities that simply ignore the evidence that does exist, they proceed as though it were a certainty in which faith could have confidence. The problem is that such procedures ignore the existential nature of theological assertions. But the problem is, additionally, that the whole line of thought is slovenly from beginning to end.

promises a survival of death. Examined carefully, this salvation is not simply continuity of self but, in one form or another, *being with God*. We can say, then, that "being with God" or "being in the presence of God" is the content as such of salvation. This, however, is formally identical to the naturalist account of salvation defended here. "God's presence to us" is nothing other than the knowledge of God given in events of grace. In this sense, openness to the future, salvation, is "eternal life." Salvation as "knowing God" or "being in the presence of God" is "beyond time" or has no temporal thickness. It is *always* good – and indeed is the best life – to know God by standing in God's presence. This is the context in which it makes sense to claim that death, the last enemy, is overcome. It is in and through God's grace, which is God's presence to us, that death is overcome. We do indeed live by faith, and we are justified by the love of God quite prior to all our attempts to acquire this gift on our own terms – even in death.

At this extreme point, the final enemy that is overcome in the promise of faith may be termed "the fear of death." Such fear is not the only way that "death" can figure in our inauthentic existence, but it does identify the way in which life can come to be dominated by death, by our being-unto-death, both by our preoccupation with it and by our deceptive evasions of it. The promise of faith is that we are freed from the domination of death over our existing. Faith knows that it may reside even under the shadow of dying in the promise of God's justifying grace. Thus, a naturalist theology, most especially a naturalist theology, can affirm and indeed celebrate that "neither death, nor life, nor angels, nor principalities, nor things present, nor things to come, nor powers, nor height, nor depth, nor anything else in all creation, will be able to separate us from the love of God in Christ Jesus our Lord" (Rom. 8:38–39).

On the referential status of transformative events

There remains a problem that cuts across the entire argument of this book. This concerns the referential status of Wieman's "creative transformation." The door is opened for a naturalist theology once it is understood that "God exists" need not refer to be objectively true. But does not Wieman's transformative event (or source of human good) have referential force? Must not transformation have ontological inventory status, and would this not make God the value of a variable?

I shall make a double response to this issue. I shall argue, first, that in the only relevant referential sense, "God" (the transformative event) has its reference within the bounds of a physicalist ontology. On the other hand, second, existentialist interpretation allows us to say that "God exists" *functions* within a valuational matrix. In this sense, it functions nonreferentially *to articulate a seeing-as appropriate to that valuational matrix* which is itself understood existentially in terms of modes of human existence: openness to the future, readiness for transformation, the giftedness of life, trust in being, and the love of God. In other words, theologically considered, "God exists" functions nonreferentially to express a theistic seeing-as within a valuational matrix – provided we can pin down more carefully the ontological standing of the notion of a transformative event.

Wieman understood the source of human good formally to denominate whatever it is in reality that we are dependent upon for the growth of value and the abundance of life. That there are such realities and that we are dependent upon them is given. Wieman then used the notion of transformation to identify our dependence for the growth of value. His analysis of faith attempts to show why we should orient ourselves according to this dependence, acknowledge and be open to the transformative powers upon which we depend. Since he is speaking of something real, something located in the world of nature, it would seem that "transformation" is a referential term of a certain

sort. But let us note that it does not require the theologian to multiply
entities to save God. It simply refers to whatever it is in nature upon
which value is dependent, and it has rather special content at the
human level of qualitative meaning.

The theologian, from the point of view I have developed, has no
stake in how far down into nature something like the notion of
transformative events can be pushed. It is possible that it can be
pushed quite far, but these have questionable valuational significance.
For instance, something very much like transformations occurred in
the first micro-seconds after the big bang in creating the universe's large-
scale structure (including its physical laws). The same is true for the
space-time fluctuations that seem to have produced the uneven
distribution of galaxies and for the processes that produce all the
heavy elements in the deaths of super-nova. Such processes become
even more evident when life appears and the mechanics of evolutionary
processes come into play at the molecular level. In all of these ways,
and in many more that could be listed, the metaphor of transformation
(if it is only a metaphor) clearly has referential status. But its status in
this sense is entirely determined by physical entities in the physicalist
inventory of what exists. No entities are multiplied, and Occam's
razor remains sharp. Furthermore, as I have just mentioned, the
theologian need have no *theological* interest in transformations at this
level because they are not valuationally determined.

The situation changes when we enter that level of nature where
what Wieman terms quality and qualitative meaning occur.[1] The
increase in value relevant to human beings (and perhaps some other
vertebrates) occurs at the level of transformations of qualitative
meaning. Following Wieman, they occur at an intercommunicative
level of shared meanings. This means that what they are – or, if you
will, how they "refer" – is determined by an interior structure of
meanings themselves. It is in this structure of qualitative meaning
that "God exists" receives its meaning, and in this relevant theological
sense "God exists" does not refer. Rather, it is a complex expression
articulating an existential self-understanding which is justified as to
its truth entirely in valuational terms. In this sense, it is a seeing-as as a
meta-expression for an existentially grounded valuational stance. It is
justified by comprehending how that existential self-understanding

[1] It is not even evident that we need to include all quality as such. It extends far more widely
into nature than qualitative meaning, perhaps, as I noted in the first chapter, being
co-extensive with life itself. It needs to be included only in so far as events of qualitative
meaning are themselves events of quality of a special kind.

requires an analysis in terms of human bondage, the giftedness of life, and the transformative process by which that existential possibility is best understood. But such transformations are themselves events of qualitative meaning. They are comprehended not referentially in any ontological sense but within a self-referencing structure of qualitative meaning articulated as a seeing-as.

Just as such a structure of qualitative meaning (and its transformations) does not multiply entities, it also, I emphasize, is entirely determined by physical entities. It is, indeed, determined largely by physical events in the brain and otherwise by those physical processes that determine human culture. These are physical processes that determine that human existence has the structure of understanding that it has, a structure of finite being-in-the-world. We saw in the analysis of Post, however, that such determination does not require reduction, does not require that the phenomena of qualitative meaning (including the temporal structure of human existing as being-toward-death) be translatable into some physical vocabulary, and does not violate the explanatory autonomy of domains of discourse outside the physical sciences. Theology is just such a domain. According to the argument presented in this work, its explanatory autonomy is constituted by an existentialist analysis of human being. Within that domain, "God exists" functions to express an existentially interpreted seeing-as which operates within a self-referential structure of qualitative meaning. In this sense, "God exists" does not refer, and when we speak of transformation here, we are speaking of something that is itself constituted within a structure of qualitative meaning. "God exists" is its interpretation.

I conclude, therefore, that Wieman's notion of transformation need not have unacceptable referential implications. In so far as it permits us to interpret God and God's action, it is compatible with the notion of a theistic seeing-as. The normative character of such a seeing-as is justified directly by the analysis of the valuational stance it expresses. In this sense, the normative argument for a *theistic* seeing-as can be made rather easily and directly simply by trying to comprehend the full scope of the Christian witness of faith existentially. From that perspective, the Christian witness of faith can easily be defended as a valuational stance which includes a theistic seeing-as. The normative argument for a theistic seeing-as is thereby included in the argument for interpreting Christianity as a valuational stance. The more demanding question is whether the normative character of the latter can be justified.

Bibliography

Abrams, M. H. (1971). *Natural Supernaturalism: Tradition and Revolution in Romantic Literature*. New York: W. W. Norton & Company.

Anderson, Bernhard W. (1951). *Rediscovering the Bible*. New York: Association Press.

Aquinas, Thomas (1953). *De potentia*. In P. Bazzi *et al.*, eds., *Questiones Disputatae*, 9th ed. Rome: Marietti Editori Ltd.

Baillie, Donald (1948). *God Was In Christ*. New York: Charles Scribner's Sons.

Barth, Karl (1933). *The Epistle to the Romans*. Translated by Edwyn C. Hoskyns. 6th ed. London: Oxford University Press.

(1953). *Rudolf Bultmann: Ein Versuch ihn zu verstehen*. 2nd ed. Zollikon-Zürich: Evangelischer Verlag.

Bergson, Henri (1935). *The Two Sources of Religion and Morality*. Translated by R. Ashley Audra and Cloudesley Brereton. New York: Holt and Company.

Braithwaite, R. B. (1955). *An Empiricist's View of Religious Belief*. Cambridge University Press.

Bretall, Robert W. ed. (1963). *The Empirical Theology of Henry Nelson Wieman*. Carbondale, Ill.: Southern Illinois University Press.

Brunner, Emil (1961). "Some remarks on Reinhold Niebuhr's work as a Christian thinker." In Charles W. Kegley and Robert W. Bretall, eds., *Reinhold Niebuhr: His Religious, Social, and Political Thought*. New York: The Macmillan Company.

Bultmann, Rudolf, (1933a). "Die Eschatologie des Johannes-Evangeliums." In Bultmann, *Glauben und Verstehen*, vol. 1 (Tübingen: J. C. B. Mohr (Paul Siebeck)), 134–152.

(1933b). "Kirche und Lehre im Neuen Testament." In Bultmann, *Glauben und Verstehen*, vol. 1 (Tübingen: J. C. B. Mohr (Paul Siebeck)), 153–187.

(1933c). "Das Problem der Natürlichen Theologie." In Bultmann, *Glauben und Verstehen*, vol. 1 (Tübingen: J. C. B. Mohr (Paul Siebeck)), 294–312.

(1933d). "Welchen Sinn hat es, von Gott zu Reden?" In Bultmann, *Glauben und Verstehen*, vol. 1 (Tübingen: J. C. B. Mohr (Paul Siebeck)), 26–37.

(1948a). "Neues Testament und Mythologie." In H. W. Bartsch, ed., *Kerygma und Mythos: Ein theologisches Gespräch*, vol. 1 (Hamburg: Herbert Reich-Evangelischer Verlag, vierte, erweiterte Auflage, 1960), 15–48. Translated by Schubert M. Ogden as "New Testament and mythology." In Bultmann, *New Testament and Mythology and Other Basic Writings*. Philadelphia: Fortress Press (1984), 1–44.

(1948b). "Zu J. Schniewinds Thesen, das Problem der Entmythologisierung betreffend." In H. W. Bartsch, ed., *Kerygma und Mythos: Ein theologisches Gespräch*, vol. 1 (Hamburg: Herbert Reich-Evangelischer Verlag, vierte, erweiterte Auflage, 1960), 122–138. Translated by Reginald H. Fuller as "A reply to the theses of J. Schniewind." In Bultmann *et al*, *Kerygma and Myth: A Theological Debate*. New York: Harper & Row Publishers (1961), 102–123.

(1951). *Theology of the New Testament*. 2 vols. Translated by Kendrick Grobel. New York: Charles Scribner's Sons.

(1952a). "Die Krise des Glaubens." In Bultmann, *Glauben und Verstehen*, vol. II (Tübingen: J. C. B. Mohr (Paul Siebeck)), 1–19. Translated by C. G. Greig as "The crisis in belief." In *Essays Philosophical and Theological*. London: SCM Press, Ltd. (1955), 1–21.

(1952b). "Das Verständnis von Welt und Mensch im Neuen Testament und im Griechentum." In Bultmann, *Glauben und Verstehen*, vol. II (Tübingen: J. C. B. Mohr (Paul Siebeck)), 59–78. Translated by C. G. Greig as "The understanding of man and the world in the New Testament and in the Greek world." In *Essays Philosophical and Theological*. London: SCM Press, Ltd. (1955), 67–89.

(1952c). "Zum Problem der Entmythologisierung." In H. W. Bartsch, ed., *Kerygma und Mythos*, vol. II (Hamburg: Herbert Reich-Evangelischer Verlag, 1952, [2nd ed., 1965]), 179–208. Translated by Schubert M. Ogden as "On the problem of demythologizing." In Bultmann, *New Testament and Mythology and Other Basic Writings*. Philadelphia: Fortress Press. (1984), 95–130.

(1956). *Primitive Christianity in Its Contemporary Setting*. Translated by R. H. Fuller. New York: The World Publishing Company.

(1960a). "The concept of revelation in the New Testament." In *Existence and Faith: Shorter Writings of Rudolf Bultmann*. Translated by Schubert M. Ogden. New York: Meridian Books, Inc., 58–91.

(1960b). "The historicity of man and faith." In *Existence and Faith: Shorter Writings of Rudolf Bultmann*. Translated by Schubert M. Ogden. New York: Meridian Books, Inc., 92–110.

(1984). "Theology as science." In Bultmann, *New Testament and Mythology and Other Basic Writings*. Translated by Schubert M. Ogden. Philadelphia: Fortress Press, 1984, 55–68.

Bultmann, Rudolf, Ernst Lohmeyer, Julius Schniewind, Helmut Thielicke, and Austin Farrer (1961a). "Bultmann replies to his critics. " In H. W. Bartsch, ed., *Kerygma and Myth: A Theological Debate*. Translated by

Reginald H. Fuller. New York: Harper & Row Publishers, 191–211.
(1961b). "New Testament and mythology." In H. W. Bartsch, ed.,
Kerygma and Myth: A Theological Debate. Translated by Reginald H.
Fuller. New York: Harper & Row Publishers, 1–44.

Buri, Fritz. (1952). "Entmythologisierung oder Entkerygmatisieriung der
Theologie." In H. W. Bartsch, ed., *Kerygma und Mythos*, vol. II
(Hamburg: Herbert Reich-Evangelischer Verlag, 1952), 85–101.

(1956–1978). *Dogmatik als Selbstverständnis des christlilchen Glaubens*. Vol. I:
Vernunft und Offenbarung (1956). Vol. II: *Der Mensch und die Gnade* (1962).
Vol. III: *Die Transzendenz der Verantwortung in die Dreifachen Schöpfung des
Dreieinigen Gottes* (1978). Bern: Verlag Paul Haupt.

Campbell, Keith (1976). *Metaphysics: An Introduction*. Encino, California:
Dickenson Publishing Co., Inc.

Camus, Albert (1955). *The Myth of Sisyphus*. Translated by Justin O'Brien.
New York: Vintage.

Cobb, John B. Jr. (1965). *A Christian Natural Theology*. Philadelphia: The
Westminster Press.

(1967). *The Structure of Christian Existence*. Philadelphia: The Westminster
Press.

(1969). *God and the World*. Philadelphia: The Westminster Press.

(1975). *Christ in a Pluralistic Age*. Philadelphia: The Westminster Press.

(1983). "Natural causality and divine action." In Owen C. Thomas, ed.,
God's Activity in the World: The Contemporary Problem. Chico, Cal.:
Scholars Press, 101–116.

Cochrane, Charles Norris (1975). *Christianity and Classical Culture: A Study of
Thought and Action From Augustus to Augustine*. Revised and corrected.
New York: Oxford University Press.

Collingwood, R. G. (1940). *Essay on Metaphysics*. London: Oxford University
Press.

Davis, Harry R. and Good, Robert C., eds. (1960). *Reinhold Niebuhr on
Politics: His Political Philosophy and Its Application to Our Age as Expressed in
His Writings*. New York: Scribner.

Dean, William (1988). *History Making History. The New Historicism in American
Religious Thought*. Albany, N.Y.: State University of New York Press.

Dreyfus, Hubert L. (1991). *Being-in-the-World. A Commentary on Heidegger's
Being and Time, Division I*. Cambridge, Mass.: M. I. T. Press.

Edwards, Rem. (1972). *Reason and Religion: An Introduction to the Philosophy of
Religion*. New York: Harcourt, Brace, Jovanovich.

Eisenstadt, S. N., ed. (1986). *The Origins and Diversity of Axial Age Civilizations*.
Albany, N.Y.: State University of New York Press.

Eliade, Mircea (1959). *The Sacred and the Profane: The Nature of Religion*.
Translated by Willard R. Trask. New York: Harcourt, Brace and
Company.

Evans, Donald (1963). *The Logic of Self-Involvement. A Philosophical Study of
Everyday Language with Special Reference to the Christian Use of Language about*

God as Creator. London: SCM Press.

Farley, Edward (1990). *Good and Evil: Interpreting a Human Condition*. Minneapolis: Fortress Press.

Ford, Lewis S. (1978). *The Lure of God: A Biblical Background for Process Theism*. Philadelphia: Fortress Press.

Gellner, Ernest (1974). *Legitimation of Belief*. Cambridge University Press.

Gerrish, B. A. (1978). *Tradition and the Modern World: Reformed Theology in the Nineteenth Century*. University of Chicago Press.

Geertz, Clifford (1973a). "Religion as a cultural system." In Geertz, *The Interpretation of Cultures: Selected Essays*. New York: Basic Books, 87–125.

(1973b). "Ethos, world view, and the analysis of sacred symbols." In Geertz, *The Interpretation of Cultures: Selected Essays*. New York: Basic Books, 126–141.

Gilkey, Langdon (1964). Review of Paul van Buren, *The Secular Meaning of the Gospel*. *The Journal of Religion*, 44, 238–243.

(1965). *Maker of Heaven and Earth: A Study of the Christian Doctrine of Creation*. Garden City, N.Y.: Doubleday and Co.

(1969). *Naming the Whirlwind: The Renewal of God-Language*. New York: The Bobbs-Merrill Co.

(1970). *Religion and the Scientific Future: Reflections on Myth, Science, and Theology*. New York: Harper & Row, Publishers.

(1974). "Reinhold Niebuhr's theology of history." *The Journal of Religion*, 54, 360–386.

(1976). *Reaping the Whirlwind: A Christian Interpretation of History*. New York: Seabury Press.

(1985). *Creationism on Trial: Evolution and God at Little Rock*. Minneapolis, Minn.: Winston Press.

Gilson, Etienne (1952). *Being and Some Philosophers*. 2nd ed. Toronto: Pontifical Institute of Medieval Studies.

(1984). *From Aristotle to Darwin and Back Again: A Journey in Final Causality, Species, and Evolution*. Translated by John Lyon. Notre Dame, Ind.: University of Notre Dame Press.

Guignon, Charles B. (1983). *Heidegger and the Problem of Knowledge*. Indianapolis, Ind.: Hackett Publishing Co., Inc.

Hall, James. (1975). *Knowledge, Belief, and Transcendence*. Boston: Houghton Miffline Co.

Hardwick, Charley D. (1972). *Faith and Objectivity. Fritz Buri and the Hermeneutical Foundations of a Radical Theology*. Preface by Van. A. Harvey. The Hague: Martinus Nijhoff.

(1987a). "Faith in a naturalist theology: Henry Nelson Wieman and American radical empiricism." In Peter Freese, ed., *Religion and Philosophy in the United States of America*, 2 vols. (Essen: Verlag die Blaue Eule), I, 369–386.

(1987b). "Naturalism, objectivity, and existentialist interpretation." In Alfred Jaeger, ed., *Weltoffenheit des christlichen Glaubens. Festgabe für Fritz*

Buri (Bern: Paul Haupt), 29–41.

(1987c). "Theological naturalism and the nature of religion: On not begging the question." *ZYGON: Journal of Science and Religion*, 22/1, 21–36.

(1988). "What is the 'Good' of religion for Wieman." *The American Journal of Theology and Philosophy*, 9/3, 165–174.

(1989). "Naturalism and existentialist interpretation: Methodological parameters for a naturalistic Christian theology." In W. Creighton Peden and Larry E. Axel, eds., *God, Values, and Empiricism. Issues in Philosophical Theology*. Macon, Ga.: Mercer University Press, 73–84.

(1991). "Review of Joseph Runzo, *Reason, Relativism and God.*" *Journal of the American Academy of Religion*, 59/4, 866–870.

Hare, R. M. (1955). "Theology and falsification." In Antony Flew and Alasdair MacIntyre, eds., *New Essays in Philosophical Theology*. London: SCM Press Ltd., 99–103.

Hartshorne, Charles (1970)."What metaphysics is." In *Creative Synthesis and Philosophic Method*. Lanham, Md.: University Press of America (2nd ed. 1983), 19–42.

Harvey, Van A. (1966). *The Historian and the Believer: The Morality of Historical Knowledge and Christian Belief*. New York: Macmillan & Co.

Harvey, Van A. and Ogden, Schubert M. (1962). "Wie neu is die 'Neue Frage nach dem historischen Jesus'?" *Zeitschrift für Theologie und Kirche*, 59, 46–87.

Hauerwas, Stanley. (1974). *Character and the Christian Life*. San Antonio; Tex.: Trinity University Press.

(1977). *Truthfulness and Tragedy: Further Investigations in Christian Ethics*. Notre Dame, Ind.: University of Notre Dame Press.

(1981a). *A Community of Character: Toward a Constructive Christian Social Ethic*. Notre Dame, Ind.: University of Notre Dame Press.

(1981b). *Vision and Virtue: Essays in Christian Ethical Reflection*. Notre Dame, Ind.: University of Notre Dame Press.

Heidegger, Martin (1927). *Sein und Zeit*. Tübingen: Max Niemeyer Verlag, 1927 [9th ed., 1960]. Translated by John Macquarrie and Edward Robinson as *Being and Time*. London: SCM Press, Ltd., (1962).

Hepburn, R. W. (1981). "Questions about the meaning of life." In Klemke, ed. *The Meaning of Life*. New York: Oxford University Press, 209–227.

Hick, John (1958). "The christology of D. M. Baillie." *Scottish Journal of Theology*, 11, 1–12.

(1979). "Is there a doctrine of the incarnation?" In Michael Goulder, ed., *Incarnation and Myth: The Debate Continued*. Grand Rapids: William B. Eerdmans Publishing Company, 47–50.

(1983). *Philosophy of Religion*. 3rd ed. Englewood Cliffs, N.J.: Prentice-Hall.

Hodges, H. A. (1953). *Languages, Standpoints, and Attitudes*. London: Oxford University Press.

Holmer, Paul L. (1978). *The Grammar of Faith*. San Francisco: Harper & Row, Publishers.

Jaspers, Karl (1932) *Philosophie, II: Existenzerhellung.* Berlin: Springer-Verlag, (3rd ed., 1956). Translated by E. B. Ashton as *Philosophy*, vol. II. Chicago: The University of Chicago Press (1970).

Jonas, Hans (1958). *The Gnostic Religion.* Boston: Beacon Press [2nd ed., enlarged, 1963].

Jones, W. T. (1952). *A History of Western Philosophy. IV: Kant and the Nineteenth Century.* New York: Harcourt Brace Jovanovich, Publishers [2nd ed., revised, 1975].

Klemke, E. D., ed. (1981). *The Meaning of Life.* New York: Oxford University Press.

Küng, Hans, (1976). *On Being a Christian.* Translated by Edward Quinn. Garden City, N.Y.: Doubleday & Co., Inc.

(1980). *Does God Exist? An Answer for Today.* Translated by Edward Quinn. Garden City, N.Y.: Doubleday & Co., Inc.

(1985a). *Eternal Life? Life After Death as a Medical, Philosophical, and Theological Problem.* Translated by Edward Quinn. Garden City, N.Y.: Doubleday & Company, Inc.

(1985b). *The Incarnation of God. An Introduction to Hegel's Theological Thought as Prolegomena to a Future Christology.* Translated by J. R. Stephenson. Edinburgh: T. & T. Clark [German ed., 1970].

Kuhn, Thomas (1970) *The Structure of Scientific Revolutions*, 2nd ed. University of Chicago Press.

Lindbeck, George A. (1984). *The Nature of Doctrine: Religion and Theology in a Postliberal Age.* Philadelphia: The Westminster Press.

Lonergan, Bernard (1972). *Method in Theology.* New York: The Seabury Press (2nd ed., 1979).

Mackie, J. L. (1977) *Ethics: Inventing Right and Wrong.* New York: Penguin Books.

Macquarrie, John (1955). *An Existentialist Theology. A Comparison of Heidegger and Bultmann.* London: SCM Press Ltd.

(1960). *The Scope of Demythologizing. Bultmann and his Critics.* London: SCM Press Ltd.

Malraux, André (1953). *The Voices of Silence.* Translated by Stuart Gilbert. New York: Doubleday & Co.

(1960). *The Metamorphosis of the Gods.* Translated by Stuart Gilbert. New York: Doubleday & Co.

Marxsen, Willi (1969). *Der Exeget als Theologe: Vorträge zum Neuen Testament.* 2nd ed. Guetersloh: Guetersloher Verlagshaus Gerd Mohn.

Miller, L. David (1974) *The New Polytheism.* New York: Harper & Row, Publishers.

Nagel, Thomas (1979). "What it is like to be a bat." In Nagel, *Mortal Questions.* Cambridge University Press, 165–180.

(1981). "The absurd." In Klemke, ed., *The Meaning of Life.* New York: Oxford University Press, 151–161.

(1986). *The View From Nowhere.* New York: Oxford University Press.

Neville, Robert C. (1980). *Creativity and God: A Challenge to Process Theology.*

New York: The Seabury Press.

(1991a). *Behind the Masks of God: An Essay Toward Comparative Theology.* Albany, N.Y.: State University of New York Press.

(1991b). *A Theology Primer.* Albany, N.Y.: State University of New York Press.

Niebuhr, H. Richard (1941). *The Meaning of Revelation.* New York: Macmillan.

(1960). *Radical Monotheism and Western Culture.* New York: Harper and Brothers.

Niebuhr, Reinhold (1935). *An Interpretation of Christian Ethics.* New York: Harper and Brothers.

(1937). *Beyond Tragedy.* New York: Charles Scribner's Sons.

(1941). *The Nature and Destiny of Man: A Christian Interpretation.* 2 vols. New York: Charles Scribner's Sons.

Nozick, Robert (1989). *The Examined Life: Philosophical Meditations.* New York: Simon and Schuster.

Oden, Thomas C. (1964). *Radical Obedience: The Ethics of Rudolf Bultmann.* Philadelphia: The Westminster Press.

Ogden, Schubert M. (1960). "Preface." In *Existence and Faith: Shorter Writings of Rudolf Bultmann.* Translated by Schubert M. Ogden. New York: Meridian Books, Inc.

(1961). *Christ without Myth: A Study Based on the Theology of Rudolf Bultmann.* New York: Harper & Row, Publishers.

(1963). *The Reality of God.* New York: Harper & Row, Publishers.

(1971). "Lonergan and the subjectivist principle." *The Journal of Religion,* 51, 155–172.

(1972). "On religion." Unpublished, mimeograph version of a paper presented to the Dartmouth College seminar on "Religion, myth, and reason," May 2–4.

(1975). "The point of christology." *The Journal of Religion,* 55, 375–395.

(1976). "Christology reconsidered: John Cobb's *Christ in a Pluralistic Age.*" *Process Studies,* 6, 116–122.

(1977). "Linguistic analysis and theology." *Theologische Zeitschrift,* 33/5, 318–335.

(1982). *The Point of Christology.* San Francisco: Harper & Row, Publishers.

(1985). "'For freedom Christ has set us free': The Christian understanding of ultimate transformation." Unpublished, mimeograph version of a paper presented to "The Buddhist-Christian Theological Encounter Group" at Vancouver School of Theology, 22–25 March.

Olafson, Frederick A. (1987). *Heidegger and the Philosophy of Mind.* New Haven: Yale University Press.

Oman, John (1931). *The Natural and the Supernatural.* New York: The Macmillan Co.

Owen, H. P. (1971). *Concepts of Deity.* New York: Herder and Herder.

Phillips, D. Z. (1970). *Death and Immortality.* London: Macmillan and Co., Ltd.

(1976). *Religion without Explanation.* Oxford: Basil Blackwell.

Post, John F. (1987). *The Faces of Existence: An Essay in Nonreductive Metaphysics.* Ithaca: Cornell University Press.

Proudfoot, Wayne (1988). "Review of Joseph Runzo, *Reason, Relativism and God.*" *The Journal of Religion,* 68/2, 305–306.

Raschke, Carl A. (1979). *The Alchemy of the Word: Language and the End of Theology.* Missoula, Mont.: Scholars Press.

Ramsey, Ian T. (1957). *Religious Language.* London: SCM Press.

Ramsey, Paul (1950). *Basic Christian Ethics.* New York: Charles Scribner's Sons.

Reiman, Jeffrey (1989). *Justice and Modern Moral Philosophy.* New Haven: Yale University Press.

Ricoeur, Paul (1965). *Fallible Man.* Translated by W. B. Barton, Jr. and Vera Deutch. Chicago: Henry Regnery Co.

(1967). *The Symbolism of Evil.* Translated by Emerson Buchanan. Boston: Beacon Press.

(1970). *Freud and Philosophy: An Essay on Interpretation.* Translated by Denis Savage. New Haven: Yale University Press.

Robinson, James M. (1959). *A New Quest of the Historical Jesus.* London; SCM Press.

Robinson, James M. and Cobb, John B., eds. (1963). *New Frontiers in Theology.* Vol. I: *The Later Heidegger and Theology.* New York: Harper & Row, Publishers.

(1964). *New Frontiers in Theology.* Vol. II: *The New Hermeneutic.* New York: Harper & Row, Publishers.

Robinson, John A. T. (1950). *In the End, God . . .: A Study of the Christian Doctrine of the Last Things.* London: James Clarke & Co., Ltd.

Ross, James (1969). *Introduction to the Philosophy of Religion.* New York: Macmillan Co.

Runzo, Joseph (1986). *Reason, Relativism and God.* New York: St. Martin's Press.

Russell, Bertrand (1981). "A free man's worship." In Klemke, ed., *The Meaning of Life.* New York: Oxford University Press, 55–62.

Santayana, George (1957). *Dialogues in Limbo.* Ann Arbor, Mich.: University of Michigan Press.

(1968). "Natural and ultimate religion." In Santayana, *The Birth of Reason and Other Essays,* Daniel Cory, ed. New York: Columbia University Press, 67–70.

Scharlemann, Robert (1964). *Thomas Aquinas and John Gerhard.* New Haven: Yale University Press.

Schleiermacher, Friedrich (1986). *The Christian Faith.* H. R. Mackintosh and J. S. Stewart, eds. Edinburgh: T. & T. Clark.

Scott, Charles E. (1990). *The Question of Ethics: Nietzsche, Foucault, Heidegger.* Bloomington, Ind.: Indiana University Press.

Scuka, Robert F. (1989). "Resurrection: Critical reflections on a doctrine in search of a meaning." *Modern Theology,* 6, 77–95.

Shaw, Marvin C. (1981). "Naturalism and the Christ: Wieman's christology." *Encounter,* 42, 379–394.

(1988). *The Paradox of Intention: Reaching the Goal by Giving Up the Attempt to Reach It.* Atlanta, Ga.: Scholars Press.

Smith, John E. (1982). "The structure of religion." In Frederick Ferre, Joseph J. Kockelmans, and John E. Smith, eds., *The Challenge of Religion: Contemporary Readings in Philosophy of Religion.* New York: Seabury Press, 27–37.

Stark, Rodney and Bainbridge, William Sims (1987). *A Theory of Religion.* Vol II, Toronto Studies in Religion. New York: Peter Lang.

Tappert, Theodore G., ed. (1959). *The Book of Concord.* Philadelphia: Muhlenberg Press.

Taylor, Charles (1975). *Hegel.* Cambridge University Press.

(1989). *Sources of the Self. The Making of Modern Identity.* Cambridge, Mass.: Harvard University Press.

(1991). *The Ethics of Authenticity.* Cambridge, Mass.: Harvard University Press.

Thomas, Owen C., ed. (1983). *God's Activity in the World: The Contemporary Problem.* Chico, Cal.: Scholars Press.

Tillich, Paul (1948). *The Protestant Era.* Translated by James Luther Adams. The University of Chicago Press.

(1952). *The Courage To Be.* New Haven: Yale University Press.

(1957). *The Dynamics of Faith.* New York: Harper and Row, Publishers.

(1967). *Systematic Theology.* 3 vols. The University of Chicago Press.

Tracy, David (1975). *Blessed Rage for Order: The New Pluralism in Theology.* New York: The Seabury Press.

Tremmel, William C. (1976). *Religion, What Is It?* New York: Holt, Rinehart and Winston.

Van Buren, Paul (1963). *The Secular Meaning of the Gospel Based on an Analysis of Its Language.* New York: The Macmillan Co.

Wallace, Anthony F. C. (1966). *Religion: An Anthropological View.* New York: Random House.

Walsh, W. H. (1963). *Metaphysics.* London: Hutchinson University Library.

Westphal, Merold (1984). *God, Guilt, and Death. An Existential Phenomenology of Religion.* Bloomington, Ind.: Indiana University Press.

Wieman, Henry Nelson (1926). *Religious Experience and Scientific Method.* Carbondale, Ill.: Southern Illinois University Press [reissue of Macmillan, 1926].

(1927). *The Wrestle of Religion with Truth.* New York: Macmillan and Co.

(1946). *The Source of Human Good.* University of Chicago Press.

(1949). "Review of Charles Hartshorne, *The Divine Relativity.*" *Philosophical Review,* 58/1, 78–82.

(1958). *Man's Ultimate Commitment.* Carbondale, Ill.: Southern Illinois University Press.

(1961). "A religious naturalist looks at Reinhold Niebuhr." In Charles W. Kegley and Robert W. Bretall, eds., *Reinhold Niebuhr: His Religious,*

Social, and Political Thought. New York: The Macmillan Company, 334–354.

(1968). "Paul Tillich's inquiry." In Wieman, *Religious Inquiry: Some Explorations.* Boston: Beacon Press.

(1975a). "Commitment for theological inquiry." In Henry Nelson Wieman, ed., and intro. Cedric L. Hepler, *Seeking a Faith for a New Age: Essays on the Interdependence of Religion, Science and Philosophy.* Metuchen, N. J.: The Scarecrow Press, Inc., 129–147.

(1975b). "The need of philosophy of religion." In Wieman, and Hepler, *Seeking a Faith for a New Age, 114–128.*

Wieman, Henry Nelson and Wieman, Regina Westhall Wieman (1935). *Normative Psychology of Religion.* New York: Thomas Y. Crowell Company.

Wiles, Maurice (1982). *Faith and the Mystery of God.* Philadelphia: Fortress Press.

Williams, D. C. (1966). *Principles of Empirical Realism.* Springfield, Ill.: Thomas Publishing Co.

Williams, Daniel Day (1963). "Wieman as a Christian theologian." In Robert W. Bretall, ed., *The Empirical Theology of Henry Nelson Wieman.* Carbondale, Ill.: Southern Illinois University Press [2nd ed., 1969]), 73–96.

Winquist, Charles. (1972). *The Transcendental Imagination: An Essay in Philosophical Theology.* The Hague: Martinus Nijhoff.

(1978). *Homecoming: Interpretation, Transformation and Individuation.* Missoula, Mont.: Scholars Press.

Wisdom, John (1965). "Gods." In Antony Flew, ed., *Logic and Language.* New York: Doubleday, 1965, 194–214.

Index